D0882499

SIGILL : COLL : CARLETON
DECLARATIO SERMONUM TUORUM ILLUMINAT
NORTHFIELD. MINN. A.D. 1866
LIBRARY
Gift of
Carolyn Selbie
in memory of
David W. Parks

ÆTHELRED THE UNREADY

Æthelred the Unready

The Ill-Counselled King

Ann Williams

Hambledon and London
London and New York

Hambledon and London

102 Gloucester Avenue
London, NW1 8HX

175 Fifth Avenue
New York, NY 10010
USA

First Published 2003

ISBN 1 85285 382 4

A description of this book is available from the
British Library and from the Library of Congress.

Typeset by Carnegie Publishing, Lancaster.
Printed and bound in Great Britain by The Bath Press.

Distributed in the United States
and Canada exclusively
by Palgrave Macmillan,
a division of St Martin's Press.

Contents

Illustrations

Between Pages 140 and 141

Tables

This book is dedicated to my faithful friends,
who over the years have ever given me the best of counsel
(though I did not always take it)

'It is a great disgrace and a shame for a man not to want to be what he is, what he has to be.'

> Ælfric the Homilist, *Colloquy*, ed. G. N. Garmondsway (2nd edn; London, 1947), pp. 112–13; translated by Michael Swanton, *Anglo-Saxon Prose* (London, 1975), pp. 113–4.

Preface

In their inestimable compendium of truly memorable history, W. C. Sellar and R. J. Yeatman entitled their eighth chapter 'Ethelread the Unready. A Weak King.'[1] The chapter is short enough to quote in full:

> Ethelread the Unready was the first Weak King of England and was thus the cause of a fresh Wave of Danes. He was called the Unready because he was never ready when the Danes were. Rather than wait for him the Danes used to fine him large sums called Danegeld, for not being ready. But though they were always ready, the Danes had very bad memories and often used to forget that they had been paid the Danegeld and come back for it almost before they had sailed away. By that time Ethelread was always unready again. Finally Ethelread was taken completely unawares by his own death and was succeeded by Canute.

1066 and All That was first published in 1930, and parodies with wicked accuracy the historical traditions which existed in its time (and for a good while later). Indeed its authors were rather kinder to Æthelred than some of their professional colleagues. In the second edition of the first volume of his *History of the Norman Conquest of England*, published in 1870, Edward Augustus Freeman roundly described Æthelred as 'a bad man and a bad King'.[2] Sir James Ramsay, in 1898, recorded Byrhtferth of Ramsey's not unfavourable description of the king ('graceful in manners, beautiful in face and comely in appearance'), but added that these are 'perhaps the only facts about him which the reader will find singled out for praise during a calamitous and disgraceful reign of eight and thirty years ... we must point out that he is the only one of all our kings whose reputation for incapacity has stamped itself upon his very name.'[3]

Such adverse judgements have been traced to the work of the twelfth-century historian, William of Malmesbury. In his *Gesta Regum Anglorum*, composed in the 1120s, William characterized Æthelred's reign as 'cruel at the outset, pitiable in mid-course, and disgraceful in its ending.'[4] William's main source for this opinion was the *Anglo-Saxon Chronicle*, which is contemporary for Æthelred's reign, and since the publication in 1978 of Simon Keynes's critical assessment of the *Chronicle*'s account, the king's reputation has begun to improve.[5] There is indeed some hope that his reign may come to be seen as 'a period of much wider and more varied interest' than has been the case heretofore.[6]

Æthelred came of a long line of notably successful monarchs. Beginning as kings of the West Saxons in the early ninth century, his forebears had extended their authority over the English kingdoms of Kent, Essex and western Mercia, and the British kingdom of Dumnonia (Devon and Cornwall). In the tenth century, the Danish settlements, established in the late ninth century throughout eastern and northern England, had been overcome and incorporated into an English kingdom which stretched from the Channel to somewhere in the neighbourhood of the Tweed, and from the North Sea to the borders of Wales.[7] Æthelred's predecessors had not only acquired these territories, but had also developed the means of governing them.[8] Many of the essential institutions of local administration originate in the stratagems devised by the tenth-century kings and their advisers, notably the shires, hundreds and vills which, with the courts and personnel attached to them, formed the backbone of local government down to (and in some respects even beyond) the eighteenth century. Nor did the rulers of the tenth century neglect the church. Under their patronage, the Benedictine reform of the late tenth century did not only reorganize English monastic life, at least in southern England, but also revitalized English intellectual and material culture, while the building of local churches by both ecclesiastics and laymen laid the foundation for the later parochial structure.

It was a comparatively united and stable kingdom which Æthelred inherited. To come of a vigorous and distinguished lineage is not, however, an unmixed advantage; the weight of accumulated honour and fame can be too heavy a burden. Whether the young Æthelred felt any such misgivings when he became king it is impossible to say. In his day no one wrote memoirs or kept journals, and though it was becoming fashionable to commission family biographies, they were more concerned with panegyric than psychobabble (and are perhaps none the worse for that). In any case the only family biography of the West Saxon kings (the *Chronicle* of Ealdorman Æthelweard) does not cover the reign of his kinsman Æthelred.[9] We do not and cannot know what kind of a man Æthelred was, only (and that in part) what he did and what happened to him. Forming judgements of character and motive from recorded actions is a dangerous hobby, which has not stopped anyone from trying. It has been said, for instance, that Æthelred's reign began under a cloud, with the murder of his half-brother Edward. The killing of a consecrated king was a weighty crime, but it had happened before; Æthelred's great-uncle Eadred became king after the murder of his full brother Edmund. Nor was bad blood between half-kin particularly uncommon; when Harthacnut succeeded Harold I in 1040, he had his half-brother's body dug up and thrown into the Thames marshes. Such occurrences do not in themselves give an unambiguous indication of the mental state of the participants, let alone the significance of the events themselves and their effects on contemporaries.

What remains to us is a story, and perhaps the best way of proceeding is simply to tell it. I freely confess to a fondness for narrative history, with an emphasis on the 'how' of things, rather than the 'why', and I have therefore given this book a chronological rather than a thematic structure. As to the sources of information, it is difficult to better the summary of E. A. Freeman, written in 1870:

> Our main authorities for this period are essentially the same as those to which we have to go for our knowledge of earlier times. The English Chronicles are still our principal guide ... Florence of Worcester gives what is essentially a Latin version of the Chronicles, with frequent explanatory additions ... The Charters and Laws of the reign of Æthelred are abundant, and, besides their primary value as illustrating laws and customs, the signatures constantly help us to the succession of offices and to a sort of skeleton biographies of the leading men of the time. These, the Chronicles, Laws, and Charters, form our primary authorities. The later Latin Chronicles, from William of Malmesbury and Henry of Huntingdon onwards, occasionally supply additional facts, but their accounts are often mixed up with romantic details, and it is dangerous to trust them, except when they show signs of following authorities now lost. Local histories, such as those of Ely, Ramsey and Abingdon, supply occasional facts, but the same sort of cautions which apply to the secondary writers of general history apply to them in a still greater degree. We now also

> begin to draw some little help from foreign sources ... The Norman writers begin to be of some importance for the events which connect England and Normandy ... Later in the period we have, in the *Encomium Emmae* ... the work of a contemporary Norman or Flemish writer, which, though throughout unfair and inaccurate, is worthy of being compared with our English writers. Occasional notices of Danish and English affairs are sometimes to be gleaned from the German writers, like Adam of Bremen and the contemporary Thietmar of Merseburg.[10]

To Freeman's 'primary authorities' should be added the works of Archbishop Wulfstan of York, Ælfric the homilist, Æthelweard the Chronicler and Byrhtferth of Ramsey. Non-English sources which he does not mention include the praise-poems composed by Icelandic skalds, many of which, though not written down till much later, seem likely to be authentic, and to them can be added the corpus of runic inscriptions, the only strictly contemporary source from late tenth- and early eleventh-century Scandinavia. Norman writers (essentially William of Jumièges) are perhaps less informative than Freeman implies, the *Encomium Emmae Reginae* and Thietmar of Merseberg rather more.

Freeman's *caveat* on the use of twelfth-century works purporting to retail the history of the tenth and eleventh centuries should be taken to heart by all historians of pre-Conquest England. The assumption that the post-Conquest chroniclers and historians had more to go on than has survived to our own day may or may not be true, but it cannot be concluded that all their additional material derives from contemporary accounts now lost. Even when the existence of such accounts can be established, problems still remain, exemplified by John of Worcester's *Chronicle* (Freeman's 'Florence').[11] It can be shown that for the period 958–92, John of Worcester, writing in the early twelfth century, used 'a now-lost Latin chronicle, which was based on a (lost) version of the *Anglo-Saxon Chronicle* and which contained information of interest to a Worcester audience', and which was also used by Byrhtferth of Ramsey, writing at the turn of the tenth and eleventh centuries.[12] It has been suggested that this lost Latin chronicle extended to 1017, and was used by John up to this date.[13] But even if this is the case, not all the additions which John makes to the *Anglo-Saxon Chronicle*'s narrative need be derived from the lost chronicle, nor, without corroboration, can we determine what has been derived from this source. Even more dubious than the postulated written sources are appeals to oral tradition, which can too easily degenerate into legends and folk-tales; some examples of the process appear in Chapter 1 below. For these reasons I have used the post-Conquest writers only sparingly and (I hope) with due caution.

The purpose of this book is simply to tell the story of Æthelred *unræd*, a king to whom posterity has not been kind. Yet even William of Malmesbury, whose malign influence on Æthelred's posthumous reputation has already been rehearsed, recorded one less damaging estimate of him, as 'a man who was, as we learn from our forebears, neither a great fool nor excessively cowardly', and, as I dug deeper into the matter, I developed a certain fondness, even a certain admiration, for him.[14] Despite all his misfortunes, some of which appear to have been of his own making, he kept his kingship to the end, which under the circumstances must be counted a considerable achievement. As was observed of another flawed hero, 'it is no small feat to have come so far, and through such dangers, still bearing the Ring'.[15]

This book could not have been completed without the help of many friends. Thanks are due, first, to Tony Morris for persuading me to undertake the task, and to Janet Nelson for reading and commenting upon the early chapters and giving me a great deal of good counsel, most of which I have actually followed. Steve Church performed a similar service, and provided much help and encouragement as I struggled with the sometimes intractable task of reducing my thoughts on Æthelred and his times to order. A version of Chapter 1 was read to the Early Medieval History seminar at the Institute of Historical Research (on 13 March 2002) and I should like to thank all those present, especially Susan Reynolds, Charlie Insley, Alan Thacker and Matt Bennett, for the ensuing discussion, which was of great help in enabling me to clarify my ideas. I am indebted to Patrick McGurk for his help with the Chronicle of John of Worcester, and to John Pullen-Appleby for his expertise on English seapower, the subject of a forthcoming book which he was kind enough to let me read in manuscript. Other friends have contributed published and unpublished articles and papers with permission to cite their findings, including David Dumville, Charlie Insley, Shashi Jayakumar, Björn Weiler and Barbara Yorke. As always, I have to thank the members of successive Battle Conferences for aid, advice and good fellowship; the number of citations to the proceedings (*Anglo-Norman Studies*) will show what an invaluable institution Battle is.

No new book can avoid being rooted in previous works. The chief prop of the present volume, as a glance at the citations will show, is the magisterial work of Simon Keynes, *The diplomas of King Æthelred 'the Unready', 978–1016*; indeed it is not too much to say that without *Diplomas*, this book could not have been written. In 1980, at the close of this mighty work, Professor Keynes outlined the lineaments of a future book on the king:

> it remains to characterize fully the institutions of royal and local government and to set in their historical context Æthelred's coinage and the extensive legislation in his name; to clarify the developments in the fortunes of the church during the reign and to assess the significance of the achievements in learning and material culture; to understand the complex but highly important prosopography of the period; to examine the web linking together all of the kingdoms of Northern Europe and the British Isles, and to discover how their respective histories interacted on one another; and to consider Æthelred's own position in relation to these different aspects of his reign, with a view to establishing his influence on and responsibility for the various developments.[16]

This, alas, is not that book. I have tried to outline some of the material relating to the first topic, royal and local government, and have touched on the fourth, at least insofar as the Scandinavian world is concerned. As for the church, its life and culture, I have left that to others, more competent than myself in such matters, to explore; my only defence is the existence of a number of excellent books and articles published on the subject in recent years. The only one of Professor Keynes's topics in which I have some personal expertise is the third, the prosopography of the period, especially as regards the lay aristocracy, who as a result probably figure rather too largely in what follows; but since they are usually under- rather than over-exposed, perhaps this is only just. For Æthelred himself, it remains true, to quote Professor Keynes again, 'that one has hardly the faintest idea of what he was really like', but I hope that at least I have given some idea of what he was up against, and how he tried to meet the challenges of his reign.[17]

Wanstead,
30 August 2002

Abbreviations

AC	John Williams, ab Ithel (ed.), *Annales Cambriae* (London, 1860)
ANS	*Anglo-Norman Studies*
AS Chron	Dorothy Whitelock, David C. Douglas and Susie I. Cooper (ed.), *The Anglo-Saxon Chronicle: a revised translation* (London, 1961, 2nd impression 1965)
ASE	*Anglo-Saxon England*
BAR	British Archaeological Reports
Barlow, *Vita Ædwardi*	Frank Barlow (ed.), *The Life of King Edward who rests at Westminster*, 2nd edn (Oxford, 1992)
Birch, *Liber de Hyde*	W. de Gray Birch (ed.), *Liber Vitae: Register and Martyrology of New Minster and Hyde Abbey, Winchester* (Winchester, 1892)
Brooks and Cubitt, *St Oswald*	Nicholas Brooks and Catherine Cubitt (ed.), *St Oswald of Worcester: life and influence* (Leicester, 1996)
ByT (Peniarth)	Thomas Jones (ed.), *Brut y Tywysogion, or The Chronicle of the Princes, Peniarth Ms 20 version* (Cardiff, 1952)
ByT (Red Book)	Thomas Jones (ed.), *Brut y Tywysogion, or The Chronicle of the Princes, Red Book of Hergest version* (Cardiff, 1955)
Campbell, *Æthelweard*	A. Campbell (ed.), *The Chronicle of Æthelweard* (London, 1962)
Chron Abingdon	J. Stevenson (ed.), *Chronicon Monasterii de Abingdon*, 2 vols, RS (London, 1858)
Chron Evesham	W. Dunn Macray (ed.), *Chronicon Abbatiae de Evesham ad annum 1418*, RS (London, 1863)

Chronicon ex Chronicis	B. Thorpe (ed.), *Florentii Wigornensis Chronicon ex Chronicis*, 2 vols (London, 1848–9)
CNMH, ii	Rosamund McKitterick (ed.), *The New Cambridge Medieval History, c. 700-c. 900*, ii, (Cambridge, 1995)
CNMH, iii	Timothy Reuter (ed.), *The New Cambridge Medieval History, c. 900-c. 1024*, iii, (Cambridge, 1999)
Cooper, *The Battle of Maldon*	Janet Cooper (ed.), *The Battle of Maldon: fiction and fact* (London, 1993)
ECEE	C. R. Hart, *The early charters of eastern England* (Leicester, 1966)
ECNENM	C. R. Hart, *The early charters of northern England and the north Midlands* (Leicester, 1975)
ECTV	Margaret Gelling, *The early charters of the Thames Valley* (Leicester, 1979)
ECWM	H. P. R. Finberg, *The early charters of the west Midlands* (Leicester, 1961)
EETS	Early English Text Society
EHD i	Dorothy Whitelock, *English Historical Documents, i, c. 500–1042* (London, 1955)
EHR	*English Historical Review*
Encomium Emmae	A. Campbell (ed.), *Encomium Emmae Reginae*, Camden Classic Reprints (Cambridge, 1998)
Fell, *St Edward*	Christine Fell, *Edward, king and martyr* (Leeds, 1971)
Freeman, *NC*	E. A. Freeman, *The history of the Norman Conquest of England*, 6 vols (Oxford, 1870–79)
GDB	R. W. H. Erskine (ed.), *Great Domesday: a facsimile* (London, 1986)
GP	N. E. S. A. Hamilton (ed.), *William of Malmesbury, De gestis pontificum Anglorum*, RS (London, 1870)
Haddan and Stubbs, *Councils*	A. W. Haddan and W. Stubbs, *Councils and ecclesiastical documents relating to Great Britain and Ireland*, 3 vols (Oxford, 1869–71)
Harmer, *Writs*	F. E. Harmer, *Anglo-Saxon Writs* (Manchester, 1952)
Haskins Soc. J.	*Haskins Society Journal*

Hemming	Thomas Hearne (ed.), *Hemingi Chartularium monachi Wigornensis* (Oxford, 1723)
HH	Diana Greenway (ed.), *Henry, Archdeacon of Huntingdon, Historia Anglorum. The History of the English People* (Oxford 1996)
Hill, *Ethelred the Unready*	David Hill (ed.), *Ethelred the Unready: papers from the Millenary Conference*, BAR British series 59 (1978)
HN	M. Rule (ed.), *Eadmeri Historia Novorum in Anglia*, RS (London, 1884), translation of Books I-IV in Geoffrey Bosanquet, *Eadmer's History of Recent Events in England* (London, 1964)
HRH	David Knowles, C. N. L. Brooke and Vera C. M. London, *The Heads of Religious Houses in England and Wales, 940–1216* (Cambridge, 1972)
Hugh Candidus	W. T. Mellows (ed.), *The Chronicle of Hugh Candidus, a monk of Peterborough* (Oxford, 1949), translation in W. T. Mellows (trans.), *The Peterborough Chronicle of Hugh Candidus* (Peterborough, 1941)
J. British Studies	*Journal of British Studies*
JBAA	*Journal of the British Archaeological Association*
JnW	R. R. Darlington and P. McGurk (ed.), *The Chronicle of John of Worcester*, 3 vols (Oxford, 1995–2001)
KCD	J. M. Kemble, *Codex Diplomaticus aevi Saxonici*, 6 vols (London, 1839–48)
Keynes, *Atlas*	Simon Keynes, *An atlas of attestations in Anglo-Saxon Charters, c. 670–1066* (Cambridge, 1995)
Keynes, *Diplomas*	Simon Keynes, *The diplomas of King Æthelred "the Unready", 978–1016* (Cambridge, 1980)
LE	E. O. Blake (ed.), *Liber Eliensis*, Camden 3rd ser., 92 (London, 1962)
Mem. St Dunstan	William Stubbs (ed.), *Memorials of Saint Dunstan, archbishop of Canterbury*, RS (London, 1874)

Monasticon	William Dugdale, *Monasticon Anglicanum*, ed. J. Caley, H. Ellis and B. Bandinel, 6 vols in 8 (London, 1817–30)
ns	new series
os	old series
OV	Marjorie Chibnall (ed.), *The Ecclesiastical History of Orderic Vitalis*, 6 vols (Oxford, 1969–80)
P&P	*Past and Present*
RS	Rolls Series
Ramsay et al., *St Dunstan*	Nigel Ramsay, Margaret Sparks and Tim Tatton-Brown (ed.), *St Dunstan: his life, times and cult* (Woodbridge, 1992)
Robertson, *Charters*	A. J. Robertson, *Anglo-Saxon Charters* (2nd edn; Cambridge, 1956)
Robertson, *Laws*	A. J. Robertson, *The laws of the kings of England from Edmund to Henry I* (Cambridge, 1925; reprinted New York, 1974)
S.	P. H. Sawyer, *Anglo-Saxon Charters: an annotated list and bibliography*, Royal Historical Society (London, 1968)
Scragg, *The Battle of Maldon*	Donald Scragg (ed.), *The Battle of Maldon, AD 991* (Oxford 1991)
Skeat, *Lives of the Saints*	W. W. Skeat (ed.), *Ælfric's Lives of the Saints*, 4 vols, EETS os 76, 82, 94, 114 (Oxford, 1881–1900)
Stafford, *Emma and Edith*	Pauline Stafford, *Queen Emma and Queen Edith: queenship and women's power in eleventh-century England* (Oxford, 1997)
Stenton, *ASE*	F. M. Stenton, *Anglo-Saxon England* (3rd edn; Oxford, 1971)
Symeon, *Libellus*	David Rollason (ed.), *Symeon of Durham, Libellus de exordio atque procursu istius hoc est Dunhelmensis Ecclesie: Tract on the origins and progress of this the church of Durham* (Oxford, 2000)
Symeon, Op. Omnia	Thomas Arnold (ed.), *Symeonis monachi Opera omnia*, 2 vols RS (London, 1882–85)

Symeon, Op. Coll.	Hinde, [J.] Hodgson, (ed.), *Symeonis Dunelmensis Opera et Collectanea*, Surtees Society 51 (1868)
Trans. Bristol and Gloucs. Arch. Soc.	*Transactions of the Bristol and Gloucestershire Archaeological Society*
VO	*Vita Oswaldi archiepiscopus Eboracensis*, in J. Raine (ed.), *The historians of the church of York and its archbishops* i, RS (London, 1879), pp. 399–475
WmJ	Elisabeth van Houts (ed.), *The Gesta Normannorum ducum of William of Jumièges, Orderic Vitalis and Robert of Torigny*, 2 vols (Oxford, 1992–95)
WmM	R. M. Thomson and M. Winterbottom (ed.), *William of Malmesbury, Gesta Regum Anglorum, The history of the English kings*, 2 vols (Oxford, 1998–99)
Wormald, *MEL*	Patrick Wormald, *The making of English law: King Alfred to the twelfth century, i, legislation and its limits* (Oxford, 1999)

1

The Gap of Corfe

'His earthly kinsmen would not avenge him, but his heavenly Father has greatly avenged him.'

Anglo-Saxon Chronicle, 'D', 'E', 978

Like his father Edgar, Æthelred 'the Unready' was a younger son. Ever since the royal house of Wessex had begun to extend its authority over all the English, it had been as common for brother to succeed brother as for son to succeed father, but the circumstances of Æthelred's succession, following the murder of his brother Edward, are sufficiently dramatic to have attracted comment both at the time and later. Indeed the events of Æthelred's reign have been seen as the direct result of its unlucky inception; medieval historians interpreted the Viking assaults as the judgement of God on a sinful nation, and their modern counterparts have discerned 'an atmosphere of suspicion which destroyed the prestige of the Crown'.[1] It is important, therefore, to understand exactly how Æthelred came to be king, and how this might have affected his reputation, both at the time and later.

All disputed royal successions (and most were disputed) arose from internal tensions within the royal family itself, and the difficulties surrounding Æthelred's succession go back to the marital history of his parents. King Edgar married Æthelred's mother, Queen Ælfthryth, in 964.[2] Their elder son Edmund, who died in 971, attests one of his father's diplomas in 966, and was probably born earlier in the same year.[3] He is presumably the unnamed ætheling who received a bequest under the will of Ælfgifu, drawn up in 966 or soon afterwards; since no other ætheling is mentioned, it can be assumed that his younger brother was not yet born.[4] Both Edmund and Æthelred, however, are mentioned by name in a genealogical tract composed in 969.[5] Æthelred's birth can therefore be dated 966 x 969, probably in 968. Both æthelings were beneficiaries under the will of Ealdorman Ælfheah, who died in 971; 'the elder ætheling' (Edmund) received a sword and thirty mancuses of silver, and 'the younger ætheling' (Æthelred) an estate at Walkhampstead (Godstone, Surrey). Their mother was also a beneficiary, and Ælfheah describes her as his *gefædera* ('gossip' in the old sense), a word denoting 'the relationship between godparents and parents, or between godparents of the same child'. It may be that the ealdorman, a kinsman of King Edgar, was godfather to one of the æthelings.[6]

Both Æthelred's parents had been married before. Ælfthryth was the widow of Æthelwold, ealdorman of East Anglia from 956 to 962.[7] By her first husband, she had a son, Leofric, possibly the Leofric who founded St Neot's (Huntingdonshire) between 979 and 984 and had a brother named Æthelnoth.[8] Relations between Ælfthryth and her first husband's family seem to have been distant and these half-brothers played no part in Æthelred's life, but his maternal uncle (*eam*) Ordwulf was to become a major figure in his nephew's reign.[9]

King Edgar's marital history is extremely difficult to unravel, not merely because of the lack of contemporary sources but also because the king's sex-life became the subject of much speculation or, to speak plainly, gossip (in the modern sense) among hagiographers and historians of a later era. The topic provides an excellent example of how these later writers interpreted, not to say embroidered their scanty sources. The starting-point is that Edward the Martyr, Edgar's son and immediate successor, was not Ælfthryth's child.[10] Edward and Edmund attest Edgar's charter of 966 for the New Minster, Winchester, as æthelings (*clitones*) but Edmund, whose attestation precedes that of his half-brother, is described as 'the king's legitimate son' (*legitimus prefati regis filius*), whereas Edward is merely 'begotten by the same king' (*eodem rege clito procreatus*).[11] Edward's anomalous position is also indicated pictorially, for he is the only member of the royal family to have an outlined cross against his name in the witness-list; the rest (Edgar, Ælfthryth, Edmund and the king's grandmother Eadgifu) are all given golden crosses.[12] Ælfthryth moreover attests as the king's 'lawful wife' (*legitima prefati regis conjuncx*), a phrase which 'might imply a distinction between herself and a wife who was not legitimate'.[13]

No earlier wife is named in the surviving tenth-century sources, and later commentators had different opinions on her identity. The first to speculate on Edward's parentage was Osbern of Canterbury, in his *vita* of St Dunstan, written in the latter part of the eleventh century.[14] He says that Edward was the son of a professed nun (*virgo velata*) of Wilton whom Edgar had seduced, thereby incurring a seven-year penance from St Dunstan, which in turn caused his royal consecration to be delayed. Osbern gives no dates, but is clearly thinking of the ceremony at Bath in 973, so that, taken literally, the seduction of the Wilton nun would have occurred in 966, but little confidence can be placed in the implied date.[15]

When Eadmer, Osbern's younger contemporary at Canterbury, came to write his version of St Dunstan's life, he was unhappy with Osbern's account of Edward's parentage, and sought advice from his friend Nicholas of Worcester. Nicholas, drawing upon chronicles and stories (*carmina*) of that time, 'written in the native tongue (i.e. English) by learned men whose names are unknown' (*a doctis patria lingua composita de his noscuntur*), and 'other writings (*scripturae*) whose testimony we believe to be true', provided Eadmer with a completely different account. In this version, Edward was the son of Æthelflæd 'the white' (*candida*), daughter of 'Ordmær, ealdorman (*dux*) of the East Angles', whom Edgar took as his lawful wife (*coniunx legitima*) while he was king of the Mercians (i.e. between 957 and 959). It was only after Æthelflæd's death 'a few years later', that Edgar married Ælfthryth, daughter of Ordgar, 'ealdorman of the West Saxons'. Nicholas also says that Æthelflæd was never crowned queen (because of Edgar's delayed coronation), though Ælfthryth was.[16] Much the same story appears (not unnaturally) in the account of Nicholas' fellow-monk, John of Worcester, though he does not specify 'Ealdorman' Ordmær's sphere of office, and adds that Æthelflæd *candida* also had the byname *eneda* (OE *ened*, 'duck').[17]

Primed with Nicholas's information, Eadmer felt able to deny that Edward was born of a consecrated nun (*ex sanctimoniali femina*). He introduces Æthelflæd *candida* in the context of Edgar's seduction of a young laywoman being brought up at Wilton, who in an unsuccessful attempt to evade his advances adopted a nun's veil ('How quickly you have become a nun!', said the king, clearly not fooled by this).[18] Edgar's offence was the greater, says Eadmer, because he already had a lawful wife (*legitimam uxorem*) in 'Ælfflæd' (*recte* Æthelflæd) *candida*, daughter of Ordmær, ealdorman of the East Angles, and mother of his son Edward. In expiation Edgar undertook a seven-year penance imposed by St Dunstan.[19]

No contemporary source mentions Æthelflæd *candida/eneda*, which is not in itself significant; there is (as we shall see) no contemporary reference to Æthelred's first wife.[20] More serious is the problem of her father Ordmær, for no contemporary ealdorman of this name is known. He may have been some junior official who has somehow slipped out of the historical record, but he was certainly not 'ealdorman of the East Angles'. Between 930 and 992, the ealdordom of East Anglia was held in turn by three members of one family, Æthelstan Half-king, who retired to become a monk at Glastonbury in 956, his son Æthelwold, first husband of Edgar's queen, who died in 962, and Æthelwold's brother Æthelwine, who died in 992.[21] This leaves no room for the tenure of the ealdordom by Ordmær. It is of course possible that Nicholas and John elevated the status of the king's supposed father-in-law, and that Ordmær was simply a wealthy thegn.[22] He has been identified as the 'powerful man' (*vir potens*) Ordmær who, in a transaction which can be dated no more closely than 932 x 956, exchanged Hatfield, Hertfordshire, with Ealdorman Æthelstan, receiving unspecified lands in Devon in return; King Edgar subsequently claimed that Hatfield had been bequeathed to him by Ordmær and his wife.[23] But even if this is the Ordmær intended by Nicholas and John of Worcester, his putative daughter remains elusive.

As well as his three sons, Edgar had a daughter, Edith, who became a nun at Wilton and was eventually canonized.[24] Her surviving seal-matrix, whose style of decoration suggests a date in the late tenth century, describes her as *regalis adelpha*, 'royal sister', the implied 'brother' being, presumably, Æthelred himself.[25] Virtually all that is known of her comes from the writings of Goscelin of Saint-Bertin, a professional hagiographer working in England in the latter half of the eleventh century. His version of Edgar's amorous adventures is rather different from those of Osbern and Eadmer. In his *vita* of St Wulfhild, abbess of Barking, he describes how, as a nun at Wilton, Wulfhild became the object of the king's attentions, but successfully resisted them, so that Edgar took instead her kinswoman Wulfthryth, a young laywoman being educated among the nuns (there is no suggestion of force, or of Wulfthryth wearing the veil to evade the king).[26] Wulfthryth, having borne the king a daughter (St Edith), returned to Wilton as a nun. In his *vita* of Edith herself, Goscelin presents Wulfthryth, whom he describes as the 'offshoot of princes and noble child of a royal duke', as Edgar's wife, their marriage ending only when she withdrew with their daughter to Wilton, of which she eventually became abbess.[27]

It is clear that by the end of the eleventh century there were a number of scandalous stories circulating about King Edgar's predilection for young nuns. Entertaining though they are, they amount to little more than anecdotal tales, and lose nothing in the telling. William of Malmesbury, for instance, appears to conflate the stories told by Osbern and Eadmer with those of Goscelin. In the *Gesta Regum*, he repeats Osbern's story of the veiled nun and the seven-year penance imposed by Dunstan, without naming either the nun herself, or her house, or any issue. He then (after a folkloric interlude about the substitution of a servant-girl for her mistress in the royal bed) conflates Goscelin's Wulfthryth, mother of St Edith, and Eadmer's young girl of Wilton who unsuccessfully wore the veil to escape the king. It is not entirely clear whether William regarded their subsequent union as a marriage; he says Wulfthryth was *lecto imperiali subacta*, 'forced into a royal marriage' (taking *lectum* to mean 'marriage-bed'), but notes Dunstan's disapproval.[28] In the *Gesta Pontificum*, it is Edgar's union with Wulfthryth, who 'had merely put on a veil as her own idea in her sudden fear of the king', which incurs the seven-year penance.[29]

It is questionable how far such tales correspond to any tenth-century reality. The writers of the Anglo-Norman period were just as prone as others before and since to draw conclusions from inadequate evidence, and pad the gaps with theories (and even inventions) of their own. Modern historians, taking much the same line as William of Malmesbury, usually give Edgar at least two wives, Æthelflæd, mother of Edward, and Ælfthryth, mother of Edmund and Æthelred; the only variation is whether St Edith's mother Wulfthryth, usually placed between the two, is regarded as a wife or a concubine.[30] This solution, however, presents a problem of chronology. The 'A' text of the *Anglo-Saxon Chronicle*, a contemporary source, describes Edward as 'a child ungrown' (*cild unweaxan*) at the time of his father's death, on 8 July 975. Taken literally, this means that he was no more than twelve or thirteen, and thus born in 962 or 963 (he can scarcely have been born after 964, the year of Edgar's marriage to Ælfthryth).[31] Edith, whom all agree to have been Wulfthryth's child, is said to have been in her twenty-third year at the time of her death, which took place on 16 September in some year between 984 and 987, placing her birth also in the period 961 x 964.[32] It seems that Eadmer may have been right to allege that Edgar's liaison with Wulfthryth was concurrent with his marriage to Æthelflæd *candida*. It should, however, be noticed that the *Passio* of Edward appears to regard him as a full brother of Edith, and therefore a son of Wulfthryth.[33]

That Edgar had a prior marital liaison less formal than his marriage with Ælfthryth is not at all unlikely. The first marriages of both Cnut and Harold II seem to have been of this kind, and, despite ecclesiastical disapproval, were not regarded by laymen as in any way unlawful; nor did such unions preclude a second marriage, even during the lifetime of the first.[34] If the traditions of the nuns of Wilton are acceptable, Edgar's previous wife was probably Wulfthryth. Conversely, the failure of the nuns of Shaftesbury, where Edward's cult was fostered, to remember (or at any rate to record) his mother's name casts doubts over the existence of Æthelflæd *candida/eneda*.[35] Her function seems to have been to absolve Edgar from the charge of carnal knowledge of a consecrated nun. Whatever the precise details, neither of Edgar's putative former wives had the same status as Ælfthryth; she alone was consecrated as queen, and she alone attested her husband's diplomas.[36]

Edgar's death on 8 July 975, at the age of only thirty-two, was probably unexpected.[37] Of his two surviving sons Æthelred, aged seven or eight at the most, was well under age; Edward was at least eleven but perhaps no more than thirteen. Two young children, especially two children born of different mothers, presented a difficult choice, the more so because there were at this time no established rules of succession.[38] Since the end of the ninth century the next king had been chosen from the closest male kin of his predecessor, latterly perhaps confined to a three-generation group defined by descent from a common grandfather, entitled to the status of æthelings. Which candidate succeeded was determined by a number of factors, among which 'designation', the stated choice of the previous king, was an important element. The

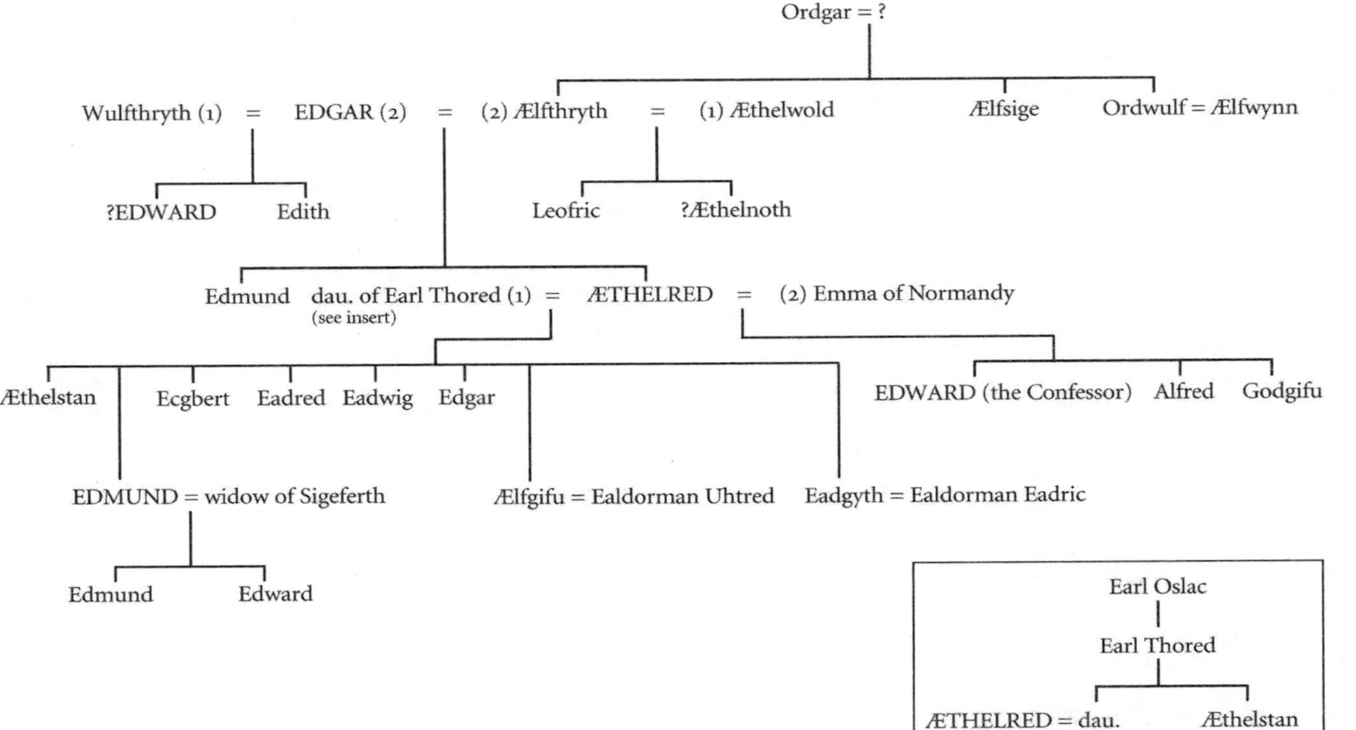

Table 1. The Family of King Æthelred

attitudes of the lay nobles also carried weight, and those most closely related to the competing æthelings, especially their mothers, had a particularly important role. The views of the church had also to be taken into account. The canons of 786, promulgated in both northern and southern England, forbade the choice of 'those begotten in adultery or incest; for just as in our times according to the canons a bastard cannot attain to the priesthood, so neither can he who was not born of a legitimate marriage be the Lord's anointed'.[39] Much, of course, depended on how 'legitimate marriage' was defined.

We do not know what arrangements Edgar himself had made, but it would be odd if he had made none, for he himself had been a younger brother whose father had died unseasonably.[40] The New Minster charter, which gives Edmund precedence over his half-brother Edward, might suggest that Edmund was then the chosen successor, but its text was drafted by Æthelwold, bishop of Winchester, an adherent of Queen Ælfthryth, and may represent her ambitions as much as the intentions of her husband.[41] A different viewpoint may be reflected in the genealogical tract produced at Glastonbury in 969, which gives Edward precedence over both Edmund and Æthelred.[42] In any event, Edmund predeceased his father, and there is no evidence to suggest that Æthelred inherited his brother's favoured position. Both the *Passio Sancti Edwardi* and John of Worcester say that Edgar chose Edward as his successor, but this may be no more than deduction based upon what actually transpired.[43]

The earliest account of the succession dispute which followed Edgar's death is that of Byrhtferth of Ramsey, in his *vita* of St Oswald, composed at the turn of the tenth and eleventh centuries.[44] He says that whereas 'the chief men of the land' wanted Edward as king, 'some of the nobles' preferred 'the king's younger son', because 'he appeared to all gentler in speech and deeds', whereas Edward 'inspired in all not only fear but even terror, for he [?afflicted them] not only with words but truly with dire blows, and especially his own men dwelling with him' (*maxime suos secum mansitantes*). Byrhtferth, writing at a time when the cult of Edward was rapidly developing, presents him as a hagiographical type of the unpleasant lout sanctified because of his unjust murder.[45] This does not necessarily invalidate his character-sketch of the young king, but it is important to remember that he may not have been speaking literally.

Character was, nonetheless, an important factor in estimating fitness to rule, and it is interesting that Byrhtferth, monk of a house whose leaders may have been among Edward's supporters, should include such a damaging estimate of the king. Especially significant is his reference to the violence shown by Edward towards members of his own household, for affability (*mansuetudo*, 'gentleness' in both its modern senses), especially towards one's subordinates and dependants, was one of the traits by which the rightful king could be known. The *Passio Sancti Edwardi*, for instance, describes Edward as the gentlest (*mansuetissimus*) of lambs.[46]

Byrhtferth records no other objection to Edward's candidacy, but Eadmer, following a hint from Nicholas of Worcester, says Edward's opponents challenged the status of his mother, who, though lawfully married, had never, unlike Ælfthryth, been crowned queen.[47] This may have been an issue in 975, but it has to be said that similar arguments were current in Eadmer's day about Henry I, as opposed to his elder brothers, and might have influenced Eadmer's interpretation of the earlier dispute.[48] Eadmer complicates the situation by alleging that at the time of Edward's birth neither his mother nor his father had been consecrated, but since he is clearly thinking of Edgar's coronation at Bath in 973 (he mentions no other) this objection would apply to Æthelred as well.[49] There is no other indication that either Edward's or his mother's legitimacy was in question in 975.

Byrhtferth does not name the participants in the dispute but it may be presumed that the queen was urging the claims of her own son, and that she had the support of Bishop Æthelwold, (to whom she seems to have been particularly close), her brother Ordwulf, and probably Ealdorman Ælfhere (brother of her *gefædera* Ælfheah), and his brother-in law, Ælfric *cild*.[50] Later writers make Archbishop Dunstan Edward's chief supporter, which is plausible enough, but unfortunately the earliest *vita* of Dunstan does not cover this part of his career.[51] John of Worcester adds Archbishop Oswald to their number, on what grounds is unclear, but Oswald is known to have been a political opponent of Ealdorman Ælfhere, and is likely to have taken a different stance; the same applies to Oswald's friend and co-founder of Ramsey, Ealdorman Æthelwine.[52] Æthelweard the Chronicler, who came from another collateral branch of the royal house, was probably also in Edward's camp; Edward made him ealdorman of the western shires (the office once held by Ælfthryth's father), and gave him land in Cornwall.[53]

A compromise was reached fairly quickly, for the *Anglo-Saxon Chronicle* implies that Edward was accepted as king before the autumn of 975.[54] One of Æthelred's diplomas, probably from the year 999, refers back to 'the time of my boyhood', when 'all the leading men of both orders unanimously chose my brother Edward to guide the government of the kingdom', adding that, as part of the agreement, Æthelred received 'the lands belonging to kings' sons'. Some of these lands had been granted by Edgar to Abingdon, but 'were at once withdrawn by force, by the decree and order of all the leading men, from the aforesaid holy monastery, and, by order of these same, placed under my power. Whether they did this thing justly or unjustly, they themselves may know'. On Edward's death, Æthelred received the royal lands as well as those of the æthelings.[55]

The diploma throws some light on the so-called 'anti-monastic reaction' of Edward's reign, when (allegedly) a group of powerful laymen led by Ælfhere of Mercia attacked the monasteries established in Edgar's reign.[56] Byrhtferth of Ramsey, who has the most extended account, says that monks were expelled in favour of the seculars whom they themselves had displaced; his sole example, Abbot Germanus of Winchcombe, is presumably singled out because he and his community found refuge at Ramsey. When the 'madness' spread to the east midlands, however, it was successfully checked by Ealdorman Æthelwine and his associates. The rivalry between the families of Æthelwine and Ælfhere was real enough and of long standing, but in other respects Byrhtferth's picture of events is too simplistic.[57] As Æthelred's diploma shows, there was more to the seizure of monastic lands than anti-monasticism. In many, perhaps most cases, it was the sharp practice involved in acquiring lands for the reformed houses that was being questioned, as the sellers (who had probably been put under considerable pressure) or their heirs sought to obtain a price closer to the actual market value.[58]

It seems that the advent in contentious circumstances of a young and inexperienced king allowed many simmering resentments, restrained by Edgar's heavy hand, to rise to the surface, but the scanty sources make it difficult to gain much idea of Edward's reign (the same is true, of course, of the reign of his father). Byrhtferth's account suggests an armed confrontation between the forces of Ælfhere and Æthelwine, but no actual violence broke out. Nor is the *Anglo-Saxon Chronicle* of much help. It records that Earl Oslac of Northumbria was exiled in 975, in circumstances which are unstated but of which all versions of the *Chronicle* seem to disapprove. The year 976 saw 'the great famine', and in 977 the king's former tutor Sidemann, bishop of Crediton, died while attending a meeting of the king and his *witan* at Kirtlington, Oxfordshire. Sidemann had wished to be buried at his episcopal see, but the king and Archbishop Dunstan, again for unstated reasons, had his body interred at Abingdon. In 978, at another *witenagemot* at Calne, Wiltshire, 'all the chief counsellors of the English people fell from an upper storey ... except Archbishop Dunstan, who alone remained standing upon a beam'. It was a serious accident: 'some were very severely injured and some did not survive it'.[59] No background is available for any of these events, which leave merely 'a vague impression of disorder', but any interpretation of Edward's reign cannot avoid being affected by its termination in the murder of the king.[60]

Edward's murder has been the subject of much discussion.[61] The bare facts are given in the various versions of the *Anglo-Saxon Chronicle*. The oldest text ('A') says merely that the king was killed (*ofslegen*) and was succeeded by his brother, the ætheling Æthelred.[62] The 'C' text, put together in the 1040s and thus after the development of Edward's cult, says that he was martyred (*gemartyrad*). The fullest account is found in 'D' and 'E' (the 'northern recension') which give the day and the time, the evening of the 18 March, and the place, 'the gap of Corfe' (*Corfes geat*); the village, now dominated by the post-Conquest castle, lies in a gap in the long, low hills which traverse the Isle of Purbeck. Both 'D' and 'E' are as they stand post-Conquest compilations, but they incorporate a tenth-century lament in alliterative verse on the king's murder (*men hine of myrðrodon*) and the development of his cult.[63] This is the only reference to 'murder' in the *Chronicle*, and the prose texts of 'D' and 'E' use the verb *ofslæn*, the significance of which is discussed below. Byrhtferth of Ramsey has a lurid and characteristically imprecise account, in which the 'zealous thegns of his brother' conceived a plot to kill the king when he visited the house where Æthelred was staying with his mother. When Edward and his entourage arrived, 'the nobles and chief men who were with the queen' came out to meet him, and stabbed him as he was dismounting from his horse.[64]

Byrhtferth's vivid narrative has provided the basis for most subsequent descriptions of Edward's murder, but it may not be all that it seems.[65] More profitable, though less immediately appealing, is the bald account of the *Anglo-Saxon Chronicle*. Both the 'A' and the 'D' and 'E' recensions use the verb *ofslæn* ('to kill, slay') of Edward's murder, a word which, in the base-text of the *Chronicle*, is used not only of death in battle, but also for assassination and killing in the course of feud; in the late 750s, for instance, the deposed West Saxon king Sigeberht 'killed (*ofslog*) the ealdorman who had dwelt with him longest', and in 787, when King Cynewulf was killed by the ætheling Cyneheard and his men, 'they were all fighting with the king until they had killed (*ofslægenne*) him'. The incident in which one of Cynewulf's reeves was killed by Vikings (*hine man ofslog*) at Portland, Dorset, may be closest of all to what happened at Corfe in 978, for the suggestion is that the reeve misread the situation and that violence erupted almost by accident: 'he wished to force them to the king's residence [as if they were unlicensed traders], *for he did not know what they were*' (my italics).[66] It is possible that King Edward's death was also 'accidental' in that, far from being planned, it arose from a provocative confrontation between the young king (prone to violent behaviour, according to Byrhtferth) and one or more of the noblemen attending on his brother. It remains curious that the perpetrator is not named; Edward's grandfather King Edmund was killed in similar circumstances but 'it was widely known how he ended his life, that Leofa stabbed (*ofstang*) him at Pucklechurch'.[67] Could it be that too many people (perhaps not all of them belonging to Ælfthryth's faction) were secretly relieved to be rid of a violent and unstable youth?[68]

Byrhtferth names no names, but by the late eleventh century Queen Ælfthryth was widely regarded as the instigator of the crime.[69] Henry of Huntingdon, writing in the twelfth century, makes her the perpetrator as well.[70] There is little contemporary support for these allegations.[71] The alliterative poem on Edward's death explicitly distinguishes his killers from his kinsmen, who are merely blamed for not avenging him.[72] It is possible that the murderers were either too powerful or too useful to the new régime for any action to be taken against them: some sixty years later, Earl Godwine of Wessex retained power during the reigns of Harthacnut and Edward the Confessor, despite suspicions that he had been involved in the murder of their brother, Alfred ætheling. But this is some way from proving, or even suggesting, that Ælfthryth was personally implicated in her stepson's death. The later accounts of her role depend partly on the 'wicked stepmother' motif, and partly on a wish to explain the misfortunes of her son's reign as God's punishment for an impious crime. Similar suspicions were entertained about Ealdorman Ælfhere, named as the killer by William of Malmesbury, and his part in the reburial of Edward's body has been seen as 'an attempt at expiation by the guilty party'.[73] In Ælfhere's case, however, the earliest accounts actually contradict the later allegations. In his description of the reburial of the king's body, Byrhtferth calls Ælfhere 'the glorious ealdorman', in strong contrast to his earlier description of him as 'the blast of the mad wind from the western territories', while the *Passio* presents him as a loyal servant of the murdered king, 'outraged that such a precious pearl should be hidden in so vile a place'.[74]

This is not to say that the murder of a consecrated king did not inspire both horror and outrage.[75] If Æthelred's consecration, on 4 May 979, did not take place until more than a year after his brother's death, then the proper interment of Edward's body may have been a necessary preliminary to the ceremony.[76] The *Anglo-Saxon Chronicle* says that the murdered king had been buried at Wareham 'without the honour due to a royal corpse' (*butan ælcum cyneslicum wurðscipe*), and Byrhtferth describes how the body was taken to the house of 'an unimportant person' and subsequently buried without the honour due to it. There it lay until it was fetched by Ealdorman Ælfhere and reburied 'with great honour' at Shaftesbury; the *Passio* gives 18 February as the day of the translation, but does not specify the year.[77] Shaftesbury was a house closely connected with the West Saxon kings; it had been founded by King Alfred, one of whose daughters was its first abbess, and more recently Ælfgifu, paternal grandmother to both Edward and Æthelred, had retired thither as as a nun, and was celebrated as a saint.[78]

The reburial of the dead king seems to have marked the resolution of the affair. There is some uncertainty about exactly what (or who) was reburied, for in 1014 Archbishop Wulfstan *lupus* was maintaining that Edward's corpse had been burned. The bones discovered at Shaftesbury in 1931 were originally identified as those of Edward, but subsequent re-examination, while confirming that they are of approximately the correct date, suggests a man in his late twenties or early thirties, rather than a youth in his mid teens.[79] Be that as it may, the reburied body was clearly accepted as that of Edward, and on 4 May 979 Æthelred was consecrated king at Kingston, Surrey, 'with much rejoicing', in the presence of both archbishops and ten diocesan bishops.[80] Whatever feelings had been aroused by Edward's murder seem to have been assuaged and the tone of both Byrhtferth and the *Chronicle* reflects not 'an atmosphere of suspicion' but one of relief at a crisis passed.

By the late tenth century, there was a long tradition in England of venerating murdered kings and princes as saints, especially when the victims were juveniles.[81] The circumstances of Edward's death made it likely, even inevitable, that he should join their number. Cults, however, must be promoted by earthly sponsors, who may have political as well as religious motives. It has been argued that Edward's cult was set up by opponents of Æthelred intent on damaging his reputation and undermining his power, but the chief mover in the establishment of Edward's veneration seems to have been Æthelred himself.[82] Indeed a clause in the code known as 'V Æthelred', which reflects royal legislation promulgated at Enham in 1008, actually commands that the feast of Edward's martyrdom (18 March) should be celebrated throughout England. This, however, is less conclusive than it seems, for the clause is a later interpolation to the code made *c.* 1018, suggesting that it was Cnut rather than Æthelred who fostered the martyr's cult.[83] Yet there is evidence, much of it admittedly circumstantial, that Æthelred was the major sponsor of his brother's sanctity. It was perhaps in the 990s that he established a monastery in Edward's honour at Cholsey, Berkshire, an estate given to him by his mother Ælfthryth; the tower of the existing parish church may incorporate part of the tenth-century building.[84] Æthelred is also said to have endowed the church of Stow-on-the-Wold, Gloucestershire (formerly 'Edward's Stow'), dedicated to Edward the Martyr.[85] Both transactions are recorded only in post-Conquest sources, but Æthelred's eldest son, Æthelstan ætheling, who predeceased his father, left a sum of £6 'to Holy Cross and St Edward at Shaftesbury'.[86]

Most telling is the timing of the cult's emergence. The annal for 978 in the contemporary 'A' text of the *Anglo-Saxon Chronicle* says merely that the king was killed; it is only the later recensions that call him saint and martyr.[87] Nor is there any mention of the cult (or indeed of Edward) in Æthelred's diploma of 984 in favour of Shaftesbury Abbey, where Edward was by then buried.[88] His feast (18 March) is included in a calendar dated to the period 979–87, but only as a later addition to the text.[89] Most significant is Byrhtferth's statement that it was not until eleven years after Edward's death, that is in 989–90, that miracles began to occur at his tomb.[90]

It has been suggested that Æthelred, whatever his own views, was unable to promote the cult in the lifetime of his mother, who died on 17 November in either 999, 1000 or 1001, but this is to assume that Ælfthryth was implicated in the murder, and, as Byrhtferth makes clear, the cult had already developed before she died.[91] More significant is the fact that Viking raids on England began to increase both in number and severity during the 990s, and the attempts of the king and his counsellors to counter this threat included spiritual as well as practical expedients; old cults were refurbished and new ones instituted, including that of Edward the Martyr. The cult of his sister St Edith is said to have been established at about the same time; Goscelin of Saint-Bertin claims that visions of Edith were seen by both Æthelred himself and his mother's brother Ordwulf, which led to the translation of her relics thirteen years after her death.[92]

The role of the nuns of Shaftesbury, the keepers of Edward's relics, should not be forgotten. According to the *Passio*, Edward appeared to an unnamed religious of the house in 1001, instructing her to tell the abbess (and through her the king) that he desired a new resting place. Æthelred received the news 'with great joy', and commanded Wulfsige, bishop of Sherborne and *Elsinus praesul* to disinter Edward's remains and rebury them in a more prominent and suitable place; he himself was not able to attend the ceremony, because of the Danish threat.[93] This reburial constitutes the 'translation' of the relics and their 'elevation', and marks the formal inauguration of the cult. The *Passio*'s account presents some difficulties. St Wulfsige (993–1002) was indeed bishop of Sherborne at the time, but there was no bishop of any see whose name might be represented by *Elsinus*; he has been identified as Abbot Ælfsige of the New Minster, Winchester (988–1007), but at the time the *Passio* was written *praesul* should mean bishop, not abbot.[94]

More seriously, the *Passio* gives dates for the martyrdom of Edward and the first burial (18 March and 18 February respectively), but not for the elevation of 1001. That feast, on 20 June, is first recorded in the thirteenth century, and does not appear in any pre-Conquest calendar, which invites the suspicion that it 'was instituted after the *Life* was composed in order to consolidate its version of events'.[95]

On the credit side, the reference to the Viking raids reflects the known circumstances in 1001.[96] On 23 May in that year, a Viking force defeated the levies of Hampshire at Dean in Sussex, and went on to harry in Devon before descending on the Isle of Wight.[97] The repercussions of these activities in Dorset may be signalled by a hoard of pennies buried just outside the walls of Shaftesbury at about this time.[98] The fears of the nuns may also be reflected in the charter of Æthelred, issued after 7 October 1001, which grants the minster and land of Bradford-on-Avon, Wiltshire, 'to Christ and his saint, my brother Edward', as a refuge for the community and its relics against the Viking raids (*adversus barbarorum insidias*).[99] Whether Bradford-on-Avon, 'located on a navigable river within easy access of the Bristol Channel' was really a safer place than the hill-top *burh* of Shaftesbury is a moot point, and it is possible that 'the idea of a refuge for the nuns and their relics was a smokescreen, introduced in order to justify a large land-grant to Shaftesbury by connecting the transaction with the requirements of the martyr's cult'.[100] The surviving church of St Laurence at Bradford, dating from the early eleventh century, may have been built to accommodate the relics of St Edward.[101]

Edward's cult is very prominent in the surviving text of the diploma, to an extent which has aroused suspicion that it was interpolated at the time when the *Passio Edwardi* was composed, though if this is the case 'one might have expected greater efforts to coordinate the charter with the *Passio Eadwardi*'.[102] The diploma, like all the pre-Conquest documentation of the abbey, survives only in the fifteenth-century cartulary (BL Harleian Ms 61), all of whose contents 'are in a generally poor state, consistent with repeated copying ... words have fallen out, and the more difficult passages are now sometimes incomprehensible'.[103] It may be this, rather than interpolation, which accounts for the clumsiness observed in the formulation of the Bradford charter. Its anxieties certainly reflect the time at which the grant was allegedly made.

Æthelred's motives in promoting Edward's cult might have included residual guilt over the nature of his half-brother's death; there had always been an element of wergeld, payment of the blood-price, in the cults of martyred princes. There were, however, positive benefits as well. Belief in the efficacy of heavenly aid in times of trouble should not be underestimated, and saintly intercessors, especially those related to the reigning king, were particularly desirable as the Viking threat intensified. The rise to sainthood of the murdered king may also have underlined his successor's position as the 'Lord's anointed'. At about the time that Edward's cult was developing, Ælfric the homilist reminded his readers that 'no man can make himself king, but the people has the choice to choose as king whom they please; but after he is consecrated as king, he then has dominion over the people, and they cannot shake his yoke from their necks'.[104] The passage occurs in a group of homilies addressed *inter alia* to Ælfric's lay patrons, Ealdorman Æthelweard and his son Æthelmær, who had perhaps been among Edward's former supporters.[105] The vital importance of this triple bond of loyalty, between king and people and between both and God, was to loom large in the reign of Æthelred *unræd*.

2

The Old Guard and the Young King

'He is no worthy king who does not have the service due to him.'

Ælfric the homilist[1]

Æthelred's byname *unræd*, first recorded in the twelfth century, is a pun on his name, 'noble counsel, no counsel'. The implication is either that he received no good advice from his counsellors (or ignored it), or that he adopted *unrædas*, ill-advised policies, which brought him and his country to ruin; speaking of the terrible events of the year 1010, the *Anglo-Saxon Chronicle* laments that 'all those disasters befell us through *unrædas*'.[2] In this the character of the king is only one factor; equally important are the characters of the men who advised him. Any estimate of Æthelred as king must also take account of the abilities of his advisers.

The king's counsellors (*witan*) who formed his council (*witenagemot*) are known mainly from the witness-lists to his diplomas. These are merely catalogues of names, and to gain any idea of the men behind them we must put some flesh on the bare bone, no easy task, especially where the lay counsellors are concerned. In diplomas preserved in later copies, the witness-lists may be truncated, and it is usually the laity who are considered unworthy of remembrance. Even when the lists survive intact, they are selective in whom to include, with a bias towards holders of high ecclesiastical and secular office.[3] Different groups among the lay witnesses can, however, be distinguished. Many of the thegns (*ministri*) who attest diplomas were members of the king's immediate entourage, the officers of his household, but others were local men, attending councils held in their own neighbourhoods. The range of participants is illustrated by the witness-list to a suit heard before a 'great synod' at London between 988 and 990. Those present included Æthelgar, archbishop of Canterbury (who presided over at least some of the proceedings), the archbishop of York, the bishops of London, Ramsbury, Rochester, Selsey, Winchester and Hereford, the ealdormen of East Anglia, Essex, the western shires, Hampshire and Northumbria, the abbots of Peterborough, Ely, Winchcombe, Westminster, Muchelney and Exeter, and twenty-two thegns. Among the last were three northern thegns, presumably attending upon their earl (Styr Ulf's son, Nafena and Northwine), the Mercian brothers Ælfhelm and Wulfric, and three men whose toponymics suggest that they were local magnates from the south east, Leofwine of Moredon (Surrey), Siward of Kent and Leofstan of Sussex.[4]

Most diplomas are dated but few include the place of issue, so that it is impossible to construct a timetable of the royal councils held in Æthelred's time, let alone an itinerary of the king's movements.[5] Times and/or places are recorded for between twenty-five and twenty-seven meetings of Æthelred's *witanegemot* (see Table 1).[6] Clearly there were many more, for diplomas are preserved for all years of the reign except 978, 988–9, 991–2 and 1010, and meetings of the *witan* were the normal venue for their production. Moreover, just as we never get a full list of who attended the *witenagemot*, neither are we given a complete picture of its proceedings. The sources which record such meetings report only the particular items in which they are interested; all we know of the *witenagemot* which met at Amesbury in 995, for instance, is that it saw the election of Ælfric as archbishop of Canterbury.[7] From such scattered and partial references, however, it is possible to gain some idea of what might be on the agenda: 'the discussion and settlement of disputes, the promulgation of legislation, the election of higher ecclesiastics, political, administrative and military decisions, internal intrigue, or the authorization of grants of land and privileges'.[8]

Attendance at the *witenagemot* ensured that the participants could not only proffer aid and counsel to their king, but also gain access to his patronage and its rewards. It was during a *witenagemot* at *Beorchore* in 1007 that the king's reeve Ælfgar offered his royal lord 300 mancuses in gold and silver for eight hides of land at Waltham St Lawrence, Berkshire; the king was pleased to grant his request, and issued a diploma.[9] The downside, of course, was the danger of incurring the king's ill-will; in

Table 2. Meetings of the witenagemot, 978-1016

Place	*Year*	*Time of Year*	*Source*
Kingston-on-Thames, Surrey	979	4 May	*AS Chron*, 'CDE', 979; 'F', 980
Cirencester	985		S.896, 937
	988	23 March	S.873
	988	16 April	S.869
London	before 988/90		S.877
London	988/90		S.877
?*Winchester: Gillingham, Dorset	993	Pentecost: 17 July	S.876
Amesbury	995	Easter	*AS Chron*, 'F', 995
*Woodstock	?997		I Atr
Calne: *Wantage	997	Easter: 'a few days later'	S.891 (=? III Atr)
	997	25 July	S.890
	998	Easter	S.893
Cookham	995 x 999		S.939
Canterbury	1002	11 July	S.905
Headington, Oxfordshire	1004	7 December	S.909
? Shropshire	1006	? Christmas	*AS Chron*, 1006
Beorchore	1007		S.915
*Enham, Hampshire	1008	Pentecost	V/VI (and ? X) Atr
*Bath	1009		VII Atr
	1010	5 May/ 9 November	*AS Chron*, 1010
London	1012	Easter	*AS Chron*, 1012
	?1012	? June/July	S.927
	1013	18-20 April	S.931a/b
*Woodstock	1014		VIII Atr (=? IX Atr)
Oxford	1015		*AS Chron*, 1015

* denotes a law-making assembly

1015 the northern thegns Sigeferth and Morcar were murdered at 'the great assembly at Oxford', clearly on the king's orders.[10]

Æthelred cannot have been above twelve years old at the time of his coronation, and his youth meant that those who dominated his earliest years had previously served his father. Chief among them were the two archbishops, Dunstan and Oswald, the ealdormen Ælfhere of Mercia and Æthelwine of East Anglia, and above all Æthelred's mother, Queen Ælfthryth, and her friend Æthelwold, bishop of Winchester. Even the young king's household was still staffed by his father's men.[11] Not surprisingly, Æthelred's first surviving diplomas are in favour of those who had been his most consistent supporters, Bishop Æthelwold and Ealdorman Ælfhere. The earliest grant, made perhaps on the very day of his coronation, was a gift to Æthelwold of land in Hampshire for the episcopal church of the Old Minster, Winchester.[12] In the same year (979) Ælfhere received land at Olney, Buckinghamshire, lying, perhaps significantly, in the debatable territory between his sphere of influence in western Mercia and that of his rival Æthelwine in East Anglia.[13]

The days of this old guard were, however, passing. The 980s and early 990s saw the deaths of many who had dominated affairs during the time of Edgar and the troubled years that followed. Ælfhere, 'prince of the Mercian people' as Byrhtferth had called him, went to meet his Maker in 983; he was buried at Glastonbury, a house which long remembered him as a benefactor.[14] The Mercian ealdordom went to his brother-in-law, Ælfric *cild*, but his place as senior ealdorman was taken by his old sparring-partner, Æthelwine of East Anglia.[15] Æthelwold died on 1 August 984, and Dunstan on 19 May 988; it was to be some time before ecclesiastics of this eminence reappeared in the king's council. In 991 Ealdorman Byrhtnoth was killed, leading the men of Essex against the Vikings at the battle of Maldon, and on 28 February 992 Archbishop Oswald departed this life, followed by his friend and ally, Ealdorman Æthelwine.

The first ealdordoms to fall vacant were those of Hampshire and Sussex. On 18 April 982, Æthelmær of Hampshire died and was buried in the New Minster at Winchester. Later in the same year came the decease of Edwin of Sussex, who had probably had authority over at least west Kent as well.[16] Both had been appointed by Edward the Martyr.

Æthelred lost no time in making his own arrangements. It was fairly unusual (though not unknown) for there to be a separate ealdorman for the south east, and Edwin was not replaced. Hampshire was a different matter; its ealdorman was responsible for the heartland of the West Saxon kings. Æthelmær left two sons but neither was chosen to succeed him, nor (so far as can be told) did either receive any official position in Æthelred's reign.[17] The shires of central Wessex were given, before the year's end, to Ælfric, whose antecedents are unknown.[18] His name is one of the commonest in tenth-century England but he might be the thegn to whom Edward the Martyr had granted land at Wylye, Wiltshire, in 977, for an estate in the same place was later given by Æthelred to Ælfric's son Ælfgar.[19] It is probably he who exchanged land at South Heighton, Sussex, with Æthelgar, bishop of Selsey (980–88), in return for the unidentified *Lamburna*.[20]

Ælfric is entitled 'ealdorman of the provinces of Winchester' (*Wentaniensium Provinciarum dux*) in a diploma of 997, and his authority certainly extended to Wiltshire as well as Hampshire.[21] He attested diplomas as senior ealdorman from 999 until he was displaced by Eadric *streona* between 1009 and 1012, and a seal-matrix of the late tenth century, bearing the inscription *Sigillum Ælfrici* and an alpha and omega motif, may have belonged to him.[22] He remained in office until 1016 when he was killed at the battle of *Assandun*, which makes him the longest-serving of all Æthelred's officials, though he had (as we shall see) some close shaves. The secret of his durability is irrecoverable but the *Chronicle*'s estimate of him as 'one of those in whom the king trusted most' is borne out by events.[23] He was sufficiently influential to procure the king's patronage for his kinsmen as well as himself. In 985 he obtained the abbacy of Abingdon for his brother Edwin (985–90), and his son Ælfgar attests royal diplomas from 982 to 992, usually in a prominent position among the thegns (*ministri*). Ælfgar was a royal reeve, and perhaps sheriff of Berkshire, which may have lain within his father's ealdordom.[24]

It was not natural wastage alone that depleted the ranks of the former establishment. By the early 980s Æthelred was of age and perhaps irked by the tutelage of his father's advisers. The death of Æthelwold in 984 seems to have marked a decisive change, for the king's mother vanishes from the witness-lists to his diplomas, to reappear only in the early 990s. Another casualty, this time permanent, was Ælfric *cild*, exiled in 985 by a council which met at Cirencester. The charge against him was apparently treason, but no details are preserved, except his seizure of certain lands belonging to a widow called Eadflæd, possibly the relict of his brother-in-law Ælfhere.[25] He may be the Ealdorman Ælfric rebuked in a papal letter for seizing lands belonging to Glastonbury Abbey 'because you cling to a dwelling close to the same place'; Ælfhere had been a benefactor of Glastonbury, and perhaps there was a dispute over the terms of his grants to the church.[26] Like Earl Oslac before him, Ælfric fled the country after his banishment, and is not heard of again. A late tradition preserved at Abingdon alleges that he returned with a band of Vikings who ravaged the countryside 'for a long time' (*multo tempore*), but since it confuses the ealdorman of Mercia both with his namesake Ælfric of Hampshire and (apparently) with his eventual successor, Eadric *streona*, little reliance can be based upon its testimony.[27]

It was probably in the mid 980s that the king married his first wife. His four eldest sons (Æthelstan, Ecgberht, Eadred and Edmund) attest a diploma in 993, and even if the youngest was a babe in arms, their parents' marriage cannot be dated later than 989, and is likely to have been earlier. A fifth son, Eadwig, attests in 997, and a sixth, Edgar, in 1001, and (to judge by the supposed dates of their marriages) the king's daughters Ælfgifu and Eadgyth must have been born (at the latest) in the early 990s.[28] No contemporary source mentions, let alone names, their mother. John of Worcester identified the mother of Edmund, Æthelstan, Eadwig and Eadgyth as Ælfgifu, daughter of Æthelberht *comes*, but no ealdorman of this name is known.[29] Ailred of Rievaulx does not name the king's first wife, but calls her the daughter of Thored, earl of Northumbria.[30] Earl Thored's existence is not in dispute, but his identity has been a matter for discussion. He might be the Thored Gunnar's son who led an expedition to Westmoreland in 966, but Ealdorman Oslac, exiled in 975, also had a son called Thored.[31] In 971 father and son attested a diploma in favour of Peterborough Abbey and both had interests in Cambridgeshire, so the fact that Æthelstan the king's brother-in-law (*aðum*) was killed in 1010 while fighting among the men of Cambridgeshire suggests that the king's father-in-law was Thored Oslac's son.[32] That this Thored was the earl of Northumbria is suggested by the latter's appearances in Æthelred's diplomas; he attests between 979 and 990, with a concentration in the years 983–5, a likely date for the king's marriage with his daughter.[33] Since Oslac's exile followed upon the election of Edward the Martyr, it may be that the family were out of favour in his reign, and that Thored was appointed to Northumbria by Æthelred, but the attestations of northern magnates are too patchy and infrequent for his absence from the witness-lists of Edward's diplomas to be conclusive.[34]

Æthelred may have been married twice before 1002, first to the daughter of Ealdorman Thored, and then to Ælfgifu.[35] It was Ælfgifu, according to John of Worcester, who bore to the king both Edmund and Æthelstan, born before 993, and Eadwig, born before 997. The later interests of the two elder æthelings, however, suggest a close connection with the thegns of the north, such as one might expect if their mother had been associated with the region, as a daughter of Thored would be.[36] What contemporary evidence exists, therefore, seems to support the testimony of Ailred rather than that of John of Worcester, and though West Saxon kings are becoming famous for 'serial monogamy', there is no need to multiply royal wives without good reason.

Other members of the king's circle are revealed by the diplomas issued between 980 and 990, most of which are in favour of laymen. Some belonged to the king's household: the *milites* Wihtgar and Æthelmær, the butler (*pincerna*) Wulfgar, the king's scribe (*scriptor*) Ælfwine, his priest (*sacerdos*) Wulfric, and his huntsman (*venator*) Leofwine.[37] The diploma for Ælfwine *scriptor* was attested by four stewards (*disciferi*) and four butlers (*pincernae*), but the copyist has omitted to preserve their names.[38] The lands granted to named officials lay in Berkshire, Hampshire, Oxfordshire, Somerset and Wiltshire and (perhaps) in Kent, and with the exception of Oxfordshire these are the shires in which the king's household officials (*taini regis*) still held land at the time of Domesday Book.[39] The *milites* Wihtgar and Æthelmær received not bookland but temporary grants of *lænland*, Wihtgar for three lives and Æthelmær for his own lifetime, in both cases with reversion to the Old Minster, Winchester, to which the estates belonged.

Wulfgar's office is revealed only in a later diploma granting the same land to Abingdon, suggesting that other *ministri* attesting diplomas might be royal servants. Some are identified elsewhere as men in the king's service. Ælfgar the reeve, son of Ealdorman Ælfric, has already been mentioned. Æthelsige, who in 987 received land at *Æsce* and Bromley, Kent, seems to have been a particular favourite of Æthelred. He attests diplomas from 984 to 997, but is especially prominent before 994.[40] A diploma of 998 refers to his *dignitas*, which may imply some official position, perhaps in Mercia, which was without an ealdorman between the exile of Ælfric *cild* in 985 and the appointment of Leofwine in 994; the Welsh annals record the participation of an Æthelsige in the expedition against Maredudd of Deheubarth in 992, and such forays were usually headed by high-ranking Mercian officials.[41]

The men who stepped into the shoes of the previous counsellors were presumably chosen by the young king, and their advice must, to a degree at least, have informed his actions. It seems that Æthelred came to regret some of the favours he bestowed in the first decade of his reign. In a group of diplomas issued in the 990s, he complains of false counsellors who took advantage of his youth and inexperience, and obtained from him lands belonging to Abingdon Abbey, the Old Minster, Winchester, and the episcopal church of Rochester.[42] Some of them are named and shamed. The attack on Abingdon's lands and liberties was blamed upon Wulfgar, bishop of Ramsbury (981–985/6) and Ealdorman Ælfric of Hampshire, who allegedly bribed the king to bestow the abbacy on Ælfric's brother Edwin.[43] Edwin and Ælfric then used the church's lands to endow their followers, including Ælfric's son Ælfgar, who received land at Moredon, Wiltshire, which he gave to his wife Ælfgifu.[44] This was not the only church land which came into Ælfgar's hands; in 986 Æthelred himself gave him land at Ebbesborne Wake, Wiltshire, which apparently belonged to the Old Minster.[45] In 993, 'the king had Ælfgar, son of Ealdorman Ælfric, blinded'; no reason is given, but the first charter of restitution to Abingdon dates from this year.[46]

The fullest and earliest account of Æthelred's spoliation of Rochester is that of Sulcard of Westminster, writing *c.* 1076 – *c.* 1085. He describes how Æthelred 'in a fit of insolent rage set on fire the city of Rochester and the church of St Andrew, and by burning and ravaging laid waste all the lands which belong to the bishop of that city'. Similar stories are told by Osbern of Canterbury and William of Malmesbury, and could be mere amplifications of the brief record in the *Anglo-Saxon Chronicle* for 986: 'the king laid waste (*fordyde*) the diocese of Rochester'. Sulcard, however, goes on to account for the king's action:

> The same king had given a manor belonging to the bishop of Rochester to one of his own retainers (*suo militi*) who asked for it. As the bishop was ignorant of this donation, he shamefully evicted the man together with his people (*cum suis*). That was the cause of the king's anger. The king used also to say that if he could have laid hands on the bishop, he would have punished him with much disgrace.[47]

Sulcard says that Dunstan reproved the king both for the illegality of the original grant and for the devastation of the church's lands, and when Æthelred was unrepentant prophesied the devastation of his kingdom 'by fire and sword'. Sulcard's source is unknown, but his account is not implausible. The ravaging of the diocese was severe enough to affect the production of the Rochester mint, and coincides with an apparent rift between the king and Ælfstan, bishop of Rochester (*c.* 964–95), who ceases to attest Æthelred's diplomas between 984 and 987.[48] Moreover, though Ælfstan was reconciled with the king, and returned to his councils from 988, it was only after his death in 995 that his successor, Bishop Godwine, was able to recover the disputed land.[49]

The histories of the Kentish estates restored by the king to Rochester are illuminated by a series of vernacular memoranda preserved in the archives of the episcopal church. The one in Sulcard's account is probably Bromley, granted by the king to Æthelsige in 987.[50] The grant post-dates the supposed quarrel between king and bishop and the recorded devastation of the diocese, but may represent the reinforcement of an earlier transaction, perhaps the transformation of a temporary *læn*, like those to the *milites* Wihtgar and Æthelmær already noticed, to a permanent gift. In his restitution of Bromley to Rochester, the king accuses Æthelsige of exploiting his youth and inexperience, and describes him as 'an enemy of Almighty God and all the people'. He is accused of unspecified acts of theft of plunder and specifically of the murder of a loyal reeve who had tried to oppose him, for which offence he has been deprived of his lands and his *dignitas*. The diploma is dated 998, and Æthelsige ceases to attest in 997 at the latest.[51] His last certain appearance is in 994, and if (as suggested above) his *dignitas* involved some official position in Mercia, his fall might be associated with the appointment in that year of Leofwine as ealdorman of the Hwiccian provinces (central Mercia).[52]

Ælfgar and Æthelsige were not the only casualties of the 990s. Ealdorman Thored is not heard of after 992 and by 993 his ealdordom was in another's hands.[53] It is possible that he simply died, but his disappearance coincides with the return of Queen Ælfthryth, who seems completely to have eclipsed the king's wife, Thored's daughter; though she must have lived into the eleventh century (her youngest son, Edgar, only begins to attest in 1001), she is never mentioned in any context, public or private.[54] It was apparently Ælfthryth who was responsible for the upbringing of the king's children. The eldest ætheling, Æthelstan, refers in his will to 'Ælfthryth my grandmother, who brought me up', and she had the use of Dean, Sussex (*Æthelingadene*), which may have been one of the estates set aside for the benefit of the æthelings.[55] In the late 990s, the Hertfordshire landholder Æthelgifu appealed to her 'royal lady', assumed to be Ælfthryth, to find a place for her kinsman Leofsige in the household of 'the ætheling' (presumably Æthelstan), and one of the witnesses, with Ælfthryth, in a Berkshire lawsuit of 990 x 992 was Æfic, steward to the æthelings (*þare æþelinga discsten*).[56] Ælfthryth may also have appointed Æthelstan's foster-mother Ælfswith, to whom he left an estate at 'Weston' (unidentified), for in the late 990s a woman of this name was instrumental, with the queen's aid, in securing her brother Leofric's tenure of land at Ruishton, Somerset, and Leofric's wife, Wulfgyth, is described as the queen's kinswoman (*gesib*).[57]

The removal of Ælfgar, Æthelsige and Thored, coupled with the denunciations of the first two, along with Ealdorman Ælfric, Bishop Wulfgar and others unnamed, for leading the young king astray might seem to bear out Æthelred's reputation for following *unrædas*, the more so since Ælfric continued to survive and prosper. There is no need, however, to swallow the royal strictures whole. Some element of scapegoating might be suspected, perhaps relating to the notoriously thin line between despoiling ecclesiastical property and using church lands for temporary grants (*læns*) to the king's men; the lands of the Old Minster at Winchester had been used in this way to provide for the *milites* Wihtgar and Æthelmær, and, in his restoration of Downton and Ebbesborne to the same house, the king revokes grants made by himself and his predecessors to their *ministri*.[58] The origin of the quarrel between the king and Bishop Ælfstan of Rochester might have been a royal *læn* of the church's land too fiercely resented by an overconfident bishop, provoking in turn an over-reaction on the king's part to injuries offered to one of his thegns. But even if we take the criticism of those prominent in the 980s at face value, it remains the case that some at least of those who succeeded them in the 990s were men of whom even the most ardent moralist might approve. If the king's youthful inexperience had led him to rely upon some unfortunate choices, at least he seems to have learnt from his mistakes.

At Pentecost 993 the king summoned his council to Winchester, to discuss 'whatever was worthy of the heavenly Creator, whatever was suited to the salvation of my soul ... and whatever was timely for the people of the English', a meeting which signals 'a new phase of the king's reign, dominated by the disciples of the previous generation's monastic reform movement'.[59] Among those present was one of the major members of the 'reform' party, Queen Ælfthryth herself. Her reappearance seems to have brought her brother Ordwulf into prominence; he attests diplomas from 980, but not until 993 is he named as one of the king's chief counsellors.[60] The family came from the west country; Ordwulf's father, Ealdorman Ordgar, freed a slave at the altar of St Petroc, Cornwall, and was buried at Exeter.[61] Ordwulf's mother and brother were buried at Tavistock, Devon, where he and his wife Ælfwynn had founded a Benedictine abbey in the 970s.[62] Ordwulf did not succeed his father as ealdorman of Devon, but John of Worcester describes him as *Domnanie primas*, perhaps 'high-reeve of Devon'. There was more than one high-reeve in the area, but Ordwulf was probably reeve of the royal manor of Lipton in Devon, which included lands in eastern Cornwall.[63]

Another royal kinsman, Æthelmær son of Ealdorman Æthelweard of the western shires, attests diplomas from 983, the year in which the king gave him land at Thames Ditton, Surrey.[64] He rose to prominence in the 990s when he helped persuade the king to ratify the will of the Essex thegn Æthelric of Bocking.[65] By 1002 he was a royal seneschal (*discðegn*).[66] His emergence into the limelight coincided with that of his father. At the beginning of Æthelred's reign, Æthelweard attests in fourth place among the ealdormen, rising to third after the death of Ælfhere in 983; only after the deaths of Byrhtnoth in 991 and Æthelwine in 992 did he become senior ealdorman.[67]

In his *Chronicle*, Æthelweard tells us that he was a great-great-grandson of King Æthelred (866–71), but gives no details of the intervening generations.[68] The fact that he omits to mention the attempt by King Æthelred's son Æthelwold to overthrow King Edward the Elder might suggest that Æthelwold was Æthelweard's ancestor, but Æthelred had another son, Æthelhelm, and there may have been unrecorded daughters.[69] No source records the name of Æthelweard's father.[70] His mother was perhaps the Æthelgifu whose daughter Ælfgifu married King Eadwig in 956/7.[71] They are the ladies with whom, according to Dunstan's earliest biographer, Eadwig was caught disporting himself when he should have been at his coronation feast, and from whose presence he was dragged by Dunstan.[72] In 958 the marriage of Eadwig and Ælfgifu was annulled by Oda, archbishop of York, on grounds of consanguinity. If Ælfgifu was Ealdorman Æthelweard's sister, she and Eadwig were 'in the degree of kinship of six men, that is within the fourth knee', within which marriage was prohibited.[73] She remained on good terms with Edgar, who in 966 issued two diplomas in her favour, in both of which she is addressed as a married woman (*matrona*) and as the king's kinswoman.[74] In her will, drawn up soon afterwards, Ælfgifu returned one of the estates, at Linslade, Buckinghamshire, to the king, and made bequests to 'the ætheling' (presumably Edmund) and to Queen Ælfthryth.[75]

Ælfgifu's will mentions a sister-in-law, Æthelflæd, implying the existence of at least one brother.[76] She leaves estates at Mongewell, Oxfordshire, and Berkhampstead, Hertfordshire, for Ælfwaru, Ælfweard and Æthelweard to hold in common and since elsewhere she calls Ælfwaru her sister it seems reasonable to conclude that the two men were also her siblings. It has to be said that the names Ælfweard and Æthelweard were very common in the tenth century and the identity of Ælfgifu's brother Æthelweard with the ealdorman rests on the fact that both were closely related to the royal kindred.[77] It may also be relevant that the ealdorman, almost alone among his contemporaries, recorded a favourable judgement on Eadwig: 'he for his great beauty got the nick-name "All-fair" from the common people [and] deserved to be loved'.[78]

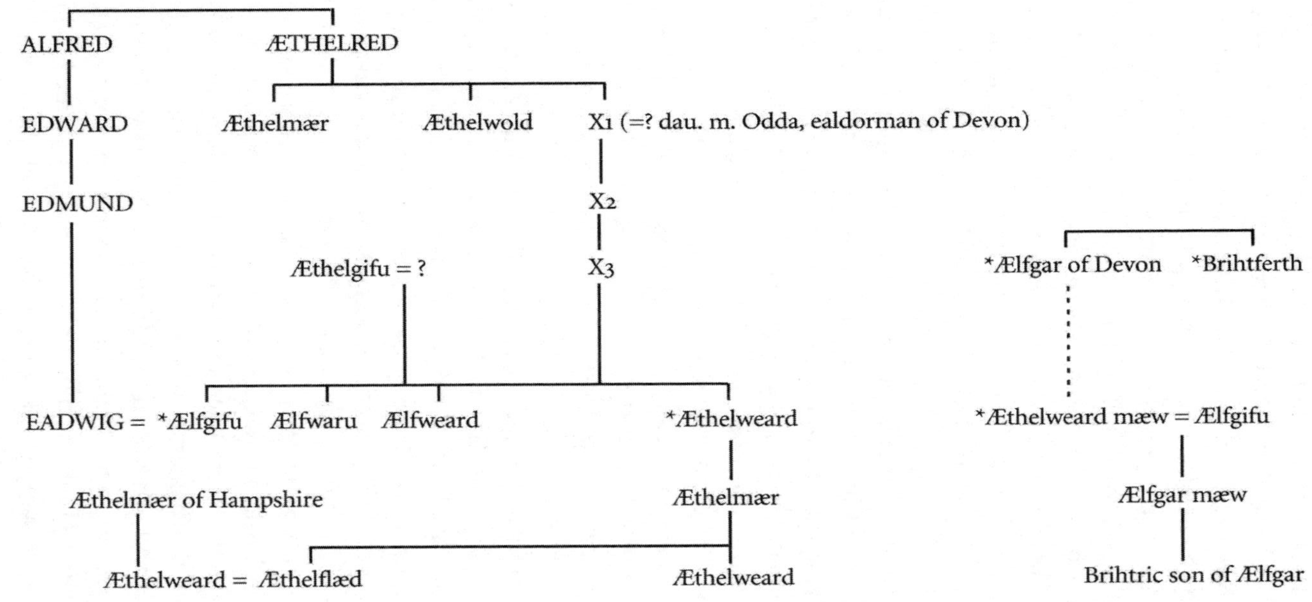

* persons addressed or described as royal kin
X1, 2, 3 generations between King Æthelred and Ealdorman Æthelweard
\- - - - - - conjectured relationship

Table 3. The Family of Ealdorman Æthelweard

Ælfgifu's estates lay predominantly in Buckinghamshire, with some in Oxfordshire, Hertfordshire and Dorset, suggesting that her family interests centred on southern Mercia rather than Wessex. Æthelmær's lands lay in the same general area, but with a stronger emphasis on Dorset. His endowment of Cerne Abbey in 987 included the reversion of Cerne itself and *Æscere* (possibly Esher, Surrey), plus lands at Minterne, Winterborne Abbas, Little and Long Bredy and Renscombe.[79] With the possible exception of *Æscere*, all the lands named lay in Dorset and seem to have belonged to Æthelmær, whereas those which he gave to his second foundation, at Eynsham, Oxfordshire, were mainly acquired from others. Eynsham itself was exchanged with his son-in-law Æthelweard for four widely-scattered estates, one of which (Lawling, Essex) was a bequest from Ælfflæd, Ealdorman Byrhtnoth's widow.[80] The only estate specifically said to come from his father, the ealdorman, was Esher, Surrey, and that had been given to the elder Æthelweard by his kinsman Brihthelm, bishop of Winchester (d. 963).[81] Other kinsmen had land in Dorset, Oxfordshire and Sussex, and included Godwine, probably the son of Ealdorman Ælfheah of Hampshire.[82]

Ordwulf and Æthelmær usually attest alongside Brihtwold, another royal kinsman whose wife Eadgifu appears as *coniunx Byrhtwoldi propinqui regis* in the New Minster *Liber Vitae*.[83] His family connexions are suggested by a sequence of names in *Ælf-* and *Briht-* found in the Devon area in the late tenth and eleventh centuries. It begins with Ælfgar, who in 958 attested a diploma of King Eadwig as the king's kinsman, immediately followed by his brother Brihtferth. They are presumably the thegns who continue to attest diplomas of Eadwig and Edgar until (in Brihtferth's case) 975.[84] The death of Ælfgar 'the king's kinsman in Devon' is recorded in the *Anglo-Saxon Chronicle* for 962. Since the *Chronicle* rarely mentions laymen below the rank of ealdorman unless they were killed in battle, he was clearly someone of importance.

Ælfgar and Brihtferth were contemporaries and perhaps relatives of Brihthelm, bishop of Winchester, who is addressed as kinsman by both Eadwig and Edgar, and was related to Ealdorman Æthelweard.[85] Ælfgar's association with Devon suggests that a younger member of the family might be Ælfgar 'the Honiton man', who attended a council held at London in 989–90, assuming (of course) that one of the Devonshire Honitons is meant.[86] This Ælfgar is probably Ælfgar *mæw* ('seagull'), who attests Æthelred's diplomas from 999 onwards. His father Æthelweard *mæw* (possibly identical with Æthelweard the Chronicler) founded the abbey of Cranborne, Dorset, and a secular minster at Tewkesbury, Gloucestershire, both of which were in the hands of Ælfgar's son Brihtric on the eve of the Norman Conquest.[87] Brihtric son of Ælfheah (or Ælfgeat) of Devon, killed on Cnut's orders in 1017, may have come from the same family.[88]

Another family which rose to prominence in the 990s was that of Wulfric *spot* Wulfrun's son, founder of Burton Abbey.[89] He and his brother Ælfhelm attest royal diplomas from the 980s and are joined in 986 by Wulfheah, Ælfhelm's son.[90] From the early 990s they appear towards the head of the witness-lists, and in 993 Ælfhelm was promoted to the ealdordom of Northumbria.[91] In 995 Æthelred confirmed Wulfric's possession of Dumbleton, Gloucestershire, exchanged with another king's thegn, and in the following year gave him land at Abbot's Bromley, Staffordshire.[92]

Wulfric's father is unknown, but his mother was the Wulfrun whose capture by the Danes at Tamworth in 940 is recorded in the *Anglo-Saxon Chronicle*.[93] The *Chronicle* rarely mentions women apart from queens and abbesses, so it seems that Wulfrun was a woman of some importance; her name is preserved in that of Wolverhampton ('Wulfrun's homestead'), given to her by King Æthelred in 985, where she founded a minster in the early 990s.[94] She was perhaps a kinswoman of the Mercian magnate Wulfsige the black (*maurus, se blaca*), to whom King Edmund granted a substantial estate in Staffordshire, where the bulk of the lands with which Wulfrun endowed Wolverhampton lay.[95] Wulfsige may have been her father, for his estate at Abbots Bromley, Staffordshire, passed first to Wulfrun and then to her son Wulfric.[96] The family had been favoured by Edgar, who in 963 gave lands at Darlaston, Staffordshire and Upper Arley, Gloucestershire, to Wulfrun's kinsman Wulfgeat; Wulfgeat attests Edgar's charters between 964 and 970.[97] Wulfric's name is too common for him to be identified among the beneficiaries of diplomas between 960 and 975, but his brother Ælfhelm may have received land at Parwich, Derbyshire, in 966, for the diploma is preserved in the Burton Abbey cartulary.[98]

The will of Wulfric, drawn up between 1002 and 1004, disposes of a huge estate, centred on the north midlands but stretching into ten shires

(Cheshire, Derbyshire, Gloucestershire, Leicestershire, Lincolnshire, Shropshire, Staffordshire, Warwickshire, Worcestershire and Yorkshire).[99] It included 'the land between Ribble and Mersey', described on the eve of 1066 as '188 manors in which there are eighty geld-paying hides', worth £145 2*s.* 2*d.*[100] Wulfric's tenure of this huge block of territory is comparable to the archbishop of York's holding in Amounderness, granted by King Æthelstan in 934.[101] He is described in the post-Conquest Burton Chronicle as *consul ac comes Merciorum*, and though this may be natural inflation of the founder's status, his heriot combines 'the money due ... from an earl with the horses and equipment due from a king's thegn'.[102] In his confirmation-charter for Burton Abbey, Æthelred describes Wulfric as 'a thegn of noble status' (*nobilis progeniei minister*) and he was perhaps the Mercian equivalent of a Northumbrian *hold*, midway between an earl and a thegn.[103]

From 993 the attestations of Wulfric and his nephew Wulfheah are accompanied by those of Wulfgeat who, though not related to them, appears to be associated with their family. His fate was certainly bound up with theirs, for he was deprived of his property in 1006, the year which saw the blinding of Wulfheah and the murder of his father, Ealdorman Ælfhelm. John of Worcester names Wulfgeat's father, Leofeca, otherwise unknown, and says that although the king loved him 'more than almost all others', he was nevertheless stripped of all his possessions and 'every dignity' (*omneque honore*) because of 'the unjust judgements and arrogant deeds' he had perpetrated.[104] He is presumably Wulfgeat 'the beloved thegn' (*dilectus minister*) named, with Ordwulf and Æthelmær, among the king's leading counsellors in 999, who encouraged him to restore the rights of Abingdon.[105]

Wulfgeat's name is common and further identification can only be tentative.[106] He may be the Wulfgeat who married Ælfgifu, widow of the blinded Ælfgar son of Ælfric, who brought to her new husband the land at Moredon given her by her first spouse. The estate was restored to Abingdon after Wulfgeat's forfeiture, and it has been objected that Wulfgeat son of Leofeca, as a friend to Abingdon, is unlikely to have been abstracting its land.[107] This is to accept the charge that Wulfgeat held Moredon illegally, whereas the diploma of restitution suggests rather that it was a three-life *læn* (Ælfgar, Ælfgifu, Wulfgeat). The allegation of illegality may have been fabricated to bolster the request

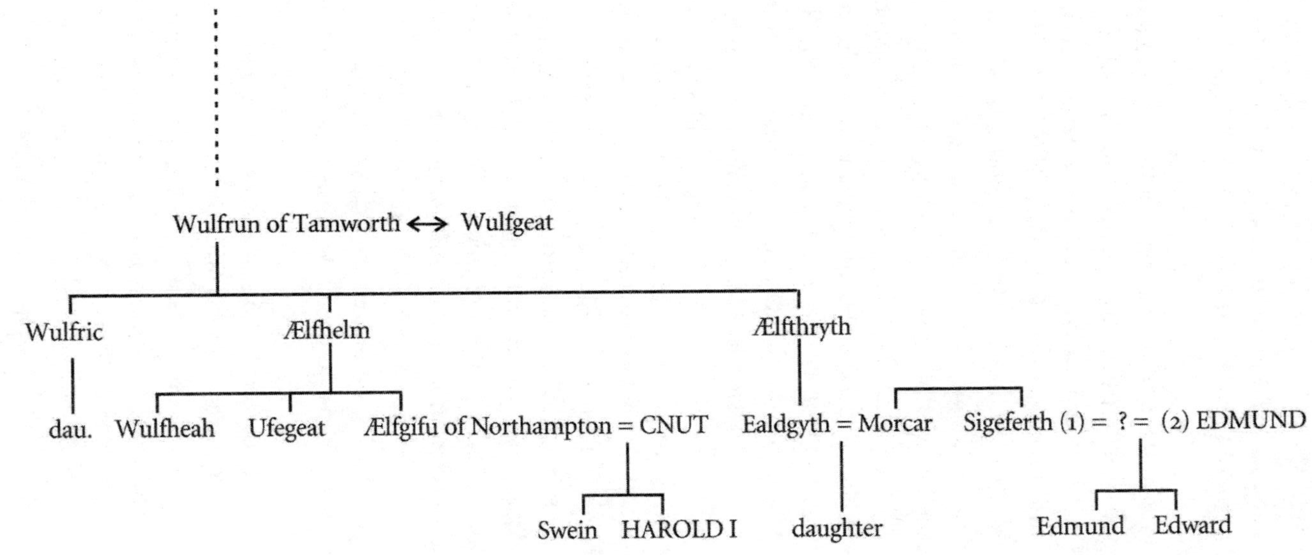

Table 4. The Family of Ealdorman Ælfhelm

of Wulfgar, abbot of Abingdon, for its return after Wulfgeat's forfeiture. It was notoriously difficult to recover *lænland*, especially if the holder had forfeited his estates; legally only his bookland should be seized, whereas his *lænland* should revert to the lessor, but this did not always happen.[108]

The landed interests of the leading magnates of the 990s seem to have lain in the south and west: Ordwulf and perhaps Brihtwold in Devon; Æthelmær and his family in central Wessex and southern Mercia; Wulfgeat perhaps in central Wessex, where Ealdorman Ælfric's known lands are also to be found; Wulfric and his family in northern Mercia. Such a distribution among the king's advisers might suggest a bias of royal interests, demonstrated in what is known of the king's itinerary, towards Wessex and western Mercia, but the appointments of Leofwine, ealdorman of central Mercia, and Leofsige, ealdorman of Essex, militate against such a conclusion, for both can be associated with the east midlands.[109] Leofwine was remembered as the donor of Alwalton, Huntingdonshire, to Peterborough Abbey.[110] Leofsige held lands in Hertfordshire and his sister Æthelflæd in Huntingdonshire. He has been identified as Leofsige, kinsman of Æthelgifu, the Hertfordshire landowner who made a will in the late 980s or 990s, but there is nothing to connect them beyond the name, which is in no way rare.[111]

It is more difficult to identify the backgrounds of the ecclesiastics in the king's council. Sigeric, archbishop of Canterbury (990–4), had been a monk of Glastonbury, abbot of St Augustine's, Canterbury and bishop of Ramsbury, and later traditions linked him with the foundation of Cholsey, Berkshire, and the promotion of St Edward's cult at Shaftesbury, Dorset. His rise was accompanied by that of his former abbot, Ælfweard of Glastonbury, who attests in a prominent position from 987 to 1009.[112] Sigeric's successor Ælfric (994–1005), a monk of Abingdon, had been abbot of St Albans and bishop of Ramsbury, a see which he continued to hold as archbishop; in his will, he left a warship to the people of Wiltshire, as well as one to Kent.[113] Both may be regarded as 'West Saxon' in sympathies and the same is probably true of Wulfsige, bishop of Sherborne (993–1002), a disciple of Dunstan, who presided over the transformation of Sherborne into a monastic chapter.[114] On the other hand, Wulfstan *lupus*, bishop of London, who from his first appearance in 996 is outranked among the episcopal witnesses only by the archbishops and the bishop of Winchester, may be associated with eastern England.[115]

Æthelred's leading ecclesiastics were a close-knit group, committed in varying ways to the ideals of the monastic reform movement. Archbishop Sigeric was the dedicatee of Ælfric's *Catholic Homilies* and the recipient of a letter from Abbot Ælfweard on the duties of an archbishop, later adapted either by Sigeric or his successor Ælfric for the benefit of Wulfsige of Sherborne.[116] Sigeric himself has left us a diary of his journey to Rome in 990, listing the churches which he visited in the city, and the staging-posts on his homeward road.[117] Ælfric the homilist wrote pastoral letters for Wulfsige of Sherborne and later for Wulfstan as bishop of Worcester (1002–16) and archbishop of York (1002–23).[118] Wulfsige himself, who continued to hold the abbacy of Westminster until 997, was in communication with Wulfstan as bishop of London.[119]

There was also a community of interest between the ecclesiastical magnates and their lay counterparts.[120] Many lay magnates were committed reformers, who patronized established houses and founded new ones. Ordwulf, Æthelmær and Wulfgeat encouraged the king to restore the lands and liberties of Abingdon Abbey, while Ealdorman Leofwine was remembered as a benefactor of Peterborough Abbey. The New Minster, Winchester, commemorated Brihtwold and his wife Eadgifu, Wulfgyth, wife of Ealdorman Ælfric, and her daughter-in-law Ælfgifu. Wulfric *spot* established a Benedictine house at Burton, and his mother a secular minster at Wolverhampton which received archiepiscopal support.[121] Ordwulf's abbey at Tavistock, described as 'Ordwulf's minster' when it was damaged by the Danes in 997, was a Benedictine house, 'for monks, not seculars but regulars, obedient to the precepts of the holy Rule'.[122] Æthelweard may have had a hand in the refoundation of Pershore Abbey, Gloucestershire, and his son Æthelmær was certainly a benefactor both of Malmesbury and of the New Minster, Winchester; he was also appointed lay advocate of the minster at Stoke-by-Nayland by its patroness, Ælfflæd, widow of Ealdorman Byrhtnoth.[123] Father and son were among the patrons of the leading scholar and writer of the age, Ælfric the homilist, who was in succession schoolmaster at Æthelmær's abbey of Cerne, and abbot of his foundation at Eynsham. Both were Benedictine houses. In the Old English preface to the first series of *Catholic Homilies*, Ælfric says that he was sent to Cerne at Æthelmær's request; his *Letter to the monks of Eynsham* makes it clear that the monastic community was constituted 'at the request of Æthelmær', and the foundation-charter commands that they 'order their lives by the Rule'.[124] Æthelmær lived in retirement at Eynsham until the crisis of Æthelred's last years brought him back to public life; Ordwulf, who retired at about the same time, seems to have ended his days in peace at Tavistock.[125]

With such advisers on hand, it is not surprising that the years on either side of the first millennium saw a resurgence in royal benefactions to reformed monasteries. It was in her son's reign that Ælfthryth established a nunnery at Wherwell and perhaps another at Amesbury.[126] It may indeed be that 'the period was one of the most prosperous for the advancement of the ecclesiastical cause before the Norman Conquest'.[127] The contribution of the laity to this advancement should not be forgotten. A substantial part of the endowment of Ramsey Abbey came from the local thegn Æthelstan Manneson and his contemporary Ælfhelm *polga* not only left his warship (*scegð*) to Ramsey, but also bestowed lands on both Ely and Westminster.[128] Nor was lay generosity lavished only on the Benedictines; the secular minsters remained 'familiar, accepted objects of patronage'.[129] The secular church has left few records of its own, and the wills of the late Old English aristocracy are often the main, or even sole, source of evidence for some minsters. We should know little of Stoke-by-Nayland, Suffolk, without the wills of Ælfflæd, widow of Ealdorman Byrhtnoth, and her family.[130]

Smaller churches also benefited from lay piety. One of the most striking developments of the late Old English period is the proliferation of estate-churches (*tunkirkan*), single-priest churches serving just one manor or vill. Not all were founded by laymen; the tenth-century church and baptistry at Potterne, Wiltshire, were probably built by the bishop of Ramsbury, who owned the manor.[131] But most of the estate-churches scattered through the countryside must have been established by the thegns to whom those estates belonged.[132] The will of the Essex thegn Æthelric of Bocking, for instance, bequeaths Bocking to Christ Church, Canterbury, 'except for one hide which I give to the priest who serves God there'.[133]

The foundation and endowment of such churches often cut into the parochial rights of the older minsters. Edgar had already legislated on the proper division of tithe in such cases, distinguishing 'old minsters', from thegnly churches, both those with graveyards and those without attached burial rights.[134] Æthelred refined the classification, listing (in descending order) 'head-minsters' (episcopal sees and great abbeys), 'median-minsters' (which would include old mother-churches), 'lesser' churches with a graveyard, and 'field-churches' which had no graveyard attached.[135] It was churches of the 'lesser' kind which eventually formed the basis of parochial organization in the later middle ages.

The king's lay counsellors included in their ranks some who were educated, even learned men. Under the will of Ælfwold, bishop of Crediton, Ordwulf received two books, 'Hrabanus and a martryology'. Given the expense involved in book-production, such a bequest would not have been made lightly and presumably Ordwulf could read or at least appreciate them.[136] Æthelweard and Æthelmær were certainly avid readers of devotional literature; they 'seem to have wanted ... in the vernacular the works which were in use in the environment of the monastic reform'.[137] Ælfric the homilist's *Lives of the Saints* was 'undertaken at the entreaty of many of the faithful ... and especially that of Ealdorman Æthelweard and of our friend Æthelmær, who most ardently favour our translations by often reading them'.[138] Æthelweard also possessed his own copy of Ælfric's *Catholic Homilies*, to which four extra pieces had been added at his own request, and a translation of Genesis was produced at his behest.[139] Nor were the ealdorman and his son the only laymen who commissioned work from Ælfric. The treatise *On the Old and New Testaments* was produced for Sigeweard of Asthall, a thegn of Oxfordshire; another thegn, Sigefrith, asked for a homily on virginity; and Ælfric also corresponded with the Warwickshire thegn, Wulfgeat of Ilmington.[140]

Æthelweard is remarkable in that he was an author in his own right, and one moreover who wrote in Latin rather than the vernacular. His *Chronicle* is often presented simply as a translation of the *Anglo-Saxon Chronicle*, and the first three books are indeed a rendering of selected passages from the *Chronicle*, with a little additional material. From the 890s, however, Æthelweard's version of events differs in important respects from all the surviving versions of the *Chronicle*, and some of the detail (like his estimate of King Eadwig, cited above) appears to reflect his own researches and opinions.[141] Even if he was merely using a *Chronicle* text unlike all others which have survived, he still presents an independent view of the tenth century.[142] Æthelweard intended to bring his work down to the time of writing (978–88) but in fact ends with the death of Edgar in 975; it is greatly to be regretted that his account of the reign of Edward the Martyr and the early years of Æthelred remained unwritten.[143]

Æthelweard's *Chronicle* is a history of his illustrious family, dedicated to his cousin Matilda, abbess of Essen (974–1011) and a great-great-granddaughter of King Alfred:

> Accordingly, sweet cousin Matilda, having gathered these things from remote antiquity, I have made communication to you, and above all I have given attention to *the history of our race* ... to you therefore I dedicate this work, most beloved, spurred by *family affection*.[144]

In his dedicatory prologue, he names among their common kindred the daughters of Edward the Elder, who married, respectively, Charles the Simple, king of the Franks, Hugh the Great, duke of the Franks, and Matilda's grandfather, Otto I. He adds Ælfthryth, daughter of King Alfred, wife of Baldwin II of Flanders, 'from [whom], as a matter of fact, Count Earnwulf [Arnulf II], who is your neighbour, is descended'.[145] Æthelweard is the only independent English witness for the identity of Elstrudis, wife of Baldwin II of Flanders, and King Alfred's daughter Ælfthryth, and the only English writer to mention, and indeed name, the daughters as well as the sons of her marriage.[146] He may have obtained this information direct from Ælfthryth's descendants, for her son Arnulf I (918–65) was the protector of Dunstan during his year of exile in Ghent in 956–7.[147]

Æthelweard's *Chronicle* belongs to a genre of 'family history' increasingly popular in the tenth and eleventh centuries. It was the first of its kind to be produced in England, and the only one written by a native Englishman.[148] Ottonian Germany, however, had already seen a number of examples, and Matilda was perhaps the moving force behind Æthelweard's work, as well as its dedicatee.[149] Certainly he asks her for further details on one of Edward's daughters who married 'a certain king near the Alps, concerning whom we have no information, because of both distance and the not inconsiderable lapse of time'.[150] Whether Matilda ever found out more and communicated it to her cousin we do not know, but she probably supplied the information on the south Italian expedition of her uncle, Otto II, in 982, and the death in the same year of her brother Otto, duke of Swabia, both of which are recorded in the *Anglo-Saxon Chronicle.* Like Æthelweard, the *Chronicle* gives the details of Duke Otto's descent from Edward the Elder: he 'was the son of the prince (*æþeling*) Leodulf (Liudolf) and this Leodulf was the son of the old Odda (Otto I) and of King Edward's daughter'.[151]

Just as laymen had literary and devotional interests, so ecclesiastics were involved in secular affairs. Churchmen are named among the leaders of armies and, even if they took no part in actual combat, they were presumably involved in strategic and tactical decisions; some were killed in the process.[152] Ecclesiastics were, of course, forbidden to bear arms but it seems that some of them did. In a private letter to Archbishop Wulfstan, Ælfric emphasizes the fact that churchmen, both monastic and secular, are called to spiritual warfare and must engage in no other: 'anyone who is ordained to this fight, if previously he has borne earthly weapons he is to lay them down at the time of ordination'.[153] Yet in his *Canons of Edgar*, composed only a year or so later, Wulfstan merely forbids priests 'to come armed within the church doors'.[154] Some ecclesiastics may have been compelled to undertake military duties (which need not include actual fighting). In his *Lives of the Saints*, Ælfric reproves 'earthly warriors' (*woruld-cempan*) who compel the 'servants of God' (i.e. monks) to 'earthly warfare' (*to þam woruld-licum gefeohte*), thereby diverting them from the spiritual struggle.[155] Since the work was produced for Æthelweard who, as ealdorman, was responsible for the military obligations of the west country – a *woruld-cempa*, in fact – the rebuke is fairly pointed. But compulsion may not have been the only factor. The more prominent churchmen, especially bishops, were not only spiritual leaders but also landholders, and landholding carried military responsibilities, though these need not be carried out in person.[156] In addition, such service was not merely a public duty to the king, imposed on all his subjects, lay or ecclesiastic, but also a spiritual obligation to God's vicar, his deputy upon earth, and it was becoming 'more difficult to place limits on what sort of service was due to him'.[157] Not all churchmen may have found this burdensome or unwelcome;

the pious lady Ælfflæd thought a tapestry depicting the warlike deeds of her husband Byrhtnoth a fitting gift for the abbey of Ely.[158]

The mixture of ecclesiastical and lay concerns is epitomized by the will of Ælfwold, bishop of Crediton (997–1012 x 1015). Not only did he leave two of his precious books to the layman Ordwulf, but he also remembered his military retainers, each of whom was given 'the horse which I have previously lent him'; gifts of armour went to his kinsman Wulfgar son of Ælfgar (three mail-coats), his brother-in-law Godric of Crediton (two mail-coats) and Cenwold (a helmet and a mail-coat). Most striking of all is his bequest to the king of a sixty-four-oared ship 'all ready except for the oarports', which he 'would like to prepare fully in a style fit for his lord, if God would allow him'.[159] This is certainly a warship, like the one bequeathed to the king by Archbishop Ælfric (995–1005), specified as 'his best ship, and the sailing-tackle with it, and sixty helmets and sixty coats of mail'.[160] The military interests of these and other churchmen were more immediate than a simple response to royal demands. The years on either side of the first millennium may have been an era of literary culture and monastic reform, but they also saw the return in force of England's old nightmare: the men of the North.

3

The Great Terror

'In that year it was determined that tribute should first be paid to the Danish men because of the great terror which they were causing along the coast.'

Anglo-Saxon Chronicle, 'C', 991

The calibre of the king and his counsellors was to be sorely tested in the years around the first millennium, which saw the return of 'the roaming fleets of seaborne heathen' who had harassed their forebears.[1] The 'northern naval force' which ravaged Cheshire in 980 and sacked St Petroc's, Cornwall, in 981 may have come from the western settlements of the northmen, and so perhaps did the force which in 988 attacked the royal vill of Watchet, Somerset, killing the Devonshire thegn Goda and many others.[2] Other raids, like those on Southampton and Thanet in 980 and on Portland, Dorset, in 982, perhaps originated in Scandinavia itself.[3] Some Viking fleets may have used Normandy as a base, for relations between Æthelred and Duke Richard I (942–96) seem to have reached breaking-point in 990. Perhaps Archbishop Sigeric, who travelled to Rome for his pallium in the spring of that year, requested papal assistance, for a few months later Pope John XV despatched an embassy headed by Leo, bishop of Trevi, to make peace between the adversaries. Bishop Leo arrived at Æthelred's court on Christmas Day 990, and messengers were despatched from the king to the duke. A formal peace was agreed at Rouen on 1 March 991; the cause of the dissension is not stated, but the agreement included a mutual undertaking not to entertain each others' enemies, among whom Viking bands might have been included.[4] Whatever their source, the early raids seem to have done only minor damage, but that was to change with the arrival of fleets led by the most powerful among the competing rulers of the northlands.

The treaty between Æthelred and Richard I was formalized on 1 March 991. On 10 or 11 August in the same year, Ealdorman Byrhtnoth was killed at Maldon by a fleet which had previously sacked Ipswich.[5] Most versions of the *Anglo-Saxon Chronicle* merely record the death of the ealdorman; only the 'A' recension, which is contemporary, says that Byrhtnoth and his army (*fyrd*) fought a battle with the Vikings, who slew the ealdorman and held the battlefield (*wælstowe ahton geweald*).[6] The traditional site of the battle is at the landward end of the causeway leading to Northey Island, in the River Blackwater, downstream of Maldon. It is identified only in the Old English poem known (since 1834) as *The Battle of Maldon*, which seems, on this point at least, to be reliable.[7] The anonymous poem, which as it stands lacks both beginning and end, describes the meeting of English and Vikings on the banks of the Blackwater ('Panta's stream'); the Viking demand for tribute (*gafol*), indignantly refused; the armed clash and Byrhtnoth's fall; the flight of the unsteadiest elements; and the heroic stand of the ealdorman's hearth-troop which fell to a man around the body of its dead lord.[8] The historicity of the poem's account is open to discussion; it is not an historical but a literary work, and in no sense an eye-witness report.[9] At the very least it illustrates the impact which the battle had on the contemporary imagination.

The loss of the second-ranking ealdorman in the kingdom was a different matter from the fall of a local reeve, and the shock caused by this disaster may be judged by its impact on all the surviving sources. It is recorded by Byrhtferth in the *Vita Oswaldi*, as well as in the *Chronicle* and the poem, and was presumably the climax of the tapestry celebrating Byrhtnoth's life and deeds which his widow Ælfflæd presented to Ely Abbey, where he was buried.[10] The reverse at Maldon required a national response, and the *Chronicle* reports that for the first time a tribute (*gafol*) was paid to the invaders 'because of the great terror that they were causing along the coasts'.[11] This may have produced a temporary respite; Ælfric, in the preface to his second set of *Catholic Homilies*, composed about this time, speaks of 'the great injuries of hostile pirates' as something now in the past.[12] But the Viking fleet did not leave English shores.

In 992, 'all the [English] ships that were of any use' were assembled at London and entrusted to Ealdormen Ælfric of Hampshire and Thored of Northumbria and Bishops Ælfstan of London and Æscwig of Dorchester, who 'were to try if they could entrap the Danish army anywhere at sea'. The ensuing débâcle is blamed by the *Chronicle* on the devious behaviour of Ealdorman Ælfric, but the implied state of unreadiness in the ships themselves may have had something to do with it, and Ælfric retained his position without impairment (it is Earl Thored who is not heard of again, though nothing suggests that he lost his rank for incompetence).[13] As for the Vikings, they moved off to attack Bamburgh in 993, after which they sailed up the Humber 'and did much damage there, both in Lindsey and in Northumbria'. The failure to provide effective opposition is blamed on the local leaders, Fræna, Godwine and Frithugist, who 'first started the flight'.[14] In 994 the fleet was back in southern England. The Viking forces attacked London on 8 September, but 'suffered more harm and injury than they ever thought any citizens (*burhwaru*) would do to them' and the city was saved.[15] The coasts of Essex, however, along with those of Kent, Sussex and Hampshire were ravaged and finally the Danes 'seized horses and rode as widely as they wished and continued to do indescribable damage'.[16]

The 994 annal gives the names of the Viking leaders as Oláf and Swein, who can be identified as the Norwegian adventurer Oláf Tryggvason and Swein Forkbeard, king of Denmark (987–1013). Whether either or both had commanded the Viking army from the beginning is uncertain. The 'A' text of the *Anglo-Saxon Chronicle* implies that Oláf had been present at the battle of Maldon in 991, but the entry (sub anno 993) has conflated the events of more than one year.[17] Swein's presence at Maldon rests upon a memorandum of the late 990s, recording the settlement of a dispute over the will of the Essex thegn Æthelric of Bocking. One of the charges against Æthelric was his alleged involvement in 'the treacherous plan that Swein should be received in Essex when first he came there with a fleet'. His crime is dated to the episcopate of Archbishop Sigeric (990–4), which would cover Swein's attack on London on 8 September 994 (Sigeric died on 28 October in that year), but the elapse of time implied suggests an earlier incursion.[18]

Oláf and Swein are well recorded in Scandinavian history and legend. Oláf Tryggvason's career is largely known from skaldic verses and rather late sagas, which make him a grandson of Harald Fairhair, king of Norway, though in fact 'his claim to royalty may have been no better than that of Perkin Warbeck'.[19] Swein Forkbeard was a more formidable figure. The runestone erected by his father, Harald Bluetooth, at the dynastic centre of Jellinge claims that Harald 'won all Denmark for himself, and Norway, and christianised the Danes'. What this meant in practice is still not entirely clear, but by 987, when Swein ousted his father and seized the kingdom, Denmark was well on the road to statehood, and the powers and resources of its kings were greater than those of any other Scandinavian leader.[20] The appearance of Swein and Oláf made the Viking threat of the 990s very different from that faced by Alfred a century earlier. While the ninth-century raiders were seeking lands in which to settle, their descendants were primarily intent on acquiring treasure to further their ambitions at home; hence their concentration upon England, the richest kingdom in the British Isles and one of the richest in northern Europe.[21]

The English response to the challenge got off to a slow start. The treaty with Richard of Normandy implies awareness of wider aspects of the Viking assault, though its practical effect is another matter; a Viking fleet found refuge in Normandy in the year 1000.[22] The *Chronicle*'s reference, sub anno 992, to 'all the ships that were of any use', suggests a fall in military preparedness since the time of Edgar. In his *Life of St Swithun*, composed in the 990s, Ælfric writes regretfully of the days of that great king, when 'no fleet was ever heard of except [that] of our own people who held this land'.[23] In such circumstances, it was sensible enough to buy time, and this was the action urged by Archbishop Sigeric after the defeat at Maldon in 991, when a tribute (*gafol*) of £10,000 was paid.[24] The ravaging and burning of 994 produced a similar response. Sigeric and the ealdormen Ælfric of Hampshire and Æthelweard of the western shires 'obtained permission from the king to purchase peace for the districts (*læppan*) which they had rule over under the king', presumably Kent, the central shires of Wessex, and the west country.[25] The payments may have amounted to £6000 between the three of them (see below); Sigeric is known to have sold the manor of Monks Risborough, Buckinghamshire, for £115 towards the redemption of Christ Church, Canterbury.[26]

It has been one of the commonest charges against King Æthelred that he preferred to pay off the Danes rather than fight them, and such criticism may have been voiced at the time.[27] In fact the king's strategy went beyond simple bribery. The *Anglo-Saxon Chronicle* says that the Viking army of 994 was paid £16,000 plus provisions, and given winter quarters at Southampton, 'on condition that they should cease that harrying'. The surviving treaty between Æthelred and the Viking army goes into more detail.[28] It refers to the earlier agreements with Sigeric, Ælfric and Æthelweard, and extends a 'general peace' (*woroldfrið*) on the same terms to the English people and the Viking army. The *gafol* is set at £22,000, as against the £16,000 of the *Chronicle*, but the difference may include the earlier sums paid by the archbishop and the two ealdormen for their regions. In return, the Viking force agreed to assist the English against any other marauders, in return for their keep. Any land which harboured the enemies of England was to be regarded as hostile by both parties to the treaty; it is difficult not to believe that Normandy was one of the intended objects of this clause. Trading ships coming to England, and English ships and traders abroad were to have protection and safe passage, and wergelds were agreed for Englishmen slain by Vikings and vice-versa; these clauses seem to imply that some at least of the Viking bands would remain in England, presumably in the king's employ.[29] Especially striking is clause 6, 1:

> With respect to all the slaughter and all the harrying and all the injuries which were committed before the truce was established, all of them are to be dismissed, and no one is to avenge it or ask for compensation.

In effect, a line was to be drawn under the recent hostilities and a new start to be made but, to judge from the sequel, this was at best temporary.

The treaty specifies the Viking leaders as Oláf (Tryggvason), *Justin* (Jósteinn, perhaps Oláf's maternal uncle) and the otherwise unrecorded Guthmund Steita's son.[30] Swein Forkbeard's name is not included, though the *Chronicle* implies that he was a party to the payoff of 994. It also records that Æthelred made a separate agreement with Oláf. Ælfheah, bishop of Winchester, and Ealdorman Æthelweard were sent to conduct Oláf to Andover, and there 'King Æthelred stood sponsor to him at confirmation and bestowed gifts on him royally. And Oláf promised – as also he performed – that he would never come back to England in hostility'.[31]

This agreement between Oláf and Æthelred may have been aimed against Swein.[32] In 995 Oláf returned to Norway with his newly-found wealth and used it in a successful bid for the kingship. The pro-Danish jarls of Lade were driven out, and found refuge at the court of their overlord, King Swein; it was in the late 990s that Erik Hákonsson married Swein's daughter Gytha, a union which was to have repercussions in England after the Danish conquest of 1016.[33] If Swein had not already returned to Denmark, Oláf's coup would have fetched him back, and he spent the next four years constructing an alliance against Oláf. His efforts bore fruit in the battle of Svold (999), in which Oláf was killed and Danish suzerainty over Norway was re-established.[34] It seems that Æthelred, by setting his two major opponents at each others' throats, successfully neutralised the immediate threat to his own kingdom, for no raids are recorded for the years 995–6.[35]

Such respite as there was proved only temporary and the *Anglo-Saxon Chronicle* for the next few years makes melancholy reading. 'In this year [997] the raiding-army (*here*) went round Devon into the mouth of the Severn and ravaged there, both in Cornwall and Wales and Devon'. It then backtracked to savage southern Devon, burning down Ordwulf's monastery at Tavistock in the process. Over the next two years it harried in Dorset, the Isle of Wight, Hampshire, Sussex and Kent, before taking itself off to Normandy in the summer of the year 1000. Who led this force we do not know, nor whence it came. If Æthelred had hired some of the members of the 994 army, then perhaps they had found their conditions of employment unsatisfactory; there is something pointed about the attack on a monastery so closely associated with the king's uncle.[36] Wherever the *here* came from, it may have received help from elsewhere in Britain. There is some numismatic evidence for raids from Ireland and other Norse colonies in the Irish Sea area in the 990s, and it was perhaps in response to such incursions that Æthelred led his army to ravage Cumberland in 1000, while his fleet did the same for the Isle of Man.[37]

In 1001 the same or another Viking force sailed up the Exe and besieged Exeter. Though the attack was successfully repelled, the levies of Devon and Somerset were defeated in battle at Pinhoe. The *here* encamped upon the Isle of Wight and in 1002 terms were arranged through Leofsige, ealdorman of Essex, and a *gafol* of £24,000 was paid. In 1003 Exeter was attacked again, and this time taken by storm; the *here* moved into Wiltshire, brushed aside the levies of Wiltshire and Hampshire, and burnt down the borough of Wilton. For the first time the identity of the leader is revealed, none other than King Swein Forkbeard. How long he had been in England is unclear, but he could have taken command as early as 1000 or 1001. In 1004 he took the fleet to Norwich and sacked the borough; three weeks later he was brought to battle near Thetford, but despite a bitter struggle the East Anglians were worsted. It was not English arms but the 'great famine' of 1005, 'such that no man ever remembered one so cruel', that sent Swein and his fleet home to Denmark.

Throughout this catalogue of disasters, the *Chronicle* lays the blame on the incompetence and vacillation of the English leaders and the loss of morale produced in the rank and file by their shilly-shallying. In 999, while the *here* was besieging Rochester, 'the Kentish levy came against them there and they then joined battle stoutly; but, alas! they too soon turned and fled because they had not the support which they should have had'. The men of Devon and Somerset fared even more ignominiously at Pinhoe in 1001: 'as soon as they joined battle, the English army gave way, and the Danes made a great slaughter there'. In 1003 the men of Wiltshire and Hampshire 'were going very resolutely towards the enemy', but their commander, Ælfric of Hampshire 'was up to his old tricks; as soon as they were so close that each army looked on the other, he feigned him sick, and began retching to vomit, and said that he was taken ill, and thus betrayed the people whom he should have led. As the saying goes, "when the leader gives way, the whole army will be very much hindered"' (*Đonne se heretoga wacað þonne bið eall se here swiðe gehindred*).

Nor was it only the local levies which put up such a poor showing. In 998 'the army (*fyrd*) was often assembled against them, but as soon as they were to have joined battle, a flight was always instigated by some means'. In 999 the king called out both the land-army (*landfyrd*) and the fleet (*scipfyrd*), but

> when the ships were ready, there was delay from day to day ... and ever as things should have been moving, they were the more delayed from one hour to the next, and ever they let their enemies' force increase, and ever the

> English retreated inland and the Danes continually followed; and in the end it effected nothing ... except the oppression of the people and the waste of money and the encouragement of their enemies.

In 1001 'the Danes went about as they pleased and nothing withstood them, and no *sciphere* on sea, nor *landfyrd*, dared go against them, no matter how far inland they went'.[38]

The description of Æthelred's reign in the *Anglo-Saxon Chronicle* has contributed most to his reputation for cowardice and foolishness, and it is therefore important to understand the nature of its account. The recensions which cover the whole of Æthelred's reign, 'C', 'D' and 'E' (and the post-Conquest 'F'), all depend for the period 983–1016 on a narrative composed, perhaps at London, between 1016 and 1023. Its author had seen the Danish conquest and the fall of the West Saxon line, and his knowledge of the outcome affects his treatment of the whole reign.[39] He implies, for instance, that the raids of 997 were unopposed, but a contemporary diploma reveals that 'the whole army' (*omnis exercitus*) had been called out in that year.[40] Even more striking is the difference between the main text of the *Chronicle* and the only independent version, the 'A' recension, represented by a single, contemporary annal for 1001.[41] It begins with the arrival of a Viking fleet off the Sussex coast, which proceeded to Dean, that 'Dean of the æthelings' which had once been held (and perhaps still was) by the king's mother, Queen Ælfthryth.[42] There, on 23 May, 'the people of Hampshire came against them, and fought against them'. The severity of the encounter is shown by the English casualty list, which included two high-reeves, Æthelweard and Leofwine, and three thegns of the bishop of Winchester, Leofric of Whitchurch, Wulfhere the bishop's thegn, and Godwine of Worthy, son of Bishop Ælfsige (d. 958).[43] In all eighty-one men were killed on the English side 'and there were far more of the Danes killed, although they had control of the field'.

The victorious Danes then moved on to Devon, where they were met by one Pallig 'with the ships which he could collect, because he had deserted King Æthelred in spite of all the pledges (*trywða*) which he had given him'; presumably he was a Viking commander who had entered the king's employ, with his personal following (*lið*), at some time after the truce of 994.[44] Having entered Devon via the Exe, the Danes journeyed to Pinhoe, and here were met by Kola the king's high-reeve and Eadsige the king's reeve (presumably of Pinhoe) 'with what army they could gather, but they were put to flight there, and many were killed, and the Danes had control of the field'. The Danes then repaired to the Isle of Wight 'and soon afterwards terms were made with them and they accepted peace'.

When the account in the 'A' text is compared with that of the other recensions, what is striking is the difference in tone. The elements are the same, the inability of the English to withstand the Danes, the existence of traitors in the ranks and the enforced truce, but here the levies put up a stout, if unsuccessful resistance, and their leaders, whether royal officers or local thegns, fight courageously, even against the odds. There is no precipitate flight at Pinhoe; Kola and Eadsige, caught by surprise and with a scratch force, do the best they can, and many men are killed before they are forced to flee.[45] There is no loss of morale in the 'A' text's account, and its existence warns against an uncritical acceptance of the lamentations found in the other recensions of the *Chronicle*.

The partiality of the author of the underlying narrative emerges in his treatment of Ælfric of Hampshire on the one hand, and the East Anglian commander, Ulfcytel, on the other. The outrageous behaviour of Ælfric in 1003 is contrasted with that of Ulfcytel in the following year. After the sack of Norwich, Ulfcytel and the East Anglian *witan* 'determined that it would be better to buy peace from the *here* before they did too much damage in the country, for they had come unexpectedly and he had not time to collect his army'. No such excuses are forthcoming for any of the West Saxon commanders. Moreover the payment of *gafol* is presented as a perfectly reasonable response to the situation, and Ulfcytel used the time bought wisely, if (in the end) unsuccessfully: he sent men to destroy the Danish ships ('but those whom he intended for this failed him'), and 'collected his army secretly, as quickly as he could'. The Danes, meanwhile, under cover of the truce, had captured and burnt Thetford, 'within three weeks after their ravaging of Norwich'. This could not be ignored and Ulfcytel, despite the fact that his levies were not fully assembled, offered battle outside the devastated town. After a bitter struggle, the East Anglians lost the day, 'but if their full strength had been there, the Danes would never have got back to their ships as they themselves said; they never met harder fighting in England than Ulfcytel dealt to them' (*hi næfre wyrsan handplegan on Angelcynne ne gemetton þonne Ulfcytel him to brohte*).

It is of course possible that Ælfric of Hampshire really was an incompetent coward and Ulfcytel a resourceful hero. Ulfcytel's reputation in Scandinavian tradition (which conferred on him his byname of *snilling*, 'the bold') bears out the words of the *Chronicle*. Sighvatr Thórðarson, one of the court poets of the Norwegian king Oláf *helgi*, calls East Anglia 'Ulfkell's land', and the contemporary *Liðsmannaflokkr*, which celebrates the exploits of the Danish leaders Thorkell and Cnut, praises the fierce resistance which he offered at the siege of London (1016).[46] As for Ælfric, the *Chronicle* has already blamed him for the débâcle in 992, when an English fleet sent against the Danes failed in its mission because the ealdorman 'sent someone to warn the enemy, and then in the night before the day on which they were to have joined battle, he absconded by night from the army, to his own great disgrace, and then the enemy escaped, except that the crew of one ship was slain'. It sounds bad, and perhaps it was, but it must be remembered that Ælfric might have had legitimate reasons for dealing with the Danes; in 994, he, along with Ealdorman Æthelweard and Archbishop Sigeric, 'bought peace' for their districts, as Ulfcytel was to do in 1004. Nor were there any repercussions; Ælfric kept his rank and office, and although his son Ælfgar was blinded in the following year, there may have been other reasons for that.[47] Ælfric himself was slain in 1016, fighting for King Edmund II Ironside at the battle of *Assandun*.[48]

Aside from the *gafol* paid in 1002, the *Chronicle* gives little idea what steps the English authorities took to combat the Viking threat. It is typical that Æthelred's expedition to Cumberland and Man in the year 1000 is presented as a botched job, in which the fleet ravages Man only because it has failed to rendezvous with the king (who was in personal command of the *landfyrd*) in Cumberland. In fact the campaign was probably aimed from the first at the Scandinavian kings of Man and the Sudreys as well as Malcolm of Strathclyde; both kingdoms had long proved troublesome to the kings of the English.

Æthelred also took steps against the enemy within. In the late summer or autumn of 1002, 'the king ordered to be slain all the Danish men who were in England [and] this was done on St Brice's Day (13 November)'. A diploma for St Frideswide's, Oxford, renewing the title-deeds destroyed when the church was burnt over the heads of the Danes of Oxford, reveals that they had taken refuge there to escape the decree 'sent out by me with the counsel of my leading men and magnates, to the effect that all the Danes who had sprung up in this island, sprouting like cockle amongst the wheat, were to be destroyed by a most just extermination'.[49] Needless to say, the decree was not aimed at the English of Scandinavian descent living in the eastern shires, who in 1004 were to give their remote cousins the hardest fighting they had ever met with in England.[50] The intended victims were probably the remnants of the Viking bands who had entered Æthelred's service in 994, and of whose loyalty he was now unsure. How they had been deployed we do not know, but the Oxford massacre suggests that they may have been used to garrison important towns.[51] As for the king's suspicions, the treacherous Pallig was almost certainly the leader of one such band, for he had received 'great gifts, in estates and gold and silver' from the king; his desertion to the Danes in 1001 was perhaps one of the factors that provoked the massacre.

Henry of Huntingdon, who has an account of the massacre based on tales heard in his boyhood from 'some very old persons', implies that the slaying was largely confined to towns, and affected only Danish men, not women or children. He clearly disapproves, but his condemnation springs (in part at least) from the fact that the killings merely inflamed the fury of the Danes, 'like a fire which someone had tried to extinguish with fat'.[52] Henry's is a sober and factual account, but it is evident that, like the murder of Edward the Martyr, the St Brice's Day massacre had by his time acquired a crop of half-truths, tales and legends, some of which surface in the writings of those keen to blacken Æthelred's already grimy reputation.[53] William of Jumièges, who seems to have believed that the entire Anglo-Danish population was the target, describes the wholesale slaughter of men, women and children; he also has the traditional survivors who bring the news to King Swein in Denmark, provoking the Danish invasion of England.[54]

William of Malmesbury also connects Swein's English campaigns with a massacre of Danes, though allowing that, as 'a man of blood', Swein scarcely needed an excuse. He says that Swein's sister Gunnhild had come to England with her husband, 'the powerful *comes* Pallig', and, having adopted Christianity (like others before and since, William assumed that the children of the Christian King Harald Bluetooth were pagans), 'offered herself as a hostage for peace'; she was nevertheless killed 'with the other Danes', as were her husband and her young son.[55] It is usually assumed that this story relates to the St Brice's Day massacre, but William is clearly speaking of Swein's campaign in 1013, and the fact that he makes Eadric *streona*, ealdorman of Mercia from 1007–17, the agent of Gunnhild's death points to a date rather later than 1002 for her murder. It is worth considering in fact whether Gunnhild ever actually existed. William is the sole source for her relationship to King Swein, her marriage to Pallig and her death at the hands of Æthelred and Eadric *streona*; Thyra, alleged to be a sister of Swein, occurs in later Scandinavian tradition, but no Pallig is recorded among her husbands.[56] As for Pallig himself, there is no reason to identify Gunnhild's husband with the turncoat of 1001, for the latter had deserted Æthelred's service before the massacre. It seems safest to conclude that William's tale of the murder of Gunnhild and Pallig in the massacre of 1002, or in some other Dane-slaying, is one of the stories which grew up around the events of St Brice's Day, to which Henry of Huntingdon bears witness.[57]

Some disapproval of the massacre was voiced, albeit obliquely, at the time. In an addition to one of his earlier homilies, Ælfric describes how the Emperor Theodosius submitted to a penance imposed by St Ambrose for having ordered the citizens of Thessalonica to be killed; the passage, added *c.* 1005, has 'an obvious contemporary parallel [in] Æthelræd's order that the Danes in England were to be killed on St Brice's Day'.[58] The *Chronicle*, however, approves the king's action or at least gives a reason for it: he 'had been informed that they would treacherously deprive him, and then all his counsellors, of life, and possess this kingdom afterwards'.[59] Nor does there appear to have been much reluctance on the part of Æthelred's subjects to comply with the king's decree; the St Frideswide diploma suggests that it was implemented with some enthusiasm. But, even in the Oxford region, the Dane-slaying was limited. Between 1006 and 1011, Toti the Dane received land at Beckley and Horton from the king, in return for 'a pound of silver pence in pure gold' as a contribution towards the tribute.[60]

In the spring of 1002, Æthelred had made another attempt to break the link between the Scandinavian raiders and Normandy, by marrying Emma, sister of the reigning duke, Richard II. Unlike his first wife, she was consecrated as queen.[61] Her dower land included Exeter, whose fall to Swein's army in 1003 is attributed in the *Chronicle* to 'the French *ceorl* Hugh, whom the queen (*seo hlefdige*) had appointed as her reeve'. It has been suggested that Swein's attack on Exeter was a 'deliberate response to the marriage, which had been designed to cut off Danish armies from Norman harbours'.[62] Exeter had already been attacked in 1001, but it may be significant that in 1004 Swein switched his assault to East Anglia, whereas the focus of attention had hitherto been the southern coasts of Wessex, the area closest to the ports of northern Frankia.

Relations between Æthelred, Duke Richard and Swein are difficult to reconstruct. William of Jumièges claims that when Swein sailed to England to avenge the dead of the St Brice's Day massacre, he entered into a pact with Richard, in which the Danes agreed to sell their English loot only in Normandy, in return for a Norman undertaking to succour wounded Danes.[63] The pact has been dated to 1003, in which year Swein is known (from the *Anglo-Saxon Chronicle*) to have been campaigning in England, but since he is said to have crossed to Rouen from Yorkshire, William of Jumièges was presumably describing the invasion of 1013.[64] William also claims that the area round Val-de-Saire on the Cotentin peninsula was ravaged by an English fleet, which was eventually driven off with huge losses by Nigel, vicomte of the Cotentin; no date is given but it is implied that Æthelred was married to Emma at the time, and the vicomte Nigel attests charters of Duke Richard in the period 1020 x 1025.[65] It is possible to ignore the details and fit the alleged events into a more logical sequence, placing, for instance, Swein's agreement with Duke Richard in the late 990s (or even 1000, when the Viking fleet was in Normandy), and seeing the English attack on the Cotentin as a response to this provocation, which would be a breach of the agreement made with Duke Richard's father; 'but that, of course, would be no more than wishful thinking'.[66]

Threatening though the Danish incursions were, they were not the only preoccupation of the king and his counsellors in the years around the first millennium and may not have been their primary concern. The massacre of St Brice's Day suggests an element of panic in the king's circle and there are other signs of stress: the burning of Wilton in 1003 caused the relocation of its moneyers to Salisbury, and the nuns of Shaftesbury may have taken temporary shelter at Bradford-on-Avon in 1001.[67] As yet, however, the raids were still localised, with primarily local effects. Even the payments of tribute may not yet have been especially burdensome; in the 990s it is possible that 'money may have flowed into England as payment for exports even faster than the Danish host could siphon it off'.[68]

The general concerns of the kingdom are not reflected in the *Anglo-Saxon Chronicle*. It gives no hint that this period saw the promulgation of 'some of the finest legislation ever produced by the Anglo-Saxon kings', which seems to 'emerge in a fairly concentrated burst' in the mid 990s.[69] Two codes are extant in full plus a fragment of a third, and a fourth is mentioned in two of the three that survive. None can be precisely dated, but the sequence is clear. The latest, known as the Wantage code (III Æthelred), may date from 997; a royal council is known to have assembled at Wantage, Berkshire, in that year, but there could have been other unrecorded meetings at the same place.[70] The Wantage code represents the application to the north east of legislation already promulgated at Woodstock (I Æthelred), which must therefore pre-date Wantage, though perhaps by months rather than years. Both codes refer back to a legislative assembly at *Bromdun*.[71] The Wantage code also appears to cite an earlier decree on the coinage, now preserved as part of the composite text known as IV Æthelred; it may be a fragment of the lost *Bromdun* legislation, or perhaps of that promulgated at the council held at Winchester on the feast of Pentecost, 993, whose existence is known only from one of the king's diplomas.[72]

The Woodstock code (I Æthelred) is the only one to have been preserved in something like the form in which it emerged from the royal council. In structure it is remarkably coherent, consisting of a series of statements of principle, each qualified by contingencies to meet deviations from the prescribed norm.[73] A similar coherence is found in the coinage decrees, 'the most sophisticated discussion of the subject in the Anglo-Saxon corpus'.[74] If clarity of expression betokens clarity of thought, then on the evidence of this legislation Æthelred and his counsellors were at the top of their form in the 990s.

Æthelred's legislation reflects the concerns addressed by his father. The Woodstock code's pronouncement on surety – 'every free man shall have trustworthy surety, that the surety hold him to all justice if he be charged' – cites almost verbatim Edgar's precept on the same subject in his Andover legislation.[75] Until the mid tenth century, surety for good behaviour (and the production of the offender in court if it was not forthcoming) had been the responsibility of families for their members and lords for their men, but thereafter the neighbourhood was increasingly brought into play. Edgar's *Wihtbordesstan* code, promulgated in the 970s, ordered the establishment of 'what amounted to neighbourhood sureties', panels of jurors in each hundred and borough to oversee commercial transactions in order to prevent trafficking in stolen goods.[76] Following on from this, Æthelred's Woodstock code 'sought to integrate the activity of lord and neighbourhood'.[77] The lord remained responsible for his men, especially those in his own household; if one of them was accused, the lord might support him in the hundred court, and receive a share in the fines if he was found guilty. If, however, the lord allowed the accused to escape, he was liable to a fine equivalent to the man's wergeld; and if he was unable to clear himself from a charge of advising the accused's flight, his own wergeld was forfeit.

It was the integration of the lord into the structure of royal and public jurisdiction which precluded the growth of 'private' justice in pre-Conquest England.[78] The most serious crimes were in any case reserved to the king's own judgement. *Mundbryce*, violation of the king's protection (*mund*), had always been a matter with which only the king could deal, and Edmund had added the offence of *hamsocn*, attack on a man in his own house.[79] By Æthelred's time, assault on the king's highway and resort to violence before seeking legal remedy were also reserved to the king, though the fines arising therefrom could be granted to privileged individuals or bodies.[80] *Mundbryce*, *hamsocn* and *foresteall* ('ambush', highway robbery) appear in the Secular code of Cnut (II Cnut) among 'the rights which the king possesses over all men in Wessex ... unless he wishes to honour anyone further'; the others are harbouring fugitives (*flymena fyrmðe*) and neglecting military service.[81]

The purpose of the Wantage code was to extend the legislation decreed 'at Woodstock in Mercia, according to English law' (*æfter Engla lage*) to the formerly Scandinavian territories in the north-east midlands.[82] The assimilation of this region had been a matter of urgency for

Æthelred's predecessors. Most of it had been overrun by Edward the Elder and his sister Æthelflæd, Lady of the Mercians, in the second decade of the tenth century. In 940, however, the region had declared for Oláf Guthfrithsson, king of York, and it was only in 942 that Edmund succeeded in retaking it, in the process successfully detaching Lincoln and its region from the control of the York kings. By 954 York itself had fallen to the West Saxons, and it was probably in the late 950s or early 960s that the north-east midlands were reorganised as 'a regional system for defence' known as the Five Boroughs (Lincoln, Stamford, Nottingham, Derby and Leicester, with their dependent regions).[83] Edmund and his successors also encouraged their adherents to acquire lands in the conquered areas; Edmund himself endowed the Mercian thegn Wulfsige the black with extensive estates in what was to become Derbyshire.[84]

Edgar's *Wihtbordesstan* code recognized the legal customs of the former kingdom of York while asserting his right to legislate for 'the whole nation, whether Englishmen or Danes or Britons, in every part of my dominion'.[85] Æthelred's Wantage code, specifically addressed to the Five Boroughs, begins with a similar assertion of the king's rights, so that 'his peace may remain as firm as it best was in the days of his ancestors'.[86] Æthelred, however, went further than Edgar. The penalties laid down in the Wantage code are harsher than those for the same offences in the 'English' legislation, implying an effort to bring the Scandinavian territories under 'English law'.[87] It may not be coincidental that, about the time that the Wantage code was issued, the bishopric of Lindsey, defunct since the Danish conquest, was revived for Bishop Sigeferth, who attests royal diplomas between 996 and 1004, nor that the ealdorman of Northumbria appointed in 993 should be Ælfhelm, a kinsman, perhaps a grandson, of that Wulfsige the black endowed by Edmund with lands in the territory of Derby.[88] The drive towards unity is suggested by the first appearance of the term 'English law' in the prologue to the Woodstock code, paralleled by the first appearance of the name 'England' in the treaty with the Viking army.[89] But the surviving text of the Wantage code is evidence of the compromises which had to be made. Its vocabulary is heavily Scandinavianised, and some of its clauses appear to be additions made by the authorities responsible for its implementation; unlike the Woodstock code, it is a composite text in which 'royal resolutions were fused with local measures and practices'.[90]

The text known as 'IV Æthelred' (the so-called 'Institutes of London') is a similar amalgam, but here the royal legislation on coinage has been grafted onto what appear to be the replies to an enquiry, probably royal, into the market dues and legal customs of London. Like the Wantage code, the text as it survives was presumably compiled by the local officials responsible for the administration of the city.[91] The coinage laws are concerned to prevent illegal minting and the circulation of defective coin.[92] The abuses covered include uttering false coin, bribing moneyers to make bad money out of good, forging dies, operating 'in woods ... or other such places', refusing to accept 'pure money of the proper weight' and bringing defective coin into the markets. Royal officials, whether bishops, earls, ealdormen or reeves, are enjoined to 'be on the watch for those who coin such base money and spread it abroad throughout the country'; the decrees envisage the possible connivance of the town-reeves in such malpractice. The effectiveness of the final injunction, that 'the coinage is to be maintained by all at the standard which I lay down in your instructions', is born out by the testimony of the surviving coins themselves, which display a remarkable uniformity in appearance, weight and purity, irrespective of where they were produced.

Minting had always been associated with urban centres, and by the tenth century it was assumed that every town should have at least one moneyer, and that moneyers should only operate in towns. Though it is convenient to use the term 'mint', this should not be taken to imply a special building. The equipment required to strike coinage was comparatively simple: 'a small forge to purify the silver, the means to hammer or roll it out and cut it, and an anvil on which to mount the dies'.[93] Most moneyers probably worked from their own houses, and though the larger towns might have several moneyers, they were independent operators, each with his own premises. Nor was minting a 'full-time' occupation, even in the great trading-centres of London, Lincoln and York. It was demand-led; the customers brought their silver to the moneyer, as bullion or obsolete coin in the case of the English, or as foreign silver (which was not legal tender in England) in the case of visiting merchants. The moneyers of Æthelred's time, like their later counterparts, were probably men of wealth and standing, merchants or goldsmiths or the like, with employees to do the actual work; indeed the coinage decrees speak of the 'workmen' (*suboperarii*) who struck the coins, and for whom the moneyers were responsible.[94]

Æthelred's coinage was a continuation of his father's, quite literally in the first instance, for the earliest coins to bear his name belong to Edgar's last issue, the 'First Small Cross' type, so called from the design on its reverse. Towards the end of his reign, Edgar had radically overhauled the English currency. There is no contemporary record of any decree on the subject (though the Andover code contains the injunction that 'one coinage shall be current through all the king's realm and no one shall refuse it') and the details have to be deduced from the surviving coins.[95] Briefly summarized, Edgar's reform involved the establishment of a single, unified coinage throughout England, in which each moneyer struck from standard dies supplied to him from centrally-appointed die-cutters.[96] The obverse of each coin bore the name of the issuing king and a stylised portrait-bust; the design on the reverse was also standardised and accompanied by the names of both the moneyer and the mint (i.e. the borough) in which it was struck. From the beginning it seems to have been envisaged that the designs would be changed every few years, and that the older issue would be withdrawn as the new one was introduced. These periodic recoinages continued from the later years of Edgar (*c.* 973) to the reign of Henry I, first at roughly six-year intervals, then (after 1035) at two- or three-year intervals. Coin-hoards deposited within England rarely contain more than one type, a demonstration of how smoothly the system worked.

The reforms instituted by Edgar continued to operate with little sign of strain throughout the reign of Æthelred. Around 979 the 'First Small Cross' type was replaced by a design bearing a Hand of Providence on the reverse, the 'First Hand' type, which in its turn gave way to a variant design, the 'Second Hand'. Between 988 and 991, the 'Hand' type was replaced by the 'Crux' issue, superseded by the 'Long Cross'. 'Long Cross' itself gave way, *c.* 1003, to the 'Helmet' issue, in which the portrait-bust of the king was shown wearing a helm, and *c.* 1009 this was replaced by the 'Last Small Cross' type, which continued throughout the reign of Edmund II (1016) and into that of Cnut.[97] Individual minting-places may, like Wilton, have been disrupted by Viking raids, but the general pattern of regular recoinages continued undisturbed, a testimony to the efficiency of at least one aspect of Æthelred's administration.[98]

At his coronation, Æthelred promised 'three things to the Christian people and my subjects: first, that God's church and the Christian people of my dominions hold true peace; the second is that I forbid robbery and all unrighteous things to all orders (*eallum hadum*); the third, that I promise and enjoin in all dooms justice and mercy'.[99] Scepticism has been expressed on the king's ability to fulfil his oath. Sir Frank Stenton described Æthelred's reign as 'a time of national degeneracy', when 'a man could betray the state without losing either office or public influence', and 'the conventions which governed the relations of different classes were breaking down'. Professor Whitelock wrote in similar vein of 'the weakness of Æthelred's régime', and its 'general disorder and bad government'.[100] The numerous references in Æthelred's diplomas to the forfeiture of land for criminal offences have been cited in evidence for such conclusions, but it seems rather that 'what was unusual under Æthelred was not forfeiture in itself, but the regular mention of an estate's prior forfeiture in royal grants'.[101]

It is a characteristic of Æthelred's diplomas that 'they quite often contain some account of how the land concerned came into the king's possession and was thus his to give away', and the diplomas which mention criminal activity are a sub-set of such texts.[102] Some incorporate memoranda drawn up when the cases were concluded, either in the original vernacular, or in a Latin translation.[103] Other such memoranda exist as separate texts. None are 'official' records, produced by the court; all were made for the successful party and represent only that party's side of the case. There was, moreover, 'a tendency to throw the (metaphorical) book at an offender', especially after conviction, as if to blacken his reputation even further.[104] A considerable body of evidence nevertheless remains for the legal practice, as opposed to theory, of Æthelred's time.[105]

The earliest authentic references to forfeiture of property for criminal offences date from the reign of Alfred. Forfeited land came into the king's hands (except for *lænland*, which reverted to the lessor) and the circumstances are recounted in diplomas re-granting the estates to new beneficiaries. The cases recorded from the early tenth century do not differ significantly either in type or frequency from those which date from Æthelred's time; one of the first to survive concerns the forfeiture of Ealdorman Wulfhere for desertion and breach of his oath to King Alfred.[106]

Wulfhere's fall is paralleled by that of Leofsige, ealdorman of Essex, in 1002. Leofsige attests for the first time in 994, and his sphere of office, Essex, is identified in 997.[107] He seems to have come from the eastern shires; he attests the will of the Cambridgeshire landowner Uvi, his only known estates lay in Hertfordshire, and his widowed sister Æthelflæd had land in Huntingdonshire, perhaps acquired from her deceased husband.[108] It has been suggested that he is the Leofsige whom the Hertfordshire landowner Æthelgifu made her chief beneficiary, but the name is a common one.[109] The Leofsige of Æthelgifu's will seems to be a young man at the start of his career; indeed Æthelgifu specifically requests 'the lady' (i.e. Queen Ælfthryth) to find him a position in the household of the ætheling (presumably Æthelstan). Given that the date of the will is probably the 990s, it is unlikely that Æthelgifu's kinsman would have been of sufficient age or status for promotion to an ealdordom in 994.[110] In one of the diplomas relating to Ealdorman Leofsige's forfeiture, the king is made to say that he had raised Leofsige from 'the rank of a satrap' to the greater dignity of an ealdorman, but, as Sir Frank Stenton observed, 'it is unsafe to give *satraps* any preciser meaning than "official" in a context like this'.[111] Ealdorman Leofsige may have had some previous office in the royal household, but to assume that this was the result of Æthelgifu's request goes beyond the evidence.[112]

Soon after his appointment as ealdorman, Leofsige was embroiled in a dispute with two royal reeves, Æthelwig of Oxford and Wynsige of Buckingham. They had allowed Christian burial to two brothers slain at Ardley, Oxfordshire, while defending one of their men against a charge of theft, an action contested by Leofsige.[113] The basis for his intervention is unknown, though Ardley lies on the borders of Oxfordshire and Buckinghamshire, which had once constituted the ealdordom of south-east Mercia, and was perhaps within Leofsige's ealdordom.[114] Nor is the legal position entirely clear. The fact that the accused thief was actually found in possession of the stolen goods calls to mind the legislation soon to be promulgated at Woodstock, which prescribed a fine equivalent to his wergeld for the lord who merely 'advised' his man to abscond after being accused; fighting in defence of a hand-having thief seems, in the circumstances, a serious offence.[115] It is therefore surprising to find the king siding with the reeves rather than the ealdorman; 'not wishing to sadden Æthelwig, who was dear and precious to me', he not only allowed their decision to stand, but also gave Æthelwig the slain brothers' land at Ardley.

Leofsige's next appearance is in 1002, as the king's envoy to the Viking force encamped on the Isle of Wight (see above). Soon afterwards he killed the high-reeve Æfic 'in his own house, without warning', and was outlawed.[116] He was convicted of *hamsocn*, one of the crimes reserved for the king's judgement. Edmund had decreed that a perpetrator of this offence should 'forfeit all that he possesses, and it shall be for the king to decide whether his life shall be preserved'.[117] The council which decided Leofsige's punishment prescribed exile and forfeiture for him and his accomplices (unnamed), and commanded that 'he who should presume to break our decree should be disinherited of all his possessions'. This fate befell the ealdorman's widowed sister Æthelflæd, who in defiance of the judgement 'tried to do everything in her power for her brother's advantage', thereby committing *flymena fyrmð*, the crime of harbouring fugitives.[118] It was presumably the status of those involved that made the murder of Æfic worthy of inclusion in the *Chronicle*, for it cannot have been unusual for disputes to end in death by violence.[119] What lay behind it is irrecoverable, but the quarrel illustrates the inevitable tensions created as powerful and ambitious men strove to acquire and keep the king's favour.[120]

The king's sympathies appear to have lain with his reeves rather than the higher officials.[121] Æfic is described as 'the chief among my chief men', and Æthelwig of Oxford as 'dear and precious to me'.[122] Royal favour to reeves was demonstrated in contemporary land-grants. The gift of Ardley to Æthelwig is one of four made to royal reeves around the turn of the millennium; Ælfgar the reeve was given land in Berkshire in 1007, Eadsige the reeve received an estate in Devon in 1005, and Æthelred the 'faithful man' (*fidelis homo*) who received a two-life lease of some Canterbury property in 1002 was probably port-reeve of Canterbury.[123] Reeves had always been the key element in the king's control not only of his own estates but also of the rights and renders due from the surrounding localities. From the latter part of the tenth century they are more visible in the surviving sources, and there are signs of growing differentiation between them.

Town-reeves in charge of trading-centres (*wicgerefan*, *portgerefan*) were distinguished by their responsibility for overseeing commercial transactions; the seventh-century laws of Hlothhere and Eadric forbade Kentishmen to buy and sell in London except in the witness of 'two or three trustworthy men or the king's *wicgerefa*'.[124] Some town-reeves were men of rank: Ealdhun, portreeve of Canterbury in the late eighth century, was a kinsman of Archbishop Jænberht, and Beornwulf, *wicgerefa* of Winchester, was numbered among the 'best thegns' of King Alfred.[125] The economic and urban growth of the tenth century probably led to an increase in the portreeves' responsibilities, and perhaps also in their status. The portreeve of London is distinguished from the lesser reeves of the region (*tungravii*) in the 'Institutes of London' (IV Atr), and the royal coinage laws assume that every town will have its portreeve.[126] Individual portreeves appear with greater frequency: Hlothwig, *portgerefa* of Canterbury, attested an agreement of 968; Brunmann *portreve* gave land in Fordwich to St Augustine's, Canterbury, in 991; Æthelred, *portgerefa* of Canterbury, attested a legal agreement between 995 and 1005; and Æthelwine, *praefectus* of Winchester, is mentioned in 1012.[127]

The new prominence of the portreeves may be a function of the availability of evidence, but this is not true of the high-reeves and shire-reeves (sheriffs), who make their first appearance in the late tenth century. The earliest reference to the high-reeve is in Edmund's Third code, which prohibits trading except in the witness of the king's high-reeve (*summus praepositus*), or the priest, treasurer (*hordarius*) or portreeve.[128] The context suggests an urban official, like the king's reeve who can deputise for the ealdorman in the court of the Five Boroughs, but the high-reeves of Æthelred's time appear as leaders of the shire-levies, a function also performed by ealdormen; Æthelweard and Leofwine were killed in 1001 at the head of the men of Hampshire, and in the same year Kola was leading the men of Somerset and Devon.[129] Given his fatal quarrel with Leofsige of Essex, Æfic may have had a similar command in the eastern shires.

The office of high-reeve seems to have fallen into abeyance after

Æthelred's time, but that of the shire-reeve was to articulate the structure of English local government for centuries to come. The earliest named sheriffs are those of Kent: Wulfsige the priest, *scirigmann*, in the 980s, and Leofsige *scyresman*, about 1000.[130] The emergence of the sheriff's office must be connected with that of the shire, and it seems to be in Æthelred's reign that the shiring of midland England between the Thames and the Tees, begun when his forebears overran the Danish settlements in the early tenth century, reached completion.[131] All the midland shires are named from their chief borough or county town, and it seems probable that the portreeves of those towns became sheriffs. It is usually assumed, for instance, that Æthelwig of Oxford and Wynsige of Buckingham were portreeves, but they may in fact have been sheriffs of the emergent shires of Oxford and Buckingham.[132]

Tenth-century kings took a keen interest in the workings of the shire and its constituent elements, the hundreds. The functions of the hundred court were laid down in the Hundred Ordinance, promulgated either late in the reign of Eadred or early in that of Edgar, and it is in Edgar's laws that the earliest reference to the shire-court appears.[133] It is from the reign of Æthelred that the link between shire-court and king becomes clear to us. In the early 990s, Æthelred sent his seal (*insegel*) to the shire-court of Berkshire, accompanied by his command to settle a lawsuit.[134] Whether the command was delivered orally or in writing is unclear, for it is not always easy to distinguish references to oral as opposed to written messages, though a clear example of the former occurs in the will of Æthelstan ætheling, which refers to the king's permission to bequeath, 'told to me in my father's words' by Ælfgar Æffa's son.[135] Æthelred's message to the shire-court of Kent, dating from around the same time as that sent to the court of Berkshire, was certainly in writing, for the court received not only the king's seal but his *gewrit* ('written message') as well.[136] These are the earliest references to legal suits heard and determined by the king's command, a process which was to have a long history in the conduct of English law.

In local administration, the years around the turn of the first millennium saw the consolidation of earlier developments and the first shoots of later ones. How far Æthelred himself was responsible we cannot know, but he does seem to have been alive to some of the dangerous forces prevalent in the reigns of his immediate predecessors. The new prominence of the king's reeves is accompanied by a diminution in the authority of his ealdormen. In the first place, Æthelred seems concerned to break the hold of powerful kindreds on particular offices. Of the ealdormen who died, or were deprived of office, between 978 and 1002, five had grown sons: Æthelmær of Hampshire (982), Ælfric *cild* (985), Æthelwine of East Anglia (992), Thored of Northumbria (992) and Æthelweard the Chronicler (998). None except (eventually) Æthelweard's son Æthelmær received his father's command, nor indeed any official position.[137] The king may have been making the point that 'the office of ealdorman was a personal one, held at his pleasure'.[138]

Nor does Æthelred seem to have been in any hurry to appoint new ealdormen to the vacant ealdordoms. Edwin of Sussex (d. 982) was never replaced. There was no ealdorman in Mercia between the exile of Ælfric *cild* in 985 and the appointment of Leofwine in 994. Æthelmær son of Æthelweard did eventually receive his father's ealdordom in the western shires in the closing years of Æthelred's reign, but between 998 and his temporary retirement in 1006 he attests among the *ministri*.[139] No one was appointed to replace Leofsige as ealdorman of Essex, and the next ealdorman of East Anglia was Thorkell the Tall, appointed by Cnut. Moreover the ealdormen appointed in the 990s had (with the exception of Northumbria) lesser spheres of influence than the great magnates of Edgar's day; Leofwine was ealdorman only of the Hwiccian territories (Worcestershire, Gloucestershire and probably Warwickshire), not of Mercia; Leofsige held only Essex and (perhaps) Oxfordshire and Buckinghamshire.[140] Gaps were presumably plugged with king's reeves and thegns; the king's favourite Æthelsige may have held some position in Mercia between the exile of Ælfric *cild* in 985 and the appointment of Leofwine in 994. Ulfcytel 'of the East Angles' certainly exercised at least some of the functions of an ealdorman between 1004 and 1016, but he attests diplomas simply as a king's thegn (*minister*).[141]

It may be presuming too much on the evidence to suggest that Æthelred was attempting to give practical force to the idea of a unified kingdom, whose officers were answerable to the king, and whom he could appoint and remove at will (this was, of course, already the case in theory).[142] Even if the dispositions described above are regarded simply as *ad hoc* arrangements which do not add up to a coherent policy, they suggest at the least that the king was not only prepared to impose his will on even the mightiest of his subjects but also had the means to enforce it. But, as the fall of Leofsige demonstrates, manipulation of royal patronage could create tensions among the ambitious men jockeying for a place in the king's favour. In a kingdom already under stress from external invasion, such tensions might have malign and eventually fatal consequences.

4

A Change of Direction

'Through an unwise king, the people will be made wretched not once but very often, because of his misdirection (*misræd*); through the king's wisdom the people will become prosperous and successful and victorious.'

Wulfstan *lupus*[1]

By the end of 1005, most of the laymen prominent in the middle years of Æthelred's reign had vanished from the witness-lists of his diplomas. Ealdorman Æthelweard ceases to attest in 998 and probably died soon afterwards; the same is perhaps true of the thegns Brihtwold and Wulfric Wulfrun's son, whose last appearances are in 999 and 1002 respectively.[2] Ordwulf and Æthelmær cease to attest in 1005, but both are recorded as living after this date. Ordwulf received a bequest under the will of Ælfwold of Crediton (1011 x 1015), when he must have been well into his sixties and perhaps living in retirement at his abbey of Tavistock.[3] Æthelmær signifies his intention to live at Eynsham in the house's foundation-charter of 1005, but it may be that his retirement was not entirely voluntary.[4] A homily of Ælfric, written in about 1007 (while he was abbot of Eynsham), seems to contain a veiled attack on his patron's enemies, and since it was produced at the request of Bishop Æthelwold II of Winchester (1006–12) for use at the New Minster, it could easily have reached the ears of the royal court.[5]

An earlier homily of Ælfric, written soon after 1000, may imply some discord among the men closest to the king; it urges the royal counsellors to speak openly rather than in whispers, and calls upon the king to heed their advice.[6] The events of 1006, as recorded in the *Chronicle*, suggest the culmination of a period of dissension, for in that year 'Wulfgeat was deprived of all his property, and Wulfheah and Ufegeat [sons of

Ealdorman Ælfhelm] were blinded, and Ealdorman Ælfhelm was killed'.[7] This disposed of almost the last of the counsellors prominent in the 990s (Leofsige of Essex had already fallen from grace in 1002). As usual the *Chronicle* gives no explanation of the circumstances. No diplomas survive for the year 1006 (which may in itself be significant), but a diploma of 1008 alleges that Wulfgeat and his wife were accused by 'the people' of 'the worst of crimes ... because of their misdeeds'.[8] Her one-time father-in-law, Ælfric of Hampshire, remained in office as senior ealdorman, the sole survivor, apart from Leofwine of the Hwicce, of the leading men of the 990s. The reticence of the sources is particularly frustrating, for the apparent exclusion of Æthelmær, followed by the downfall of Ealdorman Ælfhelm, his sons, and a thegn who may have been associated with him, looks like 'the exposed tip of an iceberg of intrigue'.[9]

Any interpretation of the events of 1006 can only be speculative, but we can at least ask the question 'who profits?'. It may not be coincidental that the fall of Ælfhelm and his associates was followed by the rise to power of Eadric *streona*, appointed ealdorman of Mercia in 1007.[10] Almost from his first appearance in the *Anglo-Saxon Chronicle*, Eadric is branded as unreliable, crafty and (in the end) treacherous, and subsequent writers have regarded him as the evil genius of Æthelred's reign.[11] His byname is not recorded until the end of the eleventh century, by the Worcester monk Hemming, who glosses it *adquisitor* ('grasping'); indeed Hemming may have coined it, for he includes Eadric among those who had despoiled the church of Worcester of its lands.[12]

Most of what we know about Eadric comes from the pages of Hemming's fellow-monk, John of Worcester. John names the ealdorman's father, Æthelric (also known as Leofwine), and his six brothers, Brihtric, Ælfric, Goda, Æthelwine, Æthelweard and Æthelmær.[13] Only Brihtric is attested in a contemporary source, but the other names (with one exception) occur among the witnesses to Æthelred's diplomas at appropriate times. An Æthelric begins to attest in 996 and continues to the end of the reign and a Goda witnesses in the early eleventh century. Æthelwine might be the thegn whose attestations are concentrated in the period 1009–12; an Æthelweard appears between 1004 and 1009 and an Æthelmær between 1009 and 1012.[14] All these names were in common usage, but their appearance at just this point in Æthelred's reign and especially their appearance in groups of two or three, following 'the well-established principle that brothers and kinsmen tend to subscribe beside one another', suggests that more than coincidence is involved.[15]

The only name missing from the witness-lists is that of Ælfric, elsewhere described by John as the father of Eadric the Wild, celebrated for his resistance to Norman encroachment in the west after the Norman Conquest.[16] That Eadric the Wild, who did indeed have a father called Ælfric, held lands in Shropshire and Herefordshire testifies to the essential accuracy of John of Worcester's information, for it is with precisely this region that the elder Eadric is associated by the *Anglo-Saxon Chronicle*; he was leading the men of the *Magonsæte* (Herefordshire and south Shropshire) at the battle of *Assandun*.[17] It is possible that Ælfric was a nephew, rather than a brother, of the ealdorman.[18]

It has been suggested that John's information on Eadric *streona* came from a lost saga on the ealdorman's deeds (or rather misdeeds).[19] The surviving family is another possible source. Eadric the Wild may have been a tenant of the church of Worcester, perhaps even the commander of the military force owed by the bishop to the king.[20] Since he was still holding land (though not of the church of Worcester) in 1086, he could have been personally known both to Hemming, and to either John or John's chief informant, Florence of Worcester, who died in 1118. Orderic Vitalis, who confirms both the ealdorman's byname and his kinship with Eadric the Wild, may likewise have known the ealdorman's grandson, Siward son of Æthelgar, patron of St Peter's, Shrewsbury, the church where Orderic had received his earliest education.[21]

The source of John of Worcester's knowledge of Eadric *streona* is of some moment, for it is John alone who implicates him in the murder of Ealdorman Ælfhelm. He says that Eadric invited the ealdorman to a great feast at Shrewsbury, and arranged for him to be killed during a hunting expedition.[22] Murder while hunting is a common topos, but such occasions were ideal for arranging 'accidents', and perhaps 'the popularity of the motif [is] merely a reflection of the frequency of its occurrence in daily life'.[23] There is some circumstantial evidence to support John's account. Though the *Anglo-Saxon Chronicle* does not implicate Eadric in Ælfhelm's murder, nor give any indication where the crime took place, it does record that the king spent the following

Christmas in Shropshire, a region associated both with the murder and with the alleged perpetrator, and one well outside the normal itineraries of the late Old English kings.[24] It may be that there was some prior enmity between the families of Eadric and Ælfhelm, which Æthelred exploited for his own ends.

Eadric *streona* was not the only beneficiary of Ælfhelm's death. His ealdordom of Northumbria passed to Uhtred, who attests Æthelred's diplomas as *dux* between 1009 and 1015.[25] He was a member of the house of Bamburgh, which had held sway in the north east since the end of the ninth century. They and the West Saxon kings had for a long time found each other useful in combating the ambitions of both the Danish kings of York and the kings of the Scots, and Osulf, high-reeve of Bamburgh, who attests diplomas of both Æthelstan and Eadred, was chosen by the latter as ealdorman of Northumbria after the fall of Scandinavian York.[26] He does not attest diplomas of Eadwig or Edgar, and by 966 at the latest had been replaced as ealdorman of Northumbria by Oslac, but his successor at Bamburgh, Ealdorman Eadulf, attests Edgar's diplomas between 968 and 970, and Ealdorman Waltheof, who is associated elsewhere with Bamburgh, attests a diploma of Æthelred in 994.[27] Eadulf and Waltheof were contemporaries of the Southumbrians appointed by the West Saxon kings as earls of Northumbria between 966 and 1006 (Oslac, Thored and Ælfhelm); whoever held overall authority, the north east was ruled by the lords of Bamburgh.

Æthelred's choice of Uhtred as ealdorman of all Northumbria marked a return to the policy adopted by King Eadred some fifty years earlier. His decision was presumably prompted as much by events in Northumbria as in southern England, but unfortunately the contemporary sources, largely of southern origin, rarely mention northern affairs. For the region beyond the Tees, we have to rely on the historical traditions of the community of St Cuthbert, most of which were written down a century or more after the event.[28] It is only Symeon of Durham, writing in the early twelfth century, who records the removal of the community from Chester-le-Street to Durham in 995.[29] According to Symeon, the place was at that time 'completely covered on all sides by a very dense forest', with only a small clearing in the midst of it. The bishop, Ealdhun (990 x 995–1016), was able to call on Uhtred, 'ealdorman of the Northumbrians' (*comes Northanhymbrorum*) for assistance in clearing the site, the attraction of which was presumably its defensibility, and the first cathedral, perched on its peninsula high above the Wear, was consecrated in 998.[30]

The relationship between Bishop Ealdhun and Ealdorman Uhtred is elaborated in an anonymous tract, *De obsessione Dunelmi* ('The siege of Durham'), produced, probably at Durham, in the late eleventh (or perhaps early twelfth) century.[31] The author describes Uhtred as the son of Waltheof, and son-in-law of the bishop, whose daughter Ecgfrida he had married.[32] When Durham was besieged by Malcolm, king of Scots, Waltheof, 'being of great age and so too old to be able to make a stand against the enemy', shut himself up in Bamburgh, and it was Uhtred who gathered 'the army of the Northumbrians and the people of York' and drove Malcolm back to Scotland. In consequence, King Æthelred 'called the aforementioned young man to him, and whilst his father Waltheof was still living, gave him as a reward ... his father's earldom, adding the earldom of York'. On his return 'home' (presumably to Bamburgh), Uhtred repudiated the bishop's daughter, who subsequently married the Yorkshire thegn Kilvert (Ketilberht) Ligulf's son. Uhtred himself took as his second wife Sige, daughter of Styr Ulf's son, 'a wealthy and prominent man'.[33]

It is hard to assess the reliability of a source like *De obsessione Dunelmi*. Its purpose was to trace the histories of the estates belonging to St Cuthbert which Bishop Ealdhun gave to his daughter and her husband, and which were still in dispute between the bishopric and the descendants of Uhtred and Ecgfrida (by their several marriages) at the end of the eleventh century.[34] Its chronology is very confused, especially in the earlier sections; in particular, the siege of Durham is given the impossible date of 969, whereas the perpetrator, Malcolm II, only succeeded to the Scottish kingdom in 1005.[35] It was not, however, uncommon for kings of the Scots to begin their reigns with forays into English territory, and a clash between Scots and English recorded under the year 1006 in the *Annals of Ulster* may be the siege of Durham described in the anonymous tract.[36] This, of course, is the earliest date at which Uhtred can have held York as well as Bamburgh.[37] Uhtred's recorded attestations to Æthelred's diplomas begin in 1009, but *De obsessione* may be correct in placing his appointment to the whole of Northumbria in the aftermath of the siege of Durham (and thus in

1006–7) and in linking that appointment to Uhtred's second marriage, to the daughter of Styr Ulf's son.

Styr was of sufficient importance to appear in contemporary as well as later sources. He attended a council at London in 989 or 990, at which Earl Thored of Northumbria was also present, and his name is followed in the list of attestations by those of two other northern magnates, Nafena and his brother Northwine.[38] Styr's name is not common and he is presumably the man who attests two diplomas of Æthelred, in 1004 and 1009 respectively.[39] The church of Durham remembered him as a benefactor and his Scandinavian name supports his identification as a thegn of York.[40] Marriage with his daughter was presumably intended to give Ealdorman Uhtred allies in the southern regions of his command. The marriage of Uhtred's former wife, Bishop Ealdhun's daughter, to a Yorkshire thegn points in the same direction. Far from marking a breach between ealdorman and bishop, the dissolution of Uhtred's first marriage enabled both men to make alliances in southern Northumbria, and 'to intrude their own influence into the political fabric of the Anglo-Scandinavian community at York'.[41]

On the king's side, Æthelred's promotion of Uhtred looks like an attempt to gain friends in the north, perhaps even to stem any repercussions arising there in the wake of Ælfhelm's murder.[42] The surviving members of Ælfhelm's family seem to have retained influence in the region even after his fall and his daughter, Ælfgifu of Northampton, was to prove enough of a catch to marry Swein Forkbeard's son, Cnut.[43] The will of Ælfhelm's brother, Wulfric Wulfrun's son, reveals the family's connection with a prominent northern kindred, for the chief beneficiary, after Burton Abbey and Ælfhelm himself, was Morcar, identified in the *Anglo-Saxon Chronicle* as one of 'the chief thegns belonging to the Seven Boroughs'.[44] His wife Ealdgyth, who was also a beneficiary (as was their unnamed daughter, Wulfric's god-child), was probably the daughter of Ælfthryth, the only sister of Wulfric and Ælfhelm.[45]

Under Wulfric's will, Morcar and his family received two estates in the West Riding of Yorkshire and a block of lands in Derbyshire. His connection with Ælfhelm's family did not hamper his advancement, for in 1009 King Æthelred himself augmented Morcar's holding in Derbyshire.[46] The diploma enshrining the gift has a long witness-list which includes a number of northern magnates, among them Ealdhun, bishop of Durham, making his only appearance as a witness to royal diplomas, Ealdorman Uhtred, Morcar's brother Sigeferth, whose name is distinguished by being capitalised, Styr, presumably Styr Ulf's son, and Thurbrand, perhaps the Yorkshire magnate Thurbrand *hold*.[47] The presence of the northerners has prompted suggestions that the grant was part of an attempt to buy their support in the crisis provoked by the arrival 'after Lammas' of the 'immense raiding-army' commanded by Thorkell the Tall.[48] Certainly Morcar and Sigeferth attest more consistently after 1009 than before.[49]

Not only did both Uhtred and Eadric *streona* rise to power on Ealdorman Ælfhelm's fall, they also share the distinction of being the king's sons-in-law.[50] The dates of their marriages are nowhere recorded. Uhtred's union with the king's daughter Ælfgifu meant the repudiation of Sige, daughter of Styr Ulf's son; it is not clear from *De obsessione* how long they were married, but two children (Eadulf and Gospatric) are recorded, which suggests that it was at least two or three years.[51] The marriage of Uhtred and Ælfgifu probably took place in or soon after 1009, the date at which he begins to attest royal diplomas.[52] As for Eadric, John of Worcester calls him the king's son in-law (*gener*) in his annal for 1009, but it is more likely that his marriage to Æthelred's daughter Eadgyth took place in or just before 1012, when Eadric displaced all other ealdormen in the witness-lists and became senior ealdorman.[53]

It was rare in the extreme for kings' daughters to be given in marriage to English noblemen. For a parallel we must look back to the union of Alfred's firstborn, Æthelflæd, to Æthelred of Mercia in the 880s, but this is not an exact comparison, for although Æthelred is almost always styled 'ealdorman', his position in Mercia was closer to that of a king. Those daughters of Alfred and Edward the Elder who did not marry into the ruling houses of Europe entered religion.[54] Subsequent marriages may have gone unrecorded, but the only certain royal daughter between the reigns of Edward the Elder and Æthelred is St Edith, who became a nun at Wilton.[55] Some quite exceptional circumstance must underlie the marriage of two royal women to English ealdormen in the closing years of Æthelred's reign, though we have no means of discovering precisely what it was.[56]

The annal for 1006 concludes with an account of the depredations of a great Danish army which savaged Wessex in that year:

> Then after midsummer the great fleet came to Sandwich, and did just as they were accustomed, ravaged, burnt and slew as they went. Then the king ordered the whole nation (*ealne ðeodscipe*) from Wessex and Mercia to be called out, and they were out on military service against the Danish army the whole autumn, yet it availed no whit more than it had often done before; for in spite of it all, the Danish army went about as it pleased, and the English levy caused the people of the country every sort of harm, so that they profited neither from the native army, nor the foreign army (*ne innhere ne uthere*). When winter approached, the English army went home and the Danish army then came after Martinmas (11 November) to its sanctuary (*fryðstol*), the Isle of Wight, and procured for themselves everywhere whatever they needed.

As the Christmas season approached, they emerged from their lair, and

> betook themselves to the entertainment waiting for them ... out through Hampshire into Berkshire to Reading; and always they observed their ancient custom, lighting their war-beacons (*herebeacen*) as they went. They then turned to Wallingford, and burnt it all, and were one night at Cholsey, and then turned along Ashdown to Cuckhamsley Barrow, and waited there for what had been proudly threatened, for it had often been said that if they went to Cuckhamsley, they would never get to the sea. They then went home another way ... There the people of Winchester could see that army, proud and undaunted, when they went past their gate to the sea, and fetched themselves food and treasures from more than fifty miles from the sea.

The annal is heavy with irony, not all of which comes through in the modern English translation; the phrase 'proudly threatened', for instance, translates *beotra gylpa*, referring to the 'boasting oath ... made formally in a prince's hall', usually to be found in heroic verse rather than prose.[57] The *Chronicle*'s use of the word *fryðstol* for the Viking camp on the Isle of Wight refers to the right of sanctuary for accused fugitives; the *fryðstol*, in fact, represents the very deepest and most inviolable sanctuary. The implication, presumably, is that the English would not dare to attack them there. The description of the Danes 'lighting their war-beacons as they went' is a more straightforward criticism of English ineptitude, for beacons were meant to be lit by the defenders as warning of enemy approach.[58] All this probably reflects the jaundiced view of the *Chronicle* rather than the attitudes of the Danes, but there is something pointed about the choice of targets, for all the places named were important sites, both strategically and symbolically. Wallingford, an Alfredian *burh*, was one of the key crossing-points of the Thames and the minster at Cholsey had probably been founded by Æthelred himself. Cuckhamsley Barrow was the meeting-place of the Berkshire shire-court, whose position in the heartlands of Wessex had probably given rise to the proverb alluded to by the *Chronicle*, which it seems was well known to the Danes.[59] As for Winchester, it was the chief residence of the West Saxon kings and the centre of their power. The unnamed leaders of the Viking force clearly included men familiar with England and English affairs.[60]

Æthelred (as we have seen) had gone into Shropshire for the Christmas season. It was presumably there, during the Christmas celebrations, that the council which decided to sue for peace was convened.[61] A truce was arranged and in 1007 a *gafol* of £36,000 was paid to the Danish host, which presumably then dispersed. It seems that Æthelred used the breathing-space thus afforded to overhaul the military administration of his kingdom. That the revival of the Mercian ealdordom in 1007 was part of such an overhaul is hinted at by the *Chronicle*'s choice of words: Eadric *streona* 'was appointed ealdorman over the *kingdom* of the Mercians' (*Myrcena rice*).[62] The rapid development of Eadric's posthumous ill-fame has precluded discussion of why Æthelred should have advanced him in the first place, but even if his chief recommendation was his willingness to do the king's dirty work for him, he might have had other qualities as well. The failure in 1006 of an army drawn, as the *Chronicle* says, 'from Wessex *and Mercia*' perhaps prompted the appointment of a man who could coordinate the defences of the region. Eadric seems to have outranked Leofwine, ealdorman since 996 of the Hwiccian provinces, for although it was usual for new ealdormen to attest diplomas at the bottom of the list of *duces*, Eadric's name precedes that of Leofwine in a diploma of 1007.[63] Moreover in 1012 the Welsh annals record a raid on St David's led by Eadric and *Ubis*, without any mention of Leofwine, and they are usually a reliable witness for the leaders of such incursions.[64]

Eadric's term of office seems to coincide with the period when the shires between the Thames and the Tees assumed something like their final form: Shropshire is mentioned for the first time in the annal for

1006; Oxfordshire, Cambridgeshire and Buckinghamshire in 1010; Hertfordshire, Bedfordshire, Huntingdonshire and Northamptonshire in 1011; Warwickshire, Gloucestershire, Staffordshire, Lincolnshire and Nottinghamshire in 1016.[65] The origins of the midland shires, unlike those of Wessex, lie in the territories assigned to the fortified *burhs* built or rebuilt by Alfred and his successors.[66] In Edgar's reign, the shrieval and burghal structures seem to have been operating in tandem, for in his third code, he claimed his royal rights (*cynescipesgerihta*) in every *burh* and every shire, and ordered that the *burh*-court should meet three times a year and the shire-court twice.[67] But it is the military rather than the legal functions of the West Saxon shire which are evident from its first appearance in the historical record, and local forces were still raised shire by shire in the reign of Æthelred.[68] The battle of Maldon in 991 was fought by 'the spearpoint of the East Saxons' (*Eastseaxena ord*). In 999 it was the turn of the Kentish levies; in 1001 the people (*folc*) of Hampshire; and in 1003 the men of Wiltshire and Hampshire, led by their ealdorman Ælfric.[69] Even within the larger hosts commanded by the king or his generals, the rank and file fought shire by shire under their own commanders. Any overhaul of the shrieval system would therefore have both administrative and military aspects.[70]

Not all the burghal territories developed into shires, nor did those which did immediately supersede the older *regiones* into which the kingdom of Mercia had been divided.[71] Nor were their boundaries always coterminous with those of the later shires. The compilers of the earliest Worcester cartulary, the *Liber Wigornensis*, which is probably no later than 1016, arranged the church's estates in order of the territories in which they lay, namely those of Gloucester, Oxford, Winchcombe, Warwick and Worcester; the suffix *-scire* was added to the first three, probably soon afterwards.[72] By 1066, however, 'Winchcombeshire' had been absorbed into Gloucestershire, though its original status is remembered in Domesday Book, which places the borough of Winchcombe immediately after that of Gloucester itself at the head of the Gloucestershire folios, and refers in the text to 'the district (*ferding*) of Winchcombe'.[73] The amalgamation is attributed to Eadric *streona* by the Worcester monk Hemming, who says that he 'presided over the whole kingdom of the English and was in all things as powerful as an underking, so that he joined vills to vills and provinces to provinces'.[74]

Hemming's testimony, if acceptable, is further evidence of Eadric's authority over Ealdorman Leofwine, for both Winchcombe and Gloucester lay in the territory of the Hwicce.

Whether Eadric had a hand in the shaping of any other west Mercian shires is less easily determined. He himself is associated with the *Magonsæte*, whose territory included Herefordshire east of the River Wye, southern Shropshire as far as Wenlock, and Gloucestershire west of the Severn; the boundaries of this ancient kingdom are partially preserved in those of the medieval diocese of Hereford, whose incumbents could still be called 'bishops of the *Magonsæte*' in the early twelfth century.[75] Northern Shropshire lay in the territory of the *Wreoconsæte*, centred on the Wrekin and Wroxeter, which is recorded as late as 963.[76] Shrewsbury, from which Shropshire is named, lay on the boundary between the two districts. Its origins are obscure but it was described as a city (*civitas*) in 901, when the lords of Mercia, Æthelred and Æthelflæd, issued a charter there for the church of Much Wenlock.[77] Since Shrewsbury articulates the structure of its dependent shire, the two must have developed hand in hand.[78] Shropshire is the earliest of the west midland shires to occur by name, in the annal for 1006 already discussed, and those who wish to make Eadric the architect of the west midland shires must argue that this is an anachronism on the part of the chronicler; given that Herefordshire does not occur by that name until the reign of Cnut, this is not unreasonable.[79] Even if Herefordshire had been separated from Shropshire before Eadric became ealdorman of Mercia, he might still have been tinkering with the boundaries.[80]

Warwick occupies a position similar to that of Shrewsbury, lying as it does on the frontiers of the Hwicce and Mercia proper, and the dioceses of Lichfield and Worcester. Not only did the lands of the church of Worcester lie exclusively in the Hwiccian part of Warwickshire but all the contributory burgesses of the borough of Warwick were attached to estates in the same region.[81] It has been suggested that this south-western region constituted the first 'Warwickshire', the north being administered from Tamworth until the early eleventh century; Eadric, who joined the territories of Winchcombe and Gloucester to form Gloucestershire, may also have united those of Warwick and Tamworth to form Warwickshire.[82] Against this, the fact that the shire-boundary between Warwickshire and Staffordshire actually bisects the ancient

Mercian centre of Tamworth supports Stenton's argument for Edward the Elder as the architect of the shrieval structure in this region.[83]

Further abroad, evidence for Eadric's participation in the shiring of the eastern and northern midlands is non-existent. It is unlikely that the north east was shired before 1015, when Sigeferth and Morcar, two of the leading thegns of the 'Seven Boroughs' were murdered at the king's command at Oxford.[84] It was Eadric *streona* who carried out the order. If he was responsible for the earlier shiring of western Mercia, perhaps he undertook the reorganization of the north east as well; but this of course is pure speculation.

The shiring of the midlands has been connected with the edict of 1008, reported in the *Chronicle*, that 'ships should be built unremittingly over all England, namely a warship (*scegð*) from 310 hides, and a helmet and a mailshirt from eight hides'.[85] It was part of the legislation enacted at Enham, Hampshire, and in the texts which relate to that legislation, the relevant clauses require the ships to be ready 'immediately after Easter'.[86] Royal edicts are rarely mentioned in the *Chronicle*, which suggests that this one had some particular significance, yet at first sight it seems to introduce little or nothing that was new. In 992, a royal council commanded that 'all the ships that were of any use should be assembled at London', language which suggests some pre-existing, if somewhat shaky, organization, and the connection between the provision of ships and that of arms for the men who were to fight them is foreshadowed in the will of Archbishop Ælfric (1002 x 1005), who bequeathed to the king not only his 'best ship' with its sailing-tackle but also sixty helmets and sixty mailshirts.[87]

The unit of 310 hides is unusual (indeed, unique), and the confusion evident in the various recensions of the *Chronicle* suggests that it may not be accurate, and that '300 hides' might be the intended reading.[88] Soon after the edict of 1008, Bishop Æthelric of Sherborne was complaining that he had ceased to receive 'shipscot' (*scypgesceote*) from thirty-three of 'the 300 hides which other bishops had for their diocese (*scyr*)'.[89] 'Shipscot' cannot be anything but a levy for the provision of ships, implying that the duty of fitting out ships (*scipfirðrunga*) had already been commuted for cash.[90] If, moreover, Bishop Æthelric's 'other bishops' refers to his predecessors at Sherborne (which is the usual interpretation), then the obligation must go back at least to the time of Bishop Æthelsige (970 x 979–991 x 993).

Bishop Æthelric's 300 hides formed what in post-Conquest sources would have been called a 'shipsoke', and though the word is not found in any pre-Conquest context, it provides too convenient a label not to be used.[91] Shipsokes were groupings of 300 hides, or (perhaps more accurately) of three hundreds each notionally containing 100 hides; not all the land within the shipsoke necessarily belonged to whoever was in charge, though this would be an obvious administrative advantage.[92] It is difficult to say how many existed at any one time. A memorandum of about 1000 lists the estates of the bishopric of London which provided 'shipmen (*scipmenn*)', presumably to the king, and it may not be coincidental that the endowment of the see at the time was in the region of 300–350 hides.[93] London's contingent was perhaps raised in 992, when Ælfstan, bishop of London, was one of the commanders of the fleet.[94] Æscwig, bishop of Dorchester-on-Thames, was among the leaders of the same force and it may be that the three hundreds in Oxfordshire found in the hands of his successors constituted another shipsoke.[95] Its contingent, which could fight on land as well as sea, may have been summoned again in 1016, for another incumbent of Dorchester, Bishop Eadnoth, was killed at *Assandun*. With him fell Wulfsige, abbot of Ramsey, to whose house the east midlands thegn Ælfhelm *polga* bequeathed a warship (*scegð*) between 975 and 1016.[96] It is hard to see the purpose of this bequest unless it was to assist the abbey in fulfilling its military obligation to the king, and it may not be coincidental that the abbey's endowment at the time of Domesday Book was approximately 320 hides.[97] The ships bequeathed to the king by Ælfric, archbishop of Canterbury and Ælfwold, bishop of Crediton (a sixty-oared ship and a sixty-four-oared *scegð* respectively) suggest that shipsokes were attached to their respective sees.[98] By the reign of Edward the Confessor, shipsokes were associated with the bishopric of Worcester and the abbey of Pershore, both of which may go back to the time of Edgar, and the abbey of St Benet's Holme, in Norfolk.[99]

The known or presumed shipsokes are all associated with religious houses but this is a by-product of the surviving evidence, which is overwhelmingly ecclesiastical in nature. Archbishop Ælfric, however, left ships to the people of Wiltshire and Kent as well as to the king, which might represent secular shipsokes. It is true that the bequest to the people of Wiltshire might reflect a shipsoke attached the bishopric of Ramsbury, held by Ælfric both before and during his tenure of Canterbury; at the time of Domesday, the lands of the former bishopric in Wiltshire amounted to 262 hides, but two of the estates concerned, Ramsbury itself (ninety hides) and Bishops Cannings (seventy hides), each constituted a single hundred.[100] There are, however, traces in Wiltshire of hundreds grouped in threes, all associated with royal manors, and on the eve of the Norman Conquest, the burgesses of Malmesbury, to which the pleas of two hundreds were attached, owed 20*s.* 'to provision the [king's] seamen' (*ad pascendos suos buzecarlos*).[101] In Kent, the archiepiscopal obligation was presumably represented by the ship left to the king, and the bequest to the Kentish people might have been intended to discharge the obligation of a secular shipsoke, but the turmoil of the Norman Conquest makes it impossible to discern any three-hundred hide units within the shire.[102] Groups of hundreds elsewhere can usually be inferred only from later sources, but some are recorded in pre-Conquest contexts.[103] In the time of Edward the Confessor, three hundreds in Devon were attached to the royal manor of Molland, and three in Herefordshire to Much Cowarne, which may have been an estate set aside for the use of the local earl.[104] The association of neighbouring hundreds for judicial purposes is known in the late tenth century, and there is no reason why the same expedient should not have been used for military assessments.[105]

Though the shipsokes probably go back to the time of Edgar, they may have been overhauled in 1008.[106] The *Chronicle*'s description of ship-building 'throughout England' suggests an extension in their range and scope. If the possible case of Ramsey is left aside, the known shipsokes are all in Wessex or south-west Mercia, which formed the heartlands of the West Saxon realm; perhaps Æthelred extended an obligation from these regions into eastern and even northern England. At the very least, the edict of 1008 is testimony to a serious attempt at reforming the military capabilities of the country. It was, moreover, a success (at least in the short term) for the *Chronicle* records that in 1009 'the ships which we mentioned above were ready and there were more of them than ever before, from what books tell us, had been in England in any king's time'. If 'any king' included Edgar, whose fleet seems to have been particularly impressive, the ship-levy at Sandwich in 1009 must have been remarkable indeed.[107] Unfortunately the *Chronicle* does not give the number of vessels involved, but does reveal that at least eighty (possibly a hundred) ships were withdrawn from the fleet, and that 'the rest' returned to London.[108] Some comparison with later levies gives the scale: in 1049 the West Saxons provided forty-two ships to a royal hosting, and there was also a Mercian contingent, of unknown size; in 1052, when Earl Godwine and his sons had creamed off the ships of central and eastern Wessex, King Edward, supported by the earls of Mercia and Northumbria, could still muster fifty ships at London to oppose his rebellious earls.[109]

The most innovatory aspect of the 1008 edict may lie not in the demand for ships but in the helmets and mail for the men who were to form the fighting contingents. It has been argued that the English forces of the 990s lacked the helmets and body armour regularly worn by the Viking invaders, and that efforts were being made in the early eleventh century to rectify this. In the poem on the battle of Maldon, only the Vikings are said to have mail-shirts, and the tactics of the English, wielding their spears from behind a wall of shields, seem designed to keep the more heavily-protected enemies at bay.[110] Moreover the wills of the great nobles of the late tenth century do not, with one exception, mention helmets and mail as part of their heriot payments to the king, whereas in later wills such items are regularly included.[111] Bequests of weapons also become more common in the early eleventh century. Archbishop Ælfric, as we have seen, included sixty helmets and sixty mail-shirts with the ship which he bequeathed to the king, and in 1014 the ætheling Æthelstan left to his royal father 'the mail-shirt which Morcar has'.[112] No arms were mentioned in connection with the sixty-four-oared *scegð* bequeathed to the king by Bishop Ælfwold of Crediton, but the bishop did leave three mail-shirts to his kinsman Wulfgar, two more to his brother-in-law Godric of Crediton and a helmet and a mail-shirt to Cenwold.[113] The concentration of references to body-armour around the time of the 1008 edict suggests that a deliberate programme was in progress, aimed at equipping the English forces with tackle comparable to that of their enemies; indeed the design of the 'Helmet' coin issue (1003–9), which shows the king himself in arms and wearing a helmet instead of the usual crown, may be part of the same programme.

Æthelred also refurbished at least some of the fortifications built by his predecessors.[114] The earliest recension of the Enham legislation commands the repair of burhs in every province, and later versions add the repair of bridges.[115] These were ancient obligations, perhaps somewhat neglected of late. Of the burhs established by Alfred and his successors, some had been abandoned and replaced by more economically viable sites; Eashing, for instance, had given way to Guildford, and Burpham to Arundel.[116] Others had overflowed their walls and ditches in the process of becoming towns, though some were still defensible, notably London, Canterbury, Exeter and Winchester. In the late Old English period, several towns had their defences strengthened. At Wallingford the northern bank was raised and crowned with stone, and the ditch was enlarged, a new stone wall was erected at Cricklade, and similar works were undertaken at Wareham, Christchurch/Twynham, Lydford, Chisbury and Malmesbury.[117] Not all these works can be precisely dated, but the danger of Viking attack seems the likeliest impetus. The clearest evidence comes from South Cadbury, Somerset, a former Iron Age hillfort already reused in the age of settlement, which was further refurbished in the early eleventh century, with a stone wall four feet in breadth surmounting a bank of earth, rubble and stone, the whole being some twenty feet high. The date is established by the South Cadbury mint, which began to operate in 1009–10, just as that of Ilchester temporarily ceased; presumably the Ilchester moneyers were moved into the safety of the new burh.[118] The moneyers of Wilton, as we have seen, were moved to Old Sarum after the sack of 1003, which suggests that one of the phases of post-Roman occupation at Old Sarum (another Iron Age hillfort) dates from Æthelred's time.[119] Both South Cadbury and Old Sarum were emergency forts, abandoned after the crisis was over. How many more such sites were temporarily reoccupied is uncertain; Cissbury, Sussex, is one possibility, if it is the site of the mint at *Sith[m]estesbyri*, die-linked with that of Chichester.[120] What is lacking is the integration of burghal garrisons with the field armies, evident in the later years of Alfred and the reigns of his successors. It seems that Æthelred's burhs were merely centres of refuge (sometimes not even that).[121]

The legislation of 1008 is the first known to have been produced under the influence of Wulfstan *lupus*, bishop of Worcester and archbishop of York.[122] If Eadric *streona* was the evil genius of Æthelred's reign, the role of 'good angel' must be assigned to Wulfstan. Given his crucial role in the latter years of Æthelred's reign (and indeed in the early years of Cnut), it is salutary to remember that our primary narrative source, the *Anglo-Saxon Chronicle*, has only two notices of him, both relating to the very end of his career.[123] Wulfstan's activities must be reconstructed from his own works, written in his idiosyncratic and easily recognisable style.

Little is known of Wulfstan's early life. His long-standing interest in the social and religious problems of eastern and northern England points to a connection with the east midlands, and it has been suggested that he was a monk at one of the Fenland monasteries.[124] It cannot have been Ely, where he was eventually buried, for the house-chronicle, which describes him as 'an excellent man, all of whose qualities and deeds served religion', would certainly have claimed him, had he been one of the brethren.[125] The same is true of Peterborough, which remembered him as a benefactor, and even preserved a tradition that he had wished to be buried there.[126] Whether Wulfstan began his ecclesiastical career as a monk or as a secular priest must remain uncertain.[127]

Whatever his origins, Wulfstan must have shown exceptional promise to have been promoted to the see of London in 996. It ranked as the third bishopric in the southern province, after Canterbury itself and Winchester. From 956, its bishop regularly attests in fourth place among the ecclesiastical witnesses, after the two archbishops and the bishop of Winchester, and this is Wulfstan's normal position from his first appearance in the witness-lists.[128] London was a secular cathedral, staffed by canons rather than monks, and its eminence was perhaps due in part to historical considerations (Gregory the Great had intended it to be the archiepiscopal see) and in part to the economic and strategic significance of the city itself.[129] The region dependent upon it, which included Essex and parts of Hertfordshire as well as Middlesex, was kept under close control by the West Saxon kings. When the structure of local administration emerges into the light of history at the time of the Domesday survey, all the hundreds of Middlesex were in the king's hands, and there were none of the so-called 'private' hundreds belonging to ecclesiastical establishments which are common elsewhere in the shires of Wessex and southern Mercia; the same is true to a lesser extent of Essex and Hertfordshire.[130] London itself was frequently chosen as a meeting-place for royal councils, which must have brought its bishop into particularly close association with the king.[131] Wulfstan's six-year tenure of the office clearly provided him with valuable experience, and the efficiency with which he discharged his duties is shown by his translation in 1002 to the double post of bishop of Worcester and archbishop of York. Only a man high in the king's confidence would have been given responsibility for the northern province, still only partially integrated into the English kingdom.

It was while bishop of London that Wulfstan adopted the pen-name *lupus* ('wolf'; a play on the first element of his name), and he was already celebrated as a writer and preacher; an anonymous letter addressed to him praises 'the most sweet sagacity of your eloquence, and the richness and simultaneous depth of your decorously set-out prose'.[132] Indeed it was as an orator that Wulfstan was long remembered; the Ely house-chronicle claimed that 'when he spoke, it was as if his listeners were hearing the very wisdom of God Himself'.[133] Even in modern translation the texts of Wulfstan's surviving homilies preserve in their structure the power and vehemence of his oratory. Their impact lies in his use of the techniques of Old English verse, 'rhyme, assonance and (above all) alliteration', and the effect of his preaching, 'almost breathless in its conciseness, imbued with a sense of radical urgency, in its very rhythmic structure hammering home the message, must have been extraordinary'.[134] The chief audience for Wulfstan's preaching was ecclesiastical, but both themes and style were carried over into his secular works.

Wulfstan's views on the duties of a bishop are set out in the *Institutes of Polity*, composed about 1008 but revised towards the end of his career:

> Bishops are heralds and teachers of God's laws and they must preach justice and forbid injustice ... and if bishops neglect to punish sins and forbid injustice, nor make known God's law, but mumble with their jaws when they ought to speak out, woe to them for that silence.[135]

His earliest homilies, composed while he was bishop of London, were categorized by their editor as the 'Eschatological Homilies', concerned as they are with the Last Judgement and especially with the coming of Antichrist which will precede it.[136] It has been argued that the imminence of the year 1000 inspired widespread millennial fears throughout all Christendom, because of the prophecy in Revelations that, after a thousand years, Satan 'shall be loosed out of his prison, and shall go out to deceive the nations'.[137] An anonymous homily of Edgar's time warns of the great terror which 'will come upon created things, in this present time, when the Judgement draws near'.[138] Wulfstan, however, cites the text from Revelations only to observe that the fateful year has gone by: 'a thousand years and more also have passed since Christ was among people in human form, and now Satan's bonds are very loose, and Antichrist's time is well at hand'.[139] This homily, like the others on the same theme, is based on the Gospel texts, which, unlike Revelations, preclude speculation on the precise date of the Apocalypse: 'of that day and that hour knoweth no man, no, not the angels which are in heaven, neither the Son, but the Father'.[140]

The signs which presage the end of the world are specified in the Gospel texts: 'nation shall rise against nation and kingdom against kingdom, and there shall be earthquakes in divers places and there shall be famine and troubles'.[141] The intensification of the Viking raids in the 990s might have caused Wulfstan to fear that he discerned the signs of the end; the connection between the Danish onslaught and the coming Apocalypse had already been made by his friend and mentor, Ælfric the homilist.[142] Nor was there any diminution of 'wars and rumours of wars' after Wulfstan's translation to York and Worcester in 1002, and, alarming though such portents might be, they were no more than 'the beginning of sorrows'.[143] The reign of Antichrist meant the appearance of false prophets, eager not to instruct the faithful but to deceive and mislead them, and to destroy those whom they could not corrupt. Under this reign of terror, all social ties would wither. Wulfstan's particular nightmare was that even family affections would break under the strain, so that 'kinsman will not protect kinsman any more than strangers'.[144] As social bonds began to give under the stress of the Danish invasions, his millennial fears can only have increased, and these intimations of doom underlie not only his preaching, but also his legislative works.[145]

In the Last Days, to live rightly would be no defence against the Antichrist, but those who held out against him would be vindicated at the Second Coming, when God, having banished the Antichrist to

Hell along with his agents and dupes, would welcome those who had faithfully endured to Heaven. It was therefore the duty of all priests to teach right doctrine and true morality, and much of Wulfstan's energy as archbishop was devoted to producing a priesthood capable of performing this task. Like London, York was a secular cathedral and its province had barely been touched by the Benedictine reform of the tenth century. Wulfstan's aim was to extend to the secular clergy the high standards of life and learning espoused by the monastic reformers of the previous generation. He was particularly concerned about the mass-priests of the 'estate-churches' (*tunkirkan*), established by lay magnates on their own lands, who were most involved in instructing the laity. It was for them that he produced the *Canons of Edgar*, a set of precepts concerned with the responsibilities of 'a parochial priest, with a lay congregation: baptism, celebration of the mass, administering penance, burial of the dead'.[146] Some of the prohibitions are quite revealing; as well as not coming armed within the church doors, a priest must not be a trader (*mangere*) nor a merchant, a tavern minstrel (*ealusceop*) nor a gleeman (*gliwige*).[147]

Wulfstan's duties as bishop and archbishop were not confined to ecclesiastical affairs, though it was this aspect which he considered of overwhelming importance. Secular demands were also attached to his office. As bishop first of London and then of Worcester, and archbishop of York, Wulfstan was a landholder, subject to the public obligations which landholding entailed. These obligations included military service. The bishopric of London (and probably of Worcester too) owed, as we have seen, a ship and its crew to the king's service, and it may not be a coincidence that the memorandum which describes how the obligation was assessed on London's estates dates from the period of Wulfstan's episcopate.[148]

Wulfstan's involvement in secular affairs went far beyond simply meeting his obligations; he wished to use the power of the king in the furtherance of his religious and moral reforms.[149] It was presumably to this end that he assembled the vast and complex corpus of legal texts upon which he drew for his own legislation. His first essay in this genre was the so-called *Peace of Edward and Guthrum*, composed between 1002 and 1005 but fathered (like the *Canons of Edgar*) on earlier royal law-makers.[150] Its purpose seems to be to provide for the north a legal tradition, almost entirely ecclesiastical in content, comparable to that of Wessex and Kent. In the present context, the interest lies in the prologue, in which the compilers are said to have 'fixed secular penalties (*woruldlice steora*) also, out of the knowledge that otherwise they would not be able to restrain many people, nor would many people otherwise submit to godly amendment as they should'.[151] The same thinking was to underlie all the legislation undertaken by Wulfstan on behalf of his royal lord, King Æthelred.

5

The Immense Raiding-Army

'The Just War is war against the cruel seamen who desire to destroy our homeland.'

Ælfric the Homilist[1]

The year 1009 began well, with the assembly at Sandwich of the ships ordered in 1008, 'more of them than ever before, from what books tell us, had been in England in any king's time'. But internal dissension brought the levy to an abrupt end, with the loss of at least eighty ships, and the remainder were taken back to London as the assembly dispersed.[2] This débâcle was followed by the arrival 'immediately after Lammas' (1 August) of 'the immense raiding-army (*se ungemetlice unfriðhere*) that we called Thorkell's army'.[3] This expedition, led by Thorkell *inn Hávi* (the Tall), is said elsewhere to have been undertaken in revenge for the death of his brother Hemming, killed in England, and although the details are found only in late and unreliable sources, the story of the dead brother (unnamed) is also in the *Encomium*, and John of Worcester records the arrival in 1009 of a second army, commanded by Hemming and Eilaf.[4]

The *Encomium Emmae* presents Thorkell as the agent of Swein Forkbeard of Denmark.[5] Scandinavian tradition, however, associates Thorkell with the semi-legendary Jomsvikings, whose historicity is still disputed; their base, if it existed, seems to have lain in the territory of the Wends, and they were perhaps one of the 'independent bands of warriors and freebooters based in the Baltic region who lived by piracy'.[6] It is unlikely that a Jomsviking would be well-disposed to Swein Forkbeard, who had overthrown his father to acquire the Danish kingdom, for both Wends and Jomsvikings are represented as supporters of Harald Bluetooth, whose second wife was the daughter of a Wendish king.[7] The known facts of Thorkell's career suggest that he was at best indifferent to the king of the Danes.[8]

The *Anglo-Saxon Chronicle* calls Thorkell's force 'the Danish army', but it was not drawn from Denmark alone. The Swedish Viking, Ulv of Borresta (Uppland), also took part and it is likely that others of his nation were also present.[9] Moreover the *Víkingavísur* of Sighvatr Thórðarson and the *Höfudlausn* of Óttarr *svarti* record the participation of the Norwegian adventurer, Oláf *helgi*, future saint and king of Norway, but at this time an unattached freelance 'following a career of desultory violence and robbery round the coasts of the Baltic and North Sea'.[10] The 'immense raiding-army' was probably made up of many such men with their personal followings; recording its departure in 1012, the *Chronicle* says that it 'dispersed as widely as it had been collected'.[11]

The arrival of 'Thorkell's army' has been described as 'one of the most catastrophic events of the reign'.[12] Its effects may be judged by the legislative enactments made at Bath in the autumn of 1009, reflected in the recensions of the code known as VII Æthelred. Like the Enham legislation of the previous year, represented by the codes known as V, VI and (probably) X Æthelred, the Bath edict bears the unmistakable imprint of Archbishop Wulfstan. To understand Wulfstan's legal texts, it is essential to remember that they cannot be treated as separate from his homilies, which express the same sentiments and share the same aims; the moral and spiritual regeneration of the English nation.[13] The events of the eleventh century's first decade can only have exacerbated the millenarian fears expressed in the early 'eschatological' homilies.[14] The great famine of 1005, recorded in the *Anglo-Saxon Chronicle*, which was felt in northern Europe as well, was immediately followed by (and perhaps contributed to) the military disasters of 1006.[15] Such apocalyptic threats demanded a moral response: 'prayer, penance and payments of alms (not to mention tithes) might manage what conventionally secular measures could not'.[16]

None of the surviving texts of the enactments associated with the archbishop represent the 'original' form of the underlying edicts; 'behind the emergence of the earliest extant version of "V" lies an evolutionary process like that which can be witnessed in the extant versions'.[17] A consequence of this is that the successive recensions give only a general idea of what was enacted, and some of the clauses may be later additions or emendations.[18] This is true of the Bath legislation, which survives in two versions, one in Old English and one a post-Conquest Latin translation, which is nevertheless probably closer to its 'original' form.[19] It describes itself as '[the edict] which was drawn up by King Æthelred and his councillors at Bath' (*hoc instituerunt Æþelredus rex et sapientes eius apud Badam*). No date is given, but the Old English version substitutes for this the heading: 'this is what was decreed when the great army (*se micele here*) came to the country', that is, in 1009.[20]

The Latin text opens with a general exhortation:

> In the first place one God shall be loved and honoured above all and all men shall show obedience to their king in accordance with the best traditions of their ancestors, and cooperate with him in defending his kingdom.

It then prescribes a general programme of fasting, almsgiving, confession and avoidance of all 'misdeeds and injustice'. A tax of 1*d.* is levied on every ploughland (*hide* in the Old English version); household dependants are also to give 1*d.* and their lords are to pay for any who cannot afford it. All thegns are to give a tithe of their property. A general three-day fast is ordered, during which all are to go daily to confession, barefoot and led by the local priest; every priest is to sing thirty masses, and every deacon and cleric thirty psalters.[21] No meat is to be served during the three days (only bread, water and raw vegetables) and what would normally have been eaten is to be distributed among the poor. Slaves are exempted from labour so that they may keep the fast, which is to be observed on the Monday, Tuesday and Wednesday immediately preceding Michaelmas (29 September, which in 1009 fell on a Thursday). Penalties are laid down for breaking the fast, whose observance is to be overseen by the priest and reeve of each vill and the heads of each tithing, who shall testify on oath that it has been properly conducted.[22] The third clause is addressed specifically to ecclesiastical communities, both monks and secular canons:

> in every religious foundation, the mass entitled 'against the heathen' shall be sung daily at Matins, by the whole community, on behalf of the king and all his people. And at the various Hours, all the members of the foundation, prostrate on the ground, shall chant the psalm: 'O Lord, how they are multiplied [that trouble me]', and the Collect against the heathen, and this

> shall be done as long as the present need continues. And in every foundation and college of monks every priest severally shall celebrate thirty masses for the king and the whole nation, and every monk shall repeat his psalter thirty times.

The final clauses concern the laity: church dues and tithes are to paid, encroachments on church property are to cease, slaves are not to be sold out of the country on pain of excommunication, and all theft is strictly forbidden; the benefit of the law is to be extended to all, both rich and poor, all stolen goods are to be restored with due emendation, and a double compensation is to be required from any reeve who has committed theft. The text ends with the command that arrears of alms are to be paid in full, and that in future all church dues are to be rendered as specified, 'so that Almighty God may show mercy towards us and grant us victory over our enemies and peace'.

Such edicts were by no means a specifically English response to the Viking threat, nor (in themselves) do they indicate any military weakness. Confronted by 'an infinite multititude of Norsemen from Denmark and the Irish region' (some of whom may once have been members of Thorkell's *ungemetlice unfriðhere*), William the Great of Aquitaine, Æthelred's contemporary, 'sent orders throughout the monasteries of Aquitaine that all should beseech the Lord's mercy with fasts and litanies, so that He should consume the strength of the enemy and should make His people victorious'.[23] William took military measures as well, but with no more success than Æthelred; defeated in the ensuing battle, from which he only narrowly escaped, he was forced to ransom his captives, sue for peace and pay over 'a huge weight of gold and silver'. Only in one respect was he luckier than Æthelred; for whatever reason, the Vikings did not return to Aquitaine.[24]

The surviving texts of the Bath legislation are exclusively ecclesiastical and, taken with the Enham enactments of the previous year, they lay down a programme for the spiritual and moral purification of the kingdom. At Enham, as we have seen, secular measures were not neglected. The *Anglo-Saxon Chronicle* records, more fully than the surviving legal texts, the measures taken to reform the ship-levy, and the Enham code also reinforces the ancient duty of repairing *burhs*.[25] The obligations of military service are emphasized by the penalties for desertion: anyone who deserts an army commanded by the king in person shall forfeit life and property, while desertion from other armies, presumably under lesser commanders, carries a fine of 120s.[26] The purity of the coinage is also addressed, and it has been suggested that the special issue of 'Agnus Dei' pennies may have been launched at Enham in 1008. The place-name seems to mean 'place where lambs are bred', and the assembly was called for Pentecost; both place-name and timing seem to be reflected by the design of the issue, which bears on the obverse not the usual portrait of the king but the Lamb of God carrying a long cross, with the inscription *a[gnus] d[e]i*, and on the reverse a dove, representing the Holy Spirit.[27] Numismatists, however, date the 'Agnus Dei' issue to the late summer or early autumn of 1009, in which case it may have been minted for the payment of the penitential tax commanded at Bath in that year.[28] What is certain is that the 'Agnus Dei' coinage was not part of the regular reminting, for this is represented by the 'Last Small Cross' issue, which replaced the 'Helmet' at about this time.[29] Whatever the precise date of origin, the 'Agnus Dei' issue, with its cross-carrying Lamb, echoes the eschatological concerns of Wulfstan's homilies.

Important though they are, the secular clauses of the Enham legislation are subordinate to its primary purpose, the moral regeneration of the country. Ecclesiastics, both monastic and secular, are exhorted to fulfil their obligations, and especially the obligation of chastity, churches are to be protected and ecclesiastical dues paid fully and promptly, saints' days are to be observed, the Sabbath kept, sinful and criminal deeds are to be confessed and emendation is to be made. The concerns underlying both the Enham and the Bath codes are similar to those of the contemporary 'Peace of God' movement in southern and central France; indeed the Enham assembly has been compared to a continental peace meeting.[30] Wulfstan's vision, reiterated throughout his works, was of king and people united in love and loyalty: 'let us loyally support one royal lord, and let each friend support the other with true fidelity'.[31] Only a people secure in its faith and united in mutual friendship could withstand its enemies, worldly or spiritual.

In the event the English nation failed to withstand its enemies and the closing decade of Æthelred's reign was one of almost unmitigated disaster, though, paradoxically, it is at this point that the organization and tactics of his forces can most clearly be seen.[32] It is not easy to explain why the English performed so badly. Despite his posthumous reputation, Æthelred was by no means militarily inactive. He is known to have led his forces in person on only four occasions (in 1000, twice in 1009 and in 1014) and the claim of his Icelandic panegyrist, Gunnlaugr Serpent's Tongue, that the army feared Æthelred no less than God is probably poetic licence, but the campaigns of 1000 and 1014 at least met with some success.[33] The military reforms implemented in 1008 (for which see Chapter 4 above) seem eminently sensible, though they were perhaps overtaken by events. It may be, as Professor Abels has argued, that the military capacity built up by Alfred and his successors was eroded during the peaceful years of Edgar (though the meagre sources for Edgar's reign may exaggerate the degree of peace), and that Æthelred's attempts to reverse the process came to nothing for lack of an 'overall coherent defensive strategy'.[34] A complementary explanation may lie in the strategy and tactics of the king's enemies, and particularly those of Thorkell the Tall between 1009 and 1012.

The *Anglo-Saxon Chronicle*'s account of Thorkell's campaigns can be supplemented by the praise-poems for Oláf *helgi*, written by Sighvatr Thórðarson and Óttarr *svarti*, the anonymous *Liðsmannaflokkr* and the German chronicler Thietmar of Merseburg.[35] The Icelandic skald Sighvatr entered Oláf's employ after his return to Norway in 1014 to claim the kingship. As 'the king's closest confidant and trusted ambassador, his opportunities for learning Oláfr's history must have been unrivalled', and his *Víkingavísur* has been described as 'the best historical document transmitted to us by the Scandinavian north'.[36] Óttarr *svarti*, by contrast, had but a brief association with Oláf, and seemingly an uneasy one at that, for his poem is a *Höfudlausn* ('head-ransom'), that is 'a poem designed to avert a king's anger by a skald in fear of execution', and Óttarr is later found in the employ of Oláf's enemy, Cnut.[37] *Liðsmannaflokkr*, composed (perhaps in England) around 1020, is an anonymous panegyric on the deeds of Thorkell and Cnut; oddly enough no skald wrote in praise of Thorkell alone (or at least nothing has survived), though he was clearly one of the greatest warriors of his age.[38] The final exploit of his first English campaign, the sack of Canterbury in 1011, is described by Thietmar of Merseburg as well as the *Anglo-Saxon Chronicle.*

The *Anglo-Saxon Chronicle* records that Thorkell's ships made landfall at Sandwich soon after Lammas (1 August) 1009. The army's first target was Canterbury, whose citizens quickly came to terms, and the men of East Kent paid a *gafol* of £3000 for a truce. The Vikings then, like others before them, occupied the Isle of Wight, launching raids into Sussex, Hampshire and Berkshire. After Martinmas (11 November), they returned to north Kent, where they 'took up winter quarters on the Thames, and lived off Essex and off the shires which were nearest, on both banks of the Thames'. Several attempts on London were beaten off; one is described by Sighvatr and Óttarr, the latter claiming that the bridge was damaged in the attack.[39]

Soon after Christmas 1009, the Vikings broke out through the Chilterns to sack Oxford and perhaps Wallingford as well.[40] They returned along both sides of the Thames as far as Staines, where the northern wing crossed the river to avoid an English force assembled at London, and came to their base on the Thames, 'and during the spring [of 1010] they were in Kent repairing their ships'. After Easter (9 April), the refurbished fleet sailed for East Anglia. Its troops landed at Ipswich 'and went straight away to where they had heard that Ulfcytel was with his army'. On 5 May English and Danes met at Ringmere Heath, some four miles north east of Thetford.[41] The *Chronicle* says that the East Angles fled 'at once', led by the otherwise unknown Thurcytel Mare's-head, but that 'the men of Cambridgeshire stood firm against them'. The Danes nevertheless held the field, and the English dead included the king's brother-in-law Æthelstan, Oswig (son-in-law of Ealdorman Byrhtnoth) and his son, Wulfric Leofwine's son, Eadwig Æfic's brother 'and many another good thegn and a countless number of the people'.[42] The Danes acquired horses 'and afterwards had control of East Anglia, and ravaged and burnt that country for three months, and even went into the wild fens, slaying the men and cattle, and burning throughout the fens; and they burnt down Thetford and Cambridge'.

The *Chronicle*'s account of the subsequent movements of the Danes is not without its ambiguities.[43] It describes how 'they turned back southwards into the Thames valley, and the mounted men rode towards the ships'. We are not told where 'the ships' were, and the Viking forces may have been returning to Ipswich, the last recorded position of their fleet, but the route described is not the most obvious or direct. In any case 'quickly afterwards they turned west again into Oxfordshire, and from there into Buckinghamshire, and so along the Ouse until they reached Bedford, and so as far as Tempsford, and ever they burnt as they went', until 'they turned back to the ships again with their booty'. Again the *Chronicle* does not say where the ships were, merely that the English force which should have been shadowing the Danes 'in case they wished to turn inland' had in fact dispersed. Nothing forbids the assumption that on this, as on the earlier occasion, the ships concerned were lying in their base on the Thames. It may have been from thence also that the final campaign of 1010 was launched 'before St Andrew's Day' (30 November), in the course of which Northampton was sacked. The host then turned southwards and 'went across the Thames into Wessex, and so towards Canning's Marsh and burnt it all', finally coming to their ships (presumably in the Thames) at Christmas.

It is unfortunate that we are not told precisely where the Viking ship base lay. In his account of Oláf *helgi*'s attack on London (presumably in 1009), Sighvatr says that some of the host had set up camp in Southwark (*Suðvirki*), but the verse exhibits some confusion with the siege of London in 1016.[44] The account in the *Anglo-Saxon Chronicle* suggests rather that the Viking host was keen to avoid London and its hinterland, though this might of course be the usual bias of the chronicler in favour of London and the Londoners. In view of the truce made with the men of east Kent, a base on Sheppey or Thanet might be possible, but neither site is 'on the Thames', and the fact that the host 'lived off Essex and off the shires which were nearest, *on both banks of the Thames*' (my italics) makes west Kent the likelier choice. A camp on the Kentish bank of the Thames would also give access to Rochester. Little is known of the city in Æthelred's reign, but its importance for the building of ships a century earlier is hinted at by the fact that some of the Viking ships captured in 893 were taken there as well as to London.[45] It was attacked in 999 and (according to John of Worcester) besieged but not, apparently, captured.[46] Some Scandinavian presence in Rochester, though perhaps of a later date, is suggested by the dedication of St Clement's, close to Rochester bridge, and the street-names Broadgate and Childergate, both incorporating the Old Norse *gata*, 'street'.[47] At the least, the Vikings' ability to operate out of their Thameside base for over two years suggests an arrangement with the men of west Kent comparable to that struck with those of east Kent in 1009.

The movements of Thorkell's army in 1009–10 suggest both an overall strategy and a familiarity with English affairs. It is significant that the *Anglo-Saxon Chronicle* has nothing to say of the English fleet after the abortive levy of 1009, though it figures largely in the accounts of earlier campaigns. Those accounts show that Sandwich was (or was becoming) the normal battle-station for the English vessels at the opening of the campaigning season, presumably because its situation at the southern outlet of the Wantsum provided 'an ideal haven well protected from the English Channel by shingle banks', in which they could be safely deployed.[48] It is equally clear that the permanent ship base was at London. It was at London that the ships were assembled in 992, and the surviving vessels of the 1009 levy were taken 'back to London' when it dispersed.[49] The ships and arms ordered in 1008 may also have been gathered there. By the mid eleventh century, the burgesses of Leicester were required to supply four horses 'as far as London, to carry weapons or other things of which there might be need' (*usque Londoniam ad comportandum arma vel alia quae opus esset*); at the same date, the burgesses of Lewes, Sussex, paid 20s. to 'those who were in charge of the arms in the ships', though in the latter case it is not clear where the ships concerned were lying.[50] Such arrangements might be a development of whatever organization had existed in Æthelred's day, when the men who were to make up the fighting-crews of the shipsokes were probably the best-equipped in the English levies, whether their gear was supplied from the king's store or by their own lords.[51]

Sandwich's significance explains the attack upon it in the 990s and, as we have seen, it was Thorkell's landfall in 1009.[52] But Thorkell went beyond merely damaging the rendezvous point for the English fleet. By establishing his base camp in the Thames downstream of London, he prevented the fleet's deployment, while ensuring freedom of action for his own vessels; in fact he used the blocking tactics which previous generations of western rulers had deployed against his own ancestors. He may also have struck at some of the fleet's infrastructure; the attack on Cannings Marsh in 1010 was perhaps intended to damage the hundredal manor of Bishops Cannings which (as we have seen) may have been part of a shipsoke associated with the bishopric of Ramsbury.[53]

The shipsoke attached to the bishopric of Sherborne may also have been targeted, for between 1007 and 1014 Bishop Æthelric was forced to sell land at Corscombe, Dorset, to Ealdorman Eadric, 'because of the attacks and ravages of the evil Danes'.[54]

As for the attack on East Anglia in 1010, this has the aspect of a grudge attack; Óttarr *svarti*'s boast that 'the people of the land fell to the ground in terror ... and many of the English *ferð* took to their heels' recalls the *Chronicle*'s entry for 1004, when Ulfcytel's men gave the Danes the hardest fighting they had ever met with in England.[55] The *Chronicle*'s claim that the Vikings deliberately sought out Ulfcytel and his army is born out by Sighvatr's statement that the ensuing battle was fought 'in Ulfcytel's land' (*á Ulfkels landi*).[56] Indeed it may be that the battles of 1004 and 1010 were fought on the same field. The *Chronicle* does not name the site of either battle, but that of 1004 was fought near Thetford, and the Scandinavian sources place the fighting in 1010 at Ringmere Heath, which can be identified as the area around Ringmere Pit, some four miles north east of Thetford.[57] The site was strategically important. A mile to the east of Ringmere runs the ancient track from Colchester to Brancaster known as the Peddars Way, and Ringmere itself lies on the road linking the Peddars Way to Thetford; from Thetford itself the Icknield Way, used since prehistory, gives access to Cambridge, Hertford and eventually London.[58] From Ringmere, therefore, warbands could be rapidly deployed to most parts of East Anglia, which raises the possibility that it may have been the marshalling-point for the local levies; in 1004, Ulfcytel gave battle before his full force had been gathered.[59]

The destruction of the East Anglian levies opened up the whole of the east midlands to the ravages of Thorkell's armies. They seem to have met with little opposition. The *Anglo-Saxon Chronicle* gives the impression of local levies overwhelmed piecemeal by a superior, rapidly-moving force. The whole nation (*eall þeodscipe*) was indeed called out in autumn of 1009, and led by the king in person; the presence of Eadric *streona* (on whom the blame for its lack of success is laid) shows that the Mercian as well as the West Saxon levies were engaged. This force did succeed in intercepting the Viking army and, although the *Chronicle* implies that nothing was achieved, it was after this that Thorkell shifted his base from the Isle of Wight to north Kent. The picture in 1010, however, is one of total disintegration:

> when they [the Vikings] were journeying to their ships, the *fyrd* should have come out again in case they wished to turn inland. Then the *fyrd* went home. And when they were in the east, the *fyrd* was in the west, and when they were in the south, then our *fyrd* was in the north. Then all the *witan* were summoned to the king, and it was to be decided how this country was to be defended. But even if anything was decided, it did not last a month. Finally there was no leader (*heafod man*) who would collect an army, but each fled as best he could, and in the end no shire would even help the next.

In the annal for 1011, the *Chronicle* returns to the same theme:

> All those disasters befell us through bad policy (*unrædas*), in that they were never offered tribute in time nor fought against; but when they had done most to our injury, peace and truce were made with them; and for all this truce and tribute they journeyed nonetheless in bands everywhere, and harried our wretched people, and plundered and killed them.

Even given the *Chronicle*'s known bias, it is hard not to read this as an accurate estimate of the position. The king and his counsellors seem like men reacting to events rather than directing them. The problem may in part have lain in the nature of the English *fyrd* itself. It is clear that from the earliest times the West Saxon *fyrd* had been raised and deployed shire by shire, and the Mercian *provinciae* probably fulfilled a similar function before this region too was shired on the West Saxon pattern.[60] Within the shire, the levies were probably summoned hundred by hundred; Æthelweard the Chronicler describes a Wiltshire force as 'the hundreds of the people' (*centuriae populi*), and the testimony of one responsible for raising the military obligation of western Wessex commands respect.[61] It is possible that one man was required from every five hides of land. The customs of Berkshire, as recorded in Domesday Book, state that one *miles* went to the king's army from every five hides, receiving £1 (4*s.* per hide) as subsistence for two month's service.[62] It has been argued that Berkshire, a region of small landholders most of whom held directly of the king, may have been a special case, but at the summoning of the fyrd (*expeditio*), the borough of Malmesbury, Wiltshire, was required either to pay 20*s.* for the support of the king's seamen (*buzecarls*) or supply one man from every five-hide holding (*unum hominem … pro honore v hidarum*), and the city of Exeter did the service of five hides (*serviebat haec civitas quantum v hidae*).[63]

It is clear that the shire-levies included contingents raised and led by the greater magnates. Domesday Book describes the system as it existed in Worcestershire on the eve of the Norman Conquest:

> When the king marches against the enemy, if anyone summoned by his edict stays behind, if he is a man so free that he has his sake and soke, and can go where he will with his land, he is at the king's mercy with all his land; but if the free man of another lord stays away from the enemy, and his lord takes another man in his place, he who was summoned shall pay a fine of 40s. to his lord. If, however, no one at all goes in his place, he himself shall give 40s. to his lord, and his lord shall pay a fine of as many shillings to the king.[64]

In the mid eleventh century, Worcestershire was dominated by three ecclesiastical lordships held by the abbots of Evesham and Pershore and the bishop of Worcester; the land of Pershore constituted a shipsoke, and another (Oswaldslow) was attached to the bishopric. It might be concluded that this unusual concentration of ecclesiastical power had affected its military organization, but in fact the customs recorded in the Domesday account have a wider provenance. The fines prescribed for the dependent defaulters are also recorded in Berkshire, a region of small landholders, though the sum involved was 50*s.* rather than 40*s.*[65] The 40*s.* fine for non-attendance is also found in Herefordshire and Shropshire, in the context of expeditions into Wales under the leadership of the sheriff; closer to the Worcestershire fine is that found in Cheshire, where the sheriff was entitled to call a man from every hide to repaid the walls and bridge of Chester, and 'the lord of any man who did not come paid 40*s.* to the king'.[66]

The penalty due from offenders among the greater lords of Worcestershire is that prescribed in the Enham legislation, which was in fact imposed on Leofric of Whitchurch, an Oxfordshire landholder, in Æthelred's time.[67] The Worcestershire customs therefore seem both to have general force, and to date back to the early eleventh century. The greater landholders, king's thegns with full rights (sake and soke) over their lands and the men dwelling upon them, and having no lord but the king (hence their freedom of commendation) were required not only to attend the king's host, but to bring their own men with them. That these men fought under their lord's command is demonstrated by the Secular code of Cnut, which reflects the legislation of Æthelred's later years: the heriot of a man who falls before his lord in battle is remitted, whereas 'the man who in his cowardice deserts his lord or his comrades, whether it is on an expedition by sea or on one on land, is to forfeit all that he owns and his own life; and the lord is to succeed to the possessions and to the land which he previously gave him'; only his bookland (granted by a royal diploma or *landboc*) is to revert to the king who gave it.[68]

Examples of such lordly warbands are occasionally to be found. In the poem on the battle of Maldon, the East Saxon levies are spearheaded by the personal following of Ealdorman Byrhtnoth.[69] If it be objected that this is too 'literary' an example, it may be compared with the Hampshire levies who fought at Dean in 1001, for the casualty list implies the presence of a contingent provided by the bishop of Winchester; the dead included Wulfhere the bishop's thegn, Godwine of Worthy, son of Bishop Ælfsige of Winchester (d. 958), and Leofric of Whitchurch, a manor belonging to the episcopal church.[70] The men of the shipsokes presumably fought under their own lords, or men appointed by them. Eadric, steersman of the bishop of Worcester's ship at the time of the Norman Conquest, is described by Hemming as 'commander of the bishop's army in the king's service' (*ductor exercitus eiusdem episcopi ad servitium regis*), and the office may go back to the tenth century.[71] Bishops of two sees with which shipsokes may reasonably be connected have already been noticed among the military commanders of Æthelred's reign (Ælfstan of London and Æscwig of Dorchester in 992, Eadnoth of Dorchester in 1016), and the military household of a third, Ælfwold of Crediton, is revealed in his will.[72] The ealdorman Æthelmær of Hampshire (d. 982) left £5 to be divided amongst his military retainers (*hiredcnihtas*).[73]

What is lacking is evidence for any more permanent force separate from the shire levies. No doubt the king, like all great lords, maintained a military household, but we know nothing of it, and the very lack of any contemporary references suggests that its numbers were too small to be of any significance; it was perhaps to compensate for this lack that Æthelred resorted to the dubious expedient of hiring Viking stipendiaries. In this respect, the situation was very different from the time of Alfred, who by the 890s had established a standing army, whose members served in rotation, fully integrated with the permanent garrisons of the burhs.[74] Nothing like this was available to Æthelred. In both the *Chronicle* and the Enham code, the distinction between 'national' and 'local' armies is one of leadership; the former were led by the king in person, the latter by local officers appointed by him.[75] Ælfric's fragmentary text, known as *Wyrdwriteras*, composed while he was abbot of Eynsham (and therefore after 1005), appears to defend this policy of delegation:

> Historians (*wyrdwriteras*) who write about kings tell us that ancient kings in former times considered how they might alleviate their burdens, because a single man cannot be everywhere and sustain all things at once, though he might have sole authority. Then the kings appointed ealdormen under them, as support for themselves, and they often sent them to many battles, as is written in heathen books and in the Bible; and the ealdormen conquered the attacking armies.

Since the context is lacking, interpretation of the piece is difficult, but Ælfric seems to approve of at least one aspect of Æthelred's policy; in 1016, however, two English armies refused to proceed unless the king himself was present to lead them.[76]

The *Chronicle*'s lament that 'in the end no shire would even help the next' points up one of the dangers in an army composed of local militias, the tendency to place self-interest above wider considerations. In his work *On the Old and New Testaments*, composed for the Oxfordshire thegn Sigeweard of Asthall, Ælfric emphasizes the thegn's duty of armed resistance to the Vikings: 'you should defend your land with weapons against the raiding *here*' (*þæt þe eowerne eard mid wæ[p]num bewerian wið onwinnende here*). He goes on to praise Judas Maccabeus and his men who 'did not want to fight just with fair words, speaking well but changing it afterwards', a phrase which recalls the complaint in *The Battle of Maldon* that 'many who spoke bravely in the meadhall would not fight when battle came'.[77] In a later homily of *c.* 1009, Ælfric reproaches Englishmen who side with the Danes and so 'betray their own nation to death'.[78] How common this was we cannot know, but a diploma of 1012 regrants land at Whitchurch, Oxfordshire, forfeited by one Leofric for 'mutinying against my soldiers on my expedition'.[79] Allegations of similar behaviour go back to the accusation against Æthelric of Bocking in the 990s (see Chapter 3 above), and the situation in the 1000s was far more alarming.

Regional feelings may also have been important. The campaigns of 1009–10 were fought in eastern Wessex and East Anglia; neither Mercia nor Northumbria were directly involved. It may be that the inhabitants of these regions were not particularly concerned with the misfortunes of East Anglians and Kentishmen.[80] The *Chronicle*'s complaint that the operation of the king's army in 1009 was hindered by Eadric *streona* 'then as it always was', might suggest that the ealdorman was reluctant to commit the levies of Mercia to the defence of the eastern regions. We are, however, almost totally ignorant of what perils might have been facing the west and north. The narrative of the *Chronicle* is focused almost exclusively on Wessex, Kent and East Anglia; it is only from Symeon of Durham that we hear of a Viking attack on Northumbria in 995, and only from the Welsh annals do we learn of Maredudd ab Owain's attack on Mercia in 991 and (of particular importance in the present context) Eadric *streona*'s raid deep into south Wales in 1012.[81] Certainly Æthelred himself was not unmindful of the importance of the north; it was just at the time of Thorkell's assault that he was cultivating the friendship of Morcar, thegn of the Seven Boroughs, and it was probably about this time also that he gave his daughter Ælfgifu in marriage to Uhtred of Bamborough.[82]

It is hard to resist the conclusion that, strive as he would, Æthelred's military reforms were a matter of too little too late; sensible in themselves, there was simply no time for them to develop the capacity for a sustained and determined resistance. Once thrown into disorder, the English were unable to regroup, and the chaos became self-perpetuating; just as nothing succeeds like success, so nothing breeds defeatism as effectively as defeat. The consequent loss of morale contributed to further disasters; and the worst was yet to come.

By the beginning of 1011, Thorkell's army 'had then overrun East Anglia, Essex, Middlesex, Oxfordshire, Cambridgeshire, Hertfordshire, Buckinghamshire, Bedfordshire, half Huntingdonshire, much of Northamptonshire, and south of the Thames all Kent, Sussex, Hastings, Surrey, Berkshire, Hampshire and much of Wiltshire'; it was perhaps the ravaging in Sussex which caused the temporary relocation of the Chichester mint to *Sith[m]estebyri*.[83] The *Chronicle*'s list does not include Somerset but it was in 1009–10 that the mint of Ilchester ceased operation, to be replaced by that of the temporary *burh* at South Cadbury.[84] Neither is Dorset mentioned, but it must be at about this time that Bishop Æthelric of Sherborne sold land at Corscombe to Ealdorman Eadric because of the ravages of the Vikings.[85]

The king and his *witan* sued for peace, offering tribute and provisions, though this did not deter the wilder elements in the Viking host from raiding and plundering at will. Then, in the late summer of 1011, the truce with the men of east Kent broke down. Between 8 and 29 September, the Viking army besieged Canterbury. Its defences seem to have been substantial enough to hold them up, for they got in only by the treachery of one Ælfmær, 'whose life Archbishop Ælfheah had saved'. Those captured included the archbishop himself, Godwine, bishop of Rochester, Ælfweard the king's reeve, Abbess Leofrun and 'all the ecclesiastics, men and women'. Ælfheah's captivity is bewailed in verse (or at least rhythmic prose):

> he was then a captive who had been head of the English people and of Christendom. There could misery be seen where happiness was often seen before, in that wretched city from which first came to us Christianity and happiness in divine and secular things.

Ælfmær, abbot of St Augustine's, however, was allowed to escape. The Vikings remained in Canterbury 'for as long as they pleased'; then, having 'ransacked the whole *burh*', they returned to their ships, taking the archbishop with them.

Once again we are not told where the ships were, though the fact that Godwine of Rochester had apparently taken refuge in Canterbury points once again to north-western Kent. By April 1012, however, the Vikings were encamped near London. Here, before Easter (13 April), the English councillors, led by Eadric *streona*, had assembled for the paying over of the tribute; the figure given in the *Chronicle* is £48,000.[86] It seems that a separate sum was demanded from the archbishop, but he refused to let it be raised.[87] His attitude 'greatly incensed' the Viking host, who were also the worse for drink, and on the Saturday after Easter (19 April), Ælfheah was murdered at a meeting of the *husting*, the formal assembly of the army, whose members

> pelted him with bones and ox-heads, and one of them struck him on the head with the back of an axe, so that he sank down with the blow, and

> his holy blood fell on the ground, and so he sent his holy soul to God's kingdom.

The next morning, Sunday 20 April, the body was carried to London, where it was received by Ealdhun, bishop of Dorchester and Ælfhun, bishop of London, and all the burgesses, and buried in St Paul's.[88]

Though Ælfheah was venerated almost from the moment of his death, there seems to have been no *vita* until that of Osbern of Canterbury, written in the 1080s. By this time virtually all that was known of Ælfheah was that he had been killed by Vikings, and doubt was being expressed whether this in itself constituted martyrdom. Osbern was concerned to demonstrate Ælfheah's sanctity, a task made easier by the paucity of information which 'allowed [him] to create the saint's life as he imagined it ought to have happened'.[89] In particular, his lurid account of the burning of Canterbury and the massacre of its people, with all the usual atrocities, looks like an amplification of the *Chronicle*'s laconic statement that the Vikings 'ransacked the whole *burh*'. Osbern's description was the direct source for John of Worcester's version, embellished with additions of his own, including the pillage of Christchurch and its destruction by fire.[90] The last detail is repeated by Eadmer, Osbern's fellow-monk, in the *Historia Novorum*.[91] The gloomy picture painted by the Canterbury monks appears not only to have been overdrawn but also to have had unfortunate consequences. By the second decade of the twelfth century, the monks of Glastonbury were claiming that members of their community had rescued the relics of St Dunstan from the ruined church and deserted city and conveyed them to Glastonbury, where they still remained. Eadmer despatched a furious letter to Glastonbury, denying that Canterbury had ever been deserted or Christchurch destroyed and abandoned after Ælfheah's murder.[92] One might suspect an element of special pleading, were it not that the Christchurch scriptorium seems to have operated normally throughout the period of the siege and its aftermath, with 'no sign of any interruption to the life of the community by the events of the year 1011'.[93]

No doubt the Viking capture of Canterbury was a violent event in which many of its inhabitants lost life, limb and property; Vikings were not noted for restraint, nor for leaving behind any valuable object which they could carry away.[94] Sighvatr says that the leaders (*portgreifar*) of the city could not defend it, and 'much sorrow befell the gallant *Partar*', while Óttarr *svarti* describes how 'fire and smoke played fiercely upon the dwellings', while his hero Oláf 'destroyed the lives of men'.[95] Some of the inhabitants, however, may have come to terms with the Vikings. The *Chronicle*'s statement that they let Abbot Ælfmær of St Augustine's escape has prompted the suggestion that he was the Ælfmær whose treachery let the besiegers into the city. John of Worcester, however, regarded this Ælfmær as a different person from the abbot; he describes him as archdeacon, and therefore a member of the archbishop's household.[96] St Augustine's, moreover, lay outside the walls, so that its abbot was not well placed to admit the Vikings into the city. But the abbey's very vulnerability to attack may have led him to negotiate his own terms in order to save his community. The only tradition preserved by the later historians of the abbey concerns a pall stolen from the tomb of St Augustine which adhered immovably to the arm of the Viking who looted it, until he confessed his guilt before the saint and the community; this so terrified his fellows that 'they not only feared to become invaders of this monastery but rather became its chief defenders'.[97] The vestigial nature of the St Augustine's tradition suggests either that the events of 1011 had made so little impact that they were not memorable, or that the community had something to hide.[98]

As for the ecclesiastics taken with Ælfheah, they were presumably ransomed; Godwine of Rochester received a grant from the king in 1012 and attests a diploma of 1013, though it is not certain how long he lived after this.[99] Abbess Leofrun, whose nuns were presumably among the female ecclesiastics mentioned in the *Chronicle*, is described as abbess of St Mildrith's by John of Worcester.[100] The minster lay on the isle of Thanet, but its community may have been living at St Mildred's, Canterbury, at this date. Within a few years, the minster and all its possessions, including St Mildred's, were in the hands of St Augustine's; perhaps raising the community's collective ransom had dealt the final blow to an already ailing house.[101]

The fall of Canterbury, cradle of the Christian faith in England, was shattering enough, but it was the murder of the archbishop that gave the event its peculiar horror. According to Sighvatr, Oláf *helgi* was raiding in the vicinity of Orford, Suffolk, at some point after the fall of Canterbury and before his departure to the Continent (probably in 1012), but the *Chronicle* says nothing of it.[102] It seems that 'provincial events subsequent to the capture and eventual murder of Ælfheah were eclipsed by the archbishop's fate'.[103] News of the martyrdom even reached the ears of Thietmar, bishop of Merseberg in eastern Saxony. The channel of transmission is unknown. Thietmar admits that English affairs are unfamiliar to him, and undertakes to describe 'only that which has been related to me by a reliable witness', subsequently identified as Sewald, but with no indication of who he was or where he came from.[104] The name could represent OE Sæweald, but although Thietmar's account of the martyrdom reflects, in general terms, that of the *Anglo-Saxon Chronicle*, he calls the archbishop Dunstan, a mistake which an English informant is unlikely to have made.[105]

However acquired, Thietmar's account is the more valuable in that it was written within six years of the event, for he died in 1018.[106] Like the *Chronicle*, he describes the anger of the Vikings at 'Dunstan's' refusal to pay ransom (though he says that the archbishop had at first agreed to pay). The furious mob surrounded him with intent to kill him, but their leader Thorkell intervened, promising them gold and silver and indeed everything that he had except his ship. But 'they could only be satisfied with the innocent blood', and pelted the archbishop with stones, sticks, and 'the skulls of cattle', until he fell dead under the onslaught. The role Thietmar assigns to Thorkell derives some support from his subsequent actions, for he was the leader of the forty-five ships which entered Æthelred's employ after the dispersal of the rest of the army.[107] He may indeed be the *Þurkytel* who attests, as the ninth of twelve *ministri*, a diploma of the king issued in 1012, in which case there is a nice irony in the fact that the recipient is Godwine, bishop of Rochester, one of the captives of 1011, and the attestation immediately preceding his own is that of his adversary of 1010, Ulfcytel of the East Angles.[108]

It is far from clear that the murder of Ælfheah was intentional, rather than the result of a bout of drunken horseplay which went badly wrong. The assembly at which the archbishop met his death is described as a *husting* (ON *husþing*), the first recorded use of the term in English, and since 'husting' came to have the meaning of a court, it has sometimes been argued that Ælfheah was tried and ritually executed. The term, however, need mean no more than 'a gathering to which a king or other leader calls men under his command'.[109] The *Chronicle* says that those present 'were also very drunk, for wine from the south had been brought there', and its *mise-en-scène* foreshadows the literary descriptions of 'murderous bone-throwing at boisterous dinner-parties' found in later sagas and tales.[110] Nor is it only Thorkell's role, as described by Thietmar, and his subsequent actions, which argues a degree of remorse, even repentance, among the Viking host. The body of Ælfheah was carried to London on the morning after the murder, and there is no suggestion in the *Chronicle* that it was fetched by the English; the bishops Ealdhun and Ælfhun, with the burgesses of London, merely receive the corpse and arrange the burial. Presumably it was the Vikings themselves who conveyed it to London. There is no indication that money changed hands; the payment of the agreed tribute is recorded quite separately, after the archbishop's interment. Whatever the circumstances, however, the space afforded by the *Chronicle* to the fall of Canterbury and the murder of its archbishop illustrates the shattering blow dealt to the collective English psyche. Nothing would ever be quite the same again.

6

A Crisis Surmounted

'They pronounced every Danish king an outlaw from England for ever.'

Anglo-Saxon Chronicle, 1014

The *gafol* of 1012 secured the departure of 'the immense raiding-army', but not of its commander. Thorkell the Tall and his forty-five ships 'came over to the king, and they promised him to defend this country, and he was to feed and clothe them'.[1] We have already seen the circumstances which caused Thorkell to change sides. Æthelred's acceptance of his service was no doubt a matter of expediency, but it had momentous consequences, for it marks the inauguration of the standing fleet of stipendiary troops (*lithesmen*), paid for by the annual *heregeld* and maintained by subsequent kings until 1051.[2] That any such thought was in Æthelred's mind is unlikely; presumably he employed Thorkell in the same way as he had once employed Pallig and other Viking leaders. His other actions in the aftermath of the raiding-army's dispersal show an understandable desire to return to some semblance of normality.

Early in 1013 the king had Lyfing, bishop of Wells, translated to Canterbury to fill the vacant archbishopric, though (as it turned out) he was unable to travel to Rome for his pallium, and for the remainder of Æthelred's reign bishops of both provinces had to be consecrated by Archbishop Wulfstan of York.[3] Other members of the royal council are revealed by the witness-lists to the diplomas issued between the spring of 1012 and the summer of 1013. No fewer than eight diplomas survive from this period (though two are of questionable authenticity), in contrast to the complete lack of diplomas for 1010 and the survival of only two from the early months of 1011.[4]

One of the first diplomas issued in 1012 is in favour of Godwine, bishop of Rochester.[5] The lands concerned, at Fen Stanton and Hilton, Huntingdonshire, are not found in Rochester's possession in 1066, and were possibly a personal gift to the bishop, perhaps in recognition of his misfortunes in 1011, or even in recompense for whatever ransom he was forced to pay.[6] The witness-list includes the attestations of the queen, Archbishop Wulfstan, ten bishops and nine abbots. Eadric *streona* heads the ealdormen, followed by Uhtred, Leofwine and Ælfric, and remains at the top of the lists for the rest of Æthelred's reign. That he had replaced Ælfric of Hampshire as senior ealdorman by 1012 is confirmed by the *Chronicle*'s description of the London assembly, attended by 'Ealdorman Eadric and all the chief counsellors (*witan*) of England, ecclesiastical and lay', but the lack of witness-lists for the years 1010 and 1011 makes it impossible to know for how long he had held this position.[7] Eadric's grip on the royal council was perhaps underpinned by the presence of his surviving kinsmen among the king's advisers; Æthelmær, Æthelweard and Æthelwine, who attest royal diplomas of 1012 and 1013 (with Æthelmær in a particularly prominent position), are probably Eadric's brothers, and Æthelric, who appears in 1013, may be their father.[8]

Northern magnates constitute another group among the counsellors. Ealdorman Uhtred, the king's other son-in-law, attests regularly from 1009 onwards, continuing a tradition established in the time of his murdered predecessor, Ælfhelm.[9] Sigeferth and his brother Morcar, whose connections with Ælfhelm's family have already been discussed, are also prominent in 1012–13, and not only as witnesses; in 1012 the king gave Morcar land at Eckington, Derbyshire, and one of the only two surviving diplomas from 1011 is in favour of the same beneficiary.[10] Godwine, who attests three diplomas of 1012–13, might be included in the 'northern' group, for he is probably the man described as 'ealdorman of Lindsey' at the time of his death in the battle of *Assandun*.[11] He appears in the same region in 993, when he was one of those accused by the *Chronicle* of starting the rout of the English.[12] His title is something of a problem, for although he can be identified as the *minister* (thegn) who attests from 996 onwards, usually well down in the list, he never appears among the *duces*.[13] If the *Chronicle*'s description of him as 'ealdorman' is not a mere slip of the pen, he probably held some local command in the Lincoln area.[14] Though the name is common, it is likely that he was one of the sons of Ealdorman Ælfheah of Hampshire, and therefore a nephew of Ælfhere of Mercia and his brother-in-law, the disgraced and exiled Ælfric *cild*; it seems that, like Ælfric's son, Ælfwine, he made his subsequent career in the east, rather than the west midlands.[15]

Also connected with the eastern shires are Ulfcytel, who attests three of the five surviving diplomas with witness-lists (once in first place), and Northman, son of Ealdorman Leofwine, who received land at Twywell, Northamptonshire, in 1013.[16] The Ælfgar who attests four diplomas may be the west country thegn Ælfgar *mæw* and the Odda who appears beside him in a diploma of 1013 might be Odda of Deerhurst, Gloucestershire, who was perhaps his kinsman.[17] Sigered, the recipient of two estates in Essex in 1013, might be Sired, brother of the Kentish thegn Siward, who was given land at Sibertswold, Kent, in 990.[18] The remaining thegns are mere names, but judging by those who can be (even tentatively) identified, Æthelred was drawing his counsellors from, and distributing his largesse over, all the regions of his kingdom.

One group of especial importance centred on the æthelings. The three eldest, Æthelstan, Edmund and Eadred, attest in 1012.[19] Eadred does not appear after 1012, and perhaps died in that year, but Æthelstan and Edmund continue to attest in 1013, and are joined by Edward, Alfred and Eadwig.[20]

Æthelstan and Edmund must by this time have been in their mid twenties, with their own households, friends and ambitions, and were beginning to make their mark on events. Something of Edmund's character and activities is revealed by his acquisition of land at Holcombe Rogus, Devon, recorded in the Sherborne lease granting him the estate and Bishop Æthelric's letter to Æthelmær, already discussed in a different context.[21] The lease shows that it was Edmund who took the initiative. When he asked for the land at Holcombe, the community 'did not dare refuse him', but temporized, saying that they needed the permission of the king and their bishop. The ætheling therefore approached his father, accompanied by the prior and the senior monks, with Archbishop Wulfstan as spokesman. The king said 'that he did not wish the estate to be given away completely' but agreed to a single-life *læn*, with reversion to the community, in return for which Edmund paid them

£20 for the estate 'with its produce and its men'. It is clear that the community were not happy about this; in his letter to Æthelmær, Bishop Æthelric remarks bitterly that, in addition to his other losses, 'we are told that we shall not be allowed to possess at Holcombe what we had in times past'.

The lease's witness-list is also interesting. The ecclesiastics are headed by Archbishop Wulfstan (who had assisted in the negotiations) and include the three west country bishops, Lyfing of Wells, Æthelric himself and Æthelsige of Cornwall, as well as the otherwise unknown Leofsunu, abbot of Cerne. The lay witnesses, apart from Eadric *streona*, seem to fall into two groups, members of the Dorset shire-court and of the ætheling's household respectively.[22] The most interesting lay signatures, however, are the two which immediately follow that of Eadric *streona*, those of Ealdorman Æthelmær and his son *Æthelfand*. The Holcombe lease survives only as a cartulary copy, and *Æthelfand* is presumably scribal error for Æthelweard.[23] The title accorded to his father may also be a later addition, for the only royal diploma attested by Æthelmær as *dux* dates from 1014.[24] Yet (as we shall presently see) the *Anglo-Saxon Chronicle* describes him as 'ealdorman' in the summer of 1013. It may be that, like Godwine of Lindsey, his was a purely local command. It is also likely that he was a friend and supporter of Bishop Æthelric of Sherborne, in whose diocese the abbey of Cerne, founded by Æthelmær, lay, in which case the title accorded him both in the Holcombe lease and in the *Chronicle* may indicate his standing in the western shires, even after his expulsion from the king's circle. It must also be significant that the only royal diploma which accords him the status of *dux* is the grant to Sherborne recording the restitution of Corscombe, recovered from Ealdorman Eadric.[25]

The Holcombe affair suggests that Edmund may not have been popular among some circles in the west of England.[26] It also hints that the king was not best pleased with his behaviour. Æthelred's favourite son seems to be the eldest, Æthelstan; he was certainly the most prominent. In two diplomas of 1004 and one of 1007, he is the only ætheling named, attesting *cum fratribus meis*, and on one occasion he is distinguished as the firstborn (*primogenitus*), all of which seems to single him out as the designated heir.[27] Edmund seems to have been particularly close to Æthelstan; in one of the diplomas attested by them both and by Eadred, he alone is described as Æthelstan's brother (*frater predicti*).[28] The same impression is given by Æthelstan's will, made on 25 June 1014.[29] It was a death-bed testament, and Edmund was certainly present, for he was one of the witnesses to the king's oral message, by the mouth of Ælfgar Æffa's son, permitting the will to be made. It was to Edmund that Æthelstan bequeathed the sword of King Offa, presumably a valued heirloom; he also received another sword with a decorated hilt, a blade (a sword without the hilts), a silver-plated horn, unspecified lands in East Anglia, and an unnamed estate in the Derbyshire Peak, from which food-rents and a charitable gift of 100*d.* to feed the poor were to be sent annually to Ely, on the feast-day of St Æthelthryth. Edmund also received directions about the £6 left to 'Holy Cross and St Edward at Shaftesbury', and was made responsible for cash payments to two of Æthelstan's retainers. Æthelstan bequeathed a sword to Eadwig, his other surviving brother of the full blood, and speaks tenderly of his 'dear father, King Æthelred' and of his grandmother Ælfthryth 'who brought me up'; there is no mention of his stepmother and her children.

The will of the ætheling is the best available evidence for the household of a lay nobleman in this period; bequests of land, money and weapons are distributed to Æthelstan's chaplain Ælfwine, his seneschal (*discþegn*) Ælfmær, his retainers (*cnihtas*) Ælfwine, Æthelwine and (another) Ælfmær, his sword-polisher Ælfnoth and his unnamed staghuntsman. It may be compared with the establishment of his brother Edmund, partially revealed in the witness-list to the Holcombe lease, which includes Lyfing the ætheling's seneschal (*discþen*), his retainers (*cnihtas*) Ælfgeat and Ælfweard and 'all the other *hiredmen*' (men of the household).[30]

Æthelstan's will is equally important as evidence of the ætheling's wider circle of acquaintance. The bequests to Edmund include land in Derbyshire, where Morcar also held estates, some granted to him by the king, others bequeathed by his wife's uncle Wufric Wulfrun's son.[31] Morcar does not appear as a beneficiary in the ætheling's will, though he might be the man who had charge of the mail shirt which Æthelstan bequeathed to his father the king, but it is probably his brother Sigeferth who received land at Hockcliffe, Bedfordshire, plus a sword, horse and shield.[32] By 1015 Edmund was a supporter of Morcar and Sigeferth's family, and an opponent of Eadric *streona*, the murderer, if John of Worcester is to be believed, of Ealdorman Ælfhelm, uncle of Morcar's wife.[33] His brother's will suggests that the association (and perhaps the enmity) may have been of some duration.

Hostility to Eadric is suggested by another bequest in Æthelstan's will, giving to Godwine Wulfnoth's son 'the estate at Compton which his father possessed'. Both the personal names and the place-name were in common usage at the time, but one Wulfnoth had already fallen foul of Eadric's family. The ship-levy of 1009 was brought to nothing by a confrontation which arose 'at the same time or a little earlier', between Brihtric, brother of Eadric *streona*, and Wulfnoth *cild*, 'the South Saxon'.[34] Brihtric came to the king and accused Wulfnoth of unspecified crimes, whereupon Wulfnoth 'enticed ships to him until he had twenty', and raided along the south coast.[35] When news of his whereabouts was brought to the levy at Sandwich, Brihtric, 'intending to make a big reputation for himself', took eighty of the assembled ships and set off to capture Wulfnoth dead or alive, but his fleet was caught in a storm and cast ashore, 'and at once Wulfnoth came and burnt up the ships'.[36]

As usual, no background is given for the dispute, but Wulfnoth's identity provides some clues. A man who could, while under a cloud, command the allegiance of twenty ships' crews was clearly of at least local importance, and this impression is confirmed both by his byname, *cild* ('boy', 'young man' and hence 'warrior', 'nobleman'), and by his toponymic description 'the South Saxon'; one of the wealthiest thegns of King Edward's day was similarly described as 'Æthelnoth *cild* the Kentishman'.[37] The most prominent Sussex family in the later eleventh century was that of Godwine, earl of Wessex under Cnut, his sons, and Edward the Confessor.[38] The 'F' recension of the *Anglo-Saxon Chronicle* describes Wulfnoth *cild* as Earl Godwine's father, and since it was written at Christchurch, Canterbury, a house closely connected with the earl, its testimony, though late, commands respect.[39]

It cannot be more than a possibility that it was Wulfnoth *cild*'s son who received Compton under the ætheling's will.[40] If, however, the Godwine of the will (whether or not he was later to become earl of Wessex) was the son of Wulfnoth *cild* of Sussex, and if, moreover, both he and his father were members of an 'æthelings' party' hostile to the growing power of Eadric *streona*, then the accusation flung at Wulfnoth *cild* by Eadric's brother Brihtric may have been politically motivated. It has been too readily assumed by modern historians that Wulfnoth *cild* was guilty as charged. He is not heard of again, and may have been dead by the time that the ætheling made his will, but Brihtric too vanishes from the witness-lists after 1009. He may be the unnamed brother of Ealdorman Eadric who, according to Osbern of Canterbury, was murdered by the men of Kent; Osbern alleges that when Eadric demanded justice from the king, Æthelred replied that the dead man had got no more than he deserved.[41] If there is any basis to this tale, it might preserve opinion of Brihtric in the south east, for the *Chronicle* appears to lay the blame for the disruption of the ship-levy on him, rather than on Wulfnoth.

It seems that a party hostile to Eadric *streona* may have been forming around the sons of the king's first marriage, one of whom was his designated heir. This is unlikely to have been unusual; the disturbances after Edgar's death imply the existence of similar parties centred on Edward the Martyr and on Æthelred himself. Other examples could be drawn from other times and places, and under normal circumstances caused only minor trouble. But the circumstances in the closing years of Æthelred's reign were not normal, and the existence of hostile factions among the circles closest to the king could only add to the dangers which faced him. Chief among these was his old adversary, Swein of Denmark.

Like his enemy Æthelred, Swein Forkbeard of Denmark has been harshly treated by historians. The German chroniclers, Thietmar of Merseburg and Adam of Bremen, are implacably hostile, despite the fact that, in Adam's case, Swein's grandson and eventual successor, Swein Estrithson, was one of his chief informants for Danish affairs. Ecclesiastical and secular politics lie at the root of this enmity. One of Adam's purposes was to assert the claims of the archbishop of Hamburg-Bremen to metropolitan authority over the Scandinavian church, which Swein Forkbeard strenuously resisted.[42] As for Thietmar, his views were perhaps coloured by Swein's marriage to the sister of Boleslav Chrobry ('the Brave'), duke of the Poles (992–1025), whose resistance to the authority of the Emperor Henry II rendered him unpopular to German opinion.[43]

A different picture of Swein emerges from the *Encomium* of Queen Emma, widow of Swein's son Cnut (and of course of King Æthelred).

Since she was an eye-witness to Swein's invasion of 1013, this might be supposed a reliable addition to our knowledge of the period, but in fact the work has its own agenda, relating to the political strife which followed Cnut's death in 1035. Its portrayal of Swein as a popular and effective king may be closer to the truth than the bilious accounts of Thietmar and Adam, but its version of what happened in 1013 is highly suspect and cannot easily be reconciled with the account in the *Anglo-Saxon Chronicle.* The *Encomium*, for instance, alleges that the motive behind Swein's invasion was his desire to punish Thorkell, described as his 'chief military commander' (*princeps milicie*), for deserting to the English king.[44] The *Chronicle*, however, presents Thorkell as an independent commander, and (as we have seen) he seems more likely to have been at best indifferent to King Swein.[45] Thietmar's reference to the 'annual census' imposed on the English by 'this filthy dog' provides a more believable motive for Swein's expedition of 1013.[46]

The *Chronicle* describes the arrival of King Swein in July 1013: he 'came with his fleet to Sandwich, and then went very quickly round East Anglia into the mouth of the Humber, and so up along the Trent until he reached Gainsborough'. Here he was met by Ealdorman Uhtred 'and all the Northumbrians', who submitted to him, as did 'all the people (*folc*) of Lindsey, and then all the people (*folc*) of the Five Boroughs, and quickly afterwards all the people (*here*) north of Watling Street, and hostages were given to him from every shire'. Swein had his army provisioned and horsed and then, leaving his son Cnut in charge at Gainsborough, turned south. Only when he had crossed Watling Street did his men begin to harry the countryside, doing 'the greatest damage that any army could do'. The aim was obviously to terrify the English into submission, and it worked; Oxford submitted and gave hostages, as did Winchester. The Londoners, however, 'resisted with full battle because King Æthelred was inside and Thorkell with him'. Many of Swein's men, incautiously trying to ford the Thames, were drowned, and he turned back to Wallingford and thence to Bath. Here he remained until 'Ealdorman Æthelmær came there, and with him the western thegns, and all submitted to Swein, and they gave him hostages'. Swein then turned back to his ships, 'and all the nation regarded him as full king' (*eall þeodscipe hine heafde for fullne cyning*).[47]

The *Chronicle*'s account raises a number of questions. The first concerns Swein's primary target; one might have expected him to head for the regions in southern and eastern England where he had previously campaigned, which were also those softened up by Thorkell's army between 1009 and 1011. But, after touching briefly at Sandwich and skirting East Anglia (as rapidly as possible), Swein made for Northumbria. Did he perhaps wish to avoid Thorkell's fleet, presumably in its base at Greenwich? Or was there another reason for establishing his base on the Trent, between York and the Five Boroughs? Later historians have had little doubt about his motives: Stenton, for instance, concluded that 'his plan of campaign turned on the expectation that the men of Danish England would be prepared to welcome a Danish king'.[48]

The idea of the 'Danelaw' as a region with its own distinctive law, custom, society and ethnic identity is a concept very deep-seated in English historiography, but one which is rarely examined.[49] The term is often used in a loose and undefined fashion, to lump together regions as disparate as the old kingdom of York, East Anglia, the east midlands and Essex, but, although 'the Danelaw' furnishes a convenient shorthand term for the regions of northern and eastern England conquered and settled by Scandinavians in the late ninth and early tenth centuries, it is salutary to remember that the first occurrences of the word 'Danelaw' (*Deone lage, Dena lage*) are found in a legal compilation by Archbishop Wulfstan and a code of laws promulgated by Æthelred as king of the English.[50] The 'Danelaw' in its legal sense was confined to York and the Five Boroughs, and while it is true that these regions had their distinctive legal customs and (which is more to the purpose) a distinctive and Scandinavianized legal terminology, the idea of 'Danish law' as something quite separate from 'English' or 'West Saxon' law (rather than an acknowledgement of local variations in custom) belongs to the world of the twelfth-century legists, rather than to tenth- or eleventh-century legislators.[51]

Whatever the concept of the 'Danelaw' was based on, it is unlikely to have been ethnicity. There is little or no evidence that the descendants of the ninth- and early tenth-century settlers continued to regard themselves as 'Danes' in the late tenth and eleventh centuries.[52] That Swein restrained his men from loot and pillage until the crossing of Watling Street need not imply any fellow-feeling between them and the local inhabitants, merely that his campaign in the north of England was conducted along diplomatic rather than military lines. An alliance may have been advantageous to both sides. Northumbria had (it seems) escaped the damage which Thorkell's army had inflicted upon East Anglia, Kent and the south-eastern shires, and it may be presumed that the inhabitants were keen to keep it that way. There were, moreover, elements among the northern nobility which might prove amenable to a sympathetic approach. It is somewhat surprising to find Ealdorman Uhtred among their number, for not only was he King Æthelred's son-in-law, but he was also of impeccably 'English' pedigree; unlike York and its region, Northumbria beyond the Tees had never been conquered or settled by Vikings.[53] Uhtred's motives in submitting to Swein are unknown, but a desire to avoid the harrying visited by Thorkell on the south and east may have been among them.

To judge by subsequent events, the brothers Sigeferth and Morcar may have played the crucial role in the submission of the north, even though they are not mentioned by name in the *Chronicle*.[54] Æthelred's efforts to cultivate this family have already been rehearsed, but Morcar's wife Ealdgyth came from a kindred which had suffered greatly at the hands of the king and (if John of Worcester is to be believed) his henchman Eadric *streona*; she was the niece of the murdered ealdorman, Ælfhelm of Northumbria. The family of Sigeferth and Morcar was influential in the Five Boroughs and in York, and if Swein could win their allegiance from Æthelred, he was in a fair way to controlling the whole area.[55] It is therefore unfortunate that we do not know the date of his son Cnut's marriage to Ælfgifu of Northampton, daughter of the murdered ealdorman and sister of his blinded sons, Wulfheah and Ufegeat; but 1013 is as likely a year as any.[56] The forbearance of Swein's army when traversing the areas north east of Watling Street may therefore have been prompted by the need to spare the estates of his new in-laws and their associates. Morcar's recorded lands centred upon Derbyshire, and Sigeferth is known to have held an estate at Peakirk, Northamptonshire, and perhaps another at Lakenheath, Suffolk.[57]

A similar situation may have applied in the south west. Swein's show of violence subdued the heartlands of royal power (Oxford, Winchester and presumably the surrounding shires), but when he arrived at Bath 'he stayed [there] with his army' until Æthelmær came to meet him, with the western thegns. Æthelmær's estrangement from Æthelred, and perhaps from Edmund also, has already been rehearsed, and his views on royal policy may be reflected in the growing criticism which has been detected in the writings of his friend Ælfric, abbot of Eynsham.[58] Æthelmær's standing in the west of England may be reflected in the title of ealdorman given to him by the *Chronicle*; as we have seen, he bears the same title in the Sherborne lease relating to Holcombe, but does not attest a royal diploma as *dux* until 1014. There may have been some local feeling that he had not received the honour which was his due. As for the 'western thegns', they are (like those of the north) anonymous. Presumably the leading men of Cornwall, Devon, Somerset and Dorset are to be included, but thegns from south-western Mercia may also have been present. Bath lies on the frontier between Wessex and Mercia (it was, of course, the site of Edgar's consecration in 973, a fact of which Swein may have been aware), and if John of Worcester's testimony is reliable, Cnut was to find allies in Gloucestershire in 1016; John adds Ælfgar *mæw*, lord of Tewkesbury, Gloucestershire, as well as Cranborne, Dorset, to the *Chronicle*'s list of Englishmen who fought on the Danish side at the battle of Sherston.[59] Leofwine, ealdorman of the Hwicce, may also have been among those who submitted to Swein at Bath.[60]

One notable omission from the *Chronicle*'s list of defectors is the lord of Mercia himself, Eadric *streona*. Given the *Chronicle*'s hostility towards him, it is inconceivable that it would not have included him had he submitted to King Swein, and the inference must be that he remained loyal to Æthelred; indeed if Cnut was already married to his victim's daughter Ælfgifu, he would have had little choice in the matter. It is curious that the *Chronicle* makes no reference to a submission by the Mercians, or for that matter of the East Angles. It seems that with the collapse of resistance in the north east, the West Saxon heartlands and the south west, Swein had achieved his end. The Londoners, 'afraid that he would destroy them', submitted and gave hostages, Queen Emma, accompanied by Ælfsige, abbot of Peterborough, fled to her brother in Normandy, and Ælfhun, bishop of London, followed with the æthelings Edward and Alfred (and presumably their sister Godgifu). Æthelred made a more leisurely withdrawal. He remained 'for a while' with Thorkell's army at Greenwich, which demanded and got pay and provisions, presumably from the south-eastern shires. Æthelred then withdrew to the Isle of Wight, where he celebrated the Christmas feast, and only then did he too cross the Channel, presumably on Thorkell's ships, to Normandy. And there he might have ended his life in exile, but for what the *Chronicle* describes as 'the happy event of Swein's death'.

King Swein Forkbeard died at Candlemas (3rd February) 1014, presumably at Gainsborough, and the fleet elected his son Cnut 'king', presumably of the English, since Denmark had been left in the hands of his elder brother Harald. Events, however, prevented Cnut from entering upon his inheritance at this time.

Archbishop Wulfstan was also in the north in February 1014; on the 16th, he consecrated Ælfwig as bishop of London.[61] It is perhaps to the period immediately following Swein's death that his most celebrated work should be dated: the *Sermo lupi* or, to give its full title, the 'Sermon of the Wolf to the English, when the Danes persecuted them most, that is in the year of Our Lord Jesus Christ 1014'.[62] It exists in three versions, the shortest of which is agreed to be the earliest, and since the second and third recensions have been dated to the period after Æthelred's reinstatement during Lent, 1014, the earliest may belong to the period before that reinstatement and after Swein's death on 3 February.[63]

The theme of the *Sermo lupi* is 'the crimes of the English against family, kindred, lords and church, and the sufferings that are the consequences of those crimes'.[64] It opens with a literally apocalyptic pronunciation:

> *Leofan men, gecnawað þæt soð is: ðeos woruld is on ofste, and hit neahlæcð þam ende; and ðy hit is on woruld a swa leng swa wyrse*: beloved men, realize what is true: this world is in haste and the end approaches; and therefore in this world things go from bad to worse, and so it must of necessity deteriorate greatly on account of the people's sins before the coming of Antichrist, and indeed it will then be dreadful and terrible far and wide throughout the world.

Having seized the attention of his audience, Wulfstan goes on to describe in general and in particular the success of the devil in leading astray the feckless English, including both offences against the church, its personnel and the Christian faith, and crimes committed by the laity against one another:

> a kinsman has not protected a kinsman any more than a stranger ...[65] nor has any one of us ordered his life as he should ... and it is the greatest treachery that a man betray his lord's soul; and a full great treachery it is also in the world that a man should betray his lord to death, or drive him in his lifetime from the land; and both have happened in this country: Edward was betrayed and then killed and afterwards burnt, and Æthelred was driven out of his country.[66]

The catalogue of the nation's sins concluded with an exhortation to repentance and amendment: 'Let us do as is necessary for us: turn to the right, and in some measure leave wrongdoing, and atone very zealously for all we have done amiss'.

Though it describes itself as a sermon, the homily may in the first instance have circulated in written form.[67] How widely it was known is a moot point, but given Wulfstan's commanding position, both as the senior archbishop and as a leading figure in the king's council, it seems likely that most of the chief men of the *witan* were among its intended recipients. It is likely too that Wulfstan took a leading role in the deliberations of 'all the councillors who were in England, ecclesiastical and lay', who decided to ignore the claims of Cnut and 'to send for King Æthelred'. The king returned 'to his own people' during the Lenten season of 1014 (16 March to 24 April) 'and he was gladly received by them all'.[68]

The agreement between the king and his counsellors is described in the *Chronicle*:

> they [the counsellors] said that no lord was dearer to them than their natural (*gecynde*) lord, if he would govern them more justly than he did before. Then the king sent his son Edward hither with his messengers and bade them greet all his people and said that he would be a gracious (*hold*) lord to them, and reform all the things which they all hated; and all the things that had been said and done against him should be forgiven on condition that they all unanimously turned to him (*to him gecyrdon*) without treachery. And complete friendship was then established with oath and pledge (*mid worde and mid wædde*) on both sides, and they pronounced every Danish king an exile from England for ever.

The *Chronicle*'s choice of words is significant, implying a renewal of the mutual oath between king and people. The two diplomas which survive for the year 1014 seem to reflect this rapprochement between the king and his errant counsellors.[69] One is a grant of land at Mathon, Herefordshire, to Ealdorman Leofwine, perhaps one of those who submitted to Swein at Bath, which has unfortunately lost its witness-list.[70] The other is the restoration to Sherborne of land at Corscombe sold to Ealdorman Eadric.[71] Both Leofwine and Uhtred attest among the *duces*, though after Eadric and Ælfric.[72] The *ministri* are headed by Ulfcytel and following him Sigeferth and Godwine (perhaps the 'ealdorman' of Lindsey). The remainder seem to be west-country thegns. This is the only diploma attested by Æthelmær as earl (*dux*), which suggests that the Æthelweard who attests in sixth place among the *ministri* may be his son. Of the other *ministri*, Ælfgar, who attests in fourth place, is perhaps Ælfgar *mæw*, and the Odda who immediately follows him may be Odda of Deerhurst; Wulfgar, who attests in seventh place, is presumably the man of the abbey who redeemed the land from Eadric *streona*.[73]

The 1014 annal contains the first acknowledgement of direct criticism against Æthelred personally; previous complaints were aimed more generally, against the ill-judged policies of the king and his advisers.[74] Some idea of what might have been included among 'the things which they all hated' may be gleaned from the legislation which followed Æthelred's reinstatement. It is now represented by the two surviving versions of the code known as VIII Æthelred.[75] Both texts have clearly been extracted from a longer set of enactments, and are purely ecclesiastical in content; one indeed contains only the clauses relating to sanctuary. The longer text also covers ecclesiastical dues, including tithe, Peter's Pence and churchscot; the proper observance of fasts and festivals; a prohibition on Sunday trading; and a section on offences committed against or by ecclesiastics (including a prohibition on the involvement of monks in feuds). Reeves are commanded to support abbots and their monasteries 'in all temporal needs'; strangers are to be protected, evildoers found and punished, excommunicates cast out. The emphasis throughout is on amendment for past misdeeds, and ends with the exhortation: 'let us loyally support one royal lord, and let each of our friends love the other with true fidelity and treat him justly', a typically Wulfstanian pronouncement found also in the *Institutes of Polity*.[76] More to the point, the legislation addresses the concerns voiced in the *Sermo lupi*: breach of sanctuary and the spoliation of churches, offences against ecclesiastics, abuse of the rights of free men (and others), non-fulfilment of charitable obligations and failure to pay ecclesiastical dues, killing of spiritual and blood kindred and the breaking of oaths and pledges.

The surviving versions of VIII Æthelred perhaps represent what Archbishop Wulfstan thought most worthy of reform. The grievances of the lay nobles may have been addressed in a lost secular counterpart to VIII Æthelred, perhaps reflected in the concluding clauses of Cnut's Secular code (II Cn 69–83).[77] The section is introduced with the words 'this is the alleviation (*lihting*) whereby I wish to secure the whole people against what has hitherto oppressed them altogether too much', words which call to mind Æthelred's promise 'to reform all the things which they all hated'. Throughout this section of II Cnut, emphasis is laid not on 'what the subject should do for authority, but on what authority could do for its subjects'.[78] Its chapters deal with abuses of lordship, including extortion by royal officials, protection for the heirs of those who die intestate, the rights of widows (including a prohibition on forced remarriage), limitation of criminal liability for an offender's kin, desertion from the army, fidelity and its just rewards, the rights of tax-paying householders to the enjoyment of their property and hunting rights.

The heriot regulations, which occupy a considerable space within the section, are of particular interest.[79] They lay down the rates for earls (ealdormen), king's thegns and lesser thegns in Wessex, Mercia, East Anglia and 'among the Danes', which must mean Northumbria and the Five Boroughs. In Wessex the earl owed eight horses, four saddled and four unsaddled, four helmets, four mailcoats, eight spears and as many shields, and four swords. This represents the equipment for four fully-armed and mounted men (with remounts) and four spear-carriers, and the ealdorman was also required to pay 200 mancuses of gold. The heriot of the king's thegn was roughly half that of the earl; four horses, two saddled and two unsaddled, two swords and four spears and as many shields, and fifty mancuses of gold. The lesser thegn gave his own horse and weapons (in Wessex); in Mercia and East Anglia he paid £2. 'Among the Danes' the king's thegn owed £4, unless he had 'a more intimate relation with the king', in which case he rendered two horses, one saddled and one unsaddled, a sword, two spears and two shields and fifty mancuses of gold; the lesser thegn owed £2.

Two things stand out from the most cursory reading: first, that in Wessex none of the payments are commuted for money, and second, that lower rates were levied in Northumbria and the north. In addition, the detail provided, coupled with the moves already noticed to improve the equipment of the king's warriors (see Chapter 4 above), especially by providing them with helmets and mailshirts, suggests that Æthelred had been demanding more than the customary rates of heriot, which had to be paid before heirs could enter upon their inheritance. Like the rest of the provisions in this section of II Cnut, the heriot regulations reflect grievances likely to have been in the minds of Æthelred's thegns in 1014. The concluding section of Cnut's Secular code (II Cn) thus probably represents, in content if not in form, 'the original specific commitments which Æthelred made in 1014'.[80]

The English magnates might reaffirm their loyalty to Æthelred, but there was still a Danish fleet at large, captained by a rival claimant to the kingship. Æthelred returned to England during Lent, but Cnut remained at Gainsborough till Easter (25 April), 'and the people of Lindsey came to an agreement that they would provide him with horses, and then go out and ravage all together'.[81] Æthelred, however, had by now a formidable force. To the resources of the English magnates, united (for the moment) behind him, he could add the forty-five ships of Thorkell the Tall under their skilful and experienced commander.

Nor had the king been idle during his enforced exile. On his arrival at Rouen, in the second week of January 1014, he had met with another member of the 'immense raiding-army', Thorkell's old ally Oláf *helgi*. Since his departure from England, Oláf had been campaigning on the Continent, where his marauding had taken him from Brittany down to northern Spain and back via Poitou to Normandy.[82] By the winter of 1013, he was in the employ of Duke Richard II, and it was allegedly at this point that he received Christian baptism from Archbishop Robert of Rouen.[83] The occasion of Oláf's engagement was Duke Richard's projected war with Odo of Chartres. When this was abandoned, Oláf was at a loose end, and his services were once more available for hire.

Precisely when he entered the service of Æthelred is unknown, but it was perhaps only after the first overtures had been made by the repentant English. Nor is it clear how payment was to be made. Oláf had of course campaigned in England before and knew how rich the pickings were, but Æthelred's withdrawal from his kingdom was anything but hasty and he may have had sufficient silver with him for at least a down payment.[84]

Óttarr *svarti* claims that his hero 'assured his realm to Æthelred', and it is probable that both he and Thorkell were present when the king, 'with his full force' (*mid fulre fyrde*), fell upon Cnut and his allies in Lindsey in the spring of 1014.[85] The region was 'ravaged and burnt, and all the men who could be got at were killed', forcing Cnut to put to sea.[86] He made for Denmark, touching only at Sandwich, where he put ashore the mutilated hostages who had been given to his father.

The *Encomium* presents Cnut's return to Denmark as a planned withdrawal 'to consult with his brother Harald, king of the Danes'.[87] This is not the impression given by the *Anglo-Saxon Chronicle*, and the *Encomium* itself retails a story about the removal of Swein Forkbeard's body to Denmark, also found in Thietmar, which suggests a much more precipitate departure. Thietmar claims that 'as his companions fled' Swein 'was buried in the place where he died', and that Æthelred, having gathered together his *milites* (perhaps a reference to the Lindsey campaign), 'made plans to disinter his enemy's corpse'. But an unnamed Englishwoman, warned by 'close friends' of the king's intention, had Swein's body taken up and returned to the north.[88] The *Encomium*'s version does not mention Æthelred's vengeful intent, but says that Swein charged Cnut to take his body home to Denmark, so that he might not be buried as 'a stranger in a foreign land; for he knew that he was hateful to that people owing to his invasion of the kingdom'. It was not, however, Cnut, but an English *matrona* (a married woman) who prepared a ship, had Swein's body embalmed and carried it to Denmark, where his sons had it interred at Holy Trinity, Roskilde.[89] The nameless Englishwoman may have been, as Freeman conjectured, a concubine of Swein, but it is tempting to equate her with Cnut's English wife, Ælfgifu of Northampton.[90]

The death of Swein Forkbeard upset the political balance in Scandinavia. His stepson Olof *Skötkonung*, king of the *Svear*, signalled his rejection of Danish suzerainty by requesting Unwan, archbishop of Hamburg-Bremen, whose authority Swein had consistently opposed, to consecrate a bishop for his people.[91] Norway too was slipping from the grasp of the Danish kings. It may have been with the proceeds of his English campaigns that Oláf *helgi* set out on his bid for the Norwegian kingship, probably in the late summer of 1015.[92] A year earlier, Æthelred had 'ordered £21,000 to be paid to the army which lay at Greenwich'. Most of this presumably represents the wages of Thorkell and his men, but some may have gone to Oláf, though perhaps not very much; according to Óttarr *svarti*, he had only two ships with him on his expedition.[93] He was nonetheless successful in defeating the pro-Danish earls of Lade, Swein and his nephew Hákon, at the battle of Nesjar, in Oslofjord, on 26 March 1016 (Swein's brother Erik was absent, campaigning with his brother-in-law Cnut in England).[94] It seems that Æthelred may have been trying to repeat the diplomacy which he had employed in 994, when he financed Oláf Tryggvasson in an attempt to embarrass Swein Forkbeard.[95] Like Olof *Skötkonung*, one of whose daughters he married, Oláf *helgi* opened negotiations with the archbishopric of Hamburg-Bremen.[96]

Even within Denmark itself, there are signs of some initial tension between Cnut and his brother Harald, who, as the elder son, had been left to govern the kingdom during Swein's absence.[97] The *Encomium*, describing Cnut's return in 1014, paints a touching picture of the tender reunion between the brothers, while hinting at underlying discord; Cnut asks Harald to share the Danish kingship with him, but Harald, 'having heard these unwelcome remarks', replies that he 'will not have [his] kingdom divided'.[98] That some power-sharing agreement was implemented is suggested by the existence of coins struck in Cnut's name at Lund certainly before the death of Harald, and perhaps as early as 1014–15.[99] Whatever arrangement the brothers made seems to have been to their mutual satisfaction, for both Thietmar and the encomiast portray them acting in concert, whether burying their father, fetching their mother from her exile among the Slavs, or preparing for a fresh assault on England.[100] It seems, however, that the English had inflicted considerable damage on the Danish forces in 1014. The *Encomium* makes Cnut request his brother's permission to over winter in Denmark 'in order that the ships and army may be renewed' (*ut … reparentur naves et exercitus*), and subsequently describes how the royal brothers 'while mending the ships, re-established the army' (*naves meliorantes exercitum restauraverunt*).[101] It was over a year before Cnut was able to return to the business of conquering England.

7

Dissent and Disaster

'He ended his days on St George's Day, and he had held his kingdom with great toil and difficulties as long as his life lasted.'

Anglo-Saxon Chronicle, 1016

Barely two years after his reinstatement as king, Æthelred died, on 23 April (St George's Day) 1016. His eldest son, Æthelstan, had predeceased him, on 25 June 1014. The loss of his designated heir must have been not only a political but a bitter personal blow to the king, who had Æthelstan buried in the royal mausoleum at the Old Minster, Winchester, the first ætheling to be interred there since Æthelweard, the younger son of King Alfred. Æthelred was succeeded by his next son, Edmund, but before the year's end he too had died, on 30 November (St Andrew's Day) 1016. Even before his passing, the English magnates, despite their proud sentence of banishment on 'every Danish king', were in negotiation with Cnut of Denmark.

The last two years of Æthelred's reign, and the brief reign of Edmund, which cannot be separated from it, illustrate both the weaknesses and the strengths of his rule. The weaknesses were political; Æthelred, as the *Chronicle* rightly says, 'had held his kingdom with great toil and difficulties as long as his life lasted'. The underlying strengths of the country are revealed in the time of Edmund who, again in the *Chronicle*'s words, 'stoutly defended his kingdom while his life lasted'.

The year 1014 ended ominously, when 'on Michaelmas Eve (28 September) the great tide of the sea flooded widely over the land, coming up higher than it had ever done before, and submerging many villages and a countless number of people'.[1] This disaster was to prove the precursor of a greater catastrophe, one caused not by uncontrollable natural forces but by a fatal (and avoidable) misjudgement. In the late spring or early summer of 1015, the king summoned a 'great assembly' (*micel gemot*) at Oxford.[2] It was the first of four meetings held in the borough during the first half of the eleventh century, and it has been argued that Oxford's situation, as 'a gateway linking Wessex to Mercia and the north', made it an especially suitable place for the affirmation of 'the essential unity of England' after periods when 'the aristocracies of the north and south had been at odds'.[3] The fabric of Oxford's society certainly seems to have included both northern and southern elements; the Mercian ealdorman Eadric *streona* had a house there, but so did the west country magnate Æthelmær, son of Ealdorman Æthelweard.[4]

In the case of the 1015 meeting, it may also be relevant that Oxford had been, with Gainsborough, Winchester and Bath, one of the centres for the submission to Swein in 1013. If, however, this 'great assembly' was meant to finalize the reconciliation between the king and his magnates, both northern and southern, it was a spectacular failure. During the course of the meeting, 'Ealdorman Eadric betrayed Sigeferth and Morcar, the chief thegns belonging to the Seven Boroughs; he enticed them into his chamber (*bur*) and they were basely killed inside it'.[5] That this gross infraction of the laws of hospitality was no private quarrel is shown by its sequel; the king seized all the property of the murdered men, some of it the result of his own largesse, and had Sigeferth's widow (Morcar's wife was presumably already dead) arrested and imprisoned at Malmesbury.[6]

The circumstances of the double murder are lost, and it is important to remember that the king may have had some reason for his actions. The possible role of the brothers in the submission to Swein has already been rehearsed; and, while Æthelred had subsequently promised that 'all the things that had been said and done against him should be forgiven', his forbearance was dependent upon the continuing loyalty of his magnates. Perhaps Sigeferth or Morcar or both had been (or were suspected of being) untrustworthy; the king's suspicions of them could have been aroused if (as suggested above), Cnut was already married to their kinswoman by marriage, Ælfgifu of Northampton. It may even be that they were not the only victims of royal paranoia in the summer of 1015. At some point after the Oxford assembly, the king gave Brihtwold, bishop of Ramsbury, the land at Chilton, Berkshire, forfeited by one Wulfgeat 'because he colluded in schemes with the king's enemies' (*munitis regis se in insidiis socium applicavit*).[7] We do not, of course, know when Wulfgeat was deprived of his property, and his fall from grace may have occurred well before 1015, but the possibility that Æthelred now thought himself secure enough to get rid of anyone he considered unreliable must be borne in mind.

When all allowances have been made, it must be said that the assassination of two leading northern magnates was (to say nothing of the ethical aspect) a serious error of judgement, and lends substance to the charge that Æthelred was prone to 'acts of spasmodic violence'.[8] The administrative structures whereby the king enforced his will on Wessex and Mercia were at best rudimentary in the north. It is unlikely that the region was as yet completely shired; Stamford was still separate from Lincolnshire in 1016, and Yorkshire is mentioned for the first time only in 1065.[9] Nor does it seem, despite the lack of firm evidence, that the king held much land in the north, though Edgar disposed of estates at Howden, Sherburn-in-Elmet and Newbald (all in Yorkshire), and Cnut gave the estate of Staindrop (County Durham) to the community of St Cuthbert.[10] There were no great royal abbeys in the region to compensate for the lack of royal estates; the reform movement of the tenth century did not reach the north. The only religious communities of any size were the cathedral churches of York and Durham (both secular houses), and only over the first did the king exercize effective patronage. This absence of royal lands and royal monasteries in the north meant that kings could not reinforce their authority by regular perambulation, as they did in Wessex and southern Mercia; West Saxon rulers were rarely to be found in the north, and then usually at the heads of armies. Æthelred's known forays to the region were both military, the ravaging of Cumberland in 1000, and the expulsion of Cnut from Lindsey in 1014. On the latter occasion he may also have stayed at York, for Styr Ulf's son's grant of Darlington to the community of St Cuthbert was made at York, in the presence of King Æthelred, Archbishop 'Ælfric' (*recte* Wulfstan), Bishop Ealdhun and the otherwise unknown Abbot Ælfwold, as well as 'all the magnates who were there that day in York with the king'.[11] Such occasions were the cement which bound king and magnates together, and the infrequency of royal visits to Northumbria meant that the links between court and locality were weaker there than in Mercia or Wessex. Royal control in Northumbria was almost entirely dependent upon the good will of the local nobility, lay and ecclesiastical, and it was therefore vital that the kings should bind the individual members of the Northumbrian establishment to their interests. Æthelred himself had pursued such a policy for a decade or more before 1015, and it is difficult to account for such a dramatic reversal.

The killing of Sigeferth and Morcar did more than upset the delicate political balance within Northumbria, for the murdered men were not influential only in the north; they also had connections with the king's own circle, and especially with the æthelings, the sons of Æthelred's first marriage. Soon after the Oxford meeting, Edmund rode to Malmesbury, released Sigeferth's widow from prison without his father's leave and married her himself. By 8 September he was in the territory of the Five Boroughs, where he 'took possession of all Sigeferth's estates and Morcar's, and the people all submitted to him' (*him to beah*); the *Chronicle's* language implies that the friends and dependants of Sigeferth and Morcar took Edmund as their lord.[12]

Two diplomas of the time illuminate the ætheling's actions.[13] The first grants land at Peakirk and Walton, Northamptonshire, to the New Minster, 'for the redemption of my soul and that of my wife and for the soul of Sigeferth', the former owner of the property; the second grants land at Lakenheath, Suffolk, to Thorney Abbey, 'for the redemption of my soul and that of my wife and for security in this present life' (*pro presentis vite sospitate*). Sigeferth is not mentioned, but the general similarity to the Peakirk diploma suggests that Lakenheath too had once belonged to him. Like his other actions in the summer of 1015, Edmund's issue of diplomas in his own name comes very close to rebellion, for the production of such documents was a prerogative of the king. The titles employed for Edmund sail very close to the wind in their quasi-regal terminology. In the Peakirk diploma he appears as 'King Edmund ætheling' (*Eadmund æðeling rex*), and in the Lakenheath diploma he is described as 'son of the king of the English and other nations round about' (*Anglorum ceterarumque gentium in circuitu triviatim persistentium basilei filius*).[14] Both grants (and there may have been more) were presumably intended to strengthen the ætheling's support both in the north and east and (if the intended recipient of the Peakirk grant is the New Minster, Winchester) in the country at large.[15] Unfortunately the diplomas survive only as cartulary copies and the witness-lists have been omitted, depriving us of any glimpse of the ecclesiastical and lay magnates who rallied to his cause.

It has been suggested that Edmund, who seems to have assumed his brother's mantle as heir, had been alarmed by the prominence given to his half-brother Edward in the negotiations of 1014, but the contemporary witness-lists do not suggest that Edward, who was still under age, was being promoted at Edmund's expense.[16] The target of his enmity seems rather to have been Eadric *streona*. Indeed the ealdorman was now in a most invidious position, for both the king's heir and the still-dangerous Cnut were married to women who had every reason to hate Eadric and to rally the resources of their powerful kin-group against him. His very survival depended solely upon that of the ageing king, and any cooperation between himself and Edmund was fatally compromised. The result, as we shall see, was disastrous for both of them.

Even as Edmund was establishing himself in the north east, Cnut's fleet was approaching the Kentish coast. It touched at Sandwich but did not linger, proceeding down the Channel as far as the Dorset Frome. While the Danish ships sheltered in Poole harbour, Cnut's army landed and ravaged in Dorset, Wiltshire and Somerset. Æthelred meanwhile 'lay sick at Cosham', on the south Hampshire coast, uncomfortably close to the Danish theatre of war.[17] It fell to his generals to raise the resistance. Eadric *streona* collected an army, presumably from Mercia, and Edmund ætheling did the same in the north, but 'when they united, the ealdorman wished to betray the ætheling, and on that account they separated without fighting, and retreated from the enemy'. The *Chronicle* would naturally blame Eadric for any trouble, but some responsibility for the débâcle should perhaps fall on Edmund also. The sequel, however, cannot be excused: 'Ealdorman Eadric seduced forty ships from the king, and they went over to Cnut'. His defection was followed by that of the West Saxons, who 'submitted and gave hostages and supplied the Danish army with horses and it then stayed there [no precise location is given] until Christmas'. No individual West Saxons are named, but their number might have included Ælfgar *mæw*, lord of Cranborne in Dorset as well as Tewkesbury in Gloucestershire.[18]

It has been assumed that the forty ships 'seduced' by Eadric constituted the *lið* of Thorkell the Tall, and that he too went over to Cnut in the autumn of 1015; this seems to have been the view of John of Worcester, who says that the ships were 'manned by Danish soldiers'.[19] The author of the *Encomium* even makes Thorkell act as a kind of fifth column for Cnut; he is said to have visited Denmark in the spring of 1015 and sworn allegiance to a suspicious Cnut, promising to join him with thirty ships as soon as he landed in England. The encomiast's version of events is marked, as usual, by chronological inexactitude and special pleading; his favourable (from a Danish viewpoint) treatment of Thorkell has more to do with the political situation at the time of writing, when a son of Thorkell was an earl in England and a potential ally of the encomiast's patron, Queen Emma, than with the events of 1015–6. Thorkell did eventually join Cnut, but there is no reason not to believe that he was loyal to Æthelred until the latter's death on 23 April 1016.[20] The forty ships which went over to Cnut with Eadric need not have been Thorkell's; they could equally well represent the Mercian ship-levy.[21]

During the Christmas season of 1015–16, Cnut and Eadric crossed from Wessex into southern Mercia and began to harry Warwickshire, where 'they ravaged and burnt and killed all they came across'. Southern Warwickshire lay within the *scir* of Ealdorman Leofwine, who was presumably still loyal to Æthelred.[22] The king had by now moved to London and it was left to Edmund to raise the English levies. It is unclear where the forces were to come from; the Mercians (or some of them) were presumably engaged against Cnut and Eadric, and the West Saxons had submitted. John of Worcester assumes, perhaps correctly, that it was the Mercian levies who were called up by Edmund and that the West Saxons were ranged alongside the Danes.[23] Whatever the difficulties, Edmund succeeded in collecting an army during the Christmas period, but 'nothing would satisfy them except that the king should be there with them and they should have the assistance of the citizens of London'. Neither requirement was forthcoming, and the levies dispersed. After Christmas was over they were ordered out again 'on pain of the full penalty', presumably the forfeiture of life or wergeld specified in the Enham legislation.[24] It must have been Edmund who issued the order, for 'word was sent to the king in London, begging him to come to join the army with the forces which he could muster'. Æthelred did indeed join his son but 'was then informed that those who should support him wished to betray him; he then left the army and returned to London'.

It seems that Edmund could not, in his father's absence, command the loyalties either of the West Saxons or the Mercians. He therefore turned to his allies in the north and sought the aid of his other brother-in-law, Ealdorman Uhtred. They made common cause as much against Eadric *streona* as against Cnut, for they concentrated their attack on the heartlands of Eadric's power, in the north Mercian shires of Stafford, Shrewsbury and Chester.[25] Their purpose was presumably to draw Eadric away from Cnut to defend his lands and men, but it was, unfortunately, a game that two could play. Cnut himself 'went out through Buckinghamshire into Bedfordshire, from there to Huntingdonshire and so into Northamptonshire, along the fen to Stamford and then into Lincolnshire; then from there to Nottinghamshire and so into Northumbria towards York'. His route took him through the eastern reaches of the Five Boroughs, so recently secured by Edmund, and into Uhtred's ealdordom. Óttarr *svarti* appears to describe the last part of Cnut's march to York in his *Knútsdrápa*, the fifth stanza of which refers to fighting in 'green Lindsey' and at *Helmingborg* 'west of the Ouse'.[26] When he heard of Cnut's advance, Uhtred 'left his ravaging and hastened northwards, and submitted then out of necessity, and with him all the Northumbrians'. The ealdorman gave hostages but was nevertheless killed, with Thurcytel Nafena's son, and Cnut gave his ealdordom to his own brother-in-law, Erik of Lade.[27]

The *Anglo-Saxon Chronicle*, which is the only contemporary source for the slaying of Uhtred, makes Eadric *streona* ('the common author of all evils') advise his brother-in-law's murder.[28] This may have been so, but it seems that Cnut was exploiting the complex politics of the northern regions for his own ends. The post-Conquest tract *De obsessione Dunelmi* says that Uhtred was killed, with forty of his men, by the English magnate Thurbrand *hold*, at the head of Cnut's own warriors.[29] There are various problems with *De obsessione*'s account, not least the fact that it places the killing of Uhtred after Cnut's conquest of England, whereas the *Chronicle* makes it quite clear that the murder preceded the death of King Æthelred. It sites the murder at *Wiheal*, which has not been satisfactorily identified; if it was Wighill (Yorkshire West Riding), just north of Tadcaster, then the ealdorman never reached York.[30] Quite another scenario is suggested by the *Knútsdrápa* of Óttarr *svarti*, which, after describing the slaughter in Lindsey and at *Helmingborg*, sends Cnut north to the Tees, where 'he made the English fall ... the deep dyke flowed over the bodies of the Northumbrians'.[31] The Tees was the boundary between the old Danish kingdom of York and 'English' Northumbria (the remnant of Bernicia), and it may be that Uhtred was attempting to reach his stronghold in Bamburgh when Cnut's men overtook and killed him.

Thurbrand *hold* himself, however, seems to be an historical personage.[32] He is usually identified with the man of the same name who, according to *De obsessione Dunelmi*, was the mortal enemy of Styr Ulf's son, Ealdorman Uhtred's one-time father-in-law; when Styr's daughter Sige married the ealdorman, part of the agreement was that Uhtred should kill Thurbrand.[33] If the *hold* and Styr's enemy are indeed one and the same then Uhtred did not honour the bargain, but the story may simply be an attempt to account for the enmity between the ealdorman and Thurbrand. This need not have had anything to do with Styr; it was not unprecedented for a Bernician nobleman to fall out with a magnate of Yorkshire.[34]

De obsessione's account of Thurbrand's family can be verified from independent sources. His descendants held property in the north as late as 1074, and their lands can be partially reassembled from the folios of *Domesday Book*.[35] On the eve of the Norman Conquest, Thurbrand's son Karl held the manor of Hunmanby (Yorkshire East Riding), assessed with its dependencies at forty-eight carucates of land worth £12.[36] Two of Karl's sons, Thurbrand and Gamall, held 144 carucates of land between them, a third son, Cnut, held three estates assessed at twelve and a half carucates, and a fourth, Sumarlid, held the manor of Crambe (Yorkshire East Riding), assessed at four carucates; he may also have held land in Lincolnshire.[37] How much of this land (if any) had belonged to Thurbrand *hold* is unknowable, but the fact that Cnut's three manors lay in Holderness may be significant, for the place-name means 'promontory of the *hold*', and it is feasible that it had once belonged to or been administered by his grandfather. Thurbrand's byname certainly implies high rank; *Norðleoda laga* equates the wergeld of a *hold* with that of a king's high-reeve, the title once born by the lords of Bamburgh.[38]

Cnut's strategy in Northumbria seems to have exploited local rivalries and tensions. Though the evidence is slight, the suggestion is that there were two factions, one based on Thurbrand *hold*, and the other, which included Styr Ulf's son and Bishop Aldhun of Durham, on Ealdorman Uhtred. That this was not a clear split between 'English' Bamburgh and 'Anglo-Scandinavian' York is demonstrated not only by Styr's presence in Uhtred's camp but also by the killing alongside the ealdorman of Thurcytel Nafena's son, whose name, along with those of his father and uncle, suggests that he came from Yorkshire.[39]

The appointment of Erik as ealdorman of Northumbria 'just as Uhtred had been' is sometimes presented as the definitive moment in the Danish conquest of the north.[40] It seems, however, that Erik did not linger long in his new command, for his panegyrist, Thórðr Kolbeinsson, gives him a major role in the siege of London, which was invested in the second week of May. Uhtred was succeeded, in northern Northumbria at least, by his brother Eadulf *cudel* ('cuttlefish'), while the major figure in York was probably Thurbrand *hold*.[41] Either or both may have been supporters of Cnut, but there is no evidence that any northern levies followed the Danish banner, though the men of Lindsey seem to have been fighting for Edmund at *Assandun* (see below). Cnut's purpose was presumably achieved by the murder of Uhtred, which not only deprived the ætheling Edmund of a major ally, but also tilted the balance of power in Northumbria; the ealdorman's faction must also have been weakened by the death, at about the same time, of Bishop Aldhun.[42] Circumstances combined to ensure that little help from the north would come to the beleaguered kings of the English.

In the spring of 1016, the theatre of war shifted to the south. By Easter (1 April) Cnut was back with his ships, presumably still lying in Poole harbour. Edmund, checked in the north as he had been in Wessex, returned to his father in London; his position in the Five Boroughs was presumably compromised by the fact that Cnut's wife Ælfgifu of Northampton had the same standing there as his own spouse, the widow of Sigeferth.[43] While Cnut was preparing for an assault on London, King Æthelred died, on 23 April. He was buried in St Paul's, and 'all the councillors (*witan*) who were in London and the citizens (*burhwaru*) chose Edmund as king'.[44]

John of Worcester reports a rival ceremony at Southampton, in which 'all the bishops, abbots, ealdormen and all the nobles of England', having 'elected Cnut as their lord and king', came to him and 'renounced and repudiated in his presence all the descendants of King Æthelred'.[45] John's authority for this statement is unknown, and it may be no more than a misplaced doublet of the general submission to Cnut after the death of Edmund in November 1016.[46] The West Saxons (or some of them) had, however, submitted to Cnut in the autumn of 1015, and perhaps had been ready to fight for him against Edmund.[47] There is also something suggestive in the wording of the renunciation of Æthelred's line, which recalls the sentence of exile on 'every Danish king' pronounced in 1014; perhaps Cnut had a point to make. These factors, coupled with the fact that it was only after Cnut arrived before London in the second week of May that Edmund (in the *Chronicle*'s phrase) 'took possession' of Wessex, suggest that the submission at Southampton has a basis in fact.[48] Whatever the precise situation, the stage was now set for the final encounter which would decide who was to hold the kingship of the English.

Cnut's fleet reached London during Rogationtide (7–9 May) 1016. Aspects of the ensuing siege are recorded not only in the *Anglo-Saxon Chronicle* but also in *Liðsmannaflokkr*, the *Eiríksdrápa* of Thórðr Kolbeinsson and Thietmar of Merseberg.[49] The *Chronicle* describes the fleet's arrival at Greenwich, where Thorkell's *lið* had once been stationed; if he and his men had not already joined Cnut, they did so at this juncture, for *Liðsmannaflokkr* implies that Thorkell was supporting Cnut during the siege of London. What the *Chronicle* calls 'a large ditch' was dug on the south bank, and the ships were dragged upstream of London bridge, presumably through the new channel thus created.[50] A second ditch encircled the city on the north bank, so that 'no man could go in or out'; one or other of these ditches may be that mentioned, out of context, by Sighvatr Thórðarson, when 'part of the host had its booths in level Southwark' (*Suðvirki*).[51]

The *Chronicle* does not name the military leaders on either side. *Liðsmannaflokkr* makes Ulfcytel the English commander, praising his skill and courage.[52] It is reasonable enough that an East Anglian commander

1. A king enthroned, Bodleian Library, MS Junius 11, fol. 57r. (*Bodleian Library*)

2. A king fighting, British Library, MS Cotton Claudius, Biv. (*British Library*)

3. Queen Emma receives the *Encomium Emmae Reginae* while her two sons look on. British Library, MS Add. 33241, fol. 1v. (*British Library*)

4. God closes Noah's Ark, Bodleian Library, MS Junius 11, fol. 66r. (*Bodleian Library*)

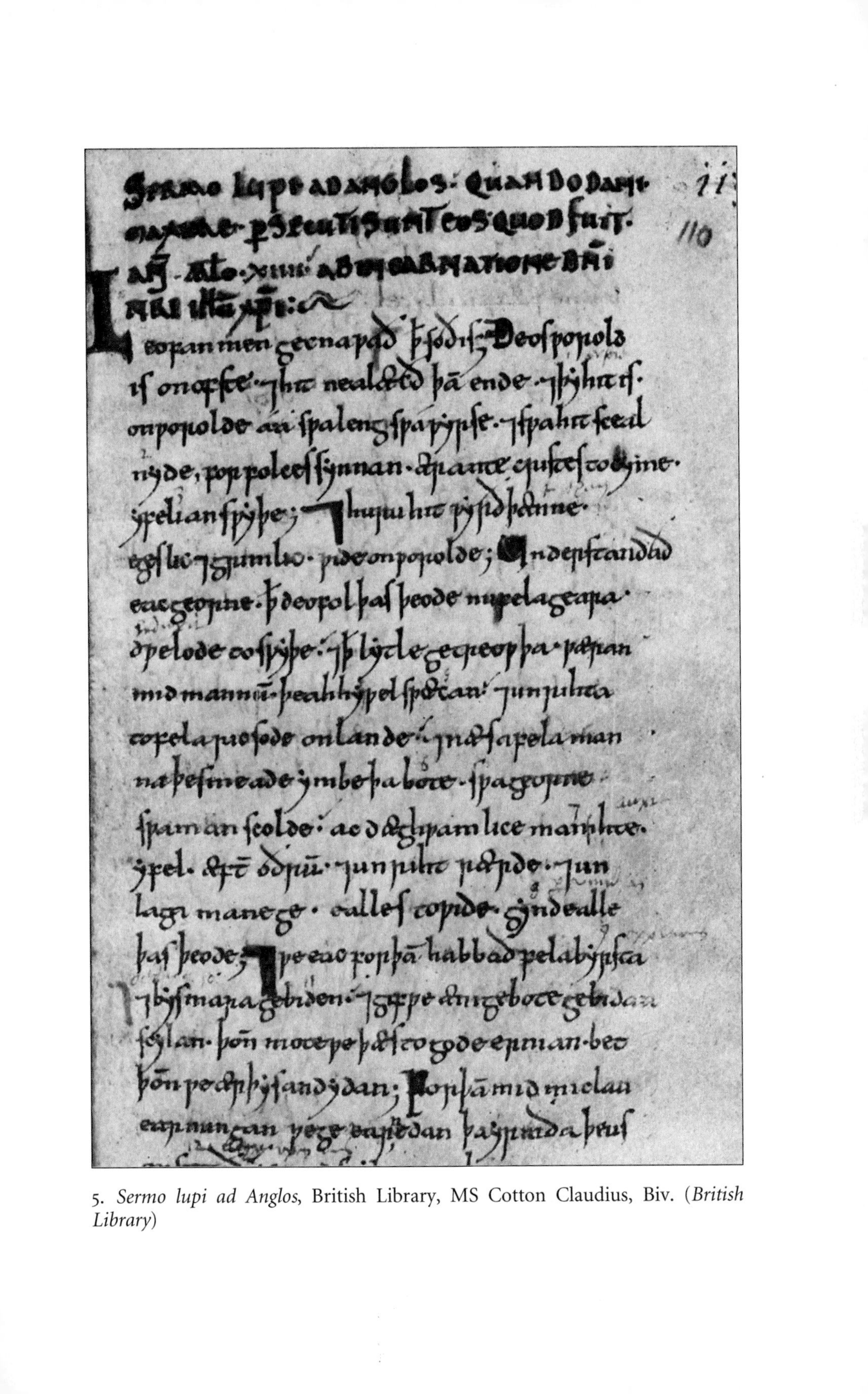

5. *Sermo lupi ad Anglos*, British Library, MS Cotton Claudius, Biv. (*British Library*)

6. Christ in Majesty, Barnack church, Northamptonshire

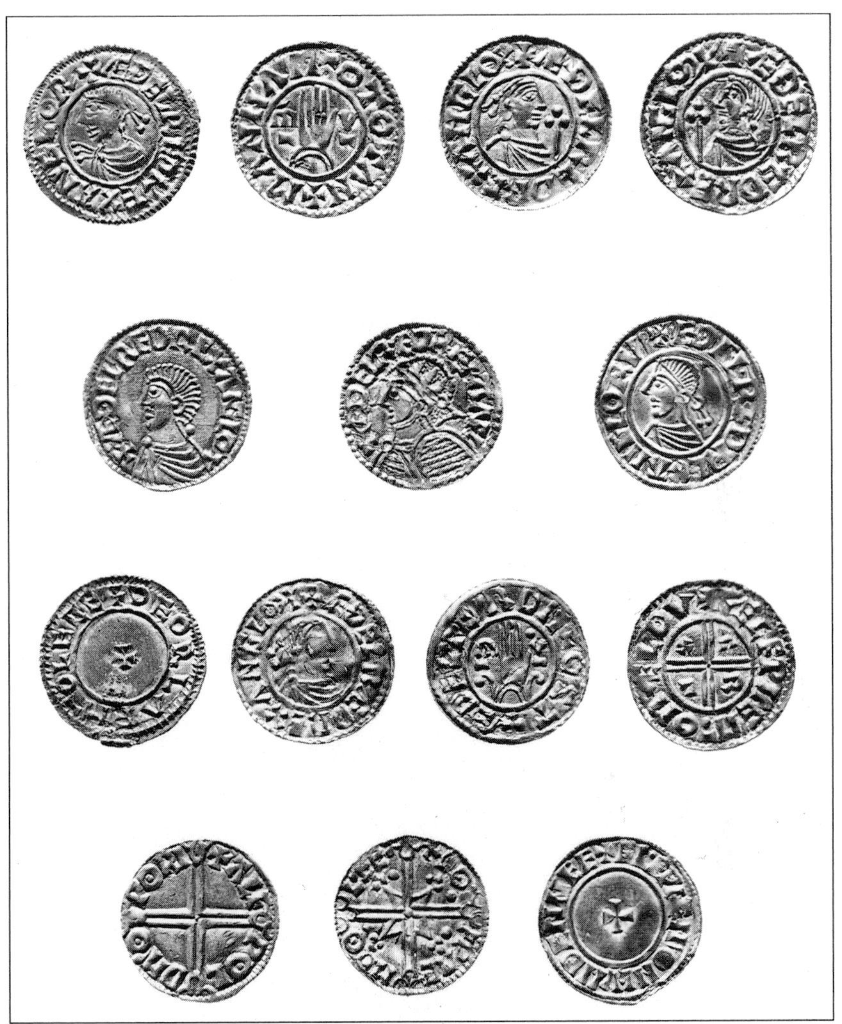

7. The seven main coins of Æthelred's reign, obverse and reverse: First Small Cross; First Hand; Second Hand; Crux (top line, left to right); Long Cross; Helmet; Last Small Cross (bottom line, left to right). (*British Museum*)

8. The 'special issue' Agnus Dei coinage, *c.* 1009: the 'Lamb of God' appears on the obverse; the reverse carries the Holy Spirit shown as a dove. (*British Museum*)

should be active in the defence of London, and his presence is borne out by *Eiríksdrápa*, which records a battle between Ulfcytel and Erik of Lade 'west of London'.[53] Erik's participation in the siege of London is itself implied in the *Encomium Emmae*.[54] The clash between Ulfcytel and Erik may have had to do with the establishment of a Danish bridgehead at Brentford, guarding the crossing-point of the Thames, though the *Knútsdrápa* of Óttarr *svarti* attributes this to Cnut himself.[55]

Thietmar gives the credit for the defence of London to Æthelred's widowed queen, presumably Emma, although she is not mentioned by name. In his version, the Danish fleet, commanded by the kings Harald and Cnut and the otherwise unrecorded 'Duke Thurgut' arrives before London in July 1016. In the city are the queen, two bishops (unnamed) and her 'sons' Æthelstan and Edmund. After a six-month siege (which brings us to January 1017), the queen sues for peace, and the Danes demand a huge ransom; £15,000 of silver for the queen, £12,000 for the bishops and £24,000 for her men, with 300 hostages to be given for security. The 'sons' however, are to be surrendered to the Danes for slaughter. The 'venerable queen', though 'greatly disturbed' by these conditions, agrees, but the sons escape from the city and begin to gather their forces. In the course of these operations they are attacked by Duke Thurgut, who is pillaging the areas around London. In the ensuing battle, both Thurgut and Edmund are killed, but 'since the bloodshed had been heavy and neither side had any prospect of victory, they parted voluntarily'. Æthelstan then collects aid from the 'Britons', and the Danes, hearing of his imminent arrival before London, take to their heels, enabling him to raise the siege.[56]

It is easy to pick holes in Thietmar's version of events. The Danes are said to have invested London in July, whereas the *Chronicle* records their arrival at Greenwich in the second week of May. Æthelstan and Edmund were the stepsons, not sons of Queen Emma; the former had been dead for nearly two years and the latter had left London before the Danes arrived. The description of the battle with 'Thurgut' has something in common with the *Chronicle*'s description of the battle of Sherston (for which see below), which was also broken off because the outcome was inconclusive. According to the *Encomium Emmae*, the Danish commander at Sherston was Thorkell the Tall, but any confusion between him and the mysterious 'Duke Thurgut' is rendered unlikely by the fact that Thietmar names Thorkell correctly in his account of the martyrdom of Ælfheah, which immediately follows that of the siege.[57] It may be that the battle mentioned by Thietmar was indeed Sherston, but neither Thorkell (if he was there at all) nor Edmund were killed therein. It has been suggested that it was Æthelstan who fell at Sherston, but even if his absence from the witness-lists after 1013 is set aside, the ætheling's will is evidence that he predeceased his father, whose verbal message conveying his consent to the testamentary dispositions is recorded therein.[58]

Despite its many blunders, which might be due to distance, garbled transmission and understandable (and acknowledged) unfamiliarity with a remote country, Thietmar's account deserves to be taken seriously. It was based on the description of 'a reliable witness', presumably the Sewald who also recounted the martyrdom of Ælfheah, and it is virtually contemporary, since Thietmar died in 1018. So far as Emma is concerned, her presence in the besieged city is implied by *Liðsmannaflokkr*, and nothing is more likely than that the queen should have taken command of the defence of London, especially in the absence of the new king, her stepson. The fact that the *Encomium* omits to mention this may be explained by Emma's unwillingness to acknowledge any connection with her first husband, even to the extent of portraying their sons as the children of Cnut; there is a fitting irony in the fact that in Thietmar's account she becomes the mother of Æthelred's sons by his first wife.[59] In the aftermath of Cnut's death in 1035, it suited Emma to imply that she had been at her brother's court in Normandy when Cnut's men, seeking an appropriately exalted bride for their newly-crowned lord, discovered there 'the most distinguished of the women of their time'.[60] Emma's version of events, as told in the *Encomium*, became the official account, but the earliest sources say or imply that she remained in England after Æthelred's death, and that her marriage with Cnut was a much more unequal affair.[61] Certainly Emma's willingness, in Thietmar's story, to abandon her 'sons' chimes with what is known of the later career of this formidable and ruthless lady, whose 'instincts for self-preservation ... seem to have been a good deal stronger than her instincts of motherly love'.[62]

With Emma left to hold off the Danes from London, Edmund rode west to rally the West Saxons and Mercians. The *Chronicle* says that he 'took possession of Wessex' (*gerad þa West Seaxan*), and that 'all the people submitted to him' (*him beah eall folc to*). The wording could imply some element of force, and it is clear from the sequel that not all the thegns of the south and west accepted his leadership.[63] His support seems to have come from the western rather than the southern shires, and from Mercia rather than Wessex. His first engagement with the Danish army took place at Penselwood, which lies on the borders of Somerset, Dorset and Wiltshire, the shires harried by Cnut in the previous year. From Penselwood Edmund moved northwards to Sherston, another peripheral settlement on the borders of Wiltshire, Somerset and Gloucestershire; the topography suggests that central Wessex was under Danish control. Both engagements seem to have been inconclusive; the *Chronicle* says of Sherston that a great slaughter was made on either side and that 'the armies separated of their own accord'.[64] The *Chronicle* also says that both Eadric *streona* and the otherwise unknown Ælfmær *deorling* were fighting on the Danish side at Sherston. John of Worcester adds the name of Ælfgar *mæw*, lord of Tewkesbury, Gloucestershire, and Cranborne, Dorset, and says that the men of Hampshire and Wiltshire were in the Danish camp.[65] This does not in itself appear unlikely, and it is clear that whatever the *Chronicle* says, not all the thegns of Wessex had as yet come over to Edmund. As for the Danes, Óttarr *svarti* claims that Cnut himself commanded the Danish forces at Sherston, whereas the *Encomium* places Thorkell the Tall in sole command; the encomiast's account is rendered suspect by its chronological dislocation, in which Sherston is dated almost a year too early, in the immediate aftermath of the Danish landfall at Sandwich in the autumn of 1015.[66]

Inconclusive though these first engagements may have been, they seem to have provided a platform from which Edmund could operate. After Sherston, he gathered his forces ('for the third time', according to the *Chronicle*) and made for London, 'keeping north of the Thames'; another indication that his support was stronger in Mercia than in central Wessex. He descended on the city from the north, via *Clayhanger* (represented by Clayhill Farm in Tottenham, Middlesex), and succeeded in driving off the Danes and raising the siege. Two days later he attacked their western encampment at Brentford, crossed the Thames and routed the Danish forces on the south bank, though many English 'were drowned there through their own carelessness'. This was not quite the end of London's ordeal, for when Edmund retired to Wessex to raise more troops the Danes made a final assault on the city 'but the Almighty God delivered it'. Cnut's fleet sailed off around the coasts of Essex as far as the Orwell, 'and went inland there, into Mercia'; the *Chronicle* presumably intends the east midland shires whose inhabitants were still known as 'east Mercians'.[67]

After raiding and harrying to the north of London, the ships returned southwards and a base was established in the Medway. Edmund, having assembled a fourth army, advanced against them. Once again he kept to the north of the Thames until he reached Brentford, where the army crossed the river (without recorded losses this time), 'and went into Kent'. John of Worcester records a battle between English and Danes at Otford, but the *Chronicle* says merely that 'the Danish army fled before him with their horses into Sheppey: the king killed as many as he could overtake'.[68] The pendulum seems at this point to have been swinging in Edmund's favour. As he pursued the fleeing Danes, he was met at Aylesford by their erstwhile ally Eadric *streona*, come to make amends for his treachery. The remarkable thing is that Edmund accepted his excuses; as the *Chronicle* says, 'no greater folly was ever agreed to than that was'. Whatever Eadric's particular qualities may have been, it was not only Æthelred who was bamboozled by him, and when this unlikely reconciliation is taken with what was about to happen, one might even deduce a degree of overconfidence in Edmund's attitude at this time.

Driven from Kent, the Danish army repaired to Essex whence it 'proceeded into Mercia and destroyed everything in its path'. Edmund, having called out the English levies for the fifth time, pursued the Danish force, and on 18 October 'overtook them in Essex at the hill which is called *Assandun* and they stoutly joined battle there'.[69] The site of *Assandun* has long been disputed between Ashingdon, in south-east Essex, and Ashdon in the north west of the shire. The long-standing consensus in favour of Ashingdon has been disputed, and the case for Ashdon put more forcibly over the last decade or so.[70] The place-name evidence is inconclusive, but the strategic and tactical aspects point to Ashdon.[71] To reach Ashingdon, the Danish fleet would have had to negotiate the River Crouch, and while this was certainly feasible, the topography is unfavourable. The river is (and presumably was) bordered with marshes and mudbanks, and there are no islands nor natural harbours for the accommodation of what was presumably a substantial number of ships. The only suitable beaching-point is just upstream of Burnham, which offers no easy route for a march into the shires of east Mercia. The commanders of the Danish force included men who were familiar with the geography of eastern England, notably Thorkell the Tall, and it is difficult to believe that they would have taken this option, given that others more favourable were available, via the Blackwater to Maldon, for instance, or the Colne to Colchester. Perhaps the likeliest hypothesis is that the Danes followed the same route they had recently taken, into the confluence of the Orwell and the Stour, where there was a natural harbour at Harwich. On the previous occasion they had got into eastern Mercia via the Orwell valley and Suffolk, but the *Chronicle*'s mention of Essex suggests that on this their second visit they went up the valley of the Stour to the headwaters of the Granta and Cam, heading for Cambridge. Ashdon lies at the head of the valley of the Bourne, which flows into the Granta. If Edmund, as seems likely, gathered his fifth force at London, and moved up Ermine Street and the Icknield Way, Ashdon would be a logical place for the meeting of the Danish and English forces. One other fragment of evidence may support this hypothesis. In the *Eiríksdrápa*, Thórðr Kolbeinsson claims that his hero 'reddened Ringmere heath' (*Hringmaraleidr*). This was once considered a misplaced reference to the battle of Ringmere in 1010 but Erik of Lade was not present at that engagement, and it has been suggested that he did lead a foray into East Anglia at some point in 1016.[72] If the route which brought the Danes to *Assandun* lay through the borders of Essex and Suffolk, it is not unfeasible that one wing of the army should have been diverted north to the traditional rallying-point of the East Anglian levies, in order to protect the Danish right flank from assault. Óttarr *svarti*'s claim that Cnut 'made corselets red in Norwich' might refer to the same incident, though it is placed after, not before, the battle of *Assandun*.[73]

The *Chronicle* describes the English army at *Assandun* as 'all the English nation' (*ealle Engla þeode*).[74] That this is no exaggeration is proven by the casualty list, which included Bishop Eadnoth of Dorchester, Abbot Wulfsige of Ramsey, Ealdorman Ælfric of Hampshire,

Godwine, 'ealdorman' of Lindsey, Ulfcytel of East Anglia and Æthelweard, son of the former ealdorman of East Anglia, Æthelwine *amicus dei*; there was also a Mercian contingent.[75] It was a far cry from the scratch force with which, according to John of Worcester, Edmund had faced the Danes at Penselwood.[76] Though his success in establishing his authority is commendable, the consequences of failure were correspondingly greater. *Assandun* was a Danish, not an English victory, 'and all the nobility of England was there destroyed'. The *Chronicle* (as usual) blames the defeat of the English on Eadric *streona*, who 'did as he had often done before: he was the first to start the flight with the *Magonsœte*, and thus betrayed his royal lord and all the English nation' (*and swa aswac his kynehlaforde and ealle þeodæ Angelcynnes*). It may be, however, that Edmund had relied too much on his rapid successes and attacked too impetuously a dangerous and powerful Danish enemy.

Edmund fell back on south-western Mercia, the ealdordom of Ealdorman Leofwine, whose bishopric was held by Archbishop Wulfstan *lupus*.[77] Cnut pursued his rival into Gloucestershire and there may have been another engagement; Óttarr *svarti* mentions a battle 'north of *Danaskógar*', perhaps the Forest of Dean, just after *Assandun*.[78] The royal counsellors, however, led by Eadric *streona*, 'advised that the kings should be reconciled'. Hostages were exchanged and a meeting arranged 'at Alney near Deerhurst'. The site, as was common for such parleys, was then an island in the River Severn, on the borders of Worcestershire and Gloucestershire; John of Worcester, who may have had some local knowledge, describes how the kings were conveyed to the island in fishing-boats, Edmund from the west and Cnut from the east.[79] It may also be relevant that Alney lay within the manor of Deerhurst, whose ancient minster was probably already in the hands of Odda, perhaps a kinsman of that Ælfgar *mæw* who (according to John of Worcester) had fought for Cnut at Sherston, alongside Eadric *streona*.[80]

The agreement reached at Alney gave Cnut the kingship of the lands north of the Thames, while Edmund retained Wessex, and (according to John of Worcester) the *regnum*, presumably meaning that Edmund remained king of the English; this was the compromise agreed in 957 between Eadwig and his brother Edgar.[81] If John's interpretation of the agreement is correct, there was presumably some acknowledgement, explicit or implicit, that in the event of the death of one party the other should succeed to the whole, and this is in fact what happened; on Edmund's death on 30 November, 'King Cnut succeeded to all the kingdom of England' (*feng Cnut cyning to eall Angelcynnes rice*).[82]

The *Chronicle* implies that Edmund's chief adviser at this time was Eadric *streona*, to whom such a compromise was not only the best but the only safe outcome.[83] He had alienated the wives of both kings and his protector Æthelred was dead; he had managed to make himself useful to Edmund, and, if the *Chronicle*'s account of his part in the English defeat at *Assandun* is correct, to Cnut as well; but he could not rely on either. A balance of power between the two was his only option. But he was merely buying time. After Cnut's accession, Eadric retained his ealdordom of Mercia for barely a year; at the Christmas court held at London in 1017, Cnut had him murdered. John of Worcester says that 'he [Cnut] feared that some day he would be entrapped by Eadric's treachery, just as Eadric's former lords Æthelred and Edmund ... were frequently deceived', and though this may be little more than inference, it is only too believable.[84]

With Eadric were killed other leading noblemen whom Cnut considered untrustworthy. He had already married Emma, thereby neutralizing her support for her sons by Æthelred, and had exiled Eadwig, the last surviving ætheling from the old king's first marriage, who was subsequently killed. In 1018 a huge tribute of £72,000 was levied, plus an additional £10,500 from the city of London, and 'the Danes and the English reached an agreement at Oxford'. A Danish dynasty was, for the moment, established over the kingdom of the English.

The *Chronicle* for Æthelred's last years paints a picture of mutual suspicion, disorder and incompetence. John of Worcester's version of events, though agreeing in content, gives on occasion a more positive account of Æthelred's actions; to give a single instance, on receiving Edmund's plea for assistance at the Christmas of 1015–16, he 'assembled many warriors (*pugnatores*) and quickly (*festinanter*) came to meet him'.[85] Perhaps (like the 'A' text for 1001) the recension on which John's account is based was less doom-laden than the surviving versions of the *Chronicle*. It has nevertheless to be said that the situation in the winter of 1015–16 could scarcely have been worse. In 1010, at the height of

Thorkell's ravaging, 'no shire would even help the next'; now only the presence of the king could unite the suspicious and divided magnates, and Æthelred himself, fearful of treachery (even, it seems, at the hands of his son and heir) and already in the throes of whatever illness it was that killed him, could not supply the leadership required. It may be that his own incautious and ill-advised actions had brought his fate upon him; 'adversity', as Freeman cuttingly remarked, 'had wrought no lasting reform; he had thrown away every advantage'.[86] Even at this pass, however, the *Chronicle* avoids any direct criticism of the king, and it is hard not to feel sympathy with his plight.

With the accession of Edmund, the picture begins to change. What qualities he might have shown had he survived to drive out Cnut and establish himself as king are both unknown and unknowable, but his undoubted military capacity has earned him a better posthumous reputation than his father. His byname, 'Ironside', was awarded him, 'because of his valour' (*for his snellscipe*) before the end of the eleventh century, and Freeman, not one to stint either praise or blame, considered him 'a hero worthy to wield the sword of Ælfred and Æthelstan'.[87] Such estimates are not wholly exaggerated. The danger he posed to Cnut is demonstrated in the *Encomium Emmae*, which sees the hand of Providence in his early death: 'God, who remembered his own ancient teaching, according to which a kingdom divided against itself cannot long stand ... took away Edmund from the body lest it should chance that if both [Edmund and Cnut] survived, neither should rule securely'.[88] Edmund's generalship was displayed in the campaigns of 1016, which also demonstrated the military strengths of the English when commanded by a determined and consistent leader. Between May and October, Edmund called out five armies, fought five general engagements, and raised the siege of London. What is more, although the final battle was a disastrous defeat for the English, he remained formidable enough to force a compromise resolved only by his death; not a mean achievement for one who had only just escaped from London as the Danish net began to close, and who had been unable in the previous year to command the loyalties of his men.

The adverse judgement passed on Æthelred by history (or at least by historians) stems from his inability to stem the Viking raids and prevent the Danish conquest. This failure cannot be denied; from 1016 to 1042

England was ruled by Cnut and his sons, and only the unexpected death of Harthacnut allowed Edward the Confessor to re-establish the West Saxon line. What should not be forgotten, however, is that the kingdom which Edward received from his Danish predecessors and transmitted to his ultimate successors, the Norman kings, was substantially the creation of his West Saxon forebears, including his father Æthelred. Even if Æthelred had done no more than maintain the institutions which had been established by the time of Edgar, this would have been, especially in view of the difficulties he had to face, a notable achievement. In fact, some of the institutions most basic to the development of the medieval English state, in particular the shire, the sheriff and the royal writ which linked both with the royal administration, were either perfected, or make their first recorded appearance in the reign of Æthelred *unræd*.[89]

It is rarely possible to identify the people responsible for such developments, but in the realm of law at least, the shaping mind of Wulfstan *lupus* can be seen at work.[90] The archbishop survived to serve Cnut as he had served Æthelred, and it was for Cnut that he produced the ecclesiastical and secular codes which sum up the legislative achievement of his West Saxon predecessors, including, of course, Æthelred himself.[91] This was to be the last legislation produced by a pre-Conquest king and when, in the early twelfth century, the laws of England began to be codified, it was Cnut's laws which became the staple and the starting-point for further endeavour.[92]

How far the administrative and legal developments of his reign should be ascribed to Æthelred himself is unknown, but it would be an error to divorce the king from the business of his kingdom. It was the king who chose and appointed the men who ran it, both in its secular and in its ecclesiastical aspects. His appointments could be disastrous, though the malign influence exercised by Eadric *streona* in his latter years may mask more positive qualities.[93] But if Æthelred is to be blamed for making Eadric ealdorman of Mercia, he must also be commended for raising Wulfstan *lupus* to the sees of London, Worcester and York.

The failures of Æthelred's kingship were political failures, an inability to control and direct the tensions and rivalries which arose between the royal councillors as they jockeyed for power. Æthelred's apparent inability to hold aloof from such conflicts may to some extent justify his reputation as *unræd*, though other aspects of his government show him amenable to good counsel as well as bad.[94] Yet the first half of his reign can show successes as well as failures, and only in the last decade did matters go fatally awry. In a kingdom less focused on its king, his personal failings would have been less disastrous, but though England at the turn of the tenth and eleventh centuries was already a 'united kingdom', its unity was centred on and symbolized by the person of its king.[95] It was precisely this king-centred unity which enabled Cnut to oust the West Saxon kings and take their kingdom from them, for once accepted as 'full king', he could exercise their regal authority for himself. In the process, however, he ensured, though perhaps unwittingly, that the English kingdom and its institutions would survive both the Danish and (eventually) the Norman conquests.

APPENDIX

A Note on 'Danegeld'

One of the more contentious aspects of Æthelred's reign in recent years has been the figures given in the *Anglo-Saxon Chronicle* for the successive tributes paid to Viking armies between 991 and 1018.[1] Without rehearsing the various arguments *in extenso*, a brief account of the points at issue may help to clarify the current state of opinion.

The term 'Danegeld' is essentially a post-Conquest coinage, used for the tax which in the pre-Conquest period was called *heregeld*; the early twelfth-century *Leges Henrici Primi*, for instance, refers to 'Danegeld, which was formerly given to the Danish forces' (*Denagildum, quod aliquando þingemannis dabatur*).[2] By this time, Danegeld was merely a tax levied annually, usually at a fairly low rate; 1*s.* or 2*s.* per hide seems to be usual, though higher rates are recorded.[3] The pre-Conquest rates are unknown, but the tax was regarded as unusually burdensome. Recording its (temporary) suspension in 1051, the *Anglo-Saxon Chronicle* complains 'this tax (*gyld, heregyld*) oppressed all the English people ... it always came before other taxes (*gyldum*) which were variously paid and it oppressed people in many ways'.[4]

The connection between the *heregeld* and the stipendiary fleet is established by the *Chronicle*'s entries for 1040 and 1041. The 'E' text records the death in 1040 of Harold I, in whose time 'sixteen ships were paid for at eight marks to each *hamule*, just as had been done in King Cnut's time'; his successor Harthacnut, however, 'decreed that sixty-two ships should be paid for', at the same rate.[5] The word *hamule* (also rendered *hamele*) is probably derived from ON *hamla*, which originally meant 'oar-loop, grommet', but which was used in Scandinavian sources of the late tenth and eleventh centuries to mean 'oarsman's place, oarport'. In contexts like that of the 1040 annal, 'oarport' signifies the man or men who plied the oar, and the meaning is presumably 'a certain number of crew', though there is no means of discovering how many men that entailed.[6] The connection between these demands and the *heregeld* is made clear by comparison with the 'C' text, which records 'a very severe tax (*swiðe strang gyld*), which was endured with difficulty, namely eight marks to the *ha*' (*hamele* in 'D').[7] Confirmation comes from 'E's entry for 1041, which records the payment of the 'army-tax' (*heregeold*), adding that it produced a sum of £21,099, 'and later £11,048 were paid for thirty-two ships'. The sums may be compared with the £21,000 paid to 'the army which lay at Greenwich' in 1014, which was presumably Thorkell's fleet of forty-five ships, hired in 1012.[8]

Such payments must be distinguished from the tributes extorted by Viking armies. The very vocabulary is different. The word used in the *Chronicle* for 'tribute' is not *geld* (and certainly not 'Danegeld') but *gafol*: thus in 991 'it was determined that tribute (*gafol*) should first be paid to the Danish men because of the great terror they were causing along the coast'.[9] In 1002, it was agreed that the Vikings 'should receive provisions and tribute' (*hi to metsunge fengon and to gafle*), and the word *gafol* is used of the payments in 1007, 1012 and 1018.[10] Only of the 994 payment is the word 'geld' used (in the form of the verb *gyldan*, 'to pay'), and there is a certain ambiguity about the arrangements on this occasion for (as we have seen) some at least of the Viking forces concerned seem to have entered Æthelred's service.[11]

In general, it is abundantly clear that '*gafol* and *heregeld* were introduced under different circumstances, raised by different means, and used for a different purpose'.[12] It is possible, perhaps even probable, that *gafol* was raised, in part at least, by a fixed levy on the hide, just as customary taxes and services had been raised since at least the eighth century.[13] It is also possible that 'a greater part would have come from the accumulated treasure-hoards and contingency funds of those whose high office made them responsible for finding the wherewithal to pay'.[14] This would certainly account for the sale and leasing of land by religious houses, and complaints from the same source of intolerable taxes necessitating the sale and melting-down of church plate.[15]

The distinction between *gafol* and *geld*, made quite clear in the contemporary sources, has not been maintained among later historians, who have used the term 'Danegeld' not only for the *heregeld* paid to stipendiary fleets in the employ of the English king but also, indeed in many cases primarily, for the *gafol* extorted from the English by victorious Viking armies.[16] It is for this reason that I have avoided using the (anachronistic) 'Danegeld' in favour of the contemporary term *gafol*. The distinction is by no means an academic one, for the confusion of geld and *gafol*, tax and tribute, lies at the root of the incredulity regarding the sums allegedly paid to successive Viking commanders between 991 and 1018. The tributes of 991 (£10,000) and 994 (£16,000) are not at issue, nor are the *heregelds* of 1014 and 1041 (£21,000 and £21,099 respectively).[17] It is the larger sums recorded for the payments between 1002 and 1018 that have provoked scepticism, chiefly because they are far in excess of any recorded sums raised by normal taxation, either by eleventh-century kings or by the (arguably) more efficient rulers of the later middle ages. But it is only to be expected that a *gafol*, extorted under the threat of further violence by an unbeaten opponent, would raise much more than a tax imposed by an English king; 'one sum was obtained under the rules of war, the other under the conventions of peace'.[18] It is true that there is a suspicious symmetry about the later gelds, which increase duodecimally from £24,000 in 1002, to £36,000 in 1007, £48,000 in 1012, and £72,000 in 1018, and true also that, in chronicles and annals of the early middle ages, numbers expressed in thousands and tens of thousands (whether of monetary units or men) tend to mean little more than 'lots and lots'. Against this it has been argued that there was enough coined money available to pay the amounts demanded: 'the volume of English mint-output was usually far in excess of the sums which had to be collected'.[19] In the end, acceptance or rejection of the *Chronicle* figures depends less on reasoned argument than on assumptions about the wealth of eleventh-century England and the powers of its kings.

Notes

Notes to Preface

1. *1066 and All That* (London, 1930), p. 12.
2. Freeman, *NC*, i, p. 259.
3. Sir James H. Ramsay, *The foundations of England, or Twelve centuries of British history, BC 55 to AD 1154*, 2 vols (London, 1898), i, p. 333; *VO*, p. 455, translated *EHD*, no 236. For this and similar opinions, see Simon Keynes, 'Anglo-Saxon history after *Anglo-Saxon England*', in David Matthew, Anne Curry and Ewen Green (ed.), *Stenton's Anglo-Saxon England fifty years on*, Reading Historical Studies, 1 (Reading, 1994), p. 187.
4. *WmM*, i, pp. 268–9. William does in fact record an alternative view of Æthelred, though only in passing (see below, at note 00).
5. Simon Keynes, 'The declining reputation of King Æthelred the Unready', in Hill, *Ethelred the Unready*, pp. 227–53; see further below, Chapter 3.
6. Keynes, 'Anglo-Saxon history after *Anglo-Saxon England*', p. 106. See also Ann Williams, *Kingship and government in pre-Conquest England. c. 500–1066* (London, 1999), p. 108.
7. The process is described with admirable clarity by Barbara Yorke, *Wessex in the early middle ages* (Leicester, 1995), pp. 94–148. For the borders with Scotland in the time of Æthelred, see Chapter 4 below.
8. For a sketch of the English administration in this period, see Williams, *Kingship and government in pre-Conquest England*, pp. 88–96.
9. See Chapter 2 below.
10. Freeman, *NC*, i, pp. 258–9, note 1.
11. The *Chronicle* of John of Worcester was formerly attributed to his older contemporary at Worcester, the monk Florence, whose contribution John acknowledges when recording his death in 1118.
12. Michael Lapidge, 'Byrhtferth and Oswald', in Brooks and Cubitt, *St Oswald*, p. 78.
13. C. R. Hart, 'The early section of the *Worcester Chronicle*', *J. Med. Hist.*, 9 (1983), pp. 251–315. Dr Hart's arguments have not been accepted by John of Worcester's most recent editor (*JnW*, ii, pp. lxxix-lxxxi).

14. *WmM*, i, pp. 276–7; see Keynes, 'Declining reputation', p. 236 and note 39, pp. 247–8.
15. J. R. R. Tolkien, *The Fellowship of the Ring* (London, 1954), p. 232.
16. Keynes, *Diplomas*, pp. 230–1.
17. Keynes, *Diplomas*, p. xviii.

Notes to Chapter 1: The Gap of Corfe

1. Stenton, *ASE*, p. 373.
2. The marriage is entered under the year 965 in *AS Chron*,'D', but S. 725 is a grant of Edgar to his queen, Ælfthryth, dated 964.
3. Edmund's birth may be marked by a grant of land to the queen in 966 (S. 742). He attests S. 745, dated 966, but not S. 739, a diploma of the same year, attested by his elder half-brother, Edward (see below, note 11); for the attestations of Æthelred's sons, some of them scarcely older than Edmund at the time, see Chapter 2 below. The various versions of the *Anglo-Saxon Chronicle* record his death two years before his father's coronation, which took place in 973 (see Keynes, *Diplomas*, p. 164). He was buried at Romsey Abbey; the English endorsement to the spurious S. 812 records his father's gifts of a golden bowl, a set of chased arm-rings and a gold-decorated scabbard to mark the occasion.
4. S. 1484. She was the divorced wife of the ætheling's uncle King Eadwig (see Chapter 2 below). It is true that the unnamed ætheling could be Edward, but Ælfgifu also bequeathed a necklace, an armlet and drinking-cup to Queen Ælfthryth, so her son Edmund is the likelier possibility; see Barbara Yorke, 'Æthelwold and the politics of the tenth century', B. Yorke (ed.), *Bishop Æthelwold: his career and influence* (Woodbridge, 1988), p. 84.
5. See note 42 below.
6. S. 1485. Ælfheah's family belonged to a collateral branch of the royal kindred, the most powerful of whom was his brother Ælfhere, ealdorman of Mercia; see Ann Williams, '*Princeps Merciorum gentis*: the family, career and connections of Ælfhere, ealdorman of Mercia, 956–83', *ASE*, 10 (1982), pp. 143–72.
7. He succeeded his father, Æthelstan 'Half-king'; for the family, see C. R. Hart, 'Athelstan "Half-king" and his family', *ASE*, 2 (1973), pp. 115–44.
8. *LE*, pp. 102–4; *ECEE*, pp. 28–9, and see previous note.
9. See below, Chapter 2. Ealdorman Æthelwine of East Anglia, brother of Ælfthryth's first husband, appears as her political opponent in 975 (see below).

10. Byrhtferth of Ramsey does indeed say that Edward was Ælfthryth's son, but later contradicts himself, at least implicitly (*VO*, pp. 429, 448).
11. S. 745, Sean Miller, *Charters of the New Minster, Winchester* (Oxford, 2001), no. 23, pp. 95–104, at p. 103; Keynes, *Atlas*, table XXXIc (2). Compare the wording in Ælfheah's will (note 6 above), in which Edmund is described as 'the elder ætheling, the king's son *and hers*' (i.e. Ælfthryth's). Edward attests S. 739, another diploma of 966, in which Ælfthryth appears as *regis coniux*, and Edmund ætheling is absent. For the titles *æðeling* and *clito*, see D. N. Dumville, 'The Ætheling: a study in Anglo-Saxon constitutional history', *ASE*, 5 (1976), pp. 1–33.
12. Miller, *Charters of the New Minster*, p. 108.
13. Keynes, *Diplomas*, p. 164.
14. It was probably written between 1089 and 1093; see Jay Rubinstein, 'The life and writings of Osbern of Canterbury', Richard Eales and Richard Sharpe (eds), *Canterbury and the Norman Conquest* (London and Rio Grande, 1995), p. 38.
15. *Mem. St Dunstan*, pp. 111–12, 114.
16. *Mem. St Dunstan*, pp. 422–4.
17. *JnW*, ii, pp. 416–17; he also makes Ordgar ealdorman of Devon. Elsewhere John describes Edgar's first wife as *Eneda femina generosissima*, 'a woman most nobly born' (*JnW*, ii, p. 417, note 5).
18. It may be relevant that Eadmer has another story in which this stratagem was used by a young girl being reared at Wilton; Matilda, daughter of Malcolm III Canmore, king of Scots, wore the veil to escape the attentions of William Rufus. In her case it was her indignant father who tore the veil off her head and carried her back to Scotland. She subsequently married Henry I, vehemently denying that she had ever intended to take religious vows (*HN*, pp. 121–3).
19. *Mem. St Dunstan*, pp. 163, 210.
20. Æthelflæd is named as the wife of Edgar in the benefactor's list of the New Minster, Winchester, the original of which is no earlier than the twelfth century (Miller, *Charters of the New Minster*, p. lviii). She is said to have given Lingfield and Sanderstead, Surrey. Land in both places was bequeathed by Ealdorman Alfred to his wife Wærburh and daughter Ealhthryth, in the late ninth century (S. 1508, *EHD*, i, no. 97); land at Sanderstead was held by the New Minster in 1066 and 1086 (*GDB* fos 32–32v).
21. Hart, 'Athelstan "Half-king" and his family', passim.
22. For a similar problem with one of the alleged fathers of Æthelred's first wife, see Chapter 2 below.

23. *LE*, p. 79; E. W. Robertson, *Historical Essays* (Edinburgh, 1872), p. 169; Hart, 'Athelstan "Half-king" and his family', pp. 129–30. It may be relevant that Edward is said to have been educated by Sidemann, abbot of Exeter (968–73) and, from 973, bishop of Crediton (*VO*, p. 448; *EHD*, i, no. 236, p. 842; *HRH*, p. 48). For Sidemann, see Patrick W. Connor, *Anglo-Saxon Exeter: a tenth-century cultural history* (Woodbridge, 1993), pp. 29–31.
24. Edith seems to have been Edgar's only daughter. The late-medieval history of St Peter's Gloucester claims that the manor of Hinton, Gloucestershire, was given to the church in 981 by an aged sister of King Æthelred called *Elfleda* (Ælfflæd or Æthelflæd), by whose entreaties the estate's assessment was cancelled; see W. H. Hart (ed.), *Historia et cartularium monasterii Sancti Petri Gloucestriae*, RS (London, 1863–7), i, p. 87. An aged sister at this date can scarcely have been a daughter of Edgar (born 943), nor of Ælfthryth. The tale was probably fabricated from a list of benefactors and the fact that by 1066 Hinton was quit of geld and forinsec service (*GDB* fo. 165); it may be a garbled legend properly relating to the Lords of Mercia, Æthelred and Æthelflæd; see Michael Hare, *The two Anglo-Saxon minsters of Gloucester*, The Deerhurst lecture 1992 (Deerhurst, 1993), pp. 12–13. Eadgifu, abbess of Nunnaminster, is called 'the king's daughter' in a memorandum dating from the closing years of Edgar's reign. If the king is Edgar, then she can have been eighteen at most, unless Edgar became sexually active at a very early age, but another case of mistaken identity seems more likely, for the memorandum is preserved in the twelfth-century *Codex Wintoniensis*, at a time when it was believed that St Edith had been abbess of Nunnaminster as well as Wilton. The names Eadgifu and Edith (Eadgyth) were frequently confused in the post-Conquest period, and the copyist probably added the description *þæs cinges dohtor* to Abbess Eadgifu's name on the assumption that she was St Edith (S. 1449, Robertson, *Charters*, no. 49, pp. 102–3, 348; *HRH*, p. 223 and note 3). For Eadgifu of Nunnaminster, see also S. 1454 (dated 990 x 992), Robertson, *Charters*, no. 66, pp. 136–7.
25. T. A. Heslop, 'English seals from the mid ninth century to 1100', *JBAA*, 133 (1980), p. 4, pl. 1A; idem, 'Twelfth-century forgeries as evidence for earlier seals: the case of St Dunstan', Ramsay et al., *St Dunstan*, p. 303. It may be that the royal brother is not Æthelred but Edward (see note 33 below).
26. Susan Ridyard, *The royal saints of Anglo-Saxon England* (Cambridge, 1988), pp. 42–3, and notes 133, 136; *Barlow, Vita Ædwardi*, p. 96. The stories are clearly variants of those told by Osbern of Canterbury and Eadmer, but the *Life* of St Edith was written *c.* 1080, and that of St Wulfhild after 1086,

the first certainly, the second probably before Goscelin's arrival at St Augustine's, Canterbury, in 1091. For St Wulfhild's family and ancestry, see now Shashi Jayakumar, 'Foundlings, ealdormen and holy women: reflections on some aristocratic families in tenth- and early eleventh-century Wiltshire', *Medieval Prosopography*, forthcoming. I am very grateful to Dr Jayakumar for allowing me to read this paper in advance of publication.

27. A. Wilmart, 'La légende de Ste Édith en prose et vers par le moine Goscelin', *Analecta Bollandiana* 56 (1938), pp. 41, 46. For the *vita*, see Ridyard, *Royal saints*, pp. 37–44.
28. *WmM*, i, pp. 258–61.
29. *GP*, pp. 27, 190–1, translated in David Preest, *William of Malmesbury: The Deeds of the Bishops of England* (Woodbridge, 2002), pp. 19, 127. In the first passage Wulfthryth is not named, but she is clearly the 'woman who had become a nun as a cover' (*eam quae vel umbratice sanctimonialis fuisset*).
30. Her wifely status was accepted by Pauline Stafford, *Queens, concubines and dowagers* (London, 1983), pp. 32, 74, 179–80, and will be argued by Barbara Yorke, 'The legitimacy of St Edith', *Haskins Soc. J.*, forthcoming (I am very grateful to Dr Yorke for allowing me to read this paper in advance of publication).
31. *AS Chron*, 'A', 975, followed by the 'B' and 'C' versions. Edgar was fourteen when he became king of the Mercians in 957.
32. Ridyard, *Royal saints*, pp. 40–1 and note 125.
33. Fell, *St Edward*, pp. 8–9: *Erat autem in eodem monasterio quaedam venerabilis virgo, soror ipsius sancti … Edgit nuncupata, quae supradicti regis gloriosissimi Edgari et eiusdem Wilfridae nondum Deo consecrate, filia fuerat.* The only other 'wife' (*coniunx*) of Edgar mentioned in the *Passio* is Ælfthryth, Edward's stepmother (pp. 1–2, 3–4). See also Pauline Stafford, 'The reign of Æthelred II: a study in the limitations on royal policy and action', in Hill, *Ethelred the Unready*, p. 21 and note 26, p. 40. If, as Dr Yorke has argued ('The legitimacy of St Edith'), Edith's seal-matrix was produced in the reign of Edward, her designation *regalis adelpha* might strengthen the possibility that she was the young king's full sister.
34. For such 'Danish marriages' (*more Danico*), otherwise known as 'handfast matches', see Freeman, *NC*, i, pp. 612–4, Robertson, *Historical essays*, pp. 172–6; Robertson regards Edgar's liaison with Wulfthryth as a 'handfast match'. Wulfstan *lupus* permitted second, but not third, marriages only if the previous spouse was dead, see the *Institutes of Polity*, translated in Michael Swanton, *Anglo-Saxon Prose* (London, 1975), p. 136, but Cnut's

marriage to Emma, his crowned queen, did not mean the end of his previous liaison with Ælfgifu of Northampton, nor is there any indication that Eadgyth Swanneck was dead when Harold II married Ealdgyth, daughter of Ealdorman Ælfgar. Cnut and Ælfgifu's son Harold nevertheless became king after his father's death (with the support of Earl Leofric of Mercia, usually regarded as a model of piety), and Earl Harold's eldest son Godwine was holding land associated with his father's family by 1066; see M. W. Campbell, 'Queen Emma and Ælfgifu of Northampton: Canute the Great's women', *Medieval Scandinavia*, 4 (1971), pp. 66–79; Marc Anthony Meyer, 'The queen's "demesne" in later Anglo-Saxon England', Marc A. Meyer (ed.), *The culture of Christendom: essays in medieval history in memory of Denis L. T. Bethel* (London and Rio Grande, 1993), pp. 79–81; Ann Williams, 'Land and power in the eleventh century: the estates of Harold Godwineson', *ANS*, 3 (1981), pp. 175–6; *GDB*, fo. 86v. See also the marriages contracted by Ealdorman Uhtred of Bamburgh, described in Chapter 4 below. It has been alleged that the first marriage of King Edward the Elder was of the same irregular kind, and even that the child of that match, King Æthelstan (924–39), was illegitimate, but see D. N. Dumville, 'Between Alfred the Great and Edgar the Peaceable: Æthelstan, first king of England', in *Wessex and England from Alfred to Edgar* (Woodbridge, 1992), pp. 150–1 and note 61.

35. Fell argued that the *Passio sancti Edwardi* was the work of Goscelin of Saint-Bertin, drawing on an earlier *vita* composed at Shaftesbury (Fell, *St Edward*, pp xviii–xx; Ridyard, *Royal Saints*, pp. 48–50); it may be, however, that the *Passio* itself was written by a nun of Shaftesbury in the late eleventh century, see Paul Hayward, 'Translation-narratives in post-Conquest hagiography and English resistance to the Norman Conquest', *ANS*, 21 (1999), pp. 85–9. In either case, the implication that Edward was Wulfthryth's son (see note 33 above) is of some moment.
36. The first wife of Æthelred never attests diplomas, whereas his queen Emma does; Cnut's first wife, Ælfgifu, was never consecrated and never attests his diplomas, as does his second wife and queen, (the same) Emma.
37. See *VO*, p. 443: 'he was suddenly taken from this world' (*EHD*, i, no. 236, p. 839).
38. For what follows, see Dumville, 'The Ætheling', pp. 1–33, especially pp. 27 ('legitimacy'), 31 (the views of the lay nobles) and 32–3 (the definition of 'ætheling').
39. *EHD*, i, no. 191, p. 771. For the 786 canons, see Patrick Wormald, 'In search of King Offa's law code', I. N. Wood and Niels Lund (ed.), *People and places in northern Europe, 500–1600*, (Woodbridge, 1991), pp. 25–45.

40. Edmund was murdered at Pucklechurch, Gloucestershire; 'it was widely known how he ended he life, that Leofa stabbed him' (*AS Chron*, 'D', 946). John of Worcester adds that Leofa was a convicted thief who was attempting to kill Edmund's steward, and that the king was killed as he went to intervene (*JnW*, ii, pp. 398–9).
41. Miller, *Charters of the New Minster*, pp. 108–9; for the relations between Ælfthryth and Æthelwold, see Yorke, 'Æthelwold and the politics of the tenth century', pp. 82–4.
42. *Eadweard and Eadmund and Æðelred æðelingas syndon Eadgares suna cyninges.* For the date and provenance, see David N. Dumville, 'The Anglian collection of royal genealogies and regnal lists', *ASE*, 5 (1976), p. 43; see also idem, 'The Ætheling', pp. 4–5. It may be significant that Archbishop Dunstan, who retained the abbacy of Glastonbury until 974–5, is credited by later writers with a crucial role in the choice of Edward as his father's successor (Nicholas Brooks, 'The career of St Dunstan', Ramsay et al., *St Dunstan*, p. 22 and see note 51 below).
43. Fell, *St Edward*, p. 2; *JnW*, ii, pp. 426–7.
44. *VO*, pp. 448–9; *EHD*, i, no. 236, p. 841.
45. André Vauchez, *Sainthood in the later Middle Ages* (Cambridge, 1997), pp. 159–60; the example given is that of St Sigismund of Burgundy (d. 523), who strangled his son Sigeric with his own hands (I owe this reference to Björn Weiler). Byrhtferth's account of Edward's murder has strongly hagiographical overtones (Michael Lapidge, 'Byrhtferth and Oswald', Brooks and Cubitt, *St Oswald*, pp. 79–80).
46. Björn Weiler, 'Kingship, usurpation and propaganda in the twelfth century: the case of Stephen', *ANS*, 23 (2001), pp. 323–4; Fell, *St Edward*, p. 9.
47. *Mem. St Dunstan*, pp. 214, 423.
48. 'He [Henry] alone of all William [I]'s sons was born a prince, and the throne seemed destined to be his' (*WmM*, i, pp. 709–10); Orderic Vitalis makes the point that Henry, unlike his elder brothers, was born after the coronation of his mother, Queen Matilda, in 1068 (*OV*, ii, pp. 214–5); see Freeman, *NC*, i, p. 626. For the connections between William and Eadmer, see Rodney M. Thomson, *William of Malmesbury* (Woodbridge, 1987), pp. 46–7, 73.
49. For an attempt to resolve this difficulty, see Janet L. Nelson, 'Inauguration rituals', Ian Wood and P. H. Sawyer (eds), *Early medieval kingship* (Leeds, 1977), p. 67. A similar argument had been advanced (unsuccessfully) in Saxony, in favour of Henry, younger son of King Henry I (d. 936), who, unlike his elder brother Otto I, was born after his father assumed the kingship; see Karl Leyser, *Rule and conflict in an early medieval society:*

Ottonian Germany (London, 1979), p. 16; idem, 'The Ottonians and Wessex', in Timothy Reuter (ed.), *Communications and power in early medieval Europe: the Carolingian and Ottonian centuries* (London, 1994), p. 88. I owe this reference to Professor Nelson.

50. The queen, her son and Ælfric *cild* (brother-in-law of Ealdorman Ælfhere) were the guests of Bishop Æthelwold at Ely soon after the resolution of the dispute (*LE*, p. 86).

51. So the *Passio* (Fell, *St Edward*, p. 2), Osbern and Eadmer (*Mem. St Dunstan*, pp. 114, 214), and John of Worcester (*JnW*, ii, pp. 262–3). The author of the first *vita* of Dunstan, identified only as 'B', was a clerk in Dunstan's household when he was abbot of Glastonbury, but left England in 960, never to return, and thus had little or no knowledge of his subject's later career (Michael Lapidge, 'B. and the *Vita S. Dunstani*', Ramsay et al., *St Dunstan*, pp. 247–59).

52. *JnW*, ii, pp. 426–7.

53. S. 832 (dated 977), translated in *EHD*, i, no. 115, pp. 522–3; Keynes, *Diplomas*, p. 175, note 84. See also L. Whitbread, 'Æthelweard and the Anglo-Saxon Chronicle', *EHR*, 74 (1959), p. 585.

54. *AS Chron*, 'D, E': 'Edgar's son Edward succeeded to the kingdom. And soon in the same year *in harvest time* there appeared the star comet' (my italics). Harvest time was normally August. The other versions of the *Chronicle* ('A', 'B', 'C') also date Edward's acceptance before the appearance of the comet, but with no indication of when that occurred.

55. S. 937; *EHD*, i, no. 123, p. 538. The lands concerned were Hurstborne Tarrant, Hampshire, and Bedwyn and Burbage, Wiltshire. Dean, Sussex ('Dean of the æthelings', *Æthelingadene*), may also have been among the 'lands belonging to kings' sons' (Keynes, *Diplomas*, p. 187, note 117). S. 937 might imply the existence of lands set aside for the use of royal sons as a group, and the existence of an official known as 'the æthelings' (plural) *discþegn*' (steward, seneschal) points in the same direction (S. 1454 and see Chapter 2, below). See also Dumville, 'The Ætheling', pp. 5–6, 32–3.

56. *AS Chron*, 975; the 'D' text, which at this point is in the style of Archbishop Wulfstan *lupus*, dates the disturbances to 976. At about this time, according to a Rochester memorandum (S. 1457, Robertson, *Charters*, no. 59, pp. 122–3), two estates were seized from the bishopric with the connivance of the local earl, Edwin, and 'that section of the people which was the enemy of God' (*þæt folc ðe wæs Godes anspreca*). For similar problems in the north, see the memorandum of Archbishop Oswald on the estates of York (S. 1453, Robertson, *Charters*, no. 54, pp. 110–13; Wormald, *MEL*, p. 193).

57. *VO*, pp. 443–7; *EHD*, i, no. 236, pp. 839–41 (for Germanus, see note 84

below); D. J. V. Fisher, 'The anti-monastic reaction in Edward the Martyr's reign', *Cambridge Historical J.*, 10 (1950–52), pp. 254–70; Hart, 'Athelstan "Half-king"' and Williams, '*Princeps Merciorum gentis*', passim; Pauline Stafford, *Unification and conquest* (London, 1989), pp. 57–8.

58. See, for example, the history of the estates acquired for Thorney Abbey (*ECEE*, pp. 277–79). For Ely, see Wormald, *MEL*, p. 156, *LE*, pp. 72–117.
59. Osbern and Eadmer make the Calne assembly the locus for a clerical complaint to Dunstan about their expulsion in favour of monks, and the collapse of the floor is interpreted as God's judgement in the latter's favour (*Mem. St Dunstan*, pp. 113–14, 213; see also Wormald, *MEL*, p. 144 and note 94).
60. Stenton, *ASE*, p. 372.
61. Keynes, *Diplomas*, pp. 166–74; Ridyard, *Royal Saints*, pp. 154–71; Simon Keynes, 'King Alfred the Great and Shaftesbury Abbey', in Laurence Keen (ed.), *Studies in the early history of Shaftesbury Abbey* (Dorchester, Dorset, 1999), pp. 48–55; Barbara Yorke, 'Edward, king and martyr: a Saxon murder mystery', ibid., pp. 99–116.
62. The annals for 973–1001 in 'A' were composed no later than the early eleventh century, see Janet M. Bately, *The Anglo-Saxon Chronicle: a collaborative edition, 3: MS A* (Cambridge, 1986), pp. xxxvii–xxxviii.
63. For the date of the lament, see Keynes, *Diplomas*, p. 167.
64. *VO*, pp. 448–9, *EHD*, i, no. 236, pp. 841–3.
65. Lapidge, 'Byrhtferth and Oswald', in Brooks and Cubitt, *St Oswald*, pp. 79–80.
66. *AS Chron*, 757, 787.
67. *AS Chron*, 'D', 946.
68. This suggestion was raised by Susan Reynolds when a version of this chapter was read to the Early Medieval seminar at the Institute of Historical Research on 13 March 2002. In the ensuing discussion it was remarked that cover-ups in themselves are frequently followed by speculative accusations of the kind inspired by the murder of Edward.
69. Ælfthryth's complicity is alleged in the *Passio Sancti Edwardi*, composed *c.* 1070–80 (see Fell, *St Edward*, p. xx), Goscelin's *Vita S. Edithe*, *c.* 1080 (see Ridyard, *Royal Saints*, pp. 37–8) and Osbern of Canterbury's *Vita Sancti Dunstani*, 1089–93 (see Robinson,'Osbern of Canterbury', p. 38); see Fell, *St Edward*, pp. 3–4; Wilmart, 'La légende de Ste Édith', p. 82; *Mem St Dunstan*, pp. 114–5. These works are not necessarily independent of each other, but the same accusation appears in the *Cronica Dunelmensis*, composed at Durham between 1072 and 1083, see H. E. Craster, 'The Red

Book of Durham', *EHR* 40 (1925), pp. 526, 529–31, and in Adam of Bremen (Tschan, *Adam of Bremen*, p. 91).

70. *HH*, pp. 324–5 and note 186; this section of the text was written between *c.* 1133 and *c.* 1140. For the development of the theme, see Fell, *St Edward*, pp. 3–6; Keynes, *Diplomas*, p. 168; Ridyard, *Royal saints*, pp. 158–9.
71. Even if the *Passio Sancti Edwardi* is based on an earlier version composed at the beginning of the eleventh century (Fell, *St Edward*, pp. xviii–xix), there is no way of knowing whether or not the hypothetical exemplar contained an accusation against Ælfthryth.
72. *AS Chron*, 'D', 'E', 978 and see the chapter-heading above; Keynes, *Diplomas*, p. 167. Byrhtferth also says that the murderers escaped earthly, though not divine, punishment (*VO*, pp. 450–1; *EHD*, i, no. 236, pp. 842–3). His statement that one of them was subsequently blinded may be a covert reference to Ælfgar son of Ealdorman Ælfric of Hampshire, blinded for an unspecified offence in 993 (Yorke, 'Edward, king and martyr', note 53, p. 115).
73. *WmM*, i, pp. 266–7, 274–5; Fisher, 'Anti-monastic reaction', p. 26. See also Yorke, 'Edward, king and martyr', pp. 106.
74. *VO*, pp. 443, 450–1; *EHD*, i, no. 236, pp. 840, 842; Fell, *St Edward*, p. 8.
75. Goscelin has an extraordinary story of the English magnates, led by Ælfhere, offering the crown to Edith after the murder of Edward because Æthelred's complicity made him unfit to rule (Wilmart, 'La légende de Ste Édith', pp. 82–3, 84–6); one can only agree with Dr Ridyard (*Royal saints*, p. 41) that this is a 'highly improbable' tale.
76. This is to accept Simon Keynes's date of 18 March 978 for the murder of Edward (*Diplomas*, p. 233, note 7), but in a forthcoming paper, 'The death of King Edward the Martyr: chronological questions', which he was kind enough to show me before publication, David Dumville argues that Edward's murder should be dated to 979 rather than 978. The 'D' and 'E' recensions of the *Chronicle*, the only ones to record the reburial at Shaftesbury, place it after Æthelred's consecration. See also next note.
77. *AS Chron*, 'D', 'E', 979, 980 (see also previous note); *VO*, pp. 450–1; Fell, *Edward*, p. 7–8. 18 February 979 would be before Æthelred's coronation, 18 February 980 (the only possibility if Edward was killed in March 979, rather than 978) would be afterwards.
78. St Ælfgifu's cult dates at the latest to the 970s, when miracles associated with her tomb were recorded by Lantfrid of Winchester (Keynes, 'King Alfred and Shaftesbury Abbey', p. 45 and note 79). It is also mentioned by Æthelweard, writing between 978 and 988 (Campbell, *Æthelweard*, p. 54; for the date, see Chapter 2 below).

79. *Sermo lupi ad Anglos*, trans. *EHD*, i, no. 240, p. 857; Keynes, 'King Alfred and Shaftesbury Abbey', pp. 53–5. By the mid eleventh century, Exeter also claimed to have relics of St Edward (Connor, *Anglo-Saxon Exeter*, p. 173, and see note 23 above).
80. *AS Chron*, 'C', 978, 'D', E', 979; for the date of Æthelred's consecration, see Keynes, *Diplomas*, p. 233, note 7. The 'rejoicing' is confirmed by Byrhtferth's account of the event, as is the presence of the two archbishops, Dunstan and Oswald (*VO*, p. 455; *EHD*, i, no. 236, p. 843).
81. D. W. Rollason, 'The cults of murdered royal saints in Anglo-Saxon England', *ASE*, 11 (1983), pp. 1–22.
82. Alan Thacker, 'Saint-making and relic collecting by Oswald and his communities', Brooks and Cubitt, *St Oswald*, pp. 247–50; Rollason, 'Cults of murdered royal saints', pp. 17–8, but see also idem, *Saints and relics in Anglo-Saxon England* (Oxford, 1989), p. 144. For Æthelred as the promoter of Edward's cult, see Keynes, *Diplomas*, pp. 169–71; idem, 'King Alfred and Shaftesbury Abbey', pp. 48–53; Ridyard, *Royal saints*, pp. 154–7; Yorke, 'Edward, king and martyr', pp. 109–12.
83. V Atr, 16; Robertson, *Laws*, pp. 84–5; Patrick Wormald, 'Æthelred the lawmaker', in Hill (ed.), *Ethelred the Unready*, pp. 49–56; idem, *MEL*, pp. 343–4, 346.
84. For Ælfthryth's gift of Cholsey to her son, see S. 877 (dated 996), translated in *EHD*, i, no. 120, pp. 531–4, at p. 532. According to Goscelin of Saint-Bertin, the house was established by Æthelred at the urging of Archbishop Sigeric (990–94), see Keynes, 'King Alfred and Shaftesbury Abbey', p. 50. Its first (and only) abbot was Germanus (*c.* 994–1013), the abbot of Winchcombe expelled in the disturbances following Edgar's death, for whom see Michael Lapidge, 'Abbot Germanus, Winchcombe, Ramsey and the Cambridge Psalter', *Anglo-Latin Literature 900–1066* (London, 1993), pp. 405–14; also *HRH*, pp. 39–40. For the church, see Richard Gem, 'Church architecture in the reign of King Æthelred', in Hill, *Ethelred the Unready*, pp. 105–9.
85. Æthelred is said to have lifted the geld assessment on the hide of land which represented the church's endowment, see *GDB*, fo. 165v; John Moore (ed.), *Domesday Book: Gloucestershire* (Chichester, 1982), no. 12, 1 and note. A spurious diploma of 1016, granting the exempt hide to Evesham Abbey, was probably forged in the course of a dispute over Maugersbury, within which Stow was then included (S. 935, *Chron Evesham*, p. 74).
86. S. 1503; this is the only reference to a 'Holy Cross' dedication at Shaftesbury. Æthelstan died in 1014.
87. See note 63 above.

88. S. 850, Susan Kelly, *The charters of Shaftesbury Abbey* (Oxford, 1996), no. 28, pp. 107–14.
89. Hayward, 'Translation-narratives', pp. 88–9, note 99.
90. *VO*, pp. 451–2. Byrhtferth cites as witness Ælfric, archbishop of Canterbury (995–1005), who had previously been bishop of Ramsbury.
91. Keynes, 'King Alfred and Shaftesbury Abbey', p. 50.
92. The date intended by Goscelin is 997, though the translation may have taken place two or three years later. See Keynes, 'King Alfred and Shaftesbury Abbey', pp. 51–3; Hayward, 'Translation-narratives', pp. 77–9. Goscelin's erroneous claim that Dunstan, who died in 988, was the agent of Edith's translation must be connected with his dedication of the *vita* to Dunstan's successor, Archbishop Lanfranc (Ridyard, *Royal saints*, pp. 40–1). There is no contemporary account of the translation, but the feast, 3 November, is attested in pre-Conquest calendars.
93. Fell, *St Edward*, pp. 12–13.
94. For Wulfsige, see Keynes, *Diplomas*, pp. 251, 258, and Frank Barlow, *The English church, 1000–1066* (2nd edn; London, 1966), pp. 222–3. He was later canonized and his *vita* was written by Goscelin of Saint-Bertin. For Abbot Ælfsige, see *HRH*, p. 81; Fell, *St Edward*, p. xix.
95. Hayward, 'Translation-narratives', pp. 86–7.
96. See Chapter 3 below.
97. *AS Chron*, 'A', 1001. For the date of the battle at Dean, see Bruce Dickins, 'The date of the battle of Æthelingadene, ASC 1001 A', *Leeds Studies in English*, 6 (1937), pp. 215–7.
98. R. H. M. Dolley, 'The Shaftesbury hoard of pence of Æthelræd II', *Numismatic Chronicle*, 6th series, 16 (1956), pp. 267–80; Keynes, 'King Alfred and Shaftesbury Abbey', pp. 52–3.
99. S. 899, Kelly, *Charters of Shaftesbury*, no. 29, pp. 214–22.
100. Kelly, *Charters of Shaftesbury*, pp. 119–20. Bradford was the most valuable estate in the abbey's very substantial endowment (*GDB* fos 17v, 67v, 75, 78v, 83v, 91).
101. Gem, 'Church architecture in the reign of King Æthelred', pp. 109–10; Eric Fernie, *The architecture of the Anglo-Saxons* (London, 1982), pp. 145–50.
102. Wormald, *MEL*, note 373, pp. 343–4; Hayward, 'Translation-narratives', note 94, p. 87.
103. Kelly, *Charters of Shaftesbury*, p. xix.
104. M. R. Godden, 'Ælfric and Anglo-Saxon kingship', *EHR*, 102 (1987), pp. 911–15, argues against interpreting this passage as a statement of 'theocratic kingship', because the compulsion in Ælfric and his source stems

not from morality but from physical incapacity; but in practical terms it comes to much the same thing.

105. *EHD*, i, no. 239B, p. 851. For Æthelweard, Æthelmær and Ælfric, see Chapter 2 below.

Notes to Chapter 2: The Old Guard and the Young King

1. Skeat (ed.), *Lives of the saints*, i, p. 6.
2. Simon Keynes, 'The declining reputation of King Æthelred the Unready', Hill, *Ethelred the Unready*', pp. 240–1.
3. Keynes, *Diplomas*, p. 155.
4. S. 877, *EHD*, i, no. 120, Robertson, *Charters*, no. 63. The northern thegns rarely attest diplomas, so their appearance is of particular interest. For Siward of Kent, see Keynes, *Diplomas*, pp. 132–4, and for similar groups at a later date, Ann Williams, 'Lost worlds: Kentish society in the eleventh century', *Medieval Prosopography*, 20 (1999), pp. 51–74.
5. This is possible only for the middle years of Æthelstan, thanks to the draughtsman 'Æthelstan A', who regularly included both date and place in his productions (Wormald, *MEL*, pp. 434–5 and note 55).
6. The table is based on Wormald, *MEL*, tables 6:1, 6:2, pp. 431, 433; Keynes, *Diplomas*, pp. 126–34, 269–72. The uncertainty arises because the Wantage code (III Atr) may or may not have been issued at the meeeting of 997 recorded in S. 891, and VIII Atr, dated 1014, may or may not relate to the same legislative assembly as IX Atr, issued at Woodstock.
7. *AS Chron*, 'F', 995, Whitelock, *The Anglo-Saxon Chronicle*, p. 84, note 2.
8. Keynes, *Diplomas*, pp. 126–7.
9. S. 915.
10. See Chapter 7 below.
11. Three stewards (*disciferi*) of Edgar (Ælfweard, Æthelweard and Ælfsige) continue to attest charters of Edward the Martyr and Æthelred. Ælfweard and Æthelweard were apparently brothers (Keynes, *Diplomas*, pp. 182–3).
12. S. 835.
13. S. 834. For the fluctuation in control of south-eastern Mercia, see Williams, '*Princeps Merciorum gentis*', pp. 164–5.
14. *AS Chron*, 983; *VO*, p. 443, *EHD*, i, p. 912.
15. Keynes, *Diplomas*, table 6.
16. *AS Chron*, 'C', 982; Æthelmær's obit is preserved in the New Minster *Liber Vitae* (Keynes, *Diplomas*, p. 240). For Edwin's activities in Kent, see Robertson, *Charters*, no. 59.
17. Under Æthelmær's will (S. 1498; Miller, *Charters of the New Minster*, no.

25), his elder son received *Igenesham* and the younger Cottesmore, Oxfordshire (*ECTV*, pp. 133–4). Neither are named, but one was the Æthelwine who received land at Clyffe Pypard, Wiltshire, in 983 (S. 848, see Keynes, *Diplomas*, p. 241, note 26), and who also held land in Gloucestershire, near Dumbleton (S. 886, trans. *EHD*, no. 119). If *Igenesham* is Eynsham, Oxfordshire (Gelling, *ECTV*, p. 133, but Inglesham, Wiltshire, is also a possibility), then the other son might be Æthelweard, who married the daughter of Æthelmær, son of Æthelweard the Chronicler, and gave the site of Eynsham Abbey to his father-in-law (S. 911 and see note 76 below). This Æthelweard became ealdorman of the western shires under Cnut; see Simon Keynes, 'Cnut's Earls', Alexander Rumble (ed.), *The reign of Cnut* (Leicester, 1994), pp. 67–70.

18. S. 842. In the Abingdon interpolations to John of Worcester's *Chronicle*, the brother of Edwin of Abingdon (i.e. Ælfric of Hampshire) is called *maior domus regiae*, which implies an office in the royal household, but Abingdon tradition confuses Ælfric of Hampshire with Ælfric *cild*, so that it is difficult to decide who is intended (see also note 27 below).
19. S. 831, 868 (dated 988). Ælfgar's land is said to have been held by Æthelwold and his brother Ælfhelm, perhaps members of the same family.
20. S. 869 (dated 988), Susan Kelly, *Charters of Selsey* (Oxford, 1998), p. 65. The reference could be to Ælfric *cild*, but his interests seem to have lain in the east midlands (Williams, '*Princeps Merciorum gentis*', p. 161 and note 90).
21. S. 891, *AS Chron*, 1003.
22. Janet Backhouse, D. H. Turner and Lesley Webster (ed.), *The Golden Age of Anglo-Saxon Art* (London, 1984), pp. 112–3.
23. *AS Chron*, 'F', 992.
24. S. 918. Ælfgar *cyninges gerefa* attests an agreement before the shire-court of Berkshire in 990 x 992 (S. 1454), in which Ælfric of Hampshire was involved as oath-helper. Ælfgar's mother Wulfgyth and wife Ælfgifu are commemorated in the New Minster *Liber Vitae*, which describes Ælfgar as *preses* and *procurator*, both titles implying some official position (Keynes, *Diplomas*, p. 184, note 110). For reeves in general, see Chapter 3 below.
25. *AS Chron*, 985, S. 937 (*EHD*, i, no. 123), S. 896; one of the estates involved had been given to Ælfhere by Edgar (S. 588). Ælfric is accused of treason (*maiestatis reum*, S. 937) and of 'committing many unheard of offences against God and against my royal authority' (*contra Deum meumque regale imperium multa et inaudita miserabiliter committens piacula*, S. 896).
26. *Mem. St Dunstan*, pp. 396–7 (*EHD*, i, no. 231). The sender is either John XIV (983–4), John XV (985–96), John XVI (997–8), John XVII (1003) or

John XVIII (1004–1009); the addressee might be Ælfric *cild* or Ælfric of Hampshire.

27. The Abingdon Chronicle says that Abbot Edwin's brother fell foul of the king, and was exiled to Denmark, returning with a Viking army, but gives the brother's name as Eadric, and makes him a son of Ealdorman Ælfhere of Mercia (*Chron Abingdon*, i, p. 357). Presumably the reference is to Ælfric *cild*, whom John of Worcester also mistakenly calls the son of Ealdorman Ælfhere (*JnW*, ii, pp. 434–5); in fact they were brothers-in-law. Abbot Edwin's brother, however, was Ælfric of Hampshire (S. 876; *JnW*, ii, p. 613; Keynes, *Diplomas*, p. 177, note 91). See also note 18 above.
28. S. 876, 891, 899; for Ælfgifu and Eadgyth, see Chapter 4 below. Pope John's letter of 991 (see Chapter 3) mentions the presence of Æthelred's 'sons and daughters' at a meeting with the papal legate at Christmas 990, but the phrase may be rhetorical; the 'sons and daughters' of Duke Richard I are likewise included as present at the meeting of the Norman ducal court in March 991 (*Mem. St Dunstan*, pp. 397–8, *EHD*, i, no. 230).
29. *Chronicon ex Chronicis*, p. 275 (the genealogical appendix). The *Æðelbriht dux* who attests S. 838 (dated 981) is a miscopying for Ealdorman Æthelweard (Keynes, *Diplomas*, table 8).
30. Keynes, *Diplomas*, p. 187, note 118. Sulcard of Westminster says she came 'of most noble English stock' (*ex nobilioribus Anglis*) but does not give her name (Bernard W. Scholz, 'Sulcard of Westminster: "Prologus de Construccione Westmonasterii"', *Traditio*, 20 (1964), pp. 74, 89).
31. *AS Chron*, 'D', 'E', 966; Dorothy Whitelock, 'The dealings of the kings of England with Northumbria in the tenth and eleventh centuries', in P. Clemoes (ed.), *The Anglo-Saxons* (London, 1959), p. 79; reprinted in *History, Law and Literature in tenth- and eleventh-century England* (London, 1981). For the various Thoreds active at the time, see Wormald, *MEL*, pp. 192–4.
32. S. 782; *LE*, pp. 95, 106; *AS Chron*, 1010 (the battle of Ringmere, see below, Chapter 5). *Aðum* can mean 'son-in-law', but kings' daughters were not usually given to local thegns (there is no suggestion that Æthelstan was more than this) and the known sons-in-law of Æthelred were powerful ealdormen, Eadric *streona* of Mercia and Uhtred of Bamburgh (see below, Chapter 4).
33. Keynes, *Diplomas*, table 8.
34. Keynes, *Diplomas*, pp. 157–8. It has been suggested that Thored seized power in the north during the crisis of 975 (Stafford, 'Reign of Æthelred II', p. 24). There is some evidence for a confrontation between Earl Thored and Archbishop Oswald (S. 1453, Robertson, *Charters*, no. 54; Wormald, *MEL*, p. 193) but this need not have occurred in 975; the 980s, when a

number of churches lost land to encroaching laymen provides an equally plausible context (Keynes, *Diplomas*, pp. 176–86).

35. Dorothy Whitelock, *The will of Æthelgifu* (Oxford, 1968), pp. 23–5. Stafford (*Emma and Edith*, pp. 72, 85, 91 note 116) dates the first marriage (Thored's daughter) *c.* 985 and the second (Ælfgifu) *c.* 990.
36. See Chapters 6 and 7 below.
37. S. 837, 851, 853, 859, 867, 871, 897.
38. S. 853; Keynes, *Diplomas*, pp. 158–61.
39. Ann Williams, *The English and the Norman Conquest* (Woodbridge, 1995), pp. 109–17.
40. S. 863–4; Keynes, *Diplomas*, pp. 184–5.
41. S. 893; David E. Thornton, 'Maredudd ab Owain: the most famous king of the Welsh', *Welsh History Review*, 18 (1997), pp. 581–3; Ann Williams, '"Cockles amongst the wheat": Danes and English in the west midlands in the first half of the eleventh century', *Midland History*, 11 (1986), note 51, pp. 19–20.
42. S. 876, 918 (Abingdon), 891 (Winchester), 885, 893 (Rochester), see Keynes, *Diplomas*, pp. 176–86. Glastonbury may also have been affected (William of Malmesbury, *Vita Dunstani*, *Mem. St Dunstan*, pp. 313–4), but it was not 'anti-monastic' sentiment which impelled the spoliators, for Rochester had a secular chapter.
43. *AS Chron*, 'C', 985; S. 876.
44. S. 876, 918 (see also below, note 107).
45. S. 861, 891; Keynes, *Diplomas*, p. 183, note 108.
46. *AS Chron*, 993; S. 876, see Keynes, *Diplomas*, pp. 250–1.
47. Scholz, 'Sulcard of Westminster', pp. 74–5, 89; *Mem. St Dunstan*, pp. 117, 310; *AS Chron*, 'CDE', 986. Sulcard's *suo militi* might be translated 'king's thegn' (J. L. Nelson, personal communication).
48. Michael Dolley, 'Æthelræd's Rochester ravaging of 986: an intriguing numismatic sidelight', *Spink's Numismatic Circular*, 75 (1967), pp. 33–4; Keynes, *Diplomas*, pp. 178–80.
49. See note 50 below. Bishop Godwine also recovered Wouldham and Littleham, the subjects of a lengthy lawsuit between the bishopric and a local Kentish family (S. 885, 1458, A Campbell, *Charters of Rochester* (London, 1973), no. 34, Robertson, *Charters*, no. 41). The estates had been adjudged to the bishopric in the time of Archbishop Dunstan, but the alleged despoilers had been able to hang on to the disputed lands with (to judge from S. 885, the diploma of restitution) the connivance of the king. Godwine also recovered Snodland, another estate with a long and contentious history (S. 1456, 1511; Campbell, *Charters of Rochester*, nos 35, 37).

50. S. 864, Keynes, *Diplomas*, p. 179, note 99. For Bromley's history, see S. 331, 671, 1457, 1511; Campbell, *Charters of Rochester*, nos 25, 29, 35–6
51. S. 893; Keynes, *Diplomas*, pp. 184–5. The Æthelsige who forfeited his land at Dumbleton, Gloucs, for pig-stealing was presumably a different individual, for the land had been regranted twice by 995 (S. 886).
52. Leofwine attests for the first time in 994. S. 891 (dated 997) describes him as *Wicciarum provinciarum dux* (Worcestershire, Gloucestershire and part of Warwickshire).
53. Ælfhelm (for whom see below) attests S. 891 (see previous note) as *Norðanhumbrensium provinciarum dux.*
54. Ælfthryth attests S. 876, dated 993; no diplomas survive for 991 or 992, but she was present at a royal gathering held at Cookham, Berkshire, in the period 990 x 992 (S. 1454). She died on 17 November in either 999, 1000 or 1001: S. 904, dated before April 1002, speaks of her as deceased (Keynes, *Diplomas*, p. 210, note 203).
55. S. 1503 (the ætheling's will); 904 (the queen's tenure of Dean). See also Chapter 1, note 55 above.
56. S. 1497, 1454. The will of Æthelgifu (S. 1497), cannot be dated more closely than *c.* 985 x 1001 but the late 990s seems most likely (Whitelock, *The will of Æthelgifu*, pp. 23–5).
57. S. 1242; Harmer, *Anglo-Saxon Writs* no. 108. Ruishton was a member of the manor of Taunton, given by Edgar to the Old Minster, Winchester (S. 806).
58. S. 891; for disputes about *lænland*, see note 108 below.
59. Wormald, *MEL*, p. 443 and see Chapter 3 below.
60. S. 876, 937; Keynes, *Diplomas*, pp. 186–7.
61. *KCD*, iv, p. 310, Haddan and Stubbs, *Councils*, i, p. 678. For the family, which still held land in Devon on the eve of the Norman Conquest, see H. P. R. Finberg, 'The house of Ordgar and the foundation of Tavistock Abbey', *EHR*, 53 (1943), pp. 190–201; idem, 'Childe's Tomb', *Lucerna* (London, 1964), pp. 186–203.
62. Æthelred's confirmation of 981 (the spurious S. 838, see Keynes, *Diplomas*, pp. 97 note 43, 180 note 101) may preserve the circumstances of the endowment; see H. P. R. Finberg, *Tavistock Abbey* (Cambridge, 1951), pp. 278–83. Ordwulf's brother is perhaps the Ælfsige for whose soul he freed a slave at St Petroc's altar (Haddan and Stubbs, *Councils*, i, p. 677).
63. *JnW*, ii, pp. 446–7; Finberg, 'Childe's Tomb', p. 193. In 1001 the men of Devon and Somerset were led into battle by the high-reeve (*heah-gerefa*) Kola (*AS Chron*, 'A', 1001, Chapter 3 below).
64. S. 847; he later gave the estate to Eynsham (S. 911).

65. S. 939, *EHD*, i, no. 121.
66. He attests the vernacular translation of S. 914 as *mines hlafordes discðegn* though in the Latin text he is simply *minister* (Keynes, *Diplomas*, pp. 161–261).
67. Keynes, *Diplomas*, table 8.
68. Campbell, *Æthelweard*, p. 39.
69. For the possibility that Æthelweard was descended from Odda, ealdorman of Devon in Alfred's reign, see Ann Williams, *Land, power and politics: the family and career of Odda of Deerhurst*, the Deerhurst Lecture, 1996 (Deerhurst, 1997), pp. 6–7.
70. C. R. Hart suggested that his father was the unnamed son of Ælfstan, a beneficiary under the will of his uncle, Ealdorman Æthelwold; see 'Athelstan Half-king', p. 118, note 5, reprinted in *The Danelaw* (London, 1992), p. 572, note 7. This would make Æthelweard the great-nephew of Æthelstan Half-king (brother of Ælfstan and Æthelwold), but Hart gives no grounds for the hypothesis, and there are no other suggestions of a connection between the two families. In the earlier version of his family-tree for the Half-king's kindred ('Athelstan Half-king', p. 117), Hart accepted the identification of Ealdorman Æthelweard as a brother of Eadwig's wife Ælfgifu, but see below, note 77.
71. Ælfgifu *þæs cininges wif* and Æthelgifu *þæs cininges wifes modur* attest S. 1292, dating from before 957 (Robertson, *Charters*, no. 31). This is the only contemporary reference to Ælfgifu as the king's wife, but she is *coniux Eadwigi regis* in the New Minster *Liber Vitae* (Birch, *Liber de Hyde*, p. 57 and see note 78 below).
72. *Mem. St Dunstan*, pp. 32, 33; the biographer had a particular animus against Æthelgifu, whom he believed was responsible for Dunstan's subsequent exile. The event was immortalized by Jerome K. Jerome (*Three Men in a Boat*): 'How poor weak-minded King Edwy must have hated Kyningestune! The coronation-feast had been too much for him ... so he slipped from the noisy revel to steal a quiet midnight hour with his beloved Elgiva. Perhaps from the casement, standing hand-in-hand, they were watching the calm moonlight on the river, while from the distant halls the boisterous revelry floated in broken bursts of faint-heard din and tumult. Then brutal Odo and St Dunstan force their rude way into the quiet room, and hurl coarse insults at the sweet-faced Queen, and drag poor Edwy back to the loud clamour of the drunken brawl'.
73. *AS Chron*, 'D', 958; VI Atr, 12; T. A. M. Charles-Edwards, 'Kinship, status and the origins of the hide', *P&P*, 52 (1972), pp. 23–4. See also Yorke, 'Æthelwold and the politics of the tenth century', p. 77.

74. S. 737–8.
75. S. 1484 (see Chapter 1, note 4 above). Other beneficiaries include the Old Minster, Winchester, where she wished to be buried, the New Minster, and Abingdon Abbey. These are the houses especially associated with Bishop Æthelwold, with whom Ælfgifu seems to have had friendly relations; she left him a personal bequest of land at *Tæfersceat* (probably in Cambridgeshire), with the request that he 'act as an advocate on my behalf and that of my mother' (Yorke, 'Æthelwold and the politics of the tenth century', pp. 76–7, 79–80, 87).
76. Not the Æthelflæd who freed a slave at St Petroc's altar for her husband Ealdorman Æthelweard (Haddan and Stubbs, *Councils*, i, pp. 678–9), who was the Chronicler's granddaughter (Keynes, 'Cnut's earls', pp. 67–70; see also note 17 above).
77. For another pair of brothers with the same names, see note 11 above. The identification of Ælfgifu's brother and the ealdorman is accepted by Yorke ('Æthelwold and the politics of the tenth century', pp. 76–7). Stafford, (*Emma and Edith*, p. 134 and note 197) and Hart ('The will of Ælfgifu', *The Danelaw*, p. 464) reject it, without, however, explaining the alleged kinship between Ælfgifu and Eadwig (and Edgar). Hart (ibid., pp. 455–65) suggests that her mother Æthelgifu was a sister of Æthelstan Half-king (and hence not the mother of Ealdorman Æthelweard, since in that case she would have to have married her nephew, see note 70 above), but the argument depends on the identification of *æt Hrisanbeorgan*, bequeathed by Ælfgifu to the Old Minster, with Monks Risborough, previously associated with Æthelstan's family. Margaret Gelling, however, has identified it as Princes Risborough (*ECTV*, p. 75). From the late tenth century, Monks Risborough belonged to the archbishopric of Canterbury (see also Chapter 3 below), whereas Ælfgifu bequeathed *æt Hrisanbeorgan* to the Old Minster. Princes Risborough first appears in Domesday Book as a royal estate (*GDB*, fo. 143v); if the terms of her will were not fully implemented, it seems likelier that one of her bequests should have been diverted to her kinsman the king than to the archbishopric.
78. Campbell, *Æthelweard*, p. 55. A slave was freed in Eadwig's memory at St Petroc's, Cornwall (Haddan and Stubbs, *Councils*, i, p. 679). Eadwig was also remembered kindly at the New Minster, Winchester, where he was buried; its history, composed in the late tenth century, describes him as a king 'mourned by many tears of his people' (Miller, *Charters of the New Minster*, pp. xxxi–xxxii). In this context, it should be remembered that the New Minster was one of the main beneficiaries of Ælfgifu's will,

and that its *Liber Vitae* is one of the few sources to call her Eadwig's wife (see note 71 above).

79. Æthelmær's charter for Cerne (S. 1217) is of dubious authenticity but probably preserves the details of the endowment; see G. D. Squibb, 'The foundation of Cerne Abbey', Barbara Yorke, 'Æthelmær: the foundation of the abbey of Cerne and the politics of the tenth century', K. Barker (ed.), *The Cerne Abbey Millennium Lectures* (Cerne Abbas, 1998), pp. 11–14, 15–20.
80. S. 911; the others were Upottery, Devon, Little Compton, Warwickshire, and Shelford, Cambridgeshire.
81. For Brihthelm, see note 85 below. Few of the lands of Ealdorman Æthelweard are recorded. Apart from Esher, he received land at Wycombe, Berkshire, under the will of his kinsman Ealdorman Ælfheah (S. 1485, Williams, '*Princeps Merciorum gentis*', p. 150), and lands in Cornwall from Edward the Martyr (S. 832 and Chapter 1 above).
82. Williams, '*Princeps Merciorum gentis*', pp. 171–2. Wulfwynn, who gave Æthelmær *Rameslege* (Brede, Sussex), part of Eynsham's endowment, might be the abbess of Wareham who died in 982 (*AS Chron*, 982; Whitbread, 'Æthelweard and the Anglo-Saxon Chronicle', p. 583).
83. Brihtwold was also commemorated at the New Minster (Keynes, *Diplomas*, pp. 188–9, 193 and notes 20, 144).
84. S. 651, Keynes, *Atlas*, table LVII (1–5). Brihtferth also attests a diploma of Edward the Martyr (table LVIII).
85. S. 615, 683, 695, 911. He may have been bishop of Selsey before his appointment to Winchester (Kelly, *Charters of Selsey*, pp. lxix, lxxvii-lxxviii, 80–1).
86. S. 877, *EHD*, i, no. 120.
87. Keynes, *Diplomas*, pp. 209, 227, note 265; *ECEE*, pp. 253–4; A. Williams, 'A west-country magnate of the eleventh century: the family, estates and patronage of Beorhtric son of Ælfgar', K. S. B. Keats-Rohan (ed.), *Family-trees and the roots of politics* (Woodbridge, 1997), pp. 43–4.
88. *AS Chron*, 1017.
89. P. H. Sawyer, *Charters of Burton Abbey* (Oxford, 1979), pp. xxxviii–xliii. Wulfric's byname *spot* is recorded only in the thirteenth century, but he is called 'Wulfrun's son' in S. 877, 886 and 939.
90. Keynes, *Diplomas*, pp. 188–9, 210–11.
91. He is *Norðanhumbrensium provinciarum dux* in S. 891 (997) and *dux Transhumbranae gentis* in S. 1380 (for which see note 121 below).
92. S. 878, 886 (*EHD*, i, no. 119) and see below, note 96. Æthelred's diploma granting Pillaton, Staffordshire, to Wulfric (S. 879, dated 996) is a post-Conquest forgery (Sawyer, *Charters of Burton*, no. 26).

93. *AS Chron*, 'D', 943, *recte* 940. Hart suggested that Wulfric's father was the man of the same name to whom Austry was granted in 958, but the diploma (S. 576) is spurious (Sawyer, *Charters of Burton*, pp. 29–30).
94. S. 860, 1380.
95. S. 479, 484, 1606, all preserved in the Burton Abbey cartulary (Sawyer, *Charters of Burton*, nos 5–7). Wulfsige also received lands in what was to become Derbyshire (see Chapter 3 below).
96. S. 878.
97. S. 720, 1380; Keynes, *Atlas*, table LVII (12–15). Wulfrun gave Upper Arley to Wolverhampton for Wulfgeat's soul.
98. S. 739; Sawyer, *Charters of Burton* no. 21. An Ælfhelm also received land at Witney Oxfordshire, in 969 (S. 771) but the name is not uncommon.
99. S. 1536; Sawyer, *Charters of Burton*, pp. xv–xxxiv, no. 29.
100. *GDB*, fo. 270. The region was appended to Cheshire in 1066 (*GDB*, fos 269v–270), and had probably been in Mercian hands from the early tenth century; see M. A. Atkin, '"The land between Ribble and Mersey" in the early tenth century', Alexander R. Rumble and A. D. Mills (ed.), *Names, Places and People: an onomastic miscellany for John McNeal Dodgson* (Stamford, 1997), pp. 8–18.
101. S. 407, Sawyer, *Charters of Burton*, p. xxiv.
102. *Monasticon*, iii, p. 47; Sawyer, *Charters of Burton*, p. xx.
103. S. 966; *Norðleoda laga*, §4, *EHD*, i, no. 52B. Compare Thurbrand *hold*, a younger contemporary of Wulfric, and perhaps lord of Holderness, Yorkshire (Williams, *The English and the Norman Conquest*, pp. 301–1, and Chapter 7 below).
104. *AS Chron*, 'CDE', 1006; *JnW*, ii, pp. 456–7. For Wulfgeat and his forfeiture, see also Chapter 7 below. A man of the same name forfeited land at Chilton, Berkshire, because 'he colluded in schemes with the king's enemies', but he may be the Wulfgeat who attested a royal diploma in 1009 (S. 934), and could not therefore be Leofeca's son; see Simon Keynes, 'Crime and punishment in the reign of King Æthelred the Unready', Wood and Lund, *People and places in northern Europe*, pp. 80–1 and note 90; Patrick Wormald, 'A handlist of Anglo-Saxon lawsuits', *ASE*, 17 (1988), pp. 256–7, note 20, and nos 72a and b; idem, *MEL*, p. 149, note 106.
105. S. 937.
106. He is unlikely to be Wulfgeat of Ilmington, Warwickshire, correspondent of Ælfric the homilist, nor Wulfgeat of Donnington, Shropshire, who made a will *c.* 1000 (S. 1534), for both seem to be Mercian thegns, whereas Wulfgeat son of Leofeca appears to have been a West Saxon; see Dorothy

Whitelock, 'Two notes on Ælfric and Wulfstan', *Modern Language Review*, 38 (1943), p. 124, reprinted in *History, Law and Literature.*

107. S. 918; Keynes, 'Crime and punishment', p. 81, note 90.

108. The principles are enunciated in II Cn 71, 71§1. The abbot of Muchelney required the king's assistance to recover a three-life *læn* at Ilminster, Somerset (S. 884); see also the arrangements about the king's men on the episcopal manor of Taunton (S. 1242, Harmer, *Anglo-Saxon Writs*, no. 108).

109. Leofwine and Leofsige were appointed in 994 (Keynes, *Diplomas*, p. 197 and table 8); for their spheres of office, see S. 891. For the king's itinerary, see David Hill, *An atlas of Anglo-Saxon England* (Oxford, 1981), p. 91.

110. W. T. Mellows (ed.), *The Chronicle of Hugh Candidus* (Peterborough, 1941), pp. 88–9. Hugh is the only source to preserve the name of Leofwine's father, Ælfwine; there is no reason to believe that this is an error for Æthelwine, ealdorman of East Anglia (d. 992).

111. S. 916, 926; F. M. Stenton, *The Latin charters of the Anglo-Saxon period* (Oxford, 1955), pp. 76–8; Chapter 3 below.

112. Keynes, *Diplomas*, pp. 190–1; Nicholas Brooks, *The early history of the church of Canterbury* (Leicester, 1984), pp. 278–83. For Cholsey and Shaftesbury, see Chapter 1 above.

113. Brooks, *The early history of the church of Canterbury*, p. 279; S. 1408 (see also note 160 below).

114. For Wulfsige, see Mary-Anne O'Donovan, *Charters of Sherborne* (Oxford, 1988), pp. xiv–xvi. The enclosure of the grounds and the division of resources between the bishop and his monks probably marks the completion of Sherborne's transformation (S. 895, O'Donovan, *Charters of Sherborne*, no. 1, dated 998).

115. Wulfstan was to become one of the most prolific and influential writers of his age, but his influence belongs more to the eleventh than to the tenth century (see Chapter 4 below).

116. Brooks, *The early history of the church of Canterbury*, pp. 281–2; *Mem. St Dunstan*, pp. 400–3, 406–8.

117. Veronica Ortenburg, 'Archbishop Sigeric's journey to Rome in 990', *ASE*, 19 (1990), pp. 197–246.

118. D. Whitelock, M. Brett and C. N. L. Brooke (ed.), *Councils and Synods, i, part 1, 871–1066* (Oxford, 1981), pp. 191–226, 255–302.

119. Dorothy Whitelock, *Some Anglo-Saxon bishops of London*, the Chambers Memorial lecture 1974 (London, 1975), pp. 22, 26–7, reprinted in *History, law and literature*; Joyce Hill, 'Monastic reform and the secular church', in Carola Hicks (ed.), *England in the eleventh century* (Stamford, 1992), pp. 104–5; O'Donovan, *Charters of Sherborne*, p. xv.

120. James Campbell, 'England, *c.* 991', Janet Cooper (ed.), *The Battle of Maldon: fiction and fact* (London, 1993), pp. 5–9.
121. Wolverhampton's foundation charter (S. 1380), attributed to Archbishop Sigeric, may come from the time of his successor Ælfric.
122. *AS Chron*, 997; S. 838.
123. *GP*, p. 298, *HRH*, p. 102 (Pershore); S. 884 (Malmesbury); Keynes, *Diplomas*, p. 193, note 144 (New Minster); S. 1486 (Stoke-by-Nayland).
124. S. 911; Jonathan Wilcox, *Ælfric's Prefaces* (Durham, 1994), pp. 108, 133. Ælfric's letter is edited by Christopher A. Jones, *Ælfric's letter to the monks of Eynsham* (Cambridge, 1999).
125. Keynes, *Diplomas*, p. 209, and see Chapter 4 below.
126. S. 904 (Wherwell); for Amesbury, see Meyer, 'The queen's "demesne" in later Anglo-Saxon England', pp. 98–9. For the queen's role in the reform movement, see Pauline Stafford, 'Queens, nunneries and reforming churchmen: gender, status and reform in tenth- and eleventh-century England', *P&P*, 163 (1999), pp. 3–35.
127. Keynes, *Diplomas*, p. 199.
128. S. 1487 (Ælhelm *polga*'s will); Andrew Wareham, 'St Oswald's family and kin', in Brooks and Cubitt, *St Oswald*, pp. 47–53 (Æthelstan Mannesune and Ramsey). See also Ann Williams, 'Thegnly piety and ecclesiastical patronage in the late Old English period', *ANS*, 24 (2002), pp. 1–24.
129. John Blair, 'Secular minster churches in Domesday Book', P. H. Sawyer (ed.), *Domesday Book: a reassessment* (London, 1985), p. 120.
130. John Blair, 'Introduction', in John Blair (ed.), *Minsters and parish churches: the local church in transition, 950–1200* (Oxford, 1988), pp. 3–5.
131. Barbara Yorke, *Wessex in the early middle ages* (Leicester, 1995), pp. 231–2.
132. 'It is above all to late Saxon thegns that the building of local churches should be ascribed': John Blair, *Early medieval Surrey* (Stroud, 1991), p. 115. See also W. J. Blair, 'Local churches in Domesday Book and before', J. C. Holt (ed.), *Domesday Studies* (Woodbridge, 1987), pp. 269–71.
133. S. 1501.
134. II Eg 2§1–2.
135. VIII Atr, 5§1.
136. S. 1422; the bequest was made after Ordwulf retired to his monastery at Tavistock. Hrabanus Maurus of Fulda (*c.* 780–856) had been a pupil of Alcuin and became one of the leading figures of the Carolingian renaissance.
137. Wilcox, *Ælfric's Prefaces*, p. 9.
138. Wilcox, *Ælfric's Prefaces*, pp. 131–2. Æthelweard particularly asked for a translation of the *passio* of St Thomas, to whose shrine in India his kinsman King Alfred had sent alms (*AS Chron*, 'C', 983).

139. Ælfric translated the first part of Genesis at Æthelweard's request and it was completed by another (anonymous) translator also writing for the ealdorman; see Mark Griffiths, 'Ælfric's preface to Genesis' *ASE*, 29 (2000), pp. 215–34.
140. Wilcox, *Ælfric's Prefaces*, pp. 14, 55, 124–5. None can be securely identified (Keynes, *Diplomas*, p. 193, note 143).
141. He gives a genealogy of the West Saxon line closer, in its upper reaches, to *Beowulf* than to the exemplar in the oldest text ('A') of the *Anglo-Saxon Chronicle; see* Sam Newton, *The origins of Beowulf and the pre-Viking kingdom of East Anglia* (Woodbridge, 1993), pp. 71–6. See also Bately, *Anglo-Saxon Chronicle, 3 MS A*, p. lxxxii; Campbell, *Æthelweard*, pp. xxvii–xxx; Whitbread, 'Æthelweard and the Anglo-Saxon Chronicle', pp. 587–9; Alfred P. Smyth, *King Alfred the Great* (Oxford, 1995), pp. 475–6; James Campbell, 'England, France, Germany and Flanders', Hill (ed.), *Ethelred the Unready*, p. 257.
142. Simon Keynes, 'England, *c.* 900–1066', *CNMH*, iii, p. 460.
143. Campbell, *Æthelweard*, p. 34. For the date of composition, see note 145 below.
144. Campbell, *Æthelweard*, p. 39 (my italics). Matilda's father was Liudolf, son of Otto I by Eadgyth, daughter of Edward the Elder.
145. Campbell, *Æthelweard*, pp. 1–2; Æthelweard's reference to Count Arnulf II (died 988) gives the *terminus ante quem* for his work, *the terminus post quem* being 978, the accession of Æthelred.
146. William of Malmesbury records the Flemish marriage of Alfred's daughter and names her sons, but mentions no daughters. Presumably he was dependent upon Æthelweard, but he gives Ælfthryth's name incorrectly as *Ethelswida* (Æthelswith) and on one occasion makes her father Edward the Elder, not Alfred (*WmM*, i, 194–5, 218–9).
147. Brooks, 'The career of St Dunstan', Ramsay et al., *St Dunstan*, p. 16. A letter from Count Arnulf to Dunstan was preserved at Canterbury (*Mem. St Dunstan*, pp. 359–61) but there is some dispute as to whether the author was Arnulf I (Brooks, 'The career of St Dunstan', p. 16, Stubbs, *Mem. St Dunstan*, p. 359, note 2) or, as argued by Elisabeth van Houts, 'Women and the writing of history in the early middle ages: the case of Abbess Matilda of Essen and Æthelweard', *Early Medieval. Europe*, 1 (1992), pp. 66–7, his grandson and successor Arnulf II.
148. The other pre-Conquest examples from England were commissioned abroad: A. Campbell (ed.), *Encomium Emmae Reginae*, Camden Classic Reprints, 4 (Cambridge, 1998); F. Barlow (ed.), *The Life of King Edward who rests at Westminster* (2nd edn; Oxford, 1992).

149. Van Houts, 'Women and the writing of history in the early middle ages', pp. 61–4.
150. William of Malmesbury names her variously as Ealdgyth (*Aldgitha*) and Ælfgifu (*Elfgiva*) (*WmM*, i, pp. 170–1, 198–9); on her second appearance, it is she who is (erroneously) wed to Otto and Eadgyth who is given to 'a certain duke near the Alps' (*cuidam duci iuxta Alpes*). She may be a doublet of Eadgifu (*Edgiva*) who (according to William) married Louis of Aquitaine, i.e. the brother of Rudolf II, king of Upper Burgundy (*WmM*, i, pp. 200–1; ii, p. 109).
151. *AS Chron*, 'C', 982. Otto II's expedition is presented as a victory for the Saxons, though in fact it was a disastrous defeat (Whitbread, 'Æthelweard and the Anglo-Saxon Chronicle', p. 578; Leyser, 'The Ottonians and Wessex', p. 98).
152. A bishop of Dorchester and an abbot of Ramsey were killed at *Assandun* in 1016 (*AS Chron*, 'CDE', 1016).
153. Whitelock et al., *Councils and synods*, p. 252.
154. Roger Fowler (ed.), *Wulfstan's Canons of Edgar* (London, 1972), chapter 46, pp. 10–11. The *Canons of Edgar* dates from the period 1005 x 1007 (Fowler, *Wulfstan's Canons of Edgar*, p. xxviii), and Ælfric's letter to Wulfstan from 1002 x 1005.
155. Skeat, *Lives of the Saints*, ii, pp. 120–2.
156. See further Chapter 4 below (for the ecclesiastical shipsokes).
157. Timothy Powell, 'The "Three Orders" of society in Anglo-Saxon England', *ASE*, 23 (1994), pp. 123–9, quotation on p. 128.
158. *LE*, p. 136. In the reign of Edward the Confessor, Leofsige, bishop of Hereford, led his men in arms against the Welsh, though this was not considered correct behaviour (*AS Chron*, 'C, D', 1056).
159. S. 1422, *EHD*, i, no. 122; the word translated 'oarport' is *ha*, for the significance of which see Appendix below. Karl Leyser remarked upon 'the extraordinary store of weapons which the prelate owned' :'The Anglo-Saxons "At Home"', Reuter (ed.), *Communications and power*, p. 107.
160. S. 1408, *EHD*, i, no. 126. He also left ships to the people of Kent, and the people of Wiltshire (see note 113 above); see also the warship bequeathed to Ramsey abbey (note 128 above). For the significance of these bequests, see Chapter 4 below.

Notes to Chapter 3: The Great Terror

1. S. 134, dated 792.
2. *AS Chron*, 'C', 980, 981; 'CDE', 988.

3. *AS Chron*, 'CDE' 980, 'C', 982; Simon Keynes, 'The historical context of the battle of Maldon', Donald Scragg (ed.), *The Battle of Maldon, AD 991* (Oxford, 1991), pp. 85–6.
4. *Mem. St Dunstan*, pp. 387–8; *WmM*, i, pp. 276–9; *EHD*, i no. 230. 'Enemies' might be disaffected persons from either country being sheltered in the other; compare Charlemagne's letter to Offa concerning the Mercian exiles whom he harboured 'for the sake of reconciliation, not from enmity' (*EHD*, i, no. 196). In the eleventh century, the counts of Flanders regularly sheltered exiled opponents of the English kings (Philip Grierson, 'The relations between England and Flanders before the Norman Conquest', *TRHS*, 4th series, 23 (1941), pp. 71–113).
5. The date is fixed by Byrhtnoth's obit, kept at Ely on 10 August and at Ramsey and Winchester on 11 August (Alan Kennedy, 'Byrhtnoth's obits and twelfth-century accounts of the battle of Maldon', Scragg, *The Battle of Maldon*, pp. 59–62).
6. *AS Chron*, 'CDE', 991, 'A', 993. 'A' seems to have conflated the events of more than one year (see note 17 below); see Janet M. Bately, 'The *Anglo-Saxon Chronicle*', in Scragg, *The Battle of Maldon*, pp. 37–50.
7. George and Susan Pretty, 'A geological reconstruction of the site of the battle of Maldon', Scragg, *The Battle of Maldon*, pp. 159–69. The topography of the site was very different in the tenth century from what it is today.
8. The standard edition of the poem is D. G. Scragg (ed.), *The Battle of Maldon* (Manchester, 1981); see also D. G. Scragg, '*The Battle of Maldon*', in Scragg, *The Battle of Maldon*, pp. 1–36.
9. There is a very extensive literature on the poem; see, in particular, the papers collected in Scragg, *The Battle of Maldon*, and in Cooper, *The Battle of Maldon*, both derived from celebratory conferences held in the battle's millenial year. See also Ann Williams, 'The battle of Maldon and *The Battle of Maldon*: history, poetry and propaganda', *Medieval History*, 2, no. 2 (1992), pp. 35–44.
10. Byrhtferth's account of the event is no more historically reliable than the Old English poem; see Michael Lapidge, 'The *Life of St Oswald*', in Scragg, *The Battle of Maldon*, pp. 51–8; idem, 'Byrhtferth and Oswald', in Brooks and Cubitt, *St Oswald*, pp. 73–8. For the tapestry, see *LE*, p. 136; Mildred Budny, 'The Byrhtnoth tapestry or embroidery', in Scragg, *The Battle of Maldon*, pp. 263–78.
11. My reasons for avoiding the anachronistic term 'Danegeld' are explained in the Appendix (below).
12. Wilcox (ed.), *Ælfric's Prefaces*, pp. 111, 128; for the date, see Keynes, 'The historical context', p. 90.

13. For the *Chronicle*'s strictures on Ealdorman Ælfric, see below.
14. *AS Chron*, 'CDE', 993. The leaders can be identified as Fræna of Rockingham, Northamptonshire, who also held land in Leicestershire, and who attested royal diplomas and private memoranda until 1004 (*ECNENM*, p. 335; Freeman, *NC*, i, pp. 624–5); Frithugist son of Cate, a Lincolnshire landholder and benefactor (like Fræna) of Peterborough Abbey (*ECEE*, p. 244); and Godwine son of Ealdorman Ælfheah of Hampshire (Williams, '*Princeps Merciorum gentis*', pp. 170–2; see also Chapter 6 below).
15. The author of the narrative underlying the main *Chronicle* text for Æthelred's reign was perhaps a Londoner (see note 39 below).
16. *AS Chron*, 'CDE', 994.
17. *AS Chron*, 'A', 993; Bately, 'The *Anglo-Saxon Chronicle 3: MS A*', pp. 42–7.
18. S. 939, *EHD*, i, no. 121; P. H. Sawyer, 'The Scandinavian background', Cooper, *The Battle of Maldon*, pp. 41–2. For the date of Sigeric's death, see note 31 below.
19. Niels Lund, 'The Danish perspective', Scragg, *The Battle of Maldon*, p. 133.
20. For Denmark in this period, see Niels Lund, '"Denemearc", "tanmarkar but" and "tanmarkar ala"', Wood and Lund, *People and places in northern Europe*, pp. 161–9; idem, 'Cnut's Danish kingdom', Rumble, *The reign of Cnut*, pp. 27–42; P. H. Sawyer, 'Cnut's Scandinavian Empire', Rumble, *The reign of Cnut*, pp. 10–22; idem, 'The Scandinavian background', Cooper, *The Battle of Maldon*, pp. 37–42.
21. Simon Keynes, 'A tale of two kings: Alfred the Great and Æthelred the Unready', *TRHS*, 5th series, 36 (1986), pp. 195–217.
22. *AS Chron*, 'CDE', 1000.
23. *EHD*, i, no. 239G; compare the *Anglo-Saxon Chronicle* ('D', 'E') for 975: 'nor was there fleet so proud nor host so strong that it got itself prey in England while that noble king held the throne'.
24. *AS Chron*, 'A', 993, 'CDE', 991; this is presumably why Sigeric acquired the posthumous byname *Danegeld*. A post-Conquest addition to the 'A' text associates Bishop Ælfheah of Winchester with the decision.
25. II Atr, 1; *EHD*, i, no. 42; Keynes, 'The historical context', pp. 104–5.
26. S. 882, dated 994, *EHD*, i, no. 118. The sum received was £90 in silver, and 200 mancuses of gold (6,000 pennies or £25). The diploma mentions 'the money which had been promised to them [the Vikings] by Archbishop Sigeric', presumably meaning the *gafol* in II Atr, 1.
27. See Byrhtnoth's reply to the Viking demand for *gafol* (tribute), in the poem on the battle of Maldon: 'we will give you spears for tribute, the poisoned point and the old sword, such heriot as will not avail you in battle': D. G. Scragg (ed.), *The Battle of Maldon* (Manchester, 1981), lines 46–8.

28. II Æthelred, Keynes, 'The historical context', pp. 103–7 and notes 72–8, pp. 112–3.
29. Freeman, *NC*, i, p. 629. Employing Viking mercenaries was not new; writing in 978–88 (before the 994 treaty) Æthelweard says that since the battle of Brunanburh (937) 'no fleet has remained here, having advanced against these shores, *except under treaty with the English*' (Campbell, *Æthelweard*, p. 54, my italics).
30. John of Worcester (*JnW*, ii, pp. 438–9) makes Jósteinn and Guthmund Steita's son the leaders at Maldon in 991, but could have been drawing on the text of the treaty (Keynes, 'The historical context', p. 90; Kennedy, 'Byrhtnoth's obits', p. 71).
31. The meeting probably post-dates the death of Sigeric on 28 October 994 (Keynes, 'The historical context', p. 103).
32. T. M. Andersson, 'The Viking policy of Ethelred the Unready', *Scandinavian Studies*, 59 (1987), pp. 284–95.
33. Lund, 'Cnut's Danish kingdom', p. 27. Erik became earl of Northumbria and Hákon, his son by Gytha (b. 998), earl of Worcestershire (Williams, 'Cockles amongst the wheat', pp. 2, 6–7).
34. The Welsh annals for 995 record an attack on the Isle of Man by Swein Harald's son, see *AC* (B), 995; *ByT* (Red Book), 995; *ByT* (Peniarth 20), 994=995. This Swein might or might not be identical with Swein Forkbeard, son of Harald Bluetooth; see Eric Christianson (ed.), *Saxo Grammaticus Gesta Danorum, Books X-XVI*, i, BAR International series, 84 (1980), note 64 p. 179; Keynes, 'The historical context', p. 92. Swein Forkbeard was in Scandinavia in or soon after 995, when he married the widow of Erik, king of the *Svear*; she was a daughter of Mieszko, duke of the Poles (Lund, 'Cnut's Danish kingdom', p. 28 and see Chapter 7 below).
35. For the possibility of a raid near Chester-le-Street in 995, see Chapter 4 below.
36. The statement (sub anno 997) that the *here* 'went round Devon into the mouth of the Severn' suggests that its starting-point was somewhere on the south coast; the Vikings had been given winter quarters in Southampton in 994.
37. Michael Dolley, 'An introduction to the coinage of Æthelræd II', Hill, *Ethelred the Unready*, p. 119.
38. It is difficult not to see a direct link between this passage and the encomium on Edgar in the 'D' and 'E' texts for 975: 'nor was there fleet so proud nor host so strong that got itself prey in England while that noble king held the throne'.
39. Keynes, 'The declining reputation of King Æthelred the Unready', pp. 229–32.

40. S. 891.
41. For the date, see Chapter 1, note 62 above.
42. Ælfthryth may not have died until 17 November 1001 (Chapter 2, note 54 above).
43. The obits of Æthelweard and his companions are commemmorated in a Winchester calendar, which also names the brothers Wulfnoth and Æthelwine (Dickins, 'The day of the battle of Æthelingadene (ASC 1001 A)', pp. 25–7).
44. For the *lið*, see Niels Lund, 'The armies of Swein Forkbeard and Cnut: *leding* or *lið*?', *ASE*, 15 (1986), pp. 105–18.
45. Eadsige may be the reeve who received land in Devon in 1005 (see note 123 below), but the name is not uncommon.
46. Sighvatr, *Víkingavísur*, stanza 7 (translated in *EHD*, i, no. 12; see further below, Chapter 5); compare the *Chronicle*'s description of Normandy as 'Richard's land' (*AS Chron*, 1000). *Liðsmannaflokkr*, see R. G. Poole, *Viking poems on war and peace* (Toronto, Buffalo and London, 1991), pp. 88, 113–5, and Chapter 7 below. Ulfcytel's posthumous reputation is discussed by Freeman, *NC*, i, pp. 639–40.
47. See Chapter 2, note 46 above. Ælfric was not the only one accused of treasonous dealings with the Danes in these years; see the case of the Essex thegn, Æthelric of Bocking (above, note 18).
48. *AS Chron*, 1016; Ulfcytel was killed in the same battle, and another casualty was Godwine, one of those accused of starting the flight in 993 (see above, note 14).
49. S. 909, *EHD*, i, no. 127. The diploma seems to have been known to William of Malmesbury (*GP*, pp. 315–6; Preest, *William of Malmesbury*, p. 212), but he connects the minster's destruction with the murder of Sigeferth and Morcar in 1015 rather than the massacre of 1002 (*WmM*, i, pp. 310–11). See also Keynes, 'Declining reputation', p. 238, and note 57 below.
50. For the assimilation of Danes and English in the eastern shires, see Cecily Clark, 'On dating *The Battle of Maldon*: certain evidence reviewed', *Nottingham Medieval Studies*, 27 (1983), pp. 1–22, reprinted in Peter Jackson (ed.), *Words. Names and History: selected writings of Cecily Clark* (Woodbridge, 1995), pp. 20–36.
51. For the possibility of a Danish garrison in Oxford, though under Cnut rather than Æthelred, see John Blair, *Anglo-Saxon Oxfordshire* (Stroud, 1994), pp. 161, 170. Henry of Huntingdon, who may have had access to local traditions, implies that the massacre was confined to towns (see note 52 below).
52. *HH*, pp. 340–1.

53. Freeman, *NC*, i, pp. 634–8. It is hard to disagree with Freeman's conclusion that the St Brice's Day material is 'a good case of the growth of legend' in which 'the massacre of St Brice got mixed up with quite different stories belonging to quite different dates'.
54. *WmJ*, ii, pp. 14–7, and see note 63 below. John of Worcester also alleges that women as well as men were slaughtered (*JnW*, ii, pp. 452–3).
55. *WmM*, i, pp. 300–1.
56. Christianson, *Saxo Grammaticus*, p. 183, note 77. L. M. Larson, *Canute the Great* (New York and London, 1912), pp. 15, 39–40, accepted the historicity of both ladies.
57. William refers to a massacre of Danes in a passage listing Æthelred's numerous crimes, but gives neither date nor context (*WmM*, i, pp. 276–7).
58. Mary Clayton, 'Of mice and men: Ælfric's second homily for the feast of a confessor', *Leeds Studies in English*, ns, 24 (1993), p. 21. The homily which received the addition is no. 28 in the second series of *Catholic Homilies.*
59. *AS Chron*, 'CDE', 1002.
60. S. 943.
61. *AS Chron*, 'CDE', 1002; the bride is called *seo hlafdige*, the normal title for a queen, and attests S. 909 (1004) as *regina.*
62. Stafford, *Emma and Edith*, p. 220.
63. *WmJ*, ii, pp. 14–17.
64. Marie Fauroux, *Recueil des actes des ducs de Normandie (911–1066)* (Caen, 1961), p. 23 and note 22; David Bates, *Normandy before 1066* (London, 1982), p. 36. If Duke Richard was in negotiation with Swein in 1003, he was clearly playing a double game.
65. *WmJ*, pp. 10–13; Fauroux, *Recueil des actes des ducs de Normandie*, p. 60, note 255. The English invasion is placed (implicitly) after the marriage of Æthelgifu and Emma (spring 1002) and before the massacre of St Brice's Day (13 November 1002) and Professor Stafford has suggested that the Cotentin lands were Emma's dowry from her brother (*Emma and Edith*, p. 218). It is possible, however, that the marriage of Æthelred is mentioned only in the way that later writers accord titles to their subjects even when recording events which occurred before those titles were acquired; if so the invasion might be earlier than 1002. William's reference to the equipment of the English *milites*, however, invites comparison with Æthelred's edict of 1008 (see Chapter 4 below).
66. Keynes, 'The historical context', pp. 94–5. For a more positive view of the evidence, see Campbell, 'England, France, Flanders and Normandy', pp. 198–203.
67. David Hill, 'Trends in the development of towns in the reign of Æthelred',

Hill, *Ethelred the Unready*, p. 223; Jeremy Haslam, 'The towns of Wiltshire', Jeremy Haslam (ed.), *Anglo-Saxon towns in southern England* (Chichester, 1984), pp. 122–8, especially p. 124. For Shaftesbury's refuge at Bradford-on-Avon, see Chapter 1 above.

68. D. M. Metcalf, 'The ranking of the boroughs: numismatic evidence for the reign of Æthelræd II', Hill, *Ethelred the Unready*', p. 180. This was to change in the last decade of Æthelred's reign; the tribute of 1007 may have amounted to 'a half to two-thirds of the country's monetary wealth' (ibid, p. 181).
69. Keynes, *Diplomas*, p. 193; Wormald, *MEL*, pp. 442–3 and table 6: 1, p. 431.
70. S. 891; Wormald, *MEL*, pp. 320–3.
71. I Atr 1§2; III Atr 4. The *Bromdun* assembly may have been as early as 984 (Wormald, 'Æthelred the lawmaker', Hill, *Ethelred the Unready*, pp. 62–3, but see idem, *MEL*, p. 328 note 296).
72. III Atr 16, apparently citing IV Atr 5§6; S. 876.
73. Wormald, *MEL*, pp. 321–2, 324–6.
74. Wormald, *MEL*, p. 328. See also H. Richardson and G. O. Sayles, *Law and legislation from Æthelberht to Magna Carta* (Edinburgh, 1966), pp. 25–6: 'as mere exercises in legislative drafting, nothing so competent had been known in England, nor was to be known until the thirteenth century'. This judgement extends to the appendix to the 994 treaty (II Æthelred), but this may be a fragment of Edgar's legislation rather than Æthelred's (Wormald, *MEL*, pp. 321, 369–70).
75. *Ælc freoman getreowne borh hæbbe, þæt se borh him to ælcon rihte gehelde gyf he betyhtlad wyrðe* (I Atr 1, translated Wormald, *MEL* p. 324); III Eg 6: *finde him ælc man þæt he borh hæbbe & se borh hine to ælcon rihte gelæde & gehealde*: 'And each man is to provide himself with a surety, and the surety is to produce and hold him to every legal duty' (translated *EHD*, i, no. 40).
76. Wormald, 'Æthelred the lawmaker', p. 36; IV Eg 2§2–6§2. For the date of the *Wihtbordesstan* code, see idem, *MEL*, pp. 378–9, 441–2.
77. Wormald, *MEL*, p. 328.
78. J Goebel, *Felony and misdemeanour* (University of Pennsylvania, 1976),pp. 339–61; Patrick Wormald, 'Lordship and justice in the early English kingdom', *Legal culture in the early medieval West* (London, 1999), pp. 313–32. The earliest references to 'private' courts in England (that is, courts held by lords for their own men) date from after the Norman Conquest.
79. II Ed 6; Roberta V. Coleman, 'Domestic peace and public order in Anglo-Saxon law', J. Douglas Woods and David A. E. Pelteret (ed.), *The*

Anglo-Saxons: synthesis and achievement, (Waterloo, Ontario, 1985), pp. 49–61.

80. IV Atr 4–4§2 claims a 30s. fine for *hamsocn*, assault on the king's highway and resort to premature violence, 'if the king will grant us [the Londoners] this concession'; see Wormald, 'Æthelred the lawmaker', pp. 65–6. For the significance of the kings' reservation of these offences to themselves, see Paul Brand, 'Feud and the state in late Anglo-Saxon England', *Journal of. British Studies*, 40 (2001), pp. 1–43, at 17–20.
81. II Cn 12, *EHD*, i, no. 50; the list includes 'only those pleas that might potentially be alienated to favourite beneficiaries, not the larger and more important matters that might *not*' (Wormald, *MEL*, p. 364, author's italics). For the application of the law on *hamsocn* and *flymena fyrmðe*, see the case of Ealdorman Leofsige and his sister Æthelflæd below.
82. Wormald, *MEL*, pp. 326, 328–9.
83. David Roffe, 'The origins of Derbyshire', *Derbyshire Archaeological Journal*, 106 (1986), pp. 102–22, quotation on p. 103.
84. S. 984, 1606, both dated 942; Sawyer, *Charters of Burton*, nos 6–7.
85. IV Eg 2a§2.
86. III Atr 1.
87. Compare III Atr 3§4–4§2 with I Atr 1§4–6; see also III Atr 8, IV Atr 5–5§3. For Æthelred's policy towards the Scandinavian territories, see Wormald, *MEL*, pp. 328–9; Niels Lund, 'King Edgar and the Danelaw', *Medieval Scandinavia*, 9 (1976), pp. 185–95, especially pp. 192–4 ; and for a contrary opinion, Stenton, *ASE*, pp. 508–12; Keynes, *Diplomas*, p. 197, note 159.
88. Wormald, *MEL*, pp. 329, 444 note 99; idem, 'Æthelred the lawmaker', pp. 61–2.
89. I Atr, Prologue, II Atr, 1§1–2; see also Ælfric's use of *engla land* in his life of St Alban (Skeat, *Lives of the Saints*, i, pp. 414–5). In subsequent codes of Æthelred and Cnut, 'English law' is paired with 'Danish law' (Wormald, *MEL*, p. 328 and note 300). See further P. Wormald, '*Engla Lond*: the making of an allegiance', *Journal of. Historical Sociology*, 7 (1994), pp. 1–24.
90. Wormald, *MEL*, p. 329; see also pp. 322–3, 326–7; idem, 'Æthelred the lawmaker', pp. 61–2.
91. Wormald, *MEL*, pp. 322, 371; Richardson and Sayles, *Law and legislation*, p. 28; David Roffe, *Domesday: the Inquest and the Book* (Oxford, 2000), p. 64.
92. IV Atr 5–9§3.
93. Mark Richardson, 'Æthelred's coinage and the payment of tribute', in Scragg, *The Battle of Maldon*, p. 164.
94. IV Atr 5–9§3.

95. III Eg 8; Wormald, *MEL*, pp. 313–6; R. H. M. Dolley and D. M. Metcalf, 'The reform of the English coinage under Eadgar', R. H. M. Dolley (ed.), *Anglo-Saxon coins* (London, 1961), pp. 136–68. See also John D. Brand, *Periodic change of type in the Anglo-Saxon and Norman periods*, (privately printed, Rochester, 1984).
96. The dies for Edgar's reform issue apparently emanate from a single centre, but a series of regional centres could also be used, as they were in the middle years of Æthelred's reign. It was control of the main design features that was crucial.
97. Michael Dolley, 'An introduction to the coinage of Æthelræd II', Hill, *Ethelred the Unready*, pp. 118–29. The sequence is well-established but the precise chronology has been subject to discussion; see C. S. S. Lyon, 'Some problems in interpreting Anglo-Saxon coinage', *ASE*, 5 (1976), pp. 196–7; Blackburn, 'Æthelred's coinage', pp. 161–2.
98. Dolley, 'An introduction to the coinage of Æthelræd II', pp. 124–5.
99. *Mem. St Dunstan*, p. 355; Wormald, *MEL*, pp. 447–8.
100. Stenton, *ASE*, pp. 394–5; Whitelock, *EHD*, i, pp. 47, 575.
101. Wormald, *MEL*, p. 149; Keynes, 'Crime and punishment', p. 81.
102. Keynes, 'Crime and punishment', p. 76; idem, *Diplomas*, pp. 95–7.
103. S. 877, 886 (vernacular); S. 883, 893, 896, 926 (Latin).
104. Wormald, *MEL*, p. 149.
105. Wormald, 'A hand-list of Anglo-Saxon lawsuits', nos 44–76; 81.
106. Wormald, 'A hand-list of Anglo-Saxon lawsuits', pp. 261–2, 279; S. 362, dated 901; Keynes, 'Crime and punishment', pp. 69–73.
107. S. 881, 891.
108. *LE*, p. 135; S. 916, 926. Æthelflæd may be the lady who bequeathed land at Laver, Essex, and Cockhampstead, Hertfordshire, to St Paul's, London (S. 1495); see C. R. Hart, 'The ealdordom of Essex', *The Danelaw* (London, 1992), p. 136. If this is the case, however, her will cannot have been allowed to stand (Keynes, 'Crime and punishment', p. 80, note 83). Æthelred's diploma confirming her bequest is a forgery (S. 908, dated 1004 x 1014) and St Paul's had no land in either place in 1066 (*LDB*, fos 30v, 31, 91; *GDB*, fo. 137v).
109. S. 1497; Hart, 'The ealdordom of Essex', pp. 136–8; Stafford, *Emma and Edith*, pp. 218–9.
110. For the date, see Chapter 2, note 56 above. Had the ealdorman been related to the testatrix, one would expect a bequest to his sister Æthelflæd (Whitelock, *Will of Æthelgifu*, pp. 22–7).
111. S. 926, Stenton, *Latin charters*, p. 79, note 2. Keynes describes *satrap* as 'a word used in glossaries as a lemma for *þegn*' (*Diplomas*, note 141, p. 192).

112. Hart ('The ealdordom of Essex', p. 137) notes that Æthelgifu's kinsman received land at Tewin, Hertfordshire, where an estate disposed of by the ætheling Æthelstan lay (S. 1497, 1503) and suggests that this estate was forfeited by the ealdorman and acquired by his former lord. However, there were two estates at Tewin (*GDB*, fos 135, 141–141v), so that 'one cannot be sure the same piece of land is in question in the two wills' (Whitelock, *Will of Æthelgifu*, p. 24). Both the ealdorman and the ætheling held estates called Norton, but the Norton of the ætheling's will (bequeathed to his father) cannot be Norton, Hertfordshire, forfeited by Ealdorman Leofsige, for that had been given to St Albans before 1006 (S. 916), and was still in the abbey's possession in 1066 (*GDB* fo. 135v).

113. S. 883 (995).

114. Hart, 'The ealdordom of Essex', p. 136; for the ealdordom of south-east Mercia, whose last recorded holder, Æthelstan *rota*, died in 970, see Williams, '*Princeps Merciorum gentis*', pp. 146–7, 158. When a Warwickshire thegn forfeited his lands for 'unlawful killing' (*unrihtum manslihte*), they went to Leofwine, ealdorman of the Hwiccian provinces, which included Warwickshire (S. 892, dated 998); perhaps Leofsige felt that he, rather than the reeve of Oxford, should have received the forfeited land at Ardley. In a similar case of manslaughter, Osgot of Castor, Northamptonshire, redeemed himself by giving his land to Abbot Ealdulf of Peterborough (Robertson, *Charters*, no. 40, pp. 76–9).

115. I Atr, 1§8, 12–13.

116. *AS Chron*, 1002; S. 926.

117. II Em, 6.

118. Stenton, *Latin charters*, pp. 70–81: 'the offences ... are covered by a Latin veil but their nature and consequences are shown for the first time in relation to an actual case'.

119. In the 980s, the widow of the Kentish thegn, Wulfbald, 'went, with her child, and killed the king's thegn Eadmær, the son of Wulfbald's father's brother, and fifteen of his companions, on the estate at Brabourne (Kent), which Wulfbald had held by robbery in the king's despite' (S. 877, *EHD*, i, no. 120; Keynes, 'Crime and punishment', pp. 78–9).

120. Hart ('The ealdordom of Essex', p. 137) suggests that Leofsige became æthelings' seneschal in succession to the Æfic recorded in 990–92, and that this Æfic was identical with the high-reeve murdered in 1002. Even if this was so (and it depends in part on the identity of the ealdorman and the kinsman of Æthelgifu, which is by no means certain), it takes us no closer to the cause of the dispute. Professor Stafford suggests a

connection with the king's marriage to Emma in the same year (*Emma and Edith*, pp. 218–9).

121. The royal favourite, Æthelsige, was exiled for killing a king's reeve (see Chapter 2 above).

122. S. 926, 883. Before his disgrace in 993, Ealdorman Ælfric's son, Ælfgar the reeve, was also *praetiosus* (S. 918).

123. S. 905, 910, 915 (Keynes, *Diplomas*, p. 183, note 110). S. 910 describes Eadsige as *minister* but in the endorsement he is *gerefa* (Keynes, *Diplomas*, p. 160, note 161); he may be the king's reeve of Pinhoe recorded in 1001 (*AS Chron*, 'A). For Æthelred the port-reeve, see note 127 below.

124. Hl, 16.

125. S. 155, *EHD*, i, no. 80 and notes; *AS Chron*, 896.

126. IV Atr, 3; 7§3.

127. S. 1215, 1654, 1456, 925. Brunmann was probably portreeve of Fordwich and Æthelred may be the *fidelis homo* who received land in Canterbury for the lives of himself and his wife in 1002 (see note 123 above). Ælfweard, the king's reeve captured by the Danes at Canterbury in 1011, may have been portreeve (*AS Chron*, 1011).

128. III Em, 5. The lords of Bamburgh also used the title *heah-gerefa*, though by Æthelred's time they were regularly styled ealdorman (*dux*), but the title is probably the equivalent of the Scots *mormaer*, 'great steward', see Alfred P. Smyth, *Warlords and Holy Men: Scotland, AD 80–1000* (London, 1984), pp. 235–6. In the north, the high-reeve ranked midway between the ealdorman and the thegn, and was equivalent to the *hold* (*Norðleoda laga*, §4, *EHD* i, no. 52B; Wormald, *MEL*, pp. 392–3).

129. III Atr, 1§1; *AS Chron*, 'A', 1001. See also Ordwulf *primas Dumnoniae* (Chapter 2, note 63 above).

130. S. 1455–56, Robertson, *Charters*, nos 41, 69; Archbishop Wulfstan forbade priests to act as reeves (Fowler, *Wulfstan's Canons of Edgar*, p. 25). Ælfgar son of Ealdorman Ælfric many have been sheriff of Berkshire at about the same time (see Chapter 2 above).

131. See Chapter 4 below.

132. Blair, *Anglo-Saxon Oxfordshire*, pp. 103–4. Later sheriffs also took the name of their shire-towns as bynames (Campbell, 'Some agents and agencies of the late Anglo-Saxon state', p. 210).

133. I Eg (the Hundred Ordinance, see Wormald, *MEL*, pp. 378–9); III Eg 5§1–2. Of the thirty-six recorded legal cases in which a shire-court was involved, none are earlier than Alfred's reign, and 'the clearest examples post-date the accession of Edgar' (Wormald, *MEL*, p. 152).

134. S. 1454, Robertson, *Charters*, no. 66.

135. S. 1503. In 1014, King Æthelred sent his son Edward and his messengers (*ærendwrecan*) to communicate with the English magnates, but it is not clear from the context whether the message was delivered orally or in written form (*AS Chron*, 1014, and see Chapter 6 below).
136. S. 1456, Robertson, *Charters*, no. 69. Two surviving writs are attributed to Æthelred, both of dubious authenticity (S. 945–6).
137. Ælfwine Ælfric's son was killed in the following of Byrhtnoth of Essex at Maldon (Scragg, *The Battle of Maldon*, lines 209–29). For the 'insignificant careers' of Ealdorman Æthelwine's sons, see Hart, 'Athelstan "Half-king"', pp. 157–8; Æthelweard was killed at *Assandun* (*AS Chron*, 1016) and there is nothing beyond the coincidence of a (common) name to connect Leofwine with the ealdorman of the Hwicce. For the sons of Æthelmær and Thored, see Chapter 2 above.
138. Keynes, *Diplomas*, p. 197, note 133. See the language used in S. 926 of Leofsige, 'whom I raised from the rank of thegn and promoted to the summit of a higher dignity by appointing him an ealdorman' (*quem de satrapis nomine tuli ad celsioris dignitatis dignum duxi promouere ducem constituendo*).
139. Æthelmær is called ealdorman in the will of Ælfflæd (1000 x 1002) but the title may be a later addition (S. 1486, Keynes, *Diplomas*, p. 210 and note 203). Æthelweard does not attest the agreement on Æthelric of Bocking's will (see note 18 above), but since it can be dated no more closely than 995 x 999, its failure to give any title to Æthelmær is inconclusive.
140. S. 891. Hart ('The ealdordom of Essex', p. 136) adds Bedfordshire, Cambridgeshire, East Anglia, Hertfordshire and Huntingdonshire to Leofsige's *scir*, but the evidence is slight.
141. *AS Chron*, 1016; Keynes, *Diplomas*, p. 208 and note 199.
142. Stafford, 'The reign of Æthelred II', p. 29: 'Æthelred was … continuing developments (too incoherent to be called policies) of the second half of the tenth century'.

Notes to Chapter 4: A Change of Direction

1. *The Institutes of Polity*, translated in Swanton, *Anglo-Saxon Prose*, p. 126.
2. For Æthelweard's death, see Keynes, *Diplomas*, pp. 192 note 139, 209; the Ealdorman Æthelweard who, with his wife Æthelflæd, freed a slave at St Petroc's altar in the time of Bishop Burhwold (1011 x 1012–1019 x 1027) is Æthelmær's son-in-law (Haddan and Stubbs, *Councils*, i, pp. 678–9 and see Chap 2 above). For Wulfric, see Sawyer, *Charters of Burton*, pp. xxxix–xl. There are no diplomas for 1003.

3. S. 1492 and see Chapter 2 above.
4. S. 911; Yorke, 'Æthelmær: the foundation of the abbey of Cerne and the politics of the tenth century', p. 20; Malcolm Godden, 'Apocalypse and invasion in late Anglo-Saxon England', M. Godden, D. Gray and T. Hoad (ed.), *From Anglo-Saxon to Middle English: studies presented to E. G. Stanley* (Oxford, 1994), pp. 131–2, 142.
5. Clayton, 'Of mice and men: Ælfric's second homily for the feast of a confessor', pp. 19–20.
6. 'The ruler's duty [is] to protect his people against an attacking army, to govern them justly and to listen to his counsellors'; see John C. Pope, *The homilies of Ælfric: a supplementary collection*, EETS, os 259–60 (London, 1967–8), i, pp. 372–5, 380–1 (the homily for the Sunday after Ascension Day).
7. John of Worcester is the only source to make Ufegeat a son of Ælfhelm, but this is plausible enough; he occurs elsewhere only in Wulfric's will (*JnW*, ii, pp. 458–9; S.1536).
8. S. 918 (see Keynes, *Diplomas*, pp. 183 and note 110, 210–11). John of Worcester (ii, pp. 456–7) says that Wulfgeat forfeited his lands 'because of the unjust judgements and arrogant deeds he had perpetrated', which gets us no further.
9. Keynes, *Diplomas*, p. 213; see also Charles Insley, 'Politics, conflict and kinship in early eleventh-century Mercia', *Midland History*, 26 (2001), pp. 28–42 (I am indebted to Dr Insley for a copy of this paper).
10. *AS Chron*, 1007.
11. *AS Chron*, 1009, 1015, 1016. For Eadric's posthumous reputation, see Freeman, *NC*, i, pp. 413–15; Keynes, 'A tale of two kings', pp. 213–17. It may be significant that Ælfric's veiled attack on his patron's enemies (see note 5 above) consists of a catalogue of examples of divine justice visited upon treachery and deceit.
12. Hemming, i, pp. 280–1. Eadric's byname is recorded, with the same gloss, by Orderic Vitalis, and (without the gloss) by John of Worcester (*OV*, ii, pp. 194–5; *JnW*, ii, pp. 456–7).
13. *JnW*, ii, pp. 460–1.
14. It is unlikely that this Æthelmær was, as John claims, the grandfather of Earl Godwine of Wessex, since he would have been too young to be the grandfather of a man who was an ealdorman by 1018, and probably of full age by 1014 (Freeman, *NC*, i, p. 701 and Chapter 6 below).
15. Keynes, *Diplomas*, pp. 212–13; for Brihtric, who attests 997–1009, see *AS Chron*, 1009.
16. *JnW*, iii, pp. 4–5, 14–15, 20–1; see also *OV*, ii, pp. 194–5. For the more

extravagant tales, see M. R. James (trans.), *Walter Map, De Nugis Curialium*, Cymmrodorion Record Series, no. 9 (London, 1923), pp. 82–4, 91–2.

17. *AS Chron*, 1016. For Eadric the Wild, see Williams, *The English and the Norman Conquest*, pp. 91–3; C. P. Lewis, 'An introduction to the Shropshire Domesday', in Ann Williams and R. W. H. Erskine (ed.), *The Shropshire Domesday* (London, 1988), p. 20.
18. Eadric the Wild belongs to the same generation as Siward son of Æthelgar, Eadric *streona*'s grandson (see note 53 below).
19. C. E. Wright, *The cultivation of saga in Anglo-Saxon England* (Edinburgh, 1939), pp. 178–212.
20. Williams, *The English and the Norman Conquest*, pp. 91–3. For the military service of the bishop of Worcester, see below.
21. *OV*, ii, pp. 194–5, iii, pp. 6–7, 142–3. For Siward son of Æthelgar, see note 53 below.
22. *JnW*, ii, pp. 456–7.
23. Wright, *Cultivation of saga*, p. 143.
24. *AS Chron*, 1006, 1016.
25. Keynes, *Diplomas*, table 8.
26. S. 407, 425, 428 (attested by Osulf as *dux*), S. 420 (as high-reeve) and S. 544 (as high-reeve of Bamburgh); see also Smyth, *Warlords and Holy Men*, pp. 195–200, 232–8. The last independent ruler of York, Eric Bloodaxe, was killed in 954 (*AS Chron* 'D', 'E'), but according to the twelfth-century *Historia Regum* it was in 952 that 'the kings of the Northumbrians came to an end and henceforth the province was administered by earls' (*Symeon Op. Omnia*, ii, p. 94; *Symeon Op. Coll*, p. 66; *EHD*, i, no. 3, p. 254). The chronology of this period is very confused; see Peter Sawyer, 'The last Scandinavian kings of York', *Northern History*, 31 (1995), pp. 39–44.
27. Keynes, *Atlas*, tables LVII, LXII. Eadulf attests S. 766, 806 (both 968), 771 (dated 969) and 779 (dated 970); Waltheof attests S. 881 (dated 994). For his connection with Bamburgh, see below.
28. The most recent discussion of the sources is by David Rollason, 'Symeon's contribution to historical writing in northern England', David Rollason, *Symeon of Durham, historian of Durham and the North* (Stamford, 1998), pp. 1–13; see also H. S. Offler, *Medieval historians of Durham* (Durham, 1958), reprinted in A. J. Piper and A. I. Doyle (ed.), *North of the Tees: studies in medieval British history* (Aldershot, 1996). For the history of St Cuthbert's community in the period, see William M. Aird, *St Cuthbert and the Normans: the church of Durham, 1071–1151* (Woodbridge, 1998), pp. 9–59.
29. In the *Libellus de exordio et procursu istius hoc est Dunelmensis ecclesie*,

composed between 1104 and 1107 x 1115 (*Symeon, Libellus*, p. xlii). According to Symeon, the move was prompted by the presence in the neighbourhood of 'pirates', usually interpreted as Vikings. The only Viking incursion recorded by the *Anglo-Saxon Chronicle* is the sack of Bamburgh in 993 (see Chapter 3 above) but this may be mentioned only because the same force then ravaged on both banks of the Humber, in 'Northumbria' (the territory of York) and in Lindsey; other raids in the north east may well have gone unrecorded. See also M. K. Lawson, *Cnut: the Danes in England in the early eleventh century* (London, 1993), pp. 21–2.

30. *Symeon, Libellus*, pp. 144–53.
31. The tract may be as early as the mid 1070s, but 'a date in the early twelfth century is no less plausible' (Richard Sharpe, 'Symeon as pamphleteer', in Rollason, *Symeon of Durham*, p. 219, note 22). It is printed in *Symeon, Op. Omnia*, i, pp. 215–20, and translated and discussed by Christopher J. Morris, *Marriage and murder in eleventh-century Northumbria: a study of 'De Obsessione Dunelmi'*, Borthwick Paper no. 82 (York, 1992); see also Richard Fletcher, *Bloodfeud: murder and revenge in Anglo-Saxon England* (London, 2002).
32. Bishop Ealdhun is said to have leased lands belonging to St Cuthbert to Earls *Ethred*, Northmann and Uhtred. *Ethred* is otherwise unknown, but Northmann *dux* attests S. 881, in company with Earl Waltheof (see note 27 above). The leased estates seem to comprise two composite manors, one centred on Gainsford and one on Bishop's Auckland; see Ted Johnson South (ed.), *Historia de Sancto Cuthberto* (Woodbridge, 2001), pp. 64–9, 112–3. The former was presumably leased to Earl Uhtred, for the latter included Escomb, given (or restored) to the church by Earl Northmann (S. 1659, Robertson, *Charters*, no. 68).
33. Morris, *Marriage and murder*, pp. 1–2.
34. The lands are sometimes described in modern works as 'Ecgfrida's dowry', but dowry, land or goods given by the bride's father to the bridegroom, is not mentioned in the Old English tract on betrothal and marriage known as *Be Wifmannes Beweddung*, printed in F. Libermann, *Die Gesetze der Angelsachsen* (Halle, 1903–16), i, pp. 442–4 (translation in *EHD*, i, no 51). Nor does it appear in either of the two surviving marriage contracts from this period (S. 1459, 1461).
35. The date may be scribal error for 949 (in Roman numerals, DCCCCLXIX for DCCCCXLIX), the year in which Malcolm I is said to have raided into England as far as the Tees; see M. O. Anderson, *Kings and kingship in early Scotland* (Edinburgh, 1973), p. 252; Morris, *Marriage and murder*, p. 11.

36. Smyth, *Warlords and Holy Men*, pp. 236–7; S. Mac Airt and G. Mac Niocall (ed.), *The Annals of Ulster* (Dublin, 1983), pp. 436–7.
37. The murder of Ealdorman Ælfhelm took place before midsummer, 1006 (*AS Chron*). When Uhtred succeeded Waltheof is another matter. Symeon implies that Uhtred was earl of the Northumbrians (*comes Northanhymbrorum*) by 995 (see above), which might suggest that Waltheof died soon after his only known attestation, to S. 881, dated before 28 October 994 (Keynes, *Diplomas*, p. 251). It is not unknown, however, for office-holders to be prematurely promoted to their honours by later writers.
38. S. 877, Robertson, *Charters*, no. 63, pp. 130–1, 375, *EHD*, i, no. 120. Thurcytel Nafena's son was murdered, along with Ealdorman Uhtred, in 1016 (*AS Chron*).
39. S. 906, 922, both from the Burton archive.
40. The mid eleventh-century *Historia de Sancto Cuthberto* records Styr Ulf's son's gift of Darlington (County Durham), in the presence and with the permission of King Æthelred, Archbishop Ælfric (*recte* Wulfstan), Bishop Ealdhun, Abbot Ælfwold and 'all the *principes* who were present with the king on that day in the city of York' (Johnson South, *Historia de Sancto Cuthberto*, pp. 66–7, 111–12; Rollason, 'Symeon's contribution', pp. 8–9). No date is given, but Æthelred's only recorded visit to the north was in 1014, when he drove Cnut's army out of Lindsey after Easter (25 April) 1014 (see Chapter 7 below); Wulfstan was in York on 16 February 1014, consecrating Ælfwig as bishop of London. The gift of Darlington is credited to Æthelred himself in the post-Conquest *Cronica monasterii Dunelmensis*, composed before 1083 (Craster, 'The Red Book of Durham', p. 526).
41. Aird, *St Cuthbert and the Normans*, p. 48; see also William E. Kapelle, *The Norman Conquest of the North* (London, 1979), pp. 16–7.
42. The families of Ælfhelm, Uhtred and Styr may have been connected. Two diplomas preserved in the Burton Abbey cartulary are in favour of an earlier Uhtred, son of Eadulf of Bamburgh (died 912); a second Uhtred, beneficiary of another diploma in the archive, may have belonged to the same kindred (S. 397, 548, 569; Sawyer, *Charters of Burton*, nos 3, 9, 13, pp. xli, 7, 22). That the only two charters attested by Styr Ulf's son are also from the Burton archive (see note 39 above) may be no more than coincidence, but Styr does attest S. 877 (see note 38 above) immediately after Ælfhelm, his son Wulfheah and his brother Wulfric Wulfrun's son.
43. See Chapter 6 below.
44. S. 1536; *AS Chron*, 1015 (see Chapter 7 below). The 'Seven Boroughs' are presumably the Five Boroughs (Lincoln, Stamford, Nottingham, Derby and Leicester), plus York and (perhaps) Bamburgh or Durham.

45. Sawyer, *Charters of Burton*, pp. xii, xl, xlii–iii. For Ælfthryth, who predeceased both her brothers, see S. 1380.
46. S. 922, Sawyer, *Charters of Burton*, no. 32; see also S. 924, 928, Sawyer, *Charters of Burton*, nos 34, 37.
47. For Styr's attestations, see notes 38 and 39 above; for Thurbrand *hold*, see Chapter 7 below.
48. Whitelock, 'Dealings', p. 87; Sawyer, *Charters of Burton*, p. 23. See Chapter 5 below.
49. Morcar attests S. 898, dated 1001, relating to land in Warks, and S. 906, the confirmation to Burton Abbey, dated 1004; both brothers attest S. 911, the foundation charter of Eynsham, Oxfordshire. Thereafter Morcar attests in 1012 (S. 926, relating to land in Huntingdonshire) and 1013 (S. 931, land in Northamptonshire), and Sigeferth in 1009 (S. 922, the diploma in favour of Morcar), 1012 (S. 926), 1013 (S. 931) and 1014 (S. 933, land in Dorset).
50. It is sometimes claimed that Ulfcytel of East Anglia was married to a daughter of King Æthelred but the evidence is late and unreliable (*Encomium Emmae*, p. 89).
51. Morris, *Marriage and murder*, pp. 2–3.
52. Fletcher (*Bloodfeud*, pp. 75–7) dates the marriage to Sige *c.* 1004 and that to Ælfgifu *c.* 1006, on the grounds that *De obsessione* says that it was Uhtred, murdered in 1016, who arranged the betrothal of his daughter by Ælfgifu (Morris, *Marriage and murder*, p. 2); but *De obsessione* is equally clear in associating his marriage to Sige with his appointment as ealdorman of all Northumbria, which cannot be earlier than 1006. It was by the marriage of their daughter Ealdgyth to Maldred Crinan's son that Uhtred and Ælfgifu became the maternal grandparents of Gospatric, earl of Bamburgh (1067–72) and ancestor of the earls of Dunbar (Morris, *Marriage and murder*, pp. 16–18).
53. *JnW*, ii, pp. 464–5; Keynes, *Diplomas*, pp. 213–4. John is the only authority for the marriage, but Eadric and Eadgyth were almost certainly the grandparents of Siward son of Æthelgar and his brother Ealdred, who still held land in Shropshire in 1086, and whose descendants can be traced into the twelfth century (Williams, *The English and the Norman Conquest*, pp. 93–6). Orderic describes the brothers as great-nephews (*pronepotes*) of Edward the Confessor, and the fact (though not the degree) of relationship is confirmed in Siward's case by Domesday Book (*OV*, ii, pp. 194–5; *GDB*, fo. 178). Siward and Ealdred were of the same generation as Eadric the Wild, which tends to suggest that Eadric's father Ælfric was a nephew rather than a brother of Eadric *streona* (see note 18 above).
54. Stafford, *Emma and Edith*, pp. 92–4.

55. An unnamed daughter of Æthelred was abbess of Wherwell in Edward the Confessor's reign (*AS Chron*, 'D', 'E', 1051); she may have been a third daughter of the king and his first wife, or perhaps either Ælfgifu or Eadgyth in widowhood. For a possible daughter of Æthelstan, see *LE*, p. 292 (Dumville, 'Æthelstan, first king of England', p. 150, note 62). For *Elfleda*, allegedly a sister of King Æthelred, and Eadgifu, abbess of Nunnaminster, supposedly a daughter of Edgar, see Chapter 1, note 24 above.
56. Cnut reverted to the earlier pattern in giving his daughter Gunnhild to the future emperor Henry III. Æthelred's youngest daughter, Godgifu, a child of his second marriage, was married abroad, first to Count Drogo of the Vexin and then to Eustace of Boulogne, but these were marriages made in exile.
57. For this and other examples of poetic irony in the *Anglo-Saxon Chronicle*, see R. I. Page, *"A most vile people": early English historians on the Vikings*, Dorothea Coke Memorial Lecture (London, 1987), pp. 26–8.
58. David Hill and Sheila Sharp, 'An Anglo-Saxon beacon-system', A. R. Rumble and A. D. Mills, *Names, places and people: an onomastic miscellany in memory of John McNeal Dodgson* (Stamford, 1997), pp. 157–65; Andrew Reynolds, *Late Anglo-Saxon England: life and landscape* (Stroud, 1999), pp. 92–6.
59. For Cholsey, see Chapter 1 above, and for Cuckhamsley, see S. 1454 (Chapter 3 above); see also their use of the Isle of Wight, already occupied by previous armies in 998 and 1001.
60. No source names the Viking leaders. The memorial stone of Ulv of Borresta in Uppland (Sweden) records that he 'took three gelds in England; first Toste paid, then Thorketil paid, then Cnut paid'. Thorketil is presumably Thorkell the Tall, who campaigned in England between 1009 and 1012, and Cnut the eventual conqueror of the English kingdom, so Toste may have been one of the leaders of the 1006 army but nothing further is known of him (Lund, 'The Danish perspective', pp. 117–8).
61. The *Chronicle* records the council of 1006 but gives neither date nor meeting-place; Christmas was, however, one of the seasons for such gatherings.
62. *AS Chron*, 'E' 1007 (my italics); 'C' and 'D' read 'throughout Mercia'.
63. S. 915; in 1009, however, these positions are reversed (S. 922). See Keynes, *Diplomas*, p. 213 and table 6.
64. *AC*(B), 1012; *ByT* (RB), 1012; *ByT* (Peniarth 20), 1011=1012. *Ubis* might stand for the OE name 'Ufi', but a sheriff of Staffordshire named Æfic is recorded in the closing years of Æthelred's reign (*Hemming*, p. 276; Williams, 'Cockles amongst the wheat', pp. 9, 19–20, note 51) .

65. See the *Anglo-Saxon Chronicle* for the dates given; Oxfordshire is also mentioned in S. 927 (dated 1012). For Oxfordshire and Buckinghamshire, see also Chapter 3, note 125 above.
66. David A. Hinton, 'The fortifications and their shires' in David Hill and Alexander Rumble (ed.), *The defence of Wessex: the Burghal Hidage and Anglo-Saxon fortification* (Manchester 1996), pp. 151–9; David Hill, 'The shiring of Mercia – again', in Nicholas J. Higham and David H. Hill (ed.), *Edward the Elder, 899–924* (London and New York, 2001), pp. 144–59; H. M. Chadwick, *Studies on Anglo-Saxon institutions* (Cambridge 1905; reprinted New York, 1963), pp. 219–27.
67. III Eg, 2a, 5§1 and see Chadwick, *Studies*, p. 220. At around the same time, a land transfer was attested by 'the court (*gemot*) of the whole host belonging to Northampton' (*ealles heres gemote on Hamtune*; see Robertson, *Charters*, no. 40, pp. 76–7). The *Libellus Æthelwoldi*, now preserved only in a twelfth-century Latin translation, refers to legal cases held in the shires (*comitatus*) of Bedford, Cambridge, Hertford and Huntingdon in the late tenth century (*LE*, pp. ix–xvii; 83–4, 98–9, 116; Wormald, *MEL*, pp. 155–6).
68. Richard Abels, *Lordship and military obligation in Anglo-Saxon England* (Berkeley, Los Angeles and London, 1988), pp. 58–9.
69. Scragg, *The Battle of Maldon*, line 69; *AS Chron*, 'A' 1001; 'CDE' 999, 1003. By contrast, it was the leading men (*se yld*) of the East Angles, not of Norfolk and Suffolk, who led the local forces in 1004 and 1010.
70. C. S. Taylor argued that the lack of any administrative division above the hundred had hampered the raising of armies in the midlands; see 'The origin of the Mercian shires', *Trans. Bristol and Gloucs Arch. Soc.*, 21 (1898), 32 (1909), reprinted in H. P. R. Finberg, *Gloucestershire Studies* (Leicester, 1957), pp. 17–51. The burghal structure, however, was even more closely entwined with military organization than was the shire.
71. The *Magonsæte* (Herefordshire and south Shropshire) appear in a diploma of 958 (S. 677) and the *Pecsæte* (the Derbyshire Peak) and *Wreocensæte* (north Shropshire) in 963 (S. 712a, 723). Leofwine became ealdorman of the Hwicce (Worcestershire, Gloucestershire and south Warwickshire) in 996, and Eadric was leading the men of the *Magonsæte* at *Assandun* in 1016.
72. Neil Ker, 'Hemming's Cartulary: a description of two Worcester cartularies in BM Cotton Tiberius A xiii', in R. W. Hunt et al. (ed.), *Studies in medieval history presented to Frederick Maurice Powicke* (Oxford, 1948), pp. 49–75, at p. 69. The *terminus post quem* is 996, the date of the latest document included. The addition of *-scire* was made by 'another scribe,

or the same scribe a little later' (H. P. R. Finberg, 'The ancient shire of Winchcombe', *ECWM*, p. 230).

73. *GDB*, fos 162v, 166. The valuation of the borough included 'the three adjoining hundreds', that is, Witley, Kiftsgate and Chelthorn.

74. *Hemming*, pp. 280–1: *omni Anglorum regno praeerat et quasi subregulus dominabatur, ut villulas vilis et provincias provinciis adjungeret.* The first part of this claim is borne out by Eadric's standing in the closing years of King Æthelred's reign (Keynes, *Diplomas*, pp. 213–24 and see Chapter 6 below). Hemming's interest in Eadric arose from his alleged theft of three estates belonging to the church of Worcester, and it is probably significant that one of them, Batsford in Witley Hundred, lay within 'Winchcombeshire'. Of the remainder, *Keingeham* is unidentified, and Eisey lay in Wiltshire, though close to the boundary with Gloucestershire. Hemming dates the loss of these lands to the time of Bishop Leofsige (1016–33) and Eadric himself was murdered at Christmas 1017 (see also Williams, 'The spoliation of Worcester', pp. 383–5).

75. Patrick Sims-Williams, *Religion and literature in western England, 600–800* (Cambridge, 1990), pp. 43–7.

76. See note 71 above. Even after the formation of the shire, northern Shropshire lay in the diocese of Lichfield, whereas the south was part of the see of Hereford (see also the situation in Warwickshire, discussed below).

77. S. 221, which survives as a single-sheet original (i.e. in a contemporary hand).

78. Margaret Gelling, *The West Midlands in the early middle ages* (Leicester, 1992), pp. 141–2, 164–7; for Shrewsbury's position in its shire, see Lewis, 'An introduction to the Shropshire Domesday', p. 1.

79. S. 1492, Robertson, *Charters*, pp. 131–2; this is a memorandum which can be dated no more closely than 1017 x 1035. See also Taylor, 'Origin of the midland shires', pp. 24–5 and note 1.

80. At some time between 1016 and 1086, the lands between the Leadon and the Severn were transferred, for secular purposes, from Herefordshire to Gloucestershire, a reorganization which probably inspired Bishop Æthelstan of Hereford (1012–56) to draw up a description of the ecclesiastical boundary between his see and that of Worcester to the east (H. P. R. Finberg, 'Bishop Athelstan's boundary', *ECWM*, pp. 225–7).

81. For the lands of Worcester, see the maps in Julian Whybra, *A lost English county: Winchcombeshire in the tenth and eleventh centuries* (Woodbridge, 1990), pp. 42, 50; the contributory burgesses of Warwick are listed in Domesday Book. This part of the shire lay in the diocese of Worcester, while the remainder was part of the see of Lichfield (see also the case of Shropshire, note 76 above).

82. T. R. Slater, 'The origins of Warwick', *Midland History*, 8 (1983), pp. 1–13.
83. Stenton, *ASE*, p. 337: 'it was certainly the work of a king who had no respect for the ancient divisions of Mercia'. See also Gelling, *West Midlands*, pp. 151–2, 156, figs. 58, 60; Hill 'The shiring of Mercia', pp. 144–5, 151.
84. Stamford and its territory was still separate from Lincolnshire in 1016, when (according to the *Anglo-Saxon Chronicle*, a Danish army went 'along the Fen to Stamford *and then* into Lincolnshire' (my italics).
85. *AS Chron*, 'C', 1008. For the variant readings in 'D' and 'E', see Whitelock, *The Anglo-Saxon Chronicle*, p. 88 note 6.
86. V Atr 27; VI Atr 33. For the Enham legislation, see Chapter 5 below.
87. *AS Chron*, 992; S. 1488, *EHD*, i, no. 126. William of Jumièges (ii, 10–13) says that the *milites* who manned the fleet which raided the Cotentin were 'properly armed with hauberks and helmets' (*loricis et galeis decenter armati*). It is unfortunate that this expedition (if it ever happened) cannot be dated (see Chapter 3 above).
88. The association of 310 hides for the ship and eight hides for the helmet and mail-shirt is particularly odd, for 310 is not divisible by eight (neither is 300); one would expect 5 hides, giving a complement of sixty-two (or sixty) armed men, as in the will of Archbishop Ælfric (see note 87 above). It might be that the original reading gave 320 hides for the ship, in which case the eight-hide unit would provide forty armed and equipped men per ship.
89. S. 1383, Harmer, *Anglo-Saxon Writs*, no. 63, O'Donovan, *Charters of Sherborne*, no. 13, pp. lvi-lvii, 46–8. The document, a letter addressed to Æthelmær, is dated only by the episcopate of Æthelric, 1002–1009 x 1014, but must be connected with the forced lease of Holcombe to the ætheling Edmund, in 1013 x 1014 (S. 1422, O'Donovan, *Charters of Sherborne*, no. 14, pp. 49–51 and see Chapter 6 below), which it mentions as imminent. It might have been written in the context of the 1008 edict and the ship-levy of 1009.
90. For *scipfirðrunga*, see V Atr, 27 (above, note 86).
91. According to the *Leges Henrici primi*, shires were divided into 'hundreds and shipsokes': L. J. Downer, *Leges Henrici primi* (Oxford, 1972), pp. 96–7. The same term is used of the bishop of Worcester's triple hundred of Oswaldslow in a diploma (S. 731) fathered on Edgar, but in fact forged in the twelfth century. For the shipsokes of Warwickshire, recorded in the Pipe Rolls of Henry II's time, see Helen Cam, 'Early groups of hundreds', *Liberties and communities in medieval England* (London, 1963), p. 93.

92. It is unlikely that the bishops of Sherborne ever possessed as much as 300 hides, but they may have had overall responsibility for three Dorset hundreds, Sherborne, Yetminster and Beaminster, though only in Sherborne Hundred was the bishopric the sole landowner (O'Donovan, *Charters of Sherborne*, p. lvii). See notes 98, 100 below for the similar positions of the bishoprics of Ramsbury and Crediton.
93. S. 1458a, Robertson, *Charters*, no. 72, pp. 144–5 (see also note 94 below). The estates named in the list provided fifty-eight men, and the full number was perhaps sixty; see Pamela Taylor, 'The endowment and military obligations of the bishopric of London', *ANS*, 14 (1992), pp. 292–3.
94. *AS Chron*, 992.
95. In 1086 the bishop of Lincoln, whither the Dorchester see had been translated, held the three hundreds of Banbury, Thame and Dorchester; unlike Sherborne (see note 92 above), all the land within the three hundreds belonged to the church (*GDB*, fos 155–155v). See Nicholas Hooper, 'Some observations on the navy in late Anglo-Saxon England', C. Harper-Bill. C. Holdsworth and J. L. Nelson (ed.), *Studies in medieval history presented to R. Allen Brown* (Woodbridge, 1989), p. 210; Frank Thorn, 'Hundreds and wapentakes', Ann Williams and R. W. H. Erskine (ed.), *The Oxfordshire Domesday* (London, 1990), p. 25; Blair, *Anglo-Saxon Oxfordshire*, p. 111.
96. *AS Chron*, 1016; S. 1487.
97. *GDB*, fos 136, 192v, 203v, 204–204v, 210v, 343v. See also Harmer, *Anglo-Saxon Writs*, p. 267.
98. S. 1488 (Ælfric), 1492 (Ælfwold); see Chapter 2 above. It may be relevant that at the time of Domesday the archbishop and his monks held some 320 sulungs (the Kentish equivalent of the hide) within the shire (*GDB*, fos 3–5). The complexities of Crediton's subsequent history (amalgamated with St German's, Cornwall, transferred to a new see at St Peter's, Exeter, and re-endowed by Bishop Leofric in the 1050s) make it impossible to estimate the endowment in Æthelred's time, but it must have included Crediton itself, which constituted a single hundred at the time of Domesday; the manor was assessed at fifteen hides, but this was clearly preferential, for it contained 185 ploughlands (*GDB*, fo. 101v); see Frank Thorn, 'Hundreds and wapentakes', Ann Williams and G. H. Martin, *The Devonshire Domesday* (London, 1991), p. 34 and note 2; Frank and Caroline Thorne, *Domesday Book: Devon* (Chichester, 1985), chapter 2, notes.
99. For Oswaldslow, the 300-hide unit associated with Worcester, and the similar unit associated with Pershore, see Ann Williams, 'An introduction to the Worcestershire Domesday', Ann Williams and R. W. H. Erskine

(ed.), *The Worcestershire Domesday* (London, 1988) pp. 17–8; for St Benet's Holme, see Hooper, 'Some observations on the navy', pp. 210–11.

100. *GDB*, fo. 66; Frank Thorn, 'Hundreds and wapentakes', Ann Williams and R. W. H. Erskine, *The Wiltshire Domesday* (London, 1989), p. 36. By 1086 the see of Ramsbury had been merged into that of Sherborne, and its *cathedra* had been moved to Old Sarum, so that the lands were in the possession of the bishop of Salisbury.
101. Thorn, 'Hundreds and Wapentakes', *The Wiltshire Domesday*, p. 40; *GDB*, fo. 64v. Obligations similar to those at Malmesbury were laid upon the boroughs of Lewes, Sussex and Warwick (*GDB*, fos 26, 238).
102. See note 98 above.
103. Helen Cam, '*Manerium cum hundredo*: the hundred and the hundred manor' and 'Early groups of hundreds', *Liberties and communities*, pp. 64–90, 91–107.
104. *GDB*, fos 101, 186; for Much Cowarne, see Ann Williams, 'The spoliation of Worcester', *ANS*, 19 (1996), p. 390.
105. See the eight hundreds of Wansford and Oundle, and the two hundreds 'at the Dykes' (Nassaborough hundred), all in Northamptonshire (Robertson, *Charters*, no. 40 and p. 331).
106. For the origins of the shipsokes, see Ann Williams, *Kingship and government in pre-Conquest England, c, 500–1066* (London, 1999), pp. 116–8.
107. For Edgar's fleet, see *AS Chron*, 'C', 'D', 973.
108. *AS Chron*, 1009; for the fate of the ships, see Chapter 6 below.
109. *AS Chron*, 'C', 'E' 1049, 'CDE', 1052. The 'E' text for 1049 distinguishes the *landesmanna scipu* from those belonging to the standing force of royal *lithesmen* (see Chapter 6 below). In the Enham legislation the vessels of the shipsokes are called *folces fyrdscipu* (VI Atr, 24).
110. Nicholas Brooks, 'Weapons and armour', in Scragg, *Battle of Maldon*, pp. 212–17.
111. Nicholas Brooks, 'Arms, status and warfare in late Anglo-Saxon England', Hill, *Ethelred the Unready*, pp. 89–93 and fig. 3. The exception is S. 1498, the will of Ealdorman Æthelmær of Hampshire (971–83), whose heriot includes four helmets and four mail-shirts.
112. S. 1488, 1503, *EHD*, i, nos 126, 130.
113. S. 1492, *EHD*, i, no. 122.
114. Hill, 'Trends in the development of towns during the reign of Ethelred II', pp. 213–26.
115. V Atr 26,1, *EHD*, i, no. 44; Wormald *MEL*, pp. 332–1, 344.
116. Peter Drewett, David Rudling and Mark Gardiner, *The south east to AD 1000* (London, 1988), pp. 333, 337.

117. Haslam, *Anglo-Saxon towns in southern England*, pp. 76, 109, 137, 153, 258.
118. Haslam, *Anglo-Saxon towns in southern England*, p. 188; Hill 'Trends in the development of towns', p. 223.
119. For the relationship between Wilton and Old Sarum, see Haslam, 'The towns of Wiltshire', pp. 122–8.
120. D. Hill, 'The origin of the Saxon towns', Peter Brandon (ed.), *The South Saxons* (Chichester, 1978), p. 187; see also Hill, 'Trends in the development of towns', pp. 224–5.
121. Richard Abels, 'From Alfred to Harold II: the military failure of the late Anglo-Saxon state', R. P. Abels and B. S. Bachrach (ed.), *The Normans and their adversaries at war: studies in memory of C. Warren Hollister* (Woodbridge, 2001), p. 23.
122. See further Chapter 5 below.
123. *AS Chron*, 'C', 1020, 'E', 1023, recording respectively his consecration of the minster at *Assandun* and his death (on 28 May); 'F', 996 (the post-Conquest recension) mentions his appointment to the bishopric of London. Wulfstan was never canonized, and there is no *vita*. A handful of charters relating to him survive, and he appears as a beneficiary in the will of Leofwine Wulfstan's son, an Essex thegn, drawn up while he was bishop of London (S. 1384–6, 1459, 1845–7; S. 1522).
124. For Wulfstan's life and career, see Dorothy Whitelock, 'Archbishop Wulfstan, homilist and statesman', *TRHS*, 4th series, 24 (1942), pp. 42–60; idem (ed.), *Sermo Lupi ad Anglos* (2nd edn, Exeter, 1976), both reprinted in *History, Law and Literature*; Dorothy Bethurum (ed.), *The Homilies of Wulfstan* (Oxford, 1957), pp. 64–87. Cecily Clark made the tentative suggestion that Wulfstan's use of Scandinavian terminology might indicate 'a man of the Southern Danelaw', meaning (in context) the Fenlands: 'On dating "The Battle of Maldon": certain evidence reviewed', in Peter Jackson (ed.), *Words, Names and History: selected writings of Cecily Clark* (Cambridge, 1995), p. 35.
125. *LE*, pp. 156–7.
126. Hugh Candidus, p. 73 (translation, p. 36).
127. Powell, 'The "Three Orders" of society in Anglo-Saxon England', p. 115 and note 45.
128. Whitelock, 'Archbishop Wulfstan', p. 21; Keynes, *Diplomas*, table 3 and p. 156, note 8.
129. London's commercial importance, and the king's interests therein, are reflected in the 'Institutes of London' (IV Atr), for which see Chapter 3 above.
130. Taylor, 'Endowment and military obligation', pp. 301–2.

131. For meetings of the *witan* at London and Westminster, see Keynes, *Diplomas*, pp. 271–2.
132. Bethurum, *Homilies of Wulfstan*, pp. 376–7; translation by Andy Orchard, 'Wulfstan I', in Michael Lapidge et al. (ed.), *The Blackwell Encyclopaedia of Anglo-Saxon England* (Oxford, 1999), p. 495.
133. *LE*, p. 156.
134. A. P. McD. Orchard, 'Crying Wolf: oral style and the Sermones Lupi', *ASE*, 21 (1992), p. 258; Milton McC. Gatch, *Preaching and Theology in Anglo-Saxon England: Ælfric and Wulfstan* (Toronto and Buffalo, 1977), p. 20.
135. Karl Jöst (ed.), *Die 'Institutes of Polity, Civil and Ecclesiastical'* (Bern, 1959); translation in Swanton, *Anglo-Saxon Prose*, pp. 125–38.
136. Bethurum, *Homilies of Wulfstan*, nos II, III, Ia, Ib, IV, V (the order is that of composition); for discussion, see Bethurum, pp. 278–82.
137. Revelations, 20: 7–8.
138. R. Morris (ed.), *Blickling Homilies of the tenth century*, EETS, os 58, 63, 73 (1874–80, reprinted 1957), pp. 115–31; translation Swanton, *Anglo-Saxon Prose*, p. 67.
139. Bethurum, *Homilies of Wulfstan*, pp. 136–7.
140. Mark, 13:32 (compare Matthew, 24:36 and 24:42). See Bethurum, *Homilies of Wulfstan*, pp. 278–9.
141. Mark, 13:8; compare Matthew, 24: 7–8.
142. See the Old English preface to the first series of *Catholic Homilies* (translated in *EHD*, i, no. 239A). For Ælfric's changing viewpoint, see Godden, 'Apocalypse and invasion in late Anglo-Saxon England', pp. 132–42.
143. Mark, 13:8.
144. Bethurum, *Homilies of Wulfstan*, no. III (*Secundum Lucam*), p. 125, and see Wormald, *MEL*, p. 451: 'the fraying of kindred ties was a variation of Wulfstan's own on the Gospel theme of mounting lawlessness and mutual hatred'. Ælfric too regarded warfare within the family as the worst kind of unjust war; 'the war … which comes from contention between citizens is very dangerous, and the … war which is between kinsmen is very wretched and endless sorrow': Ælfric, *Lives of the Saints*, cited in J. E. Cross, 'The ethic of war in Old English', Peter Clemoes and Kathleen Hughes (ed.), *England before the Conquest: studies in primary sources presented to Dorothy Whitelock* (Cambridge, 1971), pp. 272–3.
145. Wormald, *MEL*, pp. 451–3; idem, 'Archbishop Wulfstan and the holiness of society', *Legal culture in the early medieval West*, pp. 225–51.
146. Fowler, *Wulfstan's Canons of Edgar*, pp. l-li. The text is also edited, with translation, in Whitelock et al., *Councils and synods*, no. 48, pp. 313–38.

147. Fowler, *Wulfstan's Canons of Edgar*, chapters 14, 46 (see also Chapter 2 above), 59.
148. S. 1458a, see note 93 above. The first Worcester cartulary, the *Liber Wigornensis*, dating from between 996 and 1016 (see note 72 above), may also have been compiled during Wulfstan's episcopate.
149. For Wulfstan's view of the relationship between the church and the secular world, see Dorothy Bethurum, 'Regnum and Sacerdotium in the early eleventh century', Clemoes and Hughes, *England before the Conquest*, pp. 129–45.
150. F. L. Attenborough, *The laws of the earliest English kings* (Cambridge, 1922; reprinted New York, 1963). Edward and Guthrum were not, of course, contemporary as rulers (Edward succeeded to Wessex in 899 and Guthrum, king of the East Angles, died in 890), and in the prologue the peace is said to have been agreed between Alfred and Guthrum, ratified by Edward, and subsequently augmented by 'wise men' (*witan*).
151. Translation by Wormald, *MEL*, pp. 390–1.

Notes to Chapter 5: The Immense Raiding-Army

1. Skeat, *Lives of the Saints*, ii, pp. 112–4.
2. See Chapter 6 below.
3. For Thorkell's career, see *Encomium Emmae*, pp. 73–6; Poole, *Viking poems*, pp. 100–7; Keynes, 'Cnut's earls', Rumble, *Reign of Cnut*, pp. 54–7.
4. *Encomium Emmae*, pp. 10–11, 73; *JnW*, ii, pp. 462–3. Thorkell and Hemming were allegedly the sons of Strút-Haraldr, jarl of Sjælland, and Thorkell is probably the father of Earl Harald, who married Cnut's half-Wendish niece, Gunnhild, and had by her two sons, Thorkell and Hemming (Keynes, 'Cnut's earls', pp. 62 note 6, 66). Eilaf may be another Dane, the brother of Ulf, who subsequently married Swein Forkbeard's daughter Estrith (Keynes, 'Cnut's earls', pp. 58–60, 73 and note 166).
5. *Encomium Emmae*, pp. 10–11.
6. Sawyer, 'Cnut's Scandinavian empire', Rumble, *Reign of Cnut*, p. 10.
7. Tinna Damgaard-Sørensen, 'Danes and Wends: a study of Danish attitudes to the Wends', Wood and Lund, *People and places*, pp. 176–7 and note 6; see also Helen Clarke and Björn Ambrosiani, *Towns in the Viking Age* (Leicester, 1991), pp. 112–15.
8. Lund, 'The armies of Swein Forkbeard and Cnut', pp. 113–16; Niels Lund, 'Scandinavia, *c.* 700–1066', *CNMH*, ii, p. 222. See also Chapter 6 below.
9. See Chapter 4, note 60 above; Birgit Sawyer, 'Appendix: the evidence of Scandinavian runic inscriptions', Rumble, *Reign of Cnut*, pp. 23–6.
10. *Encomium Emmae*, pp. 76–7, and see Russell Poole, 'Skaldic verse and

Anglo-Saxon history: some aspects of the period 1009–1016', *Speculum*, 62 (1987), pp. 267–9; idem, *Viking poems*, pp. 92–9. For Sighvatr and Óttarr, see also below, notes 36, 37.

11. Lawson (*Cnut*, pp. 25–7) adds Swein Forkbeard himself, which on the face of it seems unlikely, and Hákon son of Jarl Erik of Lade; the evidence for the latter's presence comes from the unreliable *Translatio Sancti Ælfegi* of Osbern of Canterbury (Alexander R. Rumble and Rosemary Morris, '*Translatio Sancti Ælfegi Cantuariensis archiepiscopi et martiris*', Rumble, *Reign of Cnut*, pp. 296–7). All that can be said of this is that Osbern's account of Earl Hákon does not tally with that of the (earlier) tradition in the *Anglo-Saxon Chronicle* (*AS Chron*, 'C', 1030; Keynes, 'Cnut's earls', pp. 61–2).
12. Keynes, *Diplomas*, p. 217.
13. Wormald, *MEL*, pp. 345, 449–65.
14. See Chapter 4 above.
15. Karl Leyser, 'The tenth-century condition', in Karl Leyser (ed.), *Medieval Germany and its neighbours, 900–1250* (London, 1982), pp. 1–3.
16. Wormald, *MEL*, p. 455.
17. Wormald, *MEL*, pp. 330–5 (quotation on p. 333). For V Æthelred, see Robertson, *Laws*, pp. 78–91 (three recensions have survived, the earliest of which is printed, in translation only, in *EHD*, i, no. 44). For the OE text of VI Æthelred, Robertson, *Laws*, pp. 90–107, and for the Latin text, Whitelock et al. (ed.), *Councils and Synods*, no. 49, pp. 362–73. For the fragmentary X Æthelred, which 'may be the nearest one gets to an official text' (Wormald, *MEL*, p. 337), see Robertson, *Laws*, pp. 130–3.
18. An example is the edict commanding the veneration of Edward the Martyr, added to the Enham code (see Chapter 1 above).
19. Wormald, *MEL*, pp. 330–1. For the Latin text, see Robertson, *Laws*, pp. 108–13; for the Old English text, Robertson, *Laws*, pp. 114–17, *EHD*, i, no. 45 (translation only).
20. For the identification of the *micele here* with Thorkell's *ungemetlice here*, see Keynes, *Diplomas*, p. 217 note 224.
21. The Old English text (VII Atr, OE, 2§1) specifies that relics shall be carried in the processions, and a litany in the Winchester Troper, for the wellbeing of 'King Æthelred and the English army' (*ut aeþelredum regem et exercitum anglorum conservare digneris te rogamus*), may go back to this time (Keynes, *Diplomas*, p. 218).
22. This is one of the few references to the *tungerefa* (*tungravius*, see also IV Atr 3, Chapter 3 note 126 above) and the tithingmen, who supervised the tithings which made up the hundred (see also the *Hundred Ordinance*, I Eg 2, §4).

23. J. Chavanon (ed.), *Adémar de Chabannes, Chronique* (Paris, 1897), p. 208, cited by Jane Martindale, 'Peace and war in early eleventh-century Aquitaine', *Medieval Knighthood*, 4 (1992), p. 171; Ademar wrote *c.* 1030. For the possibility that one of William's opponents was Oláf *helgi*, see Chapter 6 below.
24. Martindale, 'Peace and war in early eleventh-century Aquitaine', pp. 172–4, quotation (from Ademar) on p. 172.
25. V Atr 26,§1 (*EHD*, i, no. 44); later recensions add the repair of bridges. For the ship-levy, see Chapter 4 above.
26. V Atr 28; later versions of the text emend the death penalty to the payment of the offender's wergeld.
27. M. K. Lawson, 'Archbishop Wulfstan and the homiletic element in the laws of Æthelred II and Cnut', Rumble, *Reign of Cnut*, pp. 152–4.
28. Michael Dolley, 'The nummular brooch from Sulgrave', Clemoes and Hughes, *England before the Conquest*, p. 388; D. M. Metcalf, *Atlas of Anglo-Saxon and Norman coin finds, c. 973–1086* (London, 1998), pp. 129–30. The issue is known to have been minted at Derby, Hereford, Leicester, Malmesbury, Northampton, Nottingham, Salisbury, Stafford and Stamford.
29. Mark Blackburn, 'Æthelred's coinage', Scragg, *Battle of Maldon*, pp. 160–1.
30. Lawson, 'Archbishop Wulfstan', pp. 152–3; see also Wormald, *MEL*, pp. 454–62.
31. *Institutes of Polity*, translated Swanton, *Anglo-Saxon Prose*, p. 138. Compare VI Atr, OE, 1.
32. Matthew Strickland, 'Military technology and conquest: the anomaly of Anglo-Saxon England', *ANS*, 19 (1997), pp. 333–82, especially pp. 376–7.
33. 'All the troops feel the same awe toward the munificent king of England as they do toward God': the translation is that of Roberta Frank, 'King Cnut in the verse of his skalds', Rumble, *Reign of Cnut*, p. 116; see also Lawson, *Cnut*, pp. 6, 37. Only the poem's refrain is cited in *Gunnlaugs saga Ormstungu*, see Margaret Ashdown, *English and Norse documents relating to the reign of Æthelred the Unready* (Cambridge, 1930), pp. 190–1. For the 1000 campaign, see Chapter 3 above, and for the events of 1014, see Chapter 6 below.
34. Abels, 'From Alfred to Harold II: the military failure of the late Anglo-Saxon state', pp. 16–28, quotation on p. 26. C. S. Taylor suggested that at least one of Æthelred's expedients backfired: 'the new shire-system from which so much had been hoped proved unavailing, and perhaps even harmful by splitting the land up into separate and self-conscious units' ('Origin of the Mercian shires', p. 35).
35. For the skaldic verses and their interpretation, see Poole, 'Skaldic verse

and Anglo-Saxon history', pp. 265–98; Judith Jesch, *Ships and men in the late Viking age: the vocabulary of runic inscriptions and skaldic verse* (Woodbridge, 2001), pp. 15–36. For Thietmar of Merseberg, see below.

36. *Encomium Emmae*, pp. 76–7; Christine Fell, '*Víkingavísur*', Ursula Dronke (ed.), *Speculum Norroenum: Norse studies in memory of Gabriel Turville-Petre* (Odense, 1981), pp. 106–22; Ashdown, *English and Norse documents*, pp. 158–61. The verses relating to England are printed (translation only) in *EHD*, i, no. 12.
37. *Encomium Emmae*, p. 77; for Óttarr's *Knútsdrápa*, written in praise of Cnut, see Chapter 7 below. *Höfudlausn* is printed and translated in Ashdown, *English and Norse documents*, pp. 157–67; for the verses relating to England (translation only), see *EHD*, i, no. 13.
38. For *Liðsmannaflokkr*, see Poole, *Viking poems*, pp. 86–90 (text), 90–115 (commentary); see also Matthew Townend, 'Contextualizing the *Knútsdrápur*: skaldic praise-poetry at the court of Cnut', *ASE*, 30 (2001), pp. 151, 161–4, 166–8.
39. Both, of course, attribute the feat to their hero Oláf; Thorkell is not mentioned.
40. The moneyers of both towns struck only the earliest coins of the 'Long Cross' issue, which replaced the 'Helmet' at about this time, and may have temporarily ceased production because of the Viking depredations (Dolley, 'Coinage of Æthelræd II', p. 126).
41. The site is not named in the *Anglo-Saxon Chronicle*, but it is identified in the Scandinavian sources and by John of Worcester (*JnW*, ii, pp. 464–7 and see note 57 below). The *Chronicle* gives the date of the battle as Ascension Day (18 May), but John of Worcester's date of 5 May is confirmed by the obituary notice of Oswig, one of the English casualties, as kept at Ely (Bruce Dickens, 'The date of Byrthnoth's death and other obits from a twelfth-century Ely Kalendar', *Leeds Studies in English*, 6 (1937), pp. 14–24).
42. For Oswig, see Margaret Locherbie-Cameron, 'Byrhtnoth and his family', Scragg, *Battle of Maldon*, pp. 255–6. Eadwig might be a brother of Æfic, the high-reeve murdered in 1002. It has been suggested that the father of Wulfric Leofwine's son might be the Leofwine Wulfstan's son, man of Wulfstan *lupus*, then bishop of London, who made his will in 998 (S. 1522); see A. S. Napier and W. H. Stevenson, *The Crawford Collection of early charters* (Oxford, 1895), p. 123, note 3. If this is the case, it is odd that the will does not mention Wulfric.
43. My reconstruction differs from Hill, *Atlas of Anglo-Saxon England*, map 121, p. 68, and also from Nicholas Hooper and Matthew Bennett, *Warfare:*

the Middle Ages (Cambridge, 1996), pp. 36–9 and map 3, who place Thorkell's base in 1010 on the Stour estuary (the border between Essex and Suffolk).

44. Fell, '*Víkingavísur*', stanza 6, p. 115; *Encomium Emmae*, p. 77 note 4.
45. *AS Chron*, 893; Williams, *Kingship and government*, pp. 77, 186 (note 98). It is perhaps not coincidental that Alfred's new fleet, incorporating both Viking and Frisian expertise, was launched in 896.
46. *AS Chron*, 999; *JnW*, ii, pp. 448–9.
47. Tim Tatton-Brown, 'The towns of Kent', Haslam, *Anglo-Saxon towns in southern England*, pp. 14–6.
48. Tatton-Brown, 'Towns of Kent', pp. 16–20 (quotation on p. 17). The Wantsum Channel, now long silted-up, was open water in the eleventh century, and Thanet was still an island.
49. *AS Chron*, 992, 1009; see also *AS Chron*, 1052.
50. *GDB*, fos 230, 26. The unspecified ship-service of Bedford (*GDB*, fo. 109) may also have been due at London.
51. Presumably the lords of the shipsokes were responsible for the arms of their own men.
52. *AS Chron*, 'A', 993; see also *AS Chron*, 1006.
53. See Chapter 4 above.
54. S. 933 (1014) is Æthelred's diploma restoring the estate, purchased from Eadric 'after a few years' by a *famulus* of the monastery called Wulfgar (see O'Donovan, *Charters of Sherborne*, no. 15). See also Chapter 6 and note 85 below.
55. *Höfudlausn*, stanza 9, translated in Poole, 'Skaldic verse and Anglo-Saxon history', p. 287.
56. Fell, '*Víkingavísur*', stanza 7, p. 116. Both Óttarr and Sighvatr give all the glory to their hero Ólaf *helgi*, but *Liðsmannaflokkr*, stanza 4, praises Thorkell (Poole, *Viking poems*, p. 87; Jesch, *Ships and men*, p. 52).
57. The name is also found in John of Worcester (*JnW*, ii, pp. 464–7). For the site, see W. H. Stevenson, 'Notes on Old English historical geography', *EHR*, 11 (1896), pp. 301–2.
58. C. R. Hart, 'The eastern Danelaw', *The Danelaw*, pp. 27, 48, maps 2.1, 2.3; idem, 'The Battles of the Holme, *Brunanburh* and Ringmere', *The Danelaw*, pp. 525–6, 530; Hill, *Atlas of Anglo-Saxon England*, p. 140, map 232.
59. *AS Chron*, 1004; Poole, 'Skaldic verse and Anglo-Saxon history', pp. 279–80. For a possible third battle at Ringmere, see Chapter 7 below.
60. C. Warren Hollister, *Anglo-Saxon military institutions on the eve of the Norman Conquest* (Oxford, 1962), pp. 91–5; Taylor, 'Origin of the Mercian shires', pp. 19–22, 35. Less is known about Mercian than about West Saxon

local organization, but the battle of Kempsford in 802 was fought between the men of Wiltshire and the Hwicce, each led by their ealdorman, and Eadric *streona* was leading the men of the *Magonsæte* at the battle of *Assandun* in 1016.

61. Campbell, *Æthelweard*, p. 28; Abels, *Lordship and military obligation*, pp. 182–3.
62. *GDB*, fo. 56v.
63. Nicholas Hooper, 'An introduction to the Berkshire Domesday', Ann Williams and R. W. H. Erskine (ed.), *The Berkshire Domesday* (London, 1988), pp. 17–21; *GDB*, fos 64v, 100; Abels, *Lordship and military obligation*, pp. 108–11.
64. *GDB*, fo. 172.
65. *GDB*, fo. 56v.
66. *GDB*, fos 179, 252, 262v. See also the burgesses of Warwick, ten of whom had to represent the rest (number unspecified) when the *landfyrd* was summoned: 'whoever was notified and did not go paid a fine of 100s (£5) to the king' (*GDB*, fo. 238).
67. V Atr 28; VI Atr 35; S. 927, and see note 79 below.
68. II Cnut, 77–8; Wormald, *MEL*, pp. 361–2 and see also Chapter 6 below.
69. Abels, *Lordship and military obligation*, pp. 146–8.
70. *AS Chron*, 'A', 1001. Whitchurch, Hants, was allegedly given to the bishopric by Edward the Elder (S. 378), and is said in Domesday always to have belonged to the church; the manor then included the subordinate holdings of Freefolk and Whitnal, one of which may have been held in 1001 by Leofric (*GDB*, fo. 41). Godwine's land, bequeathed to him by his father (S. 1491, Miller, *Charters of the New Minster*, no. 18, pp. 81–4) was probably at Martyr Worthy, held by the Old Minster, Winchester, in 1066 (*GDB*, fo. 41).
71. *GDB*, fo. 173v, Hemming, p. 81. See the *Indiculum* of Archbishop Oswald for 'the *archiductor* who presides over the bishopric' (Hemming, p. 294), but the authenticity of the *Indiculum* is not certain (though defended by Patrick Wormald, 'Lordship and justice in early English law', *Legal culture in the early medieval West*, p. 323), and the *archiductor* might in any case be the bishop himself. See also Abels, *Lordship and military obligation*, pp. 152–6.
72. For the shipsokes of London, Dorchester and Crediton, see Chapter 4 above, and for Bishop Ælfwold's will see S. 1422 and Chapter 2 above.
73. S. 1498, Miller, *Charters of the New Minster*, no. 25, p. 118.
74. Abels, 'From Alfred to Harold II: the military failure of the late Anglo-Saxon state', p. 20.

75. *AS Chron*, 1006, 1009; V Atr 28, VI Atr 35.
76. Keynes, *Diplomas*, pp. 206–8; *AS Chron*, 1016.
77. Cited in Godden, 'Apocalypse and invasion', pp. 140–2; Scragg (ed.), *The Battle of Maldon*, lines 199–201, p. 63.
78. Godden, 'Apocalypse and invasion', pp. 137–9.
79. S. 927 (see also note 67 above); Wormald, *MEL*, pp. 148–51. This is not the Leofric of Whitchurch, Hants, killed in 1001, but may be the witness to a Berkshire lawsuit of 990–2 (S. 1454).
80. Freeman, *NC*, i, p. 296.
81. For the Northumbrian expedition, see Chapter 4 above, and for Maredudd's attack on Maes Hyffaidd (probably New Radnor), see Thornton, 'Maredudd ab Owain', pp. 581–2. Eadric's raid on St David's, recorded in *AC* (B), 1012, *ByT* (RB), 1012, *ByT* (Peniarth 20), 1011=1012, may have been a response to whatever caused the relocation of the Ilchester mint to South Cadbury in 1009–10 (see Chapter 4 above). See also note 84 below.
82. See Chapter 4 above.
83. *AS Chron*, 1011. For *Sith[m]estesbyri* (operational 1009–23), perhaps the Iron Age hill-fort of Cissbury, Sussex, see Chapter 4 above.
84. See Chapter 4, and note 81 above.
85. S. 933 and note 54 above.
86. Óttarr *svarti* (*Höfudlausn*, stanza 11) speaks of the great treasure which Oláf carried off in tribute.
87. John of Worcester, following Osbern of Canterbury, gives a figure of £3000 (*JnW*, ii, pp. 470–1 and note 5).
88. The *Chronicle*'s statement that 'God now reveals there the powers of the holy martyr' shows that it was composed before the translation of Ælfheah's relics to Canterbury in 1023.
89. Rubinstein, 'The life and writings of Osbern of Canterbury', p. 36.
90. *JnW*, ii, pp. 468–71 and notes. He names the axe-thrower who actually killed Ælfheah as Thrum 'whom the archbishop had confirmed the day before'. See Keynes, 'Cnut's earls', p. 64 for 'the attractively ironic possibility' that this might be the Thrym *minister* who attests diplomas of Cnut in the early 1020s.
91. *HN*, p. 4.
92. *Mem St Dunstan*, pp. 412–22, at p. 424.
93. Brooks, *Early history of the church of Canterbury*, pp. 49, 277–8.
94. See, for an earlier period, the remarks of David N. Dumville, *The churches of north Britain in the first Viking age*, Fifth Whithorn Lecture, 1996 (Whithorn, 1997), pp. 8–9.
95. Fell, '*Víkingavísur*', stanza 8, p. 117; *Höfudlausn*, stanza 10. *Portgreifar* is a

loan from OE *portgerefa. Partar* apparently means the English (Jesch, *Ships and men*, p. 76); for some discussion of the word and its meaning, see Russell Poole, 'In search of the *Partar*', *Scandinavian Studies*, 52 (1980), pp. 264–77.

96. *JnW*, ii, pp. 468–9.
97. A. H. Davis (ed.), *William Thorne's Chronicle of Saint Augustine's Abbey* (Oxford, 1934), p. 41.
98. Richard Emms, 'The early history of St Augustine's Abbey, Canterbury', Richard Gameson (ed.), *St Augustine and the conversion of England* (Stroud, 1999), p. 419.
99. S. 926; Keynes, *Diplomas*, table 3; if the *Thurkytel miles* who attests S. 926 is Thorkell the Tall (see note 105 below), the diploma must have been issued after his defection to Æthelred. It is not certain when Godwine was succeeded by his namesake, Godwine II, who died between 1046 and 1058; see E. B Fryde, D. E. Greenway, S. Porter and I Roy (ed.), *Handbook of British Chronology* (London, 1986), p. 221.
100. *JnW*, ii, pp. 468–9.
101. Brooks, *The early history of the church of Canterbury*, pp. 84–5, 204–5; for Leofrun and some possible kinsmen, see Ann Williams, 'The Anglo-Norman abbey', Richard Gem (ed.), *St Augustine's Abbey, Canterbury* (London, 1997), p. 62.
102. Fell, '*Víkingavísur*', stanza 9, p. 118. The battle took place at *Njamóða*, perhaps the lost *Newemouthe* near Orford, Suffolk. Sighvatr says that 'the Danish army fell there where spears were thrust most fiercely against Oláf', which implies that there were losses on both sides.
103. Poole, 'Skaldic verse and Anglo-Saxon history', pp. 268–9.
104. David A Warner, *Ottonian Germany: the Chronicle of Thiemar of Merseberg* (Manchester, 2001), pp. 335, 336; extracts (in translation), *EHD*, i, no. 27.
105. Warner, *Thietmar of Merseberg*, pp. 335–6. The favourable treatment of Thorkell the Tall (see below) might suggest that his informant was one of Thorkell's following, perhaps an eastern Viking returning home after the dispersal of the army in 1012, were it not for the fact that Thietmar implies that it was the same informant who supplied him with a description of the siege of London in 1016 (see Chapter 7 below).
106. Since he calls Ælfheah Dunstan throughout, it is not quite evidence that the cult of Ælfheah was already known on the Continent as well as in England.
107. AS Chron, 1012, 1013; *Encomium Emmae*, pp. 10–11. William of Malmesbury, by contrast, presents Thorkell as the instigator of Ælfheah's murder (*GR*, pp. 300–1, 320–1).

108. S. 926; Campbell, *Charters of Rochester*, no. 33, pp. 45–7. See also note 99 above.
109. Ian McDougall, 'Serious entertainments: a peculiar type of Viking atrocity', *ASE*, 22 (1993), pp. 221–2.
110. McDougall, 'Serious entertainments', pp. 215–20.

Notes to Chapter 6: A Crisis Surmounted

1. The *Anglo-Saxon Chronicle* does not actually name Thorkell at this point, but subsequently makes it clear (*s. a.* 1013) that it was his *lið* which Æthelred employed.
2. See the account of its abolition, 'in the thirty-ninth year after it had been instituted' by King Æthelred (*AS Chron*, 'D', 1051). For the *heregeld*, see appendix below.
3. It was not until 1017 that Lyfing was able to collect his pallium from Rome, and between 1013 and 1017 he attests diplomas simply as bishop, or (occasionally) 'bishop of the church of Canterbury', in second place, after Wulfstan (Brooks, *The early history of the church of Canterbury*, p. 288).
4. Of the diplomas surviving from 1012–13, S. 926, 929 and 931 are authentic; doubts have been expressed about S. 925, 927 and 928, but on the whole opinion seems to be in their favour; S. 931a and 931b, which survive only in sixteenth-century transcripts, are not in the usual diplomatic form; S. 930 is a forgery. See Keynes, *Diplomas*, pp. 265–6; idem, 'Regenbald the chancellor (*sic*)', *ANS*, 10 (1988), p. 186 note 7 (for S. 931a and b); Susan Kelly, *The charters of Abingdon* (Oxford, 2000), no. 136 (for S. 927).
5. S. 926, Campbell, *Charters of Rochester*, no. 33. Keynes (*Diplomas*, p. 265) dates it after 17 March 1012; if the *Thurkytel miles* who attests is Thorkell the Tall (see Chapter 5 above), it must be after 19 April.
6. The estates are those forfeited by Æthelflæd, sister of Ealdorman Leofsige of Essex (see Chapter 3 above). Bishop Godwine attests S. 927, dated 1012 (but possibly early 1013), but does not appear thereafter.
7. Keynes, *Diplomas*, pp. 212–3 and table 6; the diplomas for 1011 (S. 923–4) survive only in later copies, from which the lay witnesses have been omitted. Eadric does not attest S. 931a (1013) but the last ecclesiastical witness is 'Eadric *episcopus*', which may be a mistake for 'Eadric *dux*'.
8. Æthelmær attests S. 926 at the head of the *ministri* (thegns), with Æthelweard in third and Æthelwine in tenth position, and the trio occupy the first three places among the *ministri* in S. 927, a diploma dated 1012 but probably from the early months of 1013, also attested (in sixth place) by Goda. Æthelweard does not appear again. Æthelmær does not attest S. 931

(1013), but Æthelric appears in fourth place, with Æthelwine ninth and last. Æthelmær heads the *ministri* in S. 931a and S. 931b, in both cases accompanied by Æthelric (sixth in S. 931a, fourth in S. 931b) and Æthelwine (fourth in S. 931a, seventh in S. 931b).

9. Attestations of northern ealdormen and earls had been patchy in the tenth century, but Ælfhelm regularly attests between 993 and 1006 (Keynes, *Diplomas*, table 6).
10. Sigeferth and Morcar attest S. 926, 931. The Eckington diploma (S. 928) survives in the Burton Abbey archive, as does another diploma of 1013 (S. 929), but the witness-lists of both have been truncated by the copyist with the loss of all the lay witnesses; S. 924 (1011), in Morcar's favour also survives in the Burton archive, as does the other diploma of 1011 (S. 923).
11. S. 926, 927, 931; *AS Chron*, 1016. There may be some confusion with the otherwise unknown Godric *dux* who attests S. 933 and 934, from 1014 and 1015 respectively.
12. *AS Chron*, 993 and see Chapter 3 above.
13. Keynes, *Diplomas*, table 8; Godwine Ælfheah's son may also be the recipient of S. 902, a grant of Little Haseley, Oxfordshire. S. 902, 922 are both attested by a second Godwine, in an even lower position.
14. For a similar problem with Æthelmær son of Ealdorman Æthelweard, see below.
15. Ælfheah's will (S. 1485) mentions his sons Godwine and Ælfweard and his nephew Ælfwine; the latter was killed in the entourage of Ealdorman Byrhtnoth at Maldon (Williams,' *Princeps Merciorum gentis*', pp. 168–72).
16. For Ulfcytel's attestations, see S. 926 (in eighth place), S. 931 (in first place), S. S. 931b (in eighth place). For Northman, see S. 931 and for the family's connection with the east midlands, see Chapter 2 above.
17. S. 931b and see Chapter 2 above. For the possible relationship of Odda and Ælfgar, see Williams, *Land, power and politics: Odda of Deerhurst*, pp. 4–5.
18. S. 875. For the family, see Keynes, *Diplomas*, pp. 132–4; Williams, 'Lost worlds: Kentish society in the eleventh century', pp. 61–2.
19. None of the king's sons appear in S. 926, but the names of Æthelstan, Edmund and Eadred are the only ones, apart from that of the king, in the truncated list to Æthelred's grant of land in Winchester to their stepmother the queen (S. 925), and they also attest S. 927 and 929.
20. S. 928 (Æthelstan and Edmund only), 931; none of the æthelings attest S. 931a, 931b.
21. The lease is S. 1433, Robertson, *Charters*, no. 74, O'Donovan, *Charters of*

Sherborne, no. 14; the letter (for which see also Chapter 4 above) is S. 1383, Harmer, *Writs*, no. 63, O'Donovan, *Charters of Sherborne*, no. 13. Neither can be precisely dated, though since Eadric attests the lease as ealdorman, it must be dated 1007 or later. Bishop Æthelric's last attestation is in 1011 and his successor Æthelsige attests in 1012 (Keynes, *Diplomas*, table 3).

22. The Dorset thegns (none of whom can be further identified) are Ælfgeat Hength's son, Siward, Brihtric the red 'and all the chief thegns of Dorset'. For the ætheling's men, see below.

23. The *Chronicle* (*AS Chron*, 1017) records the murder of Æthelweard, son of Æthelmær *þæs græta*, identified by John of Worcester with Ealdorman Æthelmær (*JnW*, ii, pp. 504–5); this identification has been accepted by Professor Keynes ('Cnut's earls', p. 68, note 141), but Robertson suggested that Æthelmær *þæs græta* was a different person from the ealdorman (Robertson, *Charters*, p. 387). See also note 26 below.

24. See next note.

25. S. 933 (for the circumstances see Chapter 5, note 52 above). See also note 73 below.

26. There are traces of a similar incident involving Burhwold, bishop of Cornwall (S. 951). John of Worcester (ii, 494–7) has a story about a man called Æthelweard, 'born of the most noble of English families', who was recommended to Cnut by Eadric *streona* as one who could entrap and murder Edmund's brother Eadwig ætheling (though in fact Æthelweard avoided doing any such thing). If this is not merely part of the legend of Eadric *streona*, and if this Æthelweard is the son of Ealdorman Æthelmær, then it might serve as an indication of local hostility in the west to the sons of King Æthelred's first marriage; but the name Æthelweard is very common at this time, and John's account of the incident 'read[s] more like saga' (Whitelock, *The Anglo-Saxon Chronicle*, p. 97, note 3; *JnW*, ii, p. 496, note 1). See also note 23 above.

27. S. 907, 909 (*primogenitus*), 916. The last of these attestations post-dates the birth of Emma's eldest son Edward, who attests for the first time in 1005 (Keynes, *Diplomas*, table 1).

28. S. 929.

29. S. 1503, *EHD* i, no. 130. For the date of the ætheling's death, see Keynes, *Diplomas*, p. 267.

30. S. 1433, Robertson, *Charters*, no. 74 ; O'Donovan, *Charters of Sherborne*, no. 14. Ealdwine and Wulfric, the two priests who attest immediately before Lyfing, may be Edmund's chaplains.

31. See Chapter 4 above.

32. The same or another Sigeferth was given a ploughland Hollingbourne,

Kent, which was specifically excluded from the grant of the manor to Christchurch, Canterbury. For the significance of the mailshirt, see Chapter 4 above.

33. See Chapter 7 below.
34. *AS Chron*, 1009.
35. It is not entirely clear that these ships were part of the levy, though this is the usual assumption. Whether they were or not, they may have been local vessels from one or more of the south-eastern ports. It is probably coincidental that Dover owed twenty ships annually to the king in 1066, but it is perhaps worth noticing that Wulfnoth *cild*'s descendants, Earls Godwine and Harold, had connections in the town, and may have been patrons of the refounded minster of St Mary, Dover; see Ann Williams, 'Thegnly piety and ecclesiastical patronage in the late Old English kingdom', *ANS*, 25 (2002), p. 8 and note 42. For the earls' relationship with Wulfnoth, see note 40 below.
36. The Enham legislation (1008) lays down hefty penalties for damaging a royal warship: 'if anyone damages one of the nation's warships (*folces fyrdscip*), he shall with all diligence make compensation for it, and shall pay to the king [the fine for] breach of his protection (*mund*), and if it be destroyed so as to be useless, he shall pay for it in full, and the *mundbrice* to the king' (VI Atr 24).
37. Peter A. Clarke, *The English nobility under Edward the Confessor* (Oxford, 1994), pp. 38–9, 237–8. Æthelnoth may have been port-reeve of Canterbury (Williams, 'Lost worlds: Kentish society in the eleventh century', pp. 55, 58–9).
38. The concentration of lands in Sussex held by the earl and his family in King Edward's day suggest that this was their ancestral homeland (Williams, 'Land and power in the eleventh century: the estates of Harold Godwineson', pp. 176–7, 186–7).
39. *AS Chron*, 'F', 1009; Peter S. Baker (ed.), *The Anglo-Saxon Chronicle: a collaborative edition, Ms F* (Cambridge, 2000), pp. 101–2; for the date (1100 x 1107), see pp. lxxvi-lxxxi. One of Earl Godwine's kinsmen was a monk at Christchurch and briefly archbishop-elect, though King Edward overturned the community's choice (Barlow, *Vita Ædwardi*, pp. 18–19).
40. If the estate in the will could be identified with one subsequently in the possession of the earl and his kin, the identification would be almost certain, but Compton is one of the commonest of English place-names. There are two Comptons in Sussex, where the patrimonial lands of the family lay (see note 38 above). Those who wish to identify Godwine son of Wulfnoth with the earl usually plump for Compton in Westbourne

Hundred, but this was held on the eve of the Conquest by Esbearn; admittedly he is said to hold of (*de*) Earl Godwine, but it is not certain that this implies that the land belonged to the earl, rather than indicating that Esbearn was personally commended to him or that his land owed dues to one of the earl's estates (*GDB*, fos 24, 34: a hide in Surrey also belonged to the manor). The other Compton, in Totnore Hundred, was held by Harold of the king. Admittedly he is not distinguished as the earl, but this Compton was a dependency of the manor of Laughton, in Shiplake hundred, held by Earl Godwine; it was assessed at ten hides plus the dependencies, valued at £15, and included twelve messuages in Lewes (*GDB*, fos 21, 26). Four more small dependencies of Laughton lying in Hawkesborough Hundred were held by 'Countess Goda' (*GDB*, fos 19–19v, 22–22v). John Palmer has identified her as King Edward's sister, see 'Great Domesday on CD-Rom', Elizabeth Hallam and David Bates (ed.), *Domesday Book* (Stroud, 2001), pp. 147–9, but scribal error (*Goda* for *Gida*) is also possible, and she might be Godwine's wife Gytha.

41. *Osberni precentoris Vita S. Elphegi*, H. Wharton (ed.), *Anglia Sacra* (Oxford, 1691), ii, p. 132.
42. Peter Sawyer, 'Swein Forkbeard and the historians', I. Wood and G. A. Loud (ed.), *Church and chronicle in the Middle Ages* (London and Rio Grande, 1991), pp. 28–35.
43. For German/Polish relations, see A. P. Vlasto, *The entry of the Slavs into Christendom* (Cambridge, 1970), pp. 113–42; Warner, *Thietmar*, pp. 21–36. According to Adam of Bremen Swein's wife, the mother of Harald, Cnut and their sister Estrith, was the widow of Erik, king of the *Svear*, and mother of Olof *Skötkonung*; see Francis J. Tschan (trans.), *Adam of Bremen, History of the archbishops of Hamburg-Bremen* (New York, 1959), pp. 78, 81. In fact Swein repudiated her, and she seems to have returned to her homeland, whence she was fetched, after Swein's death, by her sons Harald and Cnut (Warner, *Thietmar*, pp. 333–4; *Encomium Emmae*, pp. 18–9). Her name is not recorded. Since Boleslav ejected his stepmother and half-brothers on taking power (Warner, *Thietmar*, pp. 191–2), she may have been his full sister.
44. Campbell, *Encomium*, pp. 10–11. Thorkell is said to have deserted to the English king, but not, it may be noticed, to Æthelred; not only does the encomiast avoid the topic of Æthelred's marriage to Emma, he never even mentions him by name. William of Jumièges and William of Malmesbury present Swein's invasion as revenge for the St Brice's Day massacre, but the chronological confusion in both accounts renders their testimony unreliable (see Chapter 3 above).

45. *Encomium Emmae*, pp. lv-lvii, and see Chapter 5 note 8 above. In assessing disparities between the *Encomium*'s brief account of Swein's campaign in 1013 and that in the *Anglo-Saxon Chronicle*, the latter is to be preferred as the contemporary source.
46. Warner, *Thietmar*, pp. 332–3.
47. The phrase seems to imply *de facto* rather than *de jure* authority; see also *AS Chron*, 'E', 1036.
48. Stenton, *ASE*, pp. 384–5. Freeman came to the same conclusion (*NC*, i, pp. 355–6).
49. Notable exceptions are Dawn Hadley, '"And they proceeded to plough and to support themselves": the Scandinavian settlement of England', *ANS*, 19 (1996), pp. 69–96; Lesley Abrams, 'Edward the Elder's Danelaw', Higham and Hill, *Edward the Elder*, pp. 128–43, especially pp. 128–33.
50. *The laws of Edward and Guthrum* (EGu 7§2, see Wormald, *MEL*, pp. 889–91, and Chapter 4 above); VI Atr 37.
51. Wormald, *MEL*, pp. 466, 480.
52. Hadley. 'Scandinavian settlement', pp. 82–93, and see Wormald, '*Engla lond*: the making of an allegiance', pp. 1–24.
53. It is interesting to find the author of *De obsessione Dunelmensis* insisting on Uhtred's loyalty to Æthelred, putting into his mouth the boast that 'He [Æthelred] is both my lord and my father-in-law [and] I will never betray him'. The context, however, is Cnut's invasion in 1015; the ealdorman's behaviour in 1013 is passed over in silence (Morris, *Marriage and murder*, p. 3).
54. This seems to have been Æthelred's own belief (see Chapter 7 below).
55. They are described as 'the chief thegns of the Seven Boroughs' (*AS Chron*, 1015), presumably meaning the Five Boroughs plus York and perhaps Bamburgh; Edmund's later alliance with the family secured him the allegiance of the Five Boroughs (see Chapter 7 below).
56. She is Ælfgifu *þære Hamtunisca* in *AS Chron*, 'D', 1035, and *Ælfhelmes dohtor* in *AS Chron*, 'E', 1036. She is not mentioned in the will of her uncle Wulfric, and may have been only a child in 1002. John of Worcester says that her mother was the 'the noble lady Wulfrun' (*JnW* ii, pp. 520–1), but this may be an error for her grandmother Wulfrun, mother of Wulfric and Ælfhelm.
57. Wormald, '*Engla lond*: the making of an allegiance', p. 6. For Morcar's lands, see above and Chapter 4; for Sigeferth, S. 947–8 and Chapter 7 below.
58. Godden, 'Apocalypse and invasion', pp. 139–42 and see Chapter 4 above.
59. *AS Chron*, 1016; *JnW*, ii, pp. 486–7; for Ælfmær *deorling*, who also fought

for the Danes at Sherston, see note 73 below. For Ælfgar's lands, see Williams, 'A west-country magnate of the eleventh century', p. 43. It may also be relevant that Cnut and Edmund's parley after the battle of *Assandun* took place at 'Alney by Deerhurst' (*AS Chron*, 'D', 1016), an estate belonging to Odda, who was perhaps related both to Ælfgar and to Æthelmær (Williams, *Land, power and politics*, pp. 3–6, 12, 29, note 69; see also Chapter 7 below).

60. Hemming (*HC*, pp. 259–60) says that one of Leofwine's grandsons, Æthelwine son of Godwine,'had his hands cut off by the Danes'. Æthelwine's misfortunes are not dated, but he may have been among the hostages mutilated by Cnut after his expulsion from Lindsey in the spring of 1014 (for which see below). He survived the experience and on the eve of the Norman Conquest was holding land at Salwarpe, Worcestershire, previously held by his father; in Domesday Book he is called Æthelwine *cild* (*GDB*, fo. 176).
61. *AS Chron*, 'D', 1014.
62. Bethurum, *Homilies of Wulfstan*, no. 22; *EHD*, i, no. 240 (translation only).
63. Godden, 'Apocalypse and invasion', pp. 143–5; he dates the second recension after Æthelred's return but 'not later than 1014' (ibid., pp. 149–50, and see note 66 below).
64. Godden, 'Apocalypse and invasion', p. 147.
65. For this translation, see Godden, 'Apocalypse and invasion', p. 147 note 30.
66. The last clause quoted, relating to Æthelred's expulsion, is omitted in the two later versions of the *Sermo Lupi*, though the build-up remains. This suggests that the later versions post-date Æthelred's return, and that the omission was made to avoid offence to 'those Anglo-Saxon leaders who had accepted Swein in 1013 and were therefore implicated in the king's expulsion', but had now been reconciled with him (Godden, 'Apocalypse and invasion', p. 150).
67. Godden, 'Apocalypse and invasion', pp. 156–8.
68. *AS Chron*, 1014.
69. At least one other diploma from 1014 is recorded (S. 1602c), a grant of land at Rodden, Dorset, to one *Sealwyne* (Selewine, Seolwine or just conceivably Sæwine), otherwise unknown; see Simon Keynes, 'The lost cartulary of Abbotsbury', *ASE*, 18 (1989), pp. 227–9.
70. S. 932, printed and translated in Finberg, *ECWM*, pp. 143–5.
71. See Chapter 5, note 52 above.
72. The diploma is also attested by the mysterious Godric *dux*, whose only other attestation is to S. 934, dated 1015.
73. S. 933, O'Donovan, *Charters of Sherborne*, no. 15; the ætheling Æthelstan

does not attest, though his brothers and half-brothers do, which suggests that the diploma was issued after his death on 25 June. The remaining *ministri* are Ælfmær and Wulfweard; the former might be the Ælfmær *deorling* who later fought on the Danish side at the battle of Sherston (*AS Chron*, 1016), but the name is very common.

74. Passages in the works of both Ælfric and Wulfstan have been taken as covert criticism of the king. In a homily dating perhaps from the late 990s, Ælfric observes that 'the people will be prosperous under a prudent king but miserable under one who is unwise, suffering many misfortunes from his misdirection (*misræd*)', a sentiment expressed in almost identical terms in Wulfstan's *Institutes of Polity* (Thorpe, *The homilies of the Anglo-Saxon church*, ii, pp. 318–20; Jöst, *Die 'Institutes of Polity'*, p. 47, trans. Swanton, *Anglo-Saxon prose*, p. 126). Whether such passages were really aimed at Æthelred, or are simply general aphorisms on the theme of kingship it is difficult to say, and there is some danger of falling into a circular argument: Æthelred was an unsatisfactory king, therefore such passages are directed against his failings, therefore he was an unsatisfactory king.

75. The fragmentary IX Æthelred, of which only the opening clauses remain, may also belong to 1014; it is undated but was 'decreed at Woodstock' (Wormald, *MEL*, pp. 336–7).

76. VIII Atr 44§1, Swanton, *Anglo-Saxon prose*, pp. 137–8. IX Atr contains a fragmentary exhortation in the same terms.

77. Pauline Stafford, 'The laws of Cnut and the history of Anglo-Saxon royal promises', *ASE*, 10 (1982), pp. 173–90.

78. Wormald, *MEL*, pp. 361–2.

79. II Cn, 71–71.5.

80. Stafford, 'The laws of Cnut', p. 181.

81. *AS Chron*, 1014. Cnut's support in the region is reflected in the fact that dies struck by the Lincoln moneyers were used for the earliest coinage issued in his name as king of Denmark (Sawyer, 'Cnut's empire', p. 17 and see note 99 below).

82. Fell, '*Víkingavísur*', pp. 118–22. His Poitevin campaign, also recorded by Óttarr *svarti* (Ashdown, *English and Norse documents*, pp. 160–1), may be the same as that described by Adémar of Chabannes (Strickland, 'Military technology and conquest', p. 379, note 141; see Chapter 5, note 23 above).

83. William of Jumièges records the duke's employment of Oláf, anachronistically described as 'king of Norway', and a mysterious '*Lacmann*, king of the Swedes' (*WmJ*, ii, pp. 22–7). For the date and the source of William's information, see Elisabeth van Houts, 'Scandinavian influence in Norman literature', *ANS*, 6 (1984), pp. 118–9; see also *Encomium Emmae*, pp. 77–9.

84. William of Jumièges represents Æthelred as digging up his treasure from the earth before fleeing Winchester, but prejudice against the king has led the historian to exaggerate the speed and urgency of his removal to Normandy.
85. *Höfudlausn*, verse 6 (Ashdown, *English and Norse documents*, pp. 166–7, *EHD*, i, no. 14); the verse is displaced in the sequence. The last two verses in Sighvatr's *Víkingavísur* refer to battles in England (at unidentified places) after the continental adventures, and these may relate to engagements fought on behalf of Æthelred (*Encomium Emmae*, pp. 78–9).
86. Æthelred may have spent some time at York after the expulsion of Cnut; see Chapter 7 below.
87. *Encomium Emmae*, pp. 79–80; it also alleges that Thorkell and his men remained in England as a kind of fifth column, awaiting the opportunity to assist Cnut in the conquest of the kingdom.
88. Warner, *Thietmar*, p. 333. Swein presumably died at Gainsborough, and may have been buried there, though by the twelfth century it was believed that his body had lain at York (*Historia Regum*, *Symeon Op. Omnia*, ii, p. 146; T. D. Hardy and C. T. Martin (ed.), *Gaimar, Lestorie des Engles*, RS (London, 1888), i, p. 176).
89. *Encomium Emmae*, pp. lvii, 14–15, 18–19.
90. Freeman, *NC*, i, p. 667: 'had Swegen found his Eadgyth Swanneshals in England?'.
91. Tschan, *Adam of Bremen*, p. 95 (II. 58); Sawyer, 'Cnut's Scandinavian empire', pp. 18–19.
92. *Encomium Emmae*, pp. 69, 79–80 and note 8.
93. Ashdown, *English and Norse documents*, pp. 166–7.
94. Lund, 'Scandinavia, *c.* 700–1066', pp. 222–4. Sighvatr Thórðarson describes the settlement between Oláf and Earl Hákon, 'who had the best lineage of those who speak the Danish tongue' (Fell, '*Víkingsvísur*', p. 122).
95. Andersen, 'The Viking policy of Æthelred the Unready', p. 289.
96. Tschan, *Adam of Bremen*, pp. 94–5 (II. 57) and see note 43 above; 97 (II. 59) and note 215.
97. Lund, 'Cnut's Danish kingdom', Rumble, *Reign of Cnut*, p. 28. Harald is scarcely known outside the pages of Thietmar of Merseberg, who as he himself admits was poorly informed about Danish affairs (Warner, *Ottonian Germany*, p. 335), and the *Encomium Emmae Reginae*, whose account is coloured by the desire to present Cnut as the true heir of his father; it even makes Cnut rather than Harald the elder son. The *Anglo-Saxon Chronicle*, which ignores Harald's existence, makes the Danish fleet elect Cnut king even before the departure from England in 1014.

98. *Encomium Emmae*, pp. 16–19.
99. Kenneth Jonsson, 'Cnut's coinage', Rumble, *Reign of Cnut*, pp. 223–4; Brita Malmer, 'On the early coinage of Lund', Wood and Lund, *People and places in northern Europe*, pp. 187–93. The prototype for this earliest coinage was Æthelred's 'Last Small Cross' issue and the dies used included some from Lincoln (see note 81 above).
100. Thietmar even asserts that Harald accompanied Cnut to England, though this is mistaken (Warner, *Ottonian Germany*, p. 335). It would of course be in Harald's interest that his perhaps troublesome brother should occupy himself in foreign ventures.
101. *Encomium Emmae*, pp. 16–17, 18–19.

Notes to Chapter 7: Dissent and Disaster

1. *AS Chron*, 1014.
2. The timing can be calculated by reckoning back from the first dated event of the year, the submission of the Five Boroughs to Edmund, before 8 September (see below).
3. Stephen Baxter, 'The earls of Mercia and their commended men', *ANS*, 23 (2001), p. 37; see also Blair, *Anglo-Saxon Oxfordshire*, pp. 152–9. It was at Oxford that 'King Cnut and the Danes and the English' came to terms in 1018 (*AS Chron*).
4. Blair, *Anglo-Saxon Oxfordshire*, p. 151; Æthelmær's property, which he gave to Eynsham Abbey, included the church of St Ebb. For Eadric's house, see next note.
5. *AS Chron*, 1015. Eadric's eventual successor, Earl Leofric of Mercia (son of Ealdorman Leofwine) was also associated with Oxford, and his hall, perhaps identical with that of his predecessor, may have lain adjacent to St Michael's-at-the-North Gate (Blair, *Anglo-Saxon Oxfordshire*, pp. 159, 163–7; Baxter, 'The earls of Mercia and their commended men', pp. 22–8, 35–7).
6. John of Worcester calls her Ealdgyth, which was of course the name of Morcar's wife, the niece of Wulfric Wulfrun's son (*JnW*, ii, pp. 480–1). It is not impossible that the brothers were married to women bearing the same, rather common, name, but John may simply have given Sigeferth's wife the name of his sister-in-law. Morcar's daughter, who must have been fourteen or more at the time of her father's murder, is probably the Ælfgifu who later married Earl Leofric's son and successor, Ælfgar (Sawyer, *Charters of Burton*, pp. xli–xliii).
7. S. 934, not attested by either Sigeferth or Morcar and thus perhaps to be

dated after their murders. See Keynes, *Diplomas*, table 8; idem, 'Crime and punishment', pp. 80–1 and note 90.

8. Stenton, *ASE*, p. 374.
9. In 1016 Cnut's army went 'along the fen to Stamford *and then* into Lincolnshire' (*AS Chron*, 1016, my italics), and it is not until 1065 that the 'C' text of the *Chronicle* (the only strictly contemporary witness) records a gathering of 'all the thegns of Yorkshire' (*þa þegnas ealles on Eoforwic scire*).
10. S. 681, 712, 716; Johnson South, *Historia de Sancto Cuthberto*, pp. 68–9, 114–5. In 1066 Edward the Confessor held seven manors in Yorkshire, but none in Lincolnshire; see John Grassi, 'The lands and revenues of Edward the Confessor', *EHR*, 117 (2002), pp. 251–83, at pp. 278, 282–3.
11. Johnson South, *Historia de Sancto Cuthberto*, pp. 67, 111–12 (see also Chapter 4 above). The magnates are not named, nor is the grant dated, but it is hard to think of any other plausible context for a royal visit to the northern archbishopric.
12. The verb *gebugan* 'is regularly used with reference to commendation' (Robertson, *Charters*, p. 372).
13. S. 947–8. Their authenticity has been doubted, but it is difficult to see why anyone would forge them, for, as Dr Hart has observed (*ECEE*, pp. 200–3), 'no possible advantage could accrue ... from the possession of such documents'. Their irregular form might reflect the circumstances of their production; to quote Dr Hart again, 'the facilities of the king's writing-office could not have been at the donor's disposal', and the draughtsmen presumably used as models whatever genuine texts were to hand.
14. For the titles, see Keynes, *Diplomas*, p. 126, note 136. 'King Edmund ætheling' (S. 947) is particularly odd, for even if it was issued after Æthelred's death, why should the title of 'ætheling' be included? It is of course possible that *rex* is an insertion of the copyist.
15. Neither the New Minster, Winchester, nor Thorney Abbey held the lands concerned in 1066. There were, of course, other 'new minsters' and the small size of the property granted might suggest that the recipient was a local house.
16. Keynes, *Diplomas*, table 1; the earliest date for Edward's birth is 1003, which makes him no more than twelve in the summer of 1015. The *Life* of King Edward claims that when Emma was first pregnant, the English nobles swore to acknowledge the child, if male, as his father's heir (Barlow, *Vita Ædwardi*, pp. 7–8; 2nd edn, pp. 12–13). A similar account appears in the *Inventio* of St Vulfrann, composed soon after 1053; see Elisabeth van Houts, 'Historiography and hagiography at Saint-Wandrille: the

Inventio et Miracula Sancti Vulfranni', *ANS*, 12 (1990), pp. 247–8, 251. Edward may have made some such claim during or after the reign of Cnut, for it is implicitly denied in the *Encomium Emmae*, when Edward tells his mother that the English nobles have sworn no oath to him (*Encomium Emmae*, pp. 18–19).

17. In 1066 four hides at Cosham were appurtenant to the royal manor of Wymering, over against Portsea Island (*GDB*, fo. 38).
18. John of Worcester adds Ælfgar to the *Chronicle*'s list of Englishmen (Eadric *streona* and Ælfmær *deorling*) who fought for the Danes at the battle of Sherston in 1016 (*JnW*, ii, pp. 486–7). See also below and Chapter 6, note 60 above.
19. *JnW*, ii, pp. 480–1.
20. *Encomium Emmae*, pp. 16–19; Keynes, 'Cnut's earls', pp. 55, 74–5, 84, note 8; Poole, *Viking poems*, pp. 102–5. Campbell argued (*Encomium Emmae*, pp. 75, 84–5) that Thorkell only submitted to Cnut after the death of Edmund in November 1016 but it seems more likely that he joined the Danish force after the demise of Æthelred in April (see below, at note 45).
21. In 1049 the West Saxons raised forty-two ships, commanded by Earl Godwine; there was also a Mercian contingent, but the number of ships is not recorded (*AS Chron*, 'C', 1049).
22. For Warwickshire, see Chapter 4 above. It was to Leofwine's ealdordom that Edmund retreated after his defeat at *Assandun* (see below).
23. *JnW*, ii, pp. 482–3.
24. V Atr 28, reduced to forfeiture of property in VI Atr 35.
25. John of Worcester, assuming that Edmund and Uhtred were afraid to advance against the Danish army, criticises them for targeting the English shires (*JnW*, ii, pp. 482–3).
26. Ashdown, *English and Norse documents*, pp. 136–9; Jesch, *Ships and men*, pp. 52–3; *EHD*, i, no. 15 (translation only); see Poole, 'Skaldic verse and Anglo-Saxon history', pp. 272–3. *Helmingborg* has been identified with Hemingbrough (Yorkshire East Riding), though the town lies to the north and east, rather than the west of the Ouse.
27. Nafena and his brother Northwine attended a council at London in the 990s, along with other thegns of the north and Earl Thored (S. 877, *EHD*, i, no. 120 and see Chapter 4, note 38 above). Nothing further is known of the family.
28. The quotation is from Freeman, *NC*, i, p. 377.
29. *Symeon Op. Omnia*, ii, p. 218; Morris, *Marriage and murder*, p. 3.
30. The case for Wighill is argued by Fletcher (*Bloodfeud*, pp. 2–3), but the place-name evidence is against the identification.

31. *Knútsdrápa*, stanza 6 (Ashdown, *English and Norse documents*, pp. 136–9; *EHD*, i, no. 15; Poole, 'Skaldic verse and Anglo-Saxon history', pp. 270–8, at p. 273. See also Townend, 'Contextualizing the *Knútsdrápa*: skaldic praise-poetry at the court of Cnut', pp. 159–62). Óttarr, who was writing *c.* 1027, describes Cnut's conquest of England in unusual detail.
32. A Thurbrand attests S. 922 (dated 1009), a diploma from the Burton archive, immediately after Styr, presumably Styr Ulf's son (see Chapter 4 above).
33. Kapelle, *The Norman Conquest of the North*, pp. 17–20; Fletcher, *Bloodfeud*, pp. 51–3.
34. Compare the murder on Stainmore of York's last Viking king, Erik Bloodaxe, betrayed (according to Roger of Wendover) by Osulf of Bamburgh (*EHD*, i, no. 4, *sub anno* 950).
35. Williams, *The English and the Norman Conquest*, pp. 30–1; see also Fletcher, *Bloodfeud*, pp. 188–90.
36. *GDB*, fo. 326. By 1086 it had passed to Gilbert de Ghent, his only manor in the shire.
37. *GDB*, fos 314–314v, 332 (Thurbrand and Gamall), 324v, 374 (Cnut), 300v (Sumarlid). The figures are minimal, for men of these names are found elsewhere, and may be identical with Thurbrand *hold*'s kinsmen. The lands of Thurbrand and Gamall (all of which passed to the same Norman successor, who had no other English predecessors) were worth at least £17 5*s.* 8*d.*, but not all are given a value in the Domesday folios. Cnut's three manors were worth £6 10*s.* and Sumarlid's estate at Crambe was valued at only 2*s.*
38. For *Norðleoda laga* ('the law of the north people'), see *EHD*, i, no. 52B and Wormald, *MEL*, pp. 392–3. See also Chapter 4 above.
39. See note 27 above.
40. Freeman, *NC*, i, p. 377; Stenton, *ASE*, p. 390.
41. The succession of Eadulf is remembered only in the Durham tradition (*De obsessione Dunelmi*, for which see *Symeon Op. Omnia*, i, p. 218, Morris, *Marriage and murder*, p. 3; *De primo Saxonum adventu*, see *Symeon Op. Omnia*, ii, pp. 382–3). For Thurbrand, see Kapelle, *The Norman Conquest of the North*, pp. 21–4. For Thórð Kolbeinsson's panegyric on earl Erik, see note 49 below.
42. Aird, *St Cuthbert and the Normans*, p. 49. The see of Durham was vacant for the next three years, and when a bishop (Edmund) was finally chosen by the community, he took the unusual step of journeying to Cnut's court for the confirmation of his election.
43. Cnut's return journey to Dorset, 'keeping to the west', would have taken him through the shires of Mercia and the midlands in which Ælfgifu's

kinsmen had been landholders and it is possible that some of their descendants and dependants were still dwelling there.

44. *AS Chron*, 1016.
45. *JnW*, ii, pp. 484–5.
46. *JnW*, ii, pp. 494–5.
47. See above, note 23.
48. Freeman, who accepted the 'double election' of 1016, suggested that it was at the Southampton meeting that Thorkell the Tall defected to Cnut (*NC*, i, pp. 374–5, 378–9, 673–7); he seems to have fought on the Danish side at the siege of London and (perhaps) the battle of Sherston (see below).
49. For *Liðsmannaflokkr*, see Chapter 5, note 38 above. *Eiríksdrápa* was composed, probably in England, before the death of its hero, Erik of Lade, last heard of in 1023 (Poole, 'Skaldic verse and Anglo-Saxon history', pp. 269–71).
50. *AS Chron*, 1016: *dolfon þa ane mycele dic on ða suðhealfe and drogon heora scipa on west healfe þære brycge.* Freeman observed that the use of the verb *dragan* 'seems to mean that the ships were towed along the new-made canal' (*NC*, i, pp. 381–2 and note 6).
51. Fell, '*Víkingavísur*', p. 115 (stanza 6), translated in *EHD*, i, no. 12, and see Chapter 5, note 36 above; *buðir* are temporary dwellings, raised at peaceful gatherings as well as in military encampments. Jesch, *Ships and men*, pp. 50–1, suggests that the ditch was part of the defences and that the stanza records its successful defence by the English: *Sverð bitu völsk, en vörðu víkingar þar díki* ('Foreign swords bit and the Vikings defended the ditch'), taking *víkingar*, 'enemies', to refer to the English, the 'enemies' of Sighvatr's hero, Óláf *helgi.* Óláf was not, of course, present at the siege of London in 1016; Sighvatr's verse occurs in the description of his earlier exploits in 1009–12.
52. Poole, *Viking poems*, pp. 88 (stanza 6), 113.
53. *EHD*, i, no. 14 (stanza 11); Poole, 'Skaldic verse and Anglo-Saxon history', pp. 288–9.
54. *Encomium Emmae*, pp. 22–3, 70–1.
55. *EHD* i, no. 15 (stanza 7), Poole, 'Skaldic verse and Anglo-Saxon history', pp. 274–5. For the importance of the Brentford crossing, see below.
56. Warner, *Thietmar*, pp. 335–6.
57. For Thorkell's alleged participation in the battle of Sherston, see *Encomium Emmae*, pp. 20–3, lvii-lviii; for Thietmar's description of the martyrdom of Ælfheah (Warner, *Thietmar*, pp. 336–7), see Chapter 5 above.
58. Freeman, *NC*, i, p. 684 and see *Encomium Emmae*, p. lvi, Larson, *Cnut*, pp. 77–8; S. 1503.

59. *Encomium Emmae*, pp. 38–9. For Emma's presence in London during the siege, see Poole, *Viking poems*, pp. 89 (stanzas 8–9), 113.
60. *Encomium Emmae*, pp. 32–3.
61. Keynes, 'The æthelings in Normandy', pp. 176–7, 181–5; Stafford, *Emma and Edith*, pp. 22–4, 32, 224–7. Professor Stafford compares the marriage of Cnut and Emma to Swein's union with the widow of Erik, king of the *Svear*, which underlined the subordination of her son Olof *skötkonung* to Danish suzerainty; the parallel is not exact for Cnut's rival Edmund was a stepson, not son, of Emma, and in fact the marriage did not take place until after his death.
62. Keynes, 'The æthelings in Normandy', p. 177.
63. The verb *geridan* means 'to ride up to/over, to take (forcible) possession of'; compare the modern 'override', 'ride roughshod over'.
64. Compare the battle between Edmund and 'Thurgut' in Thietmar's account (see above). John of Worcester gives the English victory at Penselwood and the *Encomium* gives victory at Sherston to the Danes (*JnW*, ii, pp. 486–7; *Encomium Emmae*, pp. 20–3).
65. *JnW*, ii, pp. 486–9. John's account of the battle of Sherston (and that of *Assandun*) is based, like most such monastic descriptions, on literary sources and traditional motifs.
66. *Knútsdrápa*, stanza 6, *EHD*, i, no. 15, Poole, 'Skaldic verse and Anglo-Saxon history', p. 273; *Encomium Emmae*, pp. lvii-lviii, 20–3. The encomiast locates Sherston, by implication, in south-east England, whereas in fact it lies on the borders of Wessex and southern Mercia.
67. *VO*, p. 443; *EHD*, i, no. 236, p. 840.
68. *JnW*, ii, pp. 490–1.
69. The date is provided by the obits of those who died there; see Dickins, 'The day of Byrhtnoth's death and other obits', pp. 20–1.
70. Warwick Rodwell, 'The Battle of *Assandun* and its memorial church', Cooper, *The Battle of Maldon*, pp. 127–58; C. R. Hart, 'The site of *Assandun*', *The Danelaw*, pp. 553–65.
71. For what follows, see Rodwell, 'The Battle of *Assandun*', pp. 132–6.
72. *Eiríksdrápa*, stanza 12, *EHD*, i, no. 14; Poole, 'Skaldic verse and Anglo-Saxon history', pp. 276–8.
73. *Knútsdrápa*, stanza 9, *EHD*, i, no. 15. It may, however, be a displaced verse from a poem in praise of Cnut's father, Swein, for whom Óttarr is known to have worked (Townend, 'Contextualizing the *Knútsdrápur*: skaldic praise-poems at the court of Cnut', pp. 160–1).
74. *AS Chron*, 'C', 'D'; the 'E' recension has *eall Engla land*, glossed *þeode*.
75. Dr Hart has drawn attention to the eastern associations of several of the

fallen (Eadnoth, for instance, had preceded Wulfsige as abbot of Ramsey), another indication that the battle took place on the borders of Essex, East Anglia and the east midlands ('The site of *Assandun*', p. 562).

76. John says that Edmund 'had only the army which he could gather in so short a time' (*JnW*, ii, pp. 486–7).
77. It was only later in 1016 (after Edmund's death on 30 November), that Wulfstan relinquished the bishopric of Worcester to Leofsige, abbot of Thorney (*JnW*, ii, pp. 496–7).
78. *Knútsdrápa*, stanza 8, *EHD*, i, no. 15; Poole, 'Skaldic verse and Anglo-Saxon history', p. 275. Stanza 10 mentions an engagement after *Assandun* on the banks of the Thames, perhaps implying that Cnut secured London before pursuing Edmund.
79. *AS Chron*, 'D', 1016; *JnW*, ii, pp. 492–3. For the identification of *Olanige wið Deorhyrste*, see J. D. Harris, 'The site of Alney, AD 1016', *Glevensis: the Gloucester and District Archaeological Research Group Review*, 26 (1992), pp. 11–12. It is now represented by a strip of land once called the Naight (a corruption of 'Eight', that is, eyot, island) bounded on the west by the Severn and on the east by the former course of the Naight Brook.
80. For Odda and Ælfgar, see Chapter 6, note 17 above.
81. *JnW*, ii, pp. 492–3 and note 9; for the earlier agreement, see *AS Chron*, 'B', 'C', 957, 'D', 955.
82. *AS Chron*, 'CDE', 1017.
83. His role is emphasized in the *Encomium*, which makes him counsel the division of the kingdom, 'for I consider it better that our king should have half the kingdom in peace, than that he should in despite of himself lose the whole of it at the same time' (*Encomium Emmae*, pp. 28–9). Later stories implicate Eadric in Edmund's death (Wright, *Cultivation of saga*, pp. 198–210), but this is in the highest degree unlikely; murdering Edmund would serve only to increase the power of Cnut, which was not in Eadric's interests (see next note).
84. *AS Chron*, 'CDE', 1017; *JnW*, ii, pp. 504–5. The *Encomium* has an elaborate account of Eadric's murder. When the ealdorman came to Cnut seek his reward, the king asked him: '"Shall you, who have deceived your lord with guile, be capable of being true to me?" ... and summoning Eiríkr, his commander [Erik of Lade], he said: "Pay this man what we owe him" ... He indeed raised his axe without delay and cut off his head' (*Encomium Emmae*, pp. 30–3).
85. *JnW*, ii, pp. 482–3. John also omits the *Chronicle*'s sour comment that 'it availed nothing, no more than it had done often before'.
86. Freeman, *NC*, i, p. 378.

87. *AS Chron*, 'D', 1057; Freeman, *NC*, i, p. 379. For the legends which swiftly grew up around his name, see Wright, *The cultivation of saga*, pp. 184–205.
88. *Encomium Emmae*, pp. 30–1. The same providential dispensation is invoked in relation to the death of Æthelred (who remains anonymous), which allowed the triumphant Cnut to enter London (*Encomium Emmae*, pp. 22–3). Æthelred, of course, died before the siege began, and Cnut was not able to enter London until after Edmund's death.
89. For the sheriff and the writ, see above, Chapter 3; for the shire, see also Chapter 4.
90. See above, Chapters 4 and 5.
91. Taken together, I and II Cnut (respectively the 'Ecclesiastical' and the 'Secular' codes) represent 'a codification of mostly pre-existing law' (Wormald, *MEL*, p. 349).
92. Wormald, *MEL*, pp. 465–6.
93. See Chapter 4 above.
94. See above, Chapters 2 and 3.
95. Wormald, '*Engla Lond*: the making of an allegiance', passim.

Notes to Appendix A: A Note on 'Danegeld'

1. See (in order of publication) M. K. Lawson, 'The collection of Danegeld and heregeld in the reigns of Æthelred II and Cnut', *EHR*, 99 (1984), pp. 721–38; J. Gillingham, '"The most precious jewel in the English crown": levels of Danegeld and heregeld in the early eleventh century', *EHR*, 104 (1989), pp. 373–84; M. K. Lawson, '"Those stories look true": levels of taxation in the reigns of Æthelred II and Cnut', *EHR*, 104 (1989), pp. 385–406; J. Gillingham, 'Chronicles and coins as evidence for levels of tribute and taxation in late tenth-century and early eleventh-century England', *EHR*, 105 (1990), pp. 939–50; M. K. Lawson, 'Danegeld and heregeld again', *EHR*, 105 (1990), pp. 951–61.
2. Downer, *Leges Henrici primi*, pp. 120–1 (chapter 15§1): the rate is given as 12*d.* per hide per annum. See also Keynes, 'The historical background', p. 101. The use of 'thingmen' ('men of the *thing* or court') shows that the stipendiaries attached to the royal household are the intended recipients, rather than the hostile armies of invading Vikings. That some confusion between the *heregeld* and the tribute (*gafol*) paid to invaders was already creeping in during the twelfth century is shown by the posthumous byname *Danegeld* applied to Archbishop Sigeric, who died in 994 (see Chapter 3, note 24 above).
3. The *Anglo-Saxon Chronicle* records the imposition a geld of 6*s.* on the

hide in 1084 (*AS Chron*, 'E', 1083) and the Geld Rolls for the south-western shires, preserved in the *Liber Exoniensis*, record the collection of a 6*s*. geld, perhaps levied in 1086, though it is possible that they relate to the geld of 1084: see V. H. Galbraith, *The making of Domesday Book* (Oxford, 1961), pp. 87–101; R. Welldon Finn, Domesday Studies: the *Liber Exoniensis* (London, 1964, pp. 97–123). For a full survey of post-Conquest gelds, see Judith Green, 'The last century of Danegeld', *EHR*, 96 (1981), pp. 241–58.

4. *AS Chron*, 'D', 1051. The entry refers to the imposition of the tax by Æthelred, thirty-nine years earlier (i.e. in 1012).
5. *AS Chron*, 'E', 1040. The annal also records that 'the sester of wheat rose to fifty-five pence and even higher', which may be connected with the king's demands, as landowners attempted to maximise their profits in order to meet the sums demanded.
6. Jesch, *Ships and men*, pp. 156–7, 172; N. A. M. Rodger, 'Cnut's geld and the size of Danish ships', *EHR*, 110 (1995), pp. 392–403.
7. *AS Chron*, 'C', 1040; *ha* is another Scandinavian loan, ON *hár*, which has the same meaning as *hamele* (Jesch, *Ships and men*, p. 155). It is used in the literal sense of 'oarport' in the will of Ælfwold of Crediton (S. 1422, see Chapter 2 above).
8. *AS Chron*, 'E', 1041, and see Chapter 6 above.
9. *AS Chron*, CDE, 991.
10. *AS Chron*, 1002 (for the conjunction of provisions and *gafol*, see also 1006, 1011), 1007, 1012, 1018. See also the *Chronicle*'s complaint in 1011 about the ineffectiveness of 'all this truce and peace and tribute' (*griðe and friðe and gafole*).
11. See Chapter 3 above.
12. Keynes, 'The historical background', p. 101.
13. See Williams, *Kingship and government*, pp. 33–6.
14. Keynes, 'The historical background', p. 102 and note 69, p. 112; *Diplomas*, p. 202, note 182.
15. Archbishop Sigeric sold land at Monk's Risborough, Bucks, to redeem his church from sack by Vikings (S. 882 and see Chapter 3 above) and Bishop Æthelric of Sherborne sold land at Corscombe because of the ravages of the Danes (S. 933 and see Chapter 5 above); Æthelred himself is found selling land in order to raise cash to pay tribute (*uectigal*, S. 912; *tributum*, S. 943). Hemming complains that the church of Worcester had to sell and melt down church plate because of the 'unbearable burden of royal taxes' (*regalium vectigalium importabilis exactio*) and the 'huge and almost unbearable tribute' (*maximum et fere importabile tributum*) imposed on England by Æthelred during the devastation wrought by King

Swein (Hemming, p. 248). Of course the *heregeld* provoked similar complaints (see S. 1424 for the abbot of Gloucester's lease of lands to redeem the rest of his estates from 'the great *heregeld* levied throughout England').

16. The confusion occurs even in works which otherwise draw a clear distinction between tax and tribute. See, for instance, D. M. Metcalf, 'Large Danegelds in relation to war and kingship: their implications for monetary history, and some numismatic evidence', in Sonia Chadwick Hawkes (ed.), *Weapons and warfare in Anglo-Saxon England* (Oxford, 1989), p. 187: 'Words can change their meanings ... *geldum* in medieval Latin is merely tax, whereas geld in modern English carries the connotation of a heavy exaction'. Throughout this paper, the terms *geld* and *Danegeld* are used for the *gafol* paid to victorious enemies, rather than the taxes imposed by English kings, though such tributes are never confused with 'customary taxation' (see note 18 below).
17. The sum of £22,000 was paid in 994, according to II Atr (see Chapter 3 above). Compare the £16,000 which King Eadred left to his people, 'to purchase relief from hunger or a heathen army' (S. 1515).
18. Metcalf, 'Large Danegelds', p. 183; see also p. 182: 'the sums involved bore no relationship to the sums paid in customary taxation. Gelds (*sic*) were incommensurately larger' (see note 16 above).
19. Metcalf, 'Large Danegelds', p. 185. Only the tributes of 991 (the first) and 1018 (at £72,000 the largest recorded) 'required special arrangements'. In respect of the latter, Metcalf argues that 'there is positive evidence, from the coinage itself, that the geld paid to Cnut in 1018 was quite exceptionally large'.

Bibliography

PRIMARY SOURCES

Anderson, Alan Orr (ed.): *Early sources of Scottish history AD 500 to 1286*, 2 vols (Edinburgh, 1922; corrected edn, Stamford, 1990).

Arnold, Thomas (ed.): *Symeonis monachi Opera omnia*, 2 vols, RS (London, 1882–5).

Ashdown, Margaret: *English and Norse documents relating to the reign of Æthelred the Unready* (Cambridge, 1930).

Attenborough, F. L.: *The laws of the earliest English kings* (Cambridge, 1922; reprinted New York, 1963).

Baker, Peter S. (ed.): *The Anglo-Saxon Chronicle: a collaborative edition, Ms F* (Cambridge, 2000).

Barlow, F (ed.): *The life of King Edward who rests at Westminster* (2nd edn; Oxford, 1992).

Bately, Janet M. (ed.): *The Anglo-Saxon Chronicle: a collaborative edition, iii, Ms A* (Cambridge, 1986).

Bethurum, Dorothy (ed.): *The Homilies of Wulfstan* (Oxford, 1957).

Birch, W. de Gray (ed.): *Liber Vitae: Register and Martyrology of New Minster and Hyde Abbey, Winchester* (Winchester, 1892).

Blake, E. O. (ed.): *Liber Eliensis*, Camden 3rd ser., 92 (London, 1962).

Bosanquet, Geoffrey (trans.): *Eadmer's History of Recent Events in England* (London, 1964).

Campbell, A.: *Charters of Rochester* (London, 1973).

Campbell, A. (ed.): *Encomium Emmae Reginae*, Camden Classic reprints (Cambridge, 1998).

Campbell, A. (ed.): *The Chronicle of Æthelweard* (London, 1962).

Chavannon, J. (ed.): *Adémar de Chabannes, Chronique* (Paris, 1897).

Christianson, Eric (ed.): *Saxo Grammaticus Gesta Danorum, Books X-XVI*, i, BAR International series, 84 (1980).

Craster, H. H. E.: 'The Red Book of Durham', *EHR*, 40 (1925), pp. 523–9.

Darlington, R. R. and McGurk, P. (ed.): *The Chronicle of John of Worcester*, 3 vols (Oxford, 1995–2001).

Davis, A. H. (ed.): *William Thorne's Chronicle of Saint Augustine's Abbey* (Oxford, 1934).

Downer, L. J. (ed.): *Leges Henrici Primi* (Oxford, 1972).

Dugdale, William: *Monasticon Anglicanum*, ed. J. Caley, H. Ellis and B. Bandinel, 6 vols in 8 (London, 1817–30).

Erskine, R. W. H. (ed.): *Great Domesday: a facsimile* (London, 1986).

Fauroux, Marie (ed.): *Recueil des actes des ducs de Normandie (911–1066)* (Caen, 1961).

Fell, Christine: *Edward, king and martyr* (Leeds, 1971).

Fell, Christine: '*Víkingavísur*', in Ursula Dronke (ed.), *Speculum Norroenum: Norse studies in memory of Gabriel Turville-Petre* (Odense, 1981), pp. 106–22.

Fowler, Roger (ed.): *Wulfstan's Canons of Edgar* (London, 1972).

Greenway, Diana (ed.): *Henry, Archdeacon of Huntingdon, Historia Anglorum. The History of the English People* (Oxford 1996).

Haddan, A. W. and Stubbs, W.: *Councils and ecclesiastical documents relating to Great Britain and Ireland*, 3 vols (Oxford, 1869–71).

Hamilton, N. E. S. A. (ed.): *William of Malmesbury, De gestis pontificum Anglorum*, RS (London, 1870).

Harmer, F. E.: *Anglo-Saxon Writs* (Manchester, 1952).

Hardy, T. D. and Martin, C. T. (ed.): Gaimar, *Lestorie des Engles*, RS (London, 1888).

Hart, W. H. (ed.): *Historia et cartularium monasterii Sanctri Petri Gloucestriae* (London, 1863–7).

Hearne, Thomas (ed.): *Hemingi Chartularium monachi Wigornensis* (Oxford, 1723).

Hinde, [J.] Hodgson (ed.): *Symeonis Dunelmensis Opera et Collectanea*, Surtees Society, 51 (1868).

James, M. R (trans.): *Walter Map: De Nugis Curialium*, Cymmrodorion Record Series, 9 (London, 1923).

Jones, Christopher A. (ed.): *Ælfric's Letter to the monks of Evesham* (Cambridge, 1999).

Jones, Thomas (ed.): *Brut y Tywysogion, or The Chronicle of the Princes, Peniarth Ms 20 version* (Cardiff, 1952).

Jones, Thomas (ed.): *Brut y Tywysogion, or The Chronicle of the Princes, Red Book of Hergest version* (Cardiff, 1955).

Jöst, Karl: *Die 'Institutes of Polity, Civil and Ecclesiastical'* (Bern, 1959).

Kelly, Susan: *Charters of Abingdon Abbey* (Oxford, 2000).

Kelly, Susan: *Charters of Selsey* (Oxford, 1998).

Kelly, Susan: *Charters of Shaftesbury Abbey* (Oxford, 1996).

Kemble, J. M.: *Codex Diplomaticus aevi Saxonici*, 6 vols (London, 1839–48).

Liebermann, F.: *Die Gesetze der Angelsachsen*, 3 vols (Halle, 1903–16).

Mac Airt, S. and Mac Niocall, G. (ed.): *The Annals of Ulster* (Dublin, 1983).

Macray, W. Dunn (ed.): *Chronicon Abbatiae de Evesham ad annum 1418*, RS (London, 1863).

Mellows, W. T. (ed.): *The Chronicle of Hugh Candidus, a monk of Peterborough* (Oxford, 1949), translation in W. T. Mellows (trans.), *The Peterborough Chronicle of Hugh Candidus* (Peterborough, 1941).

Miller, Sean: *Charters of the New Minster, Winchester* (Oxford, 2001).

Morris, R. (ed.): *Blickling Homilies of the tenth century*, EETS os, 58, 63, 73 (1874–80; reprinted 1957).

Napier, A. S. and Stevenson, W. H.: *The Crawford Collection of early charters* (Oxford, 1895).

O'Donovan, Mary-Anne: *Charters of Sherborne* (Oxford, 1988).

Plummer, Charles: *Two of the Saxon Chronicles parallel*, 2 vols (2nd revised edn, Oxford, 1952).

Pope, John C. (ed.): *The homilies of Ælfric: a supplementary collection*, EETS os, 259–60 (London, 1967–8).

Preest, David (trans.): *William of Malmesbury: The Deeds of the Bishops of England (Gesta Pontificum Anglorum)* (Woodbridge, 2002).

Raine, J. (ed.): *The historians of the Church of York and its archbishops*, 3 vols, RS (London, 1879–94).

Ramsay, Sir James H.: *The foundations of England, or Twelve centuries of British history (BC 55 to AD 1154*, 2 vols (London, 1898)

Robertson, A. J.: *Anglo-Saxon Charters* (2nd edn, Cambridge, 1956).

Robertson, A. J.: *The laws of the kings of England from Edmund to Henry I* (Cambridge, 1925; reprinted New York, 1974).

Rollason, David (ed.): *Symeon of Durham, Libellus de exordio atque procursu istius hoc est Dunhelmensis Ecclesie: Tract on the origins and progress of this the church of Durham* (Oxford, 2000).

Rule, M. (ed.): *Eadmeri Historia Novorum in Anglia*, RS (London, 1884).

Rumble, Alexander R. and Morris, Rosemary: '*Translatio Sancti Ælfegi Cantuarensis archiepiscopi et martiris*', in Rumble, *The reign of Cnut*, pp. 283–315.

Sawyer, P. H.: *Anglo-Saxon Charters: an annotated list and bibliography*, Royal Historical Society (London, 1968); rev. edn, Susan Kelly (ed.), at www.trin.cam.ac.uk/chartwww.

Sawyer, P. H.: *Charters of Burton Abbey* (Oxford, 1979).

Scholz, Bernard: 'Sulcard of Westminster: "Prologus de Construccione Westmonasterii"', *Traditio* 20 (1964), pp. 59–91.

Scragg, Donald (ed.): *The Battle of Maldon* (Manchester, 1981).

Skeat, W. W. (ed.): *Ælfric's Lives of the Saints*, 4 vols, EETS os, 76, 82, 94, 114 (Oxford, 1881–1900).

South, Ted Johnson (ed.): *Historia de Sancto Cuthberto* (Woodbridge, 2001).

Stevenson, J. (ed.).: *Chronicon Monasterii de Abingdon*, 2 vols, RS (London, 1858).

Stubbs, William (ed.): *Memorials of Saint Dunstan, archbishop of Canterbury*, RS (London, 1874).

Swanton, Michael (trans.): *Anglo-Saxon Prose* (London, 1975).

Thomson, R. M. and Winterbottom, M. (ed.): *William of Malmesbury, Gesta Regum Anglorum, The history of the English kings*, 2 vols (Oxford, 1998–9).

Thorpe, B. (ed.): *Florentii Wigornensis Chronicon ex Chronicis*, 2 vols (London, 1848–9).

Thorpe, B. (ed.): *The homilies of the Anglo-Saxon Church* (London, 1844–6).

van Houts, Elisabeth (ed.): *The Gesta Normannorum ducum of William of Jumièges, Orderic Vitalis and Robert of Torigny*, 2 vols (Oxford, 1992–5).

Warner, David: *Ottonian Germany: the Chronicle of Thietmar of Merseberg* (Manchester, 2001).

Wharton, H.: *Anglia Sacra* (Oxford, 1691).

Whitelock, Dorothy: *Anglo-Saxon wills* (Cambridge, 1930).

Whitelock, Dorothy: *English Historical Documents i, c. 500–1042* (London, 1955).

Whitelock, Dorothy (ed.): *Sermo lupi ad Anglos* (2nd edn; Exeter, 1976), reprinted in *History, Law and Literature in tenth- and eleventh-century England.*

Whitelock, Dorothy (ed.),: *The will of Æthelgifu* (Oxford, 1968).

Whitelock, Dorothy, Brett, M. and Brooke, C. N. L.: *Councils and Synods i, part I, 871–1066* (Oxford, 1981).

Whitelock, Dorothy, Douglas, David C. and Cooper, Susie I. (ed.): *The Anglo-Saxon Chronicle: a revised translation* (2nd edn; London, 1965).

Wilcox, Jonathan: *Ælfric's Prefaces* (Durham, 1994).

Wilmart, A.: 'La légende de Ste Édith en prose et vers par le moine Goscelin', *Analecta Bollandiana*, 56 (1938), pp. 5–307.

SECONDARY SOURCES

Abels, Richard: 'English tactics, strategy and military organization in the late tenth century', in Scragg, *The Battle of Maldon*, pp. 143–55.

Abels, Richard: 'From Alfred to Harold II: the military failure of the late Anglo-Saxon state', in Abels and Bachrach, *The Normans and their adversaries at war*, pp. 15–30.

Abels, Richard: *Lordship and military obligation in Anglo-Saxon England* (Berkeley, Los Angeles and London, 1988).

Abels, Richard and Bachrach, B. S. (ed.): *The Normans and their adversaries at war: studies in memory of C. Warren Hollister* (Woodbridge, 2001).

Abrams, Lesley: 'Edward the Elder's Danelaw', in Higham and Hill, *Edward the Elder, 899–924* (London and New York, 2001), pp. 128–43.

Aird, William M.: *St Cuthbert and the Normans: the church of Durham, 1071–1151* (Woodbridge, 1998).

Anderson, M. O.: *Kings and kingship in early Scotland* (Edinburgh, 1973).

Andersson, T. M.: 'The Viking policy of Ethelred the Unready', *Scandinavian Studies*, 59 (1987), pp. 284–95.

Atkin, M. A.: '"The land between Ribble and Mersey" in the early tenth century', in Rumble and Mills, *Names, places and people*, pp. 8–18.

Backhouse, Janet, Turner, D. H. and Webster, Lesley (ed.): *The Golden Age of Anglo-Saxon art* (London, 1984).

Barker, K. (ed.): *The Cerne Abbey Millenium lectures* (Cerne Abbas, 1998).

Barlow, Frank: *The English Church 1000–1066* (2nd edn, London, 1966).

Bately, Janet: 'The *Anglo-Saxon Chronicle*', in Scragg, *The Battle of Maldon*, pp. 37–50.

Bates, David: *Normandy before 1066* (London, 1982).

Baxter, Stephen: 'The earls of Mercia and their commended men', *ANS*, 23 (2001), pp. 23–46.

Bethurum, Dorothy: 'Regnum and Sacerdotium in the early eleventh century', in Clemoes and Hughes, *England before the Conquest*, pp. 129–45.

Blackburn, Mark: 'Æthelred's coinage', in Scragg, *The Battle of Maldon*, pp. 156–69.

Blair, John: *Anglo-Saxon Gloucestershire* (Stroud, 1994).

Blair, John: *Early medieval Surrey* (Stroud, 1991).

Blair, John: 'Introduction', in John Blair (ed.), *Minsters and parish churches: the local church in transition, 950–1300* (Oxford, 1988), pp. 1–19.

Blair, John, 'Local minster churches in Domesday Book and before', in J. C. Holt (ed.), *Domesday Studies* (Woodbridge, 1987), pp. 265–78.

Blair, John: 'Secular minster churches in Domesday Book', in P. H. Sawyer (ed.), *Domesday Book: a reassessment* (London, 1985), pp. 104–42.

Brand, John D.: *Periodic change of type in the Anglo-Saxon and Norman periods*, privately printed (Rochester, 1984).

Brand, Paul: 'Feud and the state in late Anglo-Saxon England', *J. British Studies*, 40 (2001), pp. 1–43.

Brooks, Nicholas: 'Arms, status and warfare in late Anglo-Saxon England', in Hill, *Ethelred the Unready*, pp. 81–103.

Brooks, Nicholas: 'The career of St Dunstan', in Ramsay et al., *St Dunstan*, pp. 1–23.

Brooks, Nicholas: *The early history of the church of Canterbury* (Leicester, 1984).

Brooks, Nicholas: 'Weapons and armour', in Scragg, *The Battle of Maldon*, pp. 208–19.

Brooks, Nicholas, and Catherine Cubitt (ed.): *St Oswald of Worcester: life and influence* (Leicester, 1996).

Budny, Mildred: 'The Byrhtnoth tapestry or embroidery', in Scragg, *The Battle of Maldon*, pp. 263–78.

Cam, Helen: 'Early groups of hundreds', in *Liberties and communities*, pp. 91–106.

Cam, Helen: *Liberties and communities in medieval England* (London, 1963).

Cam, Helen: '*Manerium cum hundredo*: the hundred and the hundred manor', in *Liberties and communities*, pp. 64–90.

Campbell, James: 'England, *c.* 991', in Cooper, *The Battle of Maldon*, pp. 1–17.

Campbell, James: 'England, France, Germany and Flanders', in Hill, *Ethelred the Unready*, pp. 255–70.

Campbell, Miles: 'Queen Emma and Ælfgifu of Northampton: Canute the Great's women', *Medieval Scandinavia*, 4 (1971), pp. 66–79.

Chadwick, H. M.: *Studies on Anglo-Saxon institutions* (Cambridge, 1905; reprinted New York, 1963).

Charles-Edwards, T. A. M.: 'Kinship, status and the origins of the hide', *P&P*, 52 (1972), pp. 3–33.

Clark, Cecily: 'The narrative mode of *The Anglo-Saxon Chronicle* before the Conquest', in Clemoes and Hughes, *England before the Conquest*, pp. 215–35, reprinted in Peter Jackson (ed.), *Words, Names and History: selected writings of Cecily Clark* (Woodbridge, 1995), pp. 3–19.

Clark, Cecily: 'On dating *The Battle of Maldon*: certain evidence reviewed', *Nottingham Medieval Studies*, 27 (1983), pp. 1–22, reprinted in Jackson, *Words, names and history*, pp. 20–36.

Clark, Helen and Ambrosiani, Björn: *Towns in the Viking age* (Leicester, 1991).

Clayton, Mary: 'Of mice and men: Ælfric's second homily for the feast of a confessor', *Leeds Studies in English*, ns, 24 (1993), pp. 1–26.

Clemoes, Peter: 'The chronology of Ælfric's works', in Clemoes, *The Anglo-Saxons*, pp. 212–47.

Clemoes, Peter (ed.): *The Anglo-Saxons: studies in some aspects of their history and culture presented to Bruce Dickins* (London, 1959).

Clemoes, Peter and Hughes, Kathleen (ed.): *England before the Conquest: studies in primary sources presented to Dorothy Whitelock* (Cambridge, 1971).

Coleman, Roberta V.: 'Domestic peace and public order in Anglo-Saxon law', in J. Douglas Woods and David A. E. Pelteret, *The Anglo-Saxons: synthesis and achievement* (Waterloo, Ontario, 1985), pp. 49–61.

Connor, Patrick W.: *Anglo-Saxon Exeter: a tenth-century cultural history* (Woodbridge, 1993).

Cooper, Janet (ed.): *The Battle of Maldon: fiction and fact* (London, 1993).

Cross, J. E.: 'The ethic of war in Old English', in Clemoes and Hughes, *England before the Conquest*, pp. 269–82.

Damgaard-Sorensen, Tinna: 'Danes and Wends: a study of Danish attitudes to the Wends', in Wood and Lund, *People and places in northern Europe, 500–1600*, pp. 171–86.

Dickins, Bruce: 'The day of Byrhtnoth's death and other obits from a twelfth-century Ely calendar', *Leeds Studies in English*, 6 (1937), pp. 14–24.

Dickins, Bruce: 'The day of the battle of Æthelingadene, ASC 1001 A', *Leeds Studies in English*, 6 (1937), pp. 25–7.

Dolley R. H. M.: 'Æthelræd's Rochester ravaging of 986: an intriguing numismatic sidelight', *Spink's Numismatic Circular*, 75 (1967), pp. 33–4.

Dolley, R. H. M.: 'An introduction to the coinage of Æthelræd II', in Hill, *Ethelred the Unready*, pp. 118–29.

Dolley, R. H. M.: 'The nummular brooch from Sulgrave', in Clemoes and Hughes, *England before the Conquest*, pp. 333–49.

Dolley, R. H. M.: 'The Shaftesbury hoard of pence of Æthelræd II', *Numismatic Chronicle*, 6th series, 16 (1956), pp. 267–80.

Dolley, R. H. M. (ed.): *Anglo-Saxon coins* (London, 1961).

Dolley, R. H. M., and Metcalf, D. M.: 'The reform of the English coinage under Eadgar', in Dolley, *Anglo-Saxon coins*, pp. 136–68.

Drewett, Peter, Rudling, David and Gardiner, Mark: *The south east to AD 1000* (London, 1988).

Dumville, D. N.: 'Between Alfred the Great and Edgar the Peaceable: Æthelstan, first king of England', in D. N. Dumville, *Wessex and England from Alfred to Edgar* (Woodbridge, 1992), pp. 141–7.

Dumville, D. N.: *The churches of north Britain in the first Viking age*, fifth Whithorn lecture, 1996 (Whithorn, 1997).

Dumville, D. N.: 'The death of King Edward the Martyr: chronological questions', forthcoming

Dumville, D. N.: 'The Anglian collection of royal genealogies and regnal lists', *ASE*, 5 (1976), pp. 23–50.

Dumville, D. N.: 'The Ætheling: a study in Anglo-Saxon constitutional history', *ASE*, 5 (1976), pp. 1–33.

Emms, Richard: 'The early history of St Augustine's Abbey, Canterbury', in Richard Gameson (ed.), *St Augustine and the conversion of England* (Stroud, 1999), pp. 410–27.

Fernie, Eric: *The architecture of the Anglo-Saxons* (London, 1982).

Finberg, H. P. R.: 'Bishop Athelstan's boundary', in Finberg, *Early charters of the west Midlands*, pp. 225–7.

Finberg, H. P. R.: 'Childe's Tomb', *Lucerna* (London, 1964), pp. 186–203.

Finberg, H. P. R.: *Gloucestershire Studies* (Leicester, 1957).

Finberg, H. P. R.: *Tavistock Abbey* (Cambridge, 1951).

Finberg, H. P. R.: 'The ancient shire of Winchcombe', in Finberg, *Early charters of the west Midlands*, pp. 228–35.

Finberg, H. P. R.: *The early charters of the west Midlands* (Leicester, 1961).

Finberg, H. P. R.: 'The house of Ordgar and the foundation of Tavistock Abbey', *EHR*, 53 (1943), pp. 190–201.

Finn, R. Welldon: *Domesday Studies: the Liber Exoniensis* (London, 1964).

Fisher, D. J. V: 'The anti-monastic reaction in Edward the Martyr's reign', *Cambridge Hist. J.*, 10 (1950–2), pp. 254–70.

Fletcher, Richard: *Bloodfeud: murder and revenge in Anglo-Saxon England* (London, 2002).

Frank, Roberta: 'King Cnut in the verse of his skalds', in Rumble, *The reign of Cnut*, pp. 106–24.

Freeman, E. A.: *The history of the Norman Conquest of England*, 6 vols (Oxford, 1870–79).

Fryde, E. B., Greenway, Diana, Porter, S. and Roy, I. (ed.): *Handbook of British Chronology* (London, 1986).

Galbraith, V. H.: *The making of Domesday Book* (Oxford, 1961).

Gatch, Milton McC.: *Preaching and theology in Anglo-Saxon England: Ælfric and Wulfstan* (Toronto and Buffalo, 1977).

Gelling, Margaret: *The early charters of the Thames Valley* (Leicester, 1979).

Gelling, Margaret: *The west Midlands in the early middle ages* (Leicester, 1992).

Gem, Richard: 'Church architecture in the reign of King Æthelred', in Hill, *Ethelred the Unready*, pp. 105–14.

Gillingham, John: 'Chronicles and coins as evidence for levels of tribute and taxation in late tenth-century and early eleventh-century England', *EHR*, 105 (1990), pp. 939–50.

Gillingham, John: '"The most precious jewel in the English crown": levels of Danegeld and heregeld in the early eleventh century', *EHR*, 104 (1989), pp. 373–84.

Godden, Malcolm R.: 'Ælfric and Anglo-Saxon kingship', *EHR*, 102 (1987), pp. 911–15.

Godden, Malcolm R.: 'Apocalypse and invasion in late Anglo-Saxon England', in Malcolm Godden, D. Gray and T. Hoad (ed.), *From Anglo-Saxon to Middle English: studies presented to E. G. Stanley* (Oxford, 1994), pp. 130–62.

Goebel, J.: *Felony and misdemeanour* (Pennsylvania, 1976).

Grassi, John: 'The lands and revenues of Edward the Confessor', *EHR*, 117 (2002), pp. 251–83.

Green, Judith: 'The last century of Danegeld', *EHR*, 96 (1981), pp. 241–58.

Grierson, Philip: 'The relations between England and Flanders before the Norman Conquest', *TRHS*, 4th series, 23 (1941), pp. 71–113.

Hadley, Dawn: '"And they proceeded to plough and support themselves": the Scandinavian settlement of England', *ANS*, 19 (1996), pp. 69–96.

Hare, Michael: *The two Anglo-Saxon minsters of Gloucester*, the Deerhurst Lecture 1992 (Deerhurst, 1993).

Harris, J. D.: 'The site of Alney, AD 1016', *Glevensis: the Gloucester and District Archaeological Research Group Review*, 26 (1992), pp. 11–12.

Hart, C. R.: 'Athelstan "Half-king" and his family', *ASE*, 2 (1973), pp. 115–44, reprinted and revised in *The Danelaw*, pp. 569–604.

Hart, C. R.: 'The battles of the Holme, *Brunanburh* and Ringmere', in *The Danelaw*, pp. 511–32.

Hart, C. R.: *The Danelaw* (London, 1992).

Hart, C. R.: 'The ealdordom of Essex', in Kenneth Neale (ed.), *An Essex tribute: essays presented to Frederick G. Emmison* (London, 1987), pp. 57–73, 76–85, reprinted and revised in *The Danelaw*, pp. 115–40.

Hart, C. R.: *The early charters of eastern England* (Leicester, 1966).

Hart, C. R.: *The early charters of northern England and the north Midlands* (Leicester, 1975).

Hart, C. R.: 'The early section of the *Worcester Chronicle*', *Journal of Medieval History*, 9 (1983), pp. 251–315.

Hart, C. R.: 'The eastern Danelaw', in *The Danelaw*, pp. 25–113.

Hart, C. R.: 'The site of *Assandun*', *History Studies*, 1 (1968), pp. 1–12, reprinted and revised in *The Danelaw*, pp. 553–65.

Hart, C. R.: 'The will of Ælfgifu', *The Danelaw*, pp. 455–65.

Haslam, Jeremy: 'The towns of Wiltshire', in Haslam, *Anglo-Saxon towns in southern England*, pp. 87–147.

Haslam, Jeremy (ed.): *Anglo-Saxon towns in southern England* (Chichester, 1984).

Hawkes, Sonia Chadwick (ed.), *Weapons and warfare in Anglo-Saxon England* (Oxford, 1989).

Hayward, Paul, 'Translation-narratives in post-Conquest hagiography and English resistance to the Norman Conquest', *ANS*, 21 (1999), pp. 67–93.

Heslop, T. A.: 'English seals from the mid ninth century to 1100', *JBAA*, 133 (1980), pp. 1–16.

Heslop, T. A.: 'Twelfth-century forgeries as evidence for earlier seals: the case of St Dunstan', in Ramsay et al., *St Dunstan*, pp. 299–310.

Higham, Nicholas J., and Hill, David H. (ed.): *Edward the Elder, 899–924* (London and New York, 2001).

Hill, David: *An atlas of Anglo-Saxon England* (Oxford, 1981).

Hill, David: 'The origin of the Saxon towns', in Peter Brandon (ed.), *The South Saxons* (Chichester, 1978), pp. 174–89.

Hill, David: 'The shiring of Mercia – again', in Higham and Hill, *Edward the Elder*, pp. 144–59.

Hill, David: 'Trends in the development of towns in the reign of Æthelred II', in Hill, *Ethelred the Unready*, pp. 198–203.

Hill, David (ed.): *Ethelred the Unready: papers from the Millenary Conference*, BAR British series, 59 (1978).

Hill, David, and Rumble, Alexander (ed.): *The defence of Wessex: the Burghal Hidage and Anglo-Saxon fortification* (Manchester, 1996).

Hill, David, and Sharp, Sheila: 'An Anglo-Saxon beacon-system', in Rumble and Mills, *Names, places and people*, pp. 157–65.

Hill, Joyce: 'Monastic reform and the secular church', in Carola Hicks (ed.): *England in the eleventh century* (Stamford, 1992), pp. 103–18.

Hinton, David A.: 'The fortifications and their shires', in Hill and Rumble, *The defence of Wessex*, pp. 151–9.

Hollister, C. Warren: *Anglo-Saxon military institutions on the eve of the Norman Conquest* (Oxford, 1962).

Hooper, Nicholas: 'An introduction to the Berkshire Domesday', in Ann Williams and R. W. H. Erskine (ed.), *The Berkshire Domesday* (London, 1988), pp. 1–28.

Hooper, Nicholas: 'Some observations on the navy in late Anglo-Saxon England', in Christopher Harper-Bill, Christopher Holdsworth and Janet L. Nelson (ed.), *Studies in medieval history presented to R. Allen Brown* (Woodbridge, 1989) pp. 203–13.

Hooper, Nicholas, 'The Anglo-Saxons at war', in Hawkes, *Weapons and warfare*, pp. 191–202.

Hooper, Nicholas and Bennett, Matthew: *Warfare: the Middle Ages* (Cambridge, 1996).

Insley, Charles: 'Politics, conflict and kinship in early eleventh-century Mercia', *Midland History*, 26 (2001), pp. 28–42.

Jayakumar, Shashi, 'Foundlings, ealdormen and holy women: reflections on some aristocratic families in tenth- and eleventh-century Wiltshire', *Medieval Prosopography*, forthcoming.

Jesch, Judith: *Ships and men in the late Viking Age: the vocabulary of runic inscriptions and skaldic verse* (Woodbridge, 2001).

Kapelle, William E.: *The Norman Conquest of the North* (London, 1979).

Keen, Laurence (ed.), *Studies in the early history of Shaftesbury Abbey* (Dorchester, 1999).

Kennedy, Alan: 'Byrhtnoth's obits and twelfth-century accounts of the battle of Maldon', in Scragg, *The Battle of Maldon*, pp. 59–78.

Ker, Neil: 'Hemming's Cartulary: a description of two Worcester cartularies in BM Cotton Tiberius A xiii', in R. W. Hunt et al. (ed.), *Studies in medieval history presented to Frederick Maurice Powicke* (Oxford, 1948), pp. 49–75.

Keynes, Simon: 'A tale of two kings: Alfred the Great and Æthelred the Unready', *TRHS*, 5th series, 36 (1986), pp. 197–217.

Keynes, Simon: *An atlas of attestations in Anglo-Saxon Charters, c. 670–1066* (Cambridge, 1995).

Keynes, Simon: 'Anglo-Saxon history after *Anglo-Saxon England*', in Donald Matthew, Anne Curry and Ewen Green, *Stenton's Anglo-Saxon England fifty years on*, Reading Historical Studies, 1 (Reading, 1994), pp. 83–110.

Keynes, Simon, 'Cnut's earls', in Rumble, *The reign of Cnut*, pp. 43–88.

Keynes, Simon: 'Crime and punishment in the reign of King Æthelred the Unready', in Wood and Lund, *People and places in northern Europe*, pp. 67–81.

Keynes, Simon: 'England, *c.* 900–1066', in *CNMH*, iii, pp. 456–84.

Keynes, Simon, 'King Alfred the Great and Shaftesbury Abbey', in Keen, *Studies in the early history of Shaftesbury Abbey*, pp. 17–72.

Keynes, Simon: 'Regenbald the chancellor (*sic*)', *ANS*, 10 (1988), pp. 185–22.

Keynes, Simon: 'The æthelings in Normandy', *ANS*, 13 (1990), pp. 173–205.

Keynes, Simon, 'The declining reputation of King Æthelred "the Unready"', in Hill, *Ethelred the Unready*, pp. 227–53.

Keynes, Simon: *The diplomas of King Æthelred "the Unready", 978–1016* (Cambridge, 1980).

Keynes, Simon: 'The historical content of the battle of Maldon', in Scragg, *The Battle of Maldon*, pp. 81–113.

Keynes, Simon: 'The lost cartulary of Abbotsbury', *ASE*, 18 (1989), pp. 209–43.

Knowles, David, Brooke, C. N. L. and London, Vera C. M. (ed.): *The Heads of Religious Houses in England and Wales, 940–1216* (Cambridge, 1972).

Lapidge, Michael: 'Abbot Germanus, Winchcombe, Ramsey and the Cambridge Psalter', in Lapidge, *Anglo-Latin literature, 900–1066*, pp. 405–14.

Lapidge, Michael: *Anglo-Latin literature, 900–1066* (London and Rio Grande, 1993).

Lapidge, Michael, 'B. and the *Vita S. Dunstani*', in Ramsay et al., *St Dunstan*, pp. 247–59.

Lapidge, Michael: 'Byrhtferth and Oswald', in Brooks and Cubitt, *St Oswald*, pp. 64–83.

Lapidge, Michael: 'The *Life of St Oswald*', in Scragg, *The Battle of Maldon*, pp. 51–8.

Lapidge, Michael, Blair, John, Keynes, Simon and Scragg, Donald (ed.): *The Blackwell Encyclopaedia of Anglo-Saxon England* (Oxford, 1999).

Larson, L. M.: *Canute the Great* (New York and London, 1912).

Lawson, M. K.: 'Archbishop Wulfstan and the homilectic element in the laws of Æthelred II and Cnut', in Rumble, *The reign of Cnut*, pp. 141–64.

Lawson, M. K.: *Cnut: the Danes in England in the early eleventh century* (London, 1993).

Lawson, M. K.: 'Danegeld and heregeld again', *EHR* 105 (1990), pp. 951–61.

Lawson, M. K.: 'The collection of Danegeld and heregeld in the reigns of Æthelred II and Cnut', *EHR*, 99 (1984), pp. 721–38.

Lawson, M. K.: '"Those stories look true": levels of taxation in the reigns of Æthelred II and Cnut', *EHR*, 104 (1989), pp. 385–406.

Lewis, C. P.: 'An introduction to the Shropshire Domesday', in Ann Williams and R. W. H. Erskine (ed.), *The Shropshire Domesday* (London, 1990), pp. 1–27.

Leyser, Karl, 'Die Ottonen und Wessex', *Frümittelalterliche Studien*, 17 (1983), pp. 73–97, translated as 'The Ottonians and Wessex' in Reuter, *Communications and power in early medieval Europe*, pp. 73–104.

Leyser, Karl: *Medieval Germany and its neighbours, 900–1200* (London, 1982).

Leyser, Karl: *Rule and conflict in an early medieval society: Ottonian Germany* (London, 1979).

Leyser, Karl: 'The Anglo-Saxons "At Home"', in *Anglo-Saxon Studies in Archaeology and History*, BAR British series, 92 (1981), pp. 237–42; reprinted in Reuter, *Communications and power in early medieval Europe*, pp. 105–10.

Leyser, Karl: 'The tenth-century condition', in Karl Leyser, *Medieval Germany and its neighbours, 900–1200* (London, 1982), pp. 1–9.

Lockerbie-Cameron, Margaret: 'Byrhtnoth and his family', in Scragg, *The battle of Maldon*, pp. 253–62.

Lund, Niels: 'Cnut's Danish kingdom', in Rumble, *The reign of Cnut*, pp. 27–42.

Lund, Niels: 'Danish military organization', in Cooper, *The Battle of Maldon*, pp. 109–26.

Lund, Niels: '"Denemearc", "tanmarkar but" and "tanmarkar ala"', in Wood and Lund, *People and places in northern Europe, 500–1600*, pp. 161–9.

Lund, Niels: '*Expedicio* in Denmark', in Abels and Bachrach, *The Normans and their adversaries*, pp. 149–66.

Lund, Niels: 'King Edgar and the Danelaw', *Medieval Scandinavia*, 9 (1976), pp. 185–95.

Lund, Niels: 'Scandinavia, *c.* 700–1066', in *CNMH*, ii, pp. 202–27.

Lund, Niels: 'The armies of Swein Forkbeard and Cnut: *leding* or *lið*?', *ASE*, 15 (1986), pp. 105–18.

Lund, Niels: 'The Danish perspective', in Scragg, *The Battle of Maldon*, pp. 114–42.

Lyon, C. S. S.: 'Some problems in interpreting Anglo-Saxon coinage', *ASE*, 5, 1976, pp. 173–224.

Martindale, Jane: 'Peace and war in eleventh-century Aquitaine', *Medieval Knighthood*, 4 (1992), pp. 147–76.

McDougall, Ian: 'Serious entertainments: a peculiar type of Viking atrocity', *ASE*, 22 (1993), pp. 201–25.

Metcalf, D. M.: *An atlas of Anglo-Saxon and Norman coin finds, c. 973–1086* (London, 1988).

Metcalf, D. M.: 'Large Danegelds in relation to war and kingship: their implications for monetary history, and some numismatic evidence', in Hawkes, *Weapons and warfare in Anglo-Saxon England*, pp. 179–89.

Metcalf, D. M. 'The ranking of the boroughs: numismatic evidence for the reign of Æthelræd II', in Hill, *Ethelred the Unready*, pp. 159–212.

Meyer, Mark Anthony: 'The queen's "demesne" in later Anglo-Saxon England', in M. A. Meyer (ed.), *The culture of Christendom: essays in medieval history in memory of Denis L. T. Bethell* (London and Rio Grande, 1993), pp. 75–113.

Moore, John (ed.): *Domesday Book: Gloucestershire* (Chichester, 1982).

Morris, Christopher J.: *Marriage and murder in eleventh-century Northumbria: a study of 'De obsessione Dunelmi'*, Borthwick Paper 82 (York, 1992).

Nelson, Janet L.: 'Inauguration rituals', in I. N. Wood and P. H. Sawyer (ed.), *Early medieval kingship* (Leeds, 1977), pp. 50–71.

Newton, Sam: *The origins of Beowulf and the pre-Viking kingdom of East Anglia* (Woodbridge, 1993).

Offler, H. S.: *Medieval historians of Durham* (Durham, 1958); reprinted in A. J. Piper and A. I. Doyle, *North of the Tees: studies in medieval British history* (Aldershot, 1996).

Orchard, A. P. McD.:'Crying Wolf: oral style and the *Sermones Lupi*', *ASE*, 21 (1992), pp. 239–64.

Orchard, A. P. McD.:'Wulfstan I', in Lapidge et al., *The Blackwell Encyclopaedia of Anglo-Saxon England*, pp. 492–3.

Ortenburg, Veronica: 'Archbishop Sigeric's journey to Rome in 990', *ASE*, 19 (1990), pp. 197–246.

Page, R. I.: *"A most vile people": early English historians and the Vikings*, Dorothea Coke Memorial Lecture (London, 1987).

Palmer, John: 'Great Domesday on CD-Rom', in Elizabeth Hallam and David Bates (ed.), *Domesday Book* (Stroud, 2001), pp. 141–50.

Poole, R. G.: 'In search of the *Partar*', *Scandinavian Studies*, 52 (1980), pp. 264–77.

Poole, R. G.: 'Skaldic verse and Anglo-Saxon history: some aspects of the period 1009–1016', *Speculum*, 62 (1987), pp. 265–98.

Poole, R. G.: *Viking poems on war and peace* (Toronto, Buffalo and London, 1991).

Powell, Timothy: 'The "Three Orders" of society in Anglo-Saxon England', *ASE*, 23 (1994), pp. 103–32.

Pretty, George and Susan: 'A geological reconstruction of the site of the the battle of Maldon', Cooper, *The Battle of Maldon*, pp. 159–69.

Ramsay, Nigel, Sparks, Margaret, and Tatton-Brown, Tim (ed.): *St Dunstan: his life, times and cult* (Woodbridge, 1992).

Reuter, Timothy (ed.): *Communications and power in early medieval Europe: the Carolingian and Ottonian centuries* (London and Rio Grande, 1994)

Reynolds, Andrew: *Late Anglo-Saxon England: life and landscape* (Stroud, 1999)

Richardson, H. G., and Sayles, G. O.: *Law and legislation from Æthelberht to Magna Carta* (Edinburgh, 1966).

Richardson, Mark: 'Æthelred's coinage and the payment of tribute', in Scragg, *The Battle of Maldon, AD 991*, pp. 156–69.

Ridyard, Susan: *The royal saints of Anglo-Saxon England* (Cambridge, 1988).

Robertson, E. W.: *Historical Essays* (Edinburgh, 1872).

Rodger, N. A. M.: 'Cnut's geld and the size of Danish ships', *EHR*, 110 (1995), pp. 392–403.

Rodwell, Warwick: 'The Battle of *Assandun* and its memorial church', in Cooper, *The battle of Maldon*, pp. 127–58.

Roffe, David: *Domesday: the Inquest and the Book* (Oxford, 2000).

Roffe, David: 'The origins of Derbyshire', *Derbyshire Archaeological Journal*, 106 (1986), pp. 102–22.

Rollason, D. W.: *Saints and relics in Anglo-Saxon England* (Oxford, 1989).

Rollason, D. W.: 'Symeon's contribution to historical writing in northern England', in Rollason, *Symeon of Durham*, pp. 1–13.

Rollason, D. W.: 'The cults of murdered royal saints in Anglo-Saxon England', *ASE*, 11 (1983), pp. 1–22.

Rollason, D. W. (ed.): *Symeon of Durham, historian of Durham and the North* (Stamford, 1998).

Rubinstein, J.: 'The life and writings of Osbern of Canterbury', in Richard Eales and Richard Sharpe (ed.), *Canterbury and the Norman Conquest: churches, saints and scholars, 1066–1109* (London and Rio Grande, 1995), pp. 27–40.

Rumble, Alexander R. (ed.): *The reign of Cnut* (Leicester, 1994).

Rumble, Alexander and Mills, A. D. (ed.): *Names, places and people: an onomastic miscellany for John McNeal Dodgson* (Stamford, 1997).

Sawyer, Birgit: 'Appendix: the evidence of Scandinavian runic inscriptions', in Rumble, *The reign of Cnut*, pp. 23–6.

Sawyer, P. H.: 'Cnut's Scandinavian empire', in Rumble, *The reign of Cnut*, pp. 10–22.

Sawyer, P. H.: 'Swein Forkbeard and the historians', in I. Wood and G. A. Loud (ed.), *Church and Chronicle in the Middle Ages* (London and Rio Grande, 1991), pp. 28–35.

Sawyer, P. H.: 'The last Scandinavian kings of York', *Northern History*, 31 (1995), pp. 39–44.

Sawyer, P. H.: 'The Scandinavian background', in Cooper, *The Battle of Maldon*, pp. 33–42.

Scragg, Donald, '*The Battle of Maldon*', in Scragg, *The Battle of Maldon*, pp. 1–36.

Scragg, Donald (ed.): *The Battle of Maldon AD 991* (Oxford, 1991).

Sharpe, Richard: 'Symeon as pamphleteer', in Rollason, *Symeon of Durham*, pp. 214–29.

Sims-Williams, Patrick: *Religion and literature in western England, 600–800* (Cambridge, 1990).

Slater, T. R.: 'The origins of Warwick', *Midland History*, 8 (1983), pp. 1–13.

Smyth, Alfred P.: *King Alfred the Great* (Oxford, 1995).

Smyth, Alfred P.: *Warlords and Holy Men: Scotland, AD 80–1000* (London, 1984).

Squibb, G. D.: 'The foundation of Cerne Abbey', in Barker, *The Cerne Abbey Millenium lectures*, pp. 11–14.

Stafford, Pauline: 'The laws of Cnut and the history of Anglo-Saxon royal promises', *ASE*, 10 (1982), pp. 173–90.

Stafford, Pauline: *Queen Emma and Queen Edith: queenship and women's power in eleventh-century England* (Oxford, 1997).

Stafford, Pauline: *Queens, concubines and dowagers* (London, 1983).

Stafford, Pauline: 'Queens, nunneries and reforming churchmen: gender, status and reform in tenth- and eleventh-century England', *P&P*, 163 (1999), pp. 3–35.

Stafford, Pauline: 'The reign of Æthelred II: a study in the limitations on royal policy and action', in Hill, *Ethelred the Unready*, pp. 15–46.

Stafford, Pauline: *Unification and conquest: a political and social history of England in the tenth and eleventh centuries* (London, 1989).

Stenton, F. M.: *Anglo-Saxon England* (3rd edn, Oxford, 1971).

Stenton, F. M.: *The Latin charters of the Anglo-Saxon period* (Oxford, 1955).

Stevenson, W. H.: 'Notes on Old English historical geography', *EHR*, 11 (1896), pp. 301–2.

Strickland, Matthew: 'Military technology and conquest: the anomaly of Anglo-Saxon England', *ANS*, 19 (1997), pp. 333–82.

Tatton-Brown, Tim: 'The towns of Kent', in Haslam, *Anglo-Saxon towns in southern England*, pp. 1–36.

Taylor, C. S.: 'The origin of the Mercian shires', *Trans. Bristol and Gloucs. Arch. Soc.*, 21 (1898), 32 (1909); reprinted in Finberg, *Gloucestershire Studies*, pp. 17–51.

Taylor, Pamela: 'The endowment and military obligations of the bishopric of London', *ANS*, 14 (1992), pp. 287–312.

Thacker, Alan: 'Saint-making and relic-collecting by Oswald and his communities', in Brooks and Cubitt, *St Oswald*, pp. 244–68.

Thomson, Rodney M.: *William of Malmesbury* (Woodbridge, 1987).

Thorn, Frank: 'Hundreds and wapentakes', in Ann Williams and R. W. H. Erskine (ed.), *The Oxfordshire Domesday* (London, 1990), pp. 20–9.

Thorn, Frank: 'Hundreds and wapentakes', in Ann Williams and R. W. H. Erskine (ed.), *The Wiltshire Domesday* (London, 1989), pp. 31–42.

Thorn, Frank: 'Hundreds and wapentakes', in Ann Williams and G. H. Martin (ed.), *The Devonshire Domesday* (London, 1991), pp. 26–42.

Thorn, Frank, and Thorn Caroline (ed.): *Domesday Book: Devon* (Chichester, 1985).

Thornton, David E.: 'Maredudd ab Owain: the most famous king of the Welsh', *Welsh History Review*, 18 (1997), pp. 567–91.

Townend, Matthew: 'Contextualizing the *Knútsdrápur*: skaldic praise-poetry at the court of Cnut', *ASE*, 30 (2001), pp. 145–79.

van Houts, Elisabeth: 'Scandinavian influence in Norman literature', *ANS*, 6 (1984), pp. 107–21.

van Houts, Elisabeth: 'Women and the writing of history in the early middle ages: the case of Abbess Matilda of Essen and Æthelweard', *Early Medieval Europe*, 1 (1992), pp. 53–68.

Vauchez, André: *Sainthood in the later middle ages* (Cambridge, 1997).

Vlasto, A. P.: *The entry of the Slavs into Christendom* (Cambridge, 1970).

Wareham, Andrew: 'St Oswald's family and kin', in Brooks and Cubitt, *St Oswald*, pp. 46–63.

Weiler, Björn: 'Kingship, usurpation and propaganda in the twelfth century: the case of Stephen', *ANS*, 23 (2001), pp. 299–26.

Whitbread, L.: 'Æthelweard and the Anglo-Saxon Chronicle', *EHR*, 74 (1959), pp. 577–89.

Whitelock, Dorothy: 'Archbishop Wulfstan, homilist and statesman', *TRHS*, 4th series, 24 (1942), pp. 42–60; reprinted in *History, Law and Literature in tenth- and eleventh-century England.*

Whitelock, Dorothy: *History, Law and Literature in tenth- and eleventh-century England* (London, 1981).

Whitelock, Dorothy: *Some Anglo-Saxon bishops of London*, the Chambers Memorial Lecture, 1974 (London, 1975); reprinted in *History, Law and Literature in tenth- and eleventh-century England.*

Whitelock, Dorothy: 'The dealings of the kings of England with Northumbria in the tenth and eleventh centuries', in Clemoes, *The Anglo-Saxons*, pp. 70–88; reprinted in *History, Law and Literature in tenth- and eleventh-century England.*

Whitelock, Dorothy: 'Two notes on Ælfric and Wulfstan', *Modern Language Review*, 38 (1943), pp. 122–6; reprinted in *History, Law and Literature in tenth- and eleventh-century England*

Whybra, Julian: *A lost English county: Winchcombeshire in the tenth and eleventh centuries* (Woodbridge, 1990).

Williams, Ann: 'A west-country magnate of the eleventh century: the family, estates and patronage of Beorhtric son of Ælfgar', in K. S. B. Keats-Rohan (ed.), *Family-trees and the roots of politics* (Woodbridge, 1997), pp. 41–68.

Williams, Ann: 'An introduction to the Worcestershire Domesday', in Ann Williams and R. W. H. Erskine (ed.), *The Worcestershire Domesday* (London, 1988), pp. 1–31.

Williams, Ann, '"Cockles amongst the wheat": Danes and English in the west midlands in the first half of the eleventh century', *Midland History*, 11 (1986), pp. 1–22.

Williams, Ann: *Kingship and government in pre-Conquest England, c. 500–1066* (London, 1999).

Williams, Ann: 'Land and power in the eleventh century: the estates of Harold Godwineson', *ANS*, 3 (1981), pp. 171–87.

Williams, Ann: *Land, power and politics: the family and career of Odda of Deerhurst*, the Deerhurst Lecture, 1996 (Deerhurst, 1997).

Williams, Ann: 'Lost worlds: Kentish society in the eleventh century', *Medieval Prosopography*, 20 (1999), pp. 51–74.

Williams, Ann: '*Princeps Merciorum gentis*: the family, career and connections of Ælfhere, ealdorman of Mercia', *ASE*, 10 (1982), pp. 143–72.

Williams, Ann: 'The Anglo-Norman abbey', in Richard Gem (ed.), *St Augustine's Abbey, Canterbury* (London, 1997), pp. 50–66.

Williams, Ann: 'The battle of Maldon and *The Battle of Maldon*: history, poetry and propaganda', *Medieval History*, 2, no2 (1992), pp. 35–44.

Williams, Ann: *The English and the Norman Conquest* (Woodbridge, 1995).

Williams, Ann: 'The spoliation of Worcester', *ANS*, 19 (1996), pp. 303–408 .

Williams, Ann: 'Thegnly piety and ecclesiastical patronage in the late Old English period', *ANS*, 24 (2002), pp. 1–24.

Wood, I. N., and Lund, Niels (ed.): *People and places in northern Europe, 500–1600* (Woodbridge, 1991).

Wood, I. N. and Sawyer, P. (ed.): *Early medieval kingship* (Leeds, 1977)

Wormald, Patrick: 'Æthelred the lawmaker', in Hill, *Ethelred the Unready*, pp. 47–80.

Wormald, Patrick: 'A hand-list of Anglo-Saxon lawsuits', *ASE*, 17 (1988), pp. 247–81.

Wormald, Patrick: 'Archbishop Wulfstan and the holiness of society', in *Legal culture in the medieval West*, pp. 225–51.

Wormald, Patrick: '*Engla Lond*: the making of an allegiance', *Journal of Historical Sociology*, 7 (1994), pp. 1–24.

Wormald, Patrick: 'In search of King Offa's law-code', in Wood and Lund, *People and places in northern Europe*, pp. 25–45.

Wormald, Patrick: *Legal culture in the early medieval West* (London, 1999).

Wormald, Patrick: 'Lordship and justice in the early English kingdom', in *Legal culture in the early medieval West*, pp. 313–32.

Wormald, Patrick, *The making of English law: King Alfred to the twelfth century, i, legislation and its limits* (Oxford, 1999).

Wright, C. E.: *The cultivation of saga in Anglo-Saxon England* (Edinburgh, 1939).

Yorke, Barbara: 'Æthelmær: the foundation of Cerne Abbey and the politics of the tenth century', in Barker, *The Cerne Abbey Millenium lectures*, pp. 15–20.

Yorke, Barbara: 'Æthelwold and the politics of the tenth century', in Yorke, *Bishop Æthelwold: his career and influence*, pp. 65–88.

Yorke, 'Edward, king and martyr', in Keen, *Studies in the early history of Shaftesbury Abbey*, pp. 99–116.

Yorke, Barbara: 'The legitimacy of St Edith', *Haskins Soc. J.* forthcoming.

Yorke, Barbara: *Wessex in the early middle ages* (Leicester, 1995).

Yorke, Barbara (ed.): *Bishop Æthelwold: his career and influence* (Woodbridge, 1988).

Index